Praise for *The Iliad*

"Stephen Mitchell's translation of the *Iliad* is a mammoth, enlivening achievement. In this masterwork that is both immediate and timeless, Mitchell reaches into the heart of things, as he has done so many times, and lets the unmitigated complexity and paradoxical dimensions of life pulse and tug at each other in a way that reminds us we are alive and responsible for what we do. In his muscular and tender rendition of Homer, he cautions us against our own warrior culture. He has taken the dust off a classic so it can breathe."

> —Mark Nepo, author of *The Book of Awakening* and *As Far As the Heart Can See*

"Stephen Mitchell has translated the *Iliad*'s 'serene music' with a serenity and musicianship worthy of the original. His love of Homer's humanity and his deep insight into this most timeless of poems radiate from every line of verse. Mitchell's *Iliad* is a glorious achievement, free-flowing and natural but also carefully researched. It promises to become the foremost version of Homer's epic in modern English."

> —James Romm, Professor of Classics, Bard College, and author of *Ghost on the Throne: The Death of Alexander the Great and the War for Crown and Empire*

"Mitchell has done more than any other translator to fill Matthew Arnold's criteria for rendering Homer. This translation is 'eminently rapid,' 'eminently plain and direct,' and 'eminently noble.' In remarkably straightforward English, free of pretense and other distractions, the story keeps much of its original excitement and seriousness. Mitchell has completed a labor of true love and driven hard toward the real thing."

> —Sarah Ruden, Department of Classics, Wesleyan University, and translator of the *Aeneid*

"Mitchell's powerful verse allows us to read the *Iliad* as it was read in the ancient world, as an exciting narrative about war, anger, and regret, with a lucidity that reveals the poet's profound insight into the tragic nature of the human condition."

> —Mary Lefkowitz, Professor Emerita of Classical Studies, Wellesley College, and author of *Greek Gods, Human Lives*

"In a lifetime of conspicuously successful translations, this is Stephen Mitchell's greatest achievement."

> —Victor H. Mair, Professor of Chinese Language and Literature, University of Pennsylvania

*f*P

BY STEPHEN MITCHELL

POETRY

Parables and Portraits

FICTION

The Frog Prince
Meetings with the Archangel

NONFICTION

A Thousand Names for Joy (with Byron Katie)
Loving What Is (with Byron Katie)
The Gospel According to Jesus

TRANSLATIONS AND ADAPTATIONS

The Iliad
Duino Elegies and The Sonnets to Orpheus
The Second Book of the Tao
Gilgamesh
Bhagavad Gita
Real Power: Business Lessons from the Tao Te Ching (with James A. Autry)
Full Woman, Fleshly Apple, Hot Moon: Selected Poems of Pablo Neruda
Genesis
Ahead of All Parting: The Selected Poetry and Prose of Rainer Maria Rilke
A Book of Psalms
The Selected Poetry of Dan Pagis
Tao Te Ching
The Book of Job
The Selected Poetry of Yehuda Amichai (with Chana Bloch)

The Sonnets to Orpheus
The Lay of the Love and Death of Cornet Christoph Rilke
Letters to a Young Poet
The Notebooks of Malte Laurids Brigge
The Selected Poetry of Rainer Maria Rilke

EDITED BY STEPHEN MITCHELL

Question Your Thinking, Change the World: Quotations from Byron Katie
The Essence of Wisdom
Bestiary: An Anthology of Poems about Animals
Song of Myself
Into the Garden: A Wedding Anthology (with Robert Hass)
The Enlightened Mind: An Anthology of Sacred Prose
The Enlightened Heart: An Anthology of Sacred Poetry
Dropping Ashes on the Buddha: The Teaching of Zen Master Seung Sahn

FOR CHILDREN

The Ugly Duckling, by Hans Christian Andersen (illustrated by
Steve Johnson and Lou Fancher)

Iron Hans (illustrated by Matt Tavares)

Genies, Meanies, and Magic Rings (illustrated by Tom Pohrt)

The Tinderbox, by Hans Christian Andersen (illustrated by
Bagram Ibatoulline)

The Wishing Bone and Other Poems (illustrated by Tom Pohrt)

The Nightingale, by Hans Christian Andersen (illustrated by
Bagram Ibatoulline)

Jesus: What He Really Said and Did

The Creation (illustrated by Ori Sherman)

Homer

The Iliad

Translated, with an Introduction and Notes,
by Stephen Mitchell

FREE PRESS

New York London Toronto Sydney New Delhi

Free Press
A Division of Simon & Schuster, Inc.
1230 Avenue of the Americas
New York, NY 10020

First Free Press hardcover edition October 2011

FREE PRESS and colophon are trademarks of Simon & Schuster, Inc.

For information about special discounts for bulk purchases, please contact Simon &
Schuster Special Sales at 1-866-506-1949 or business@simonandschuster.com.

The Simon & Schuster Speakers Bureau can bring authors to your live event.
For more information or to book an event contact the Simon & Schuster Speakers
Bureau at 1-866-248-3049 or visit our website at www.simonspeakers.com.

Map copyright © 2011 by Jeffrey L. Ward

Book design by Ellen R. Sasahara

Manufactured in the United States of America

1   3   5   7   9   10   8   6   4   2

Library of Congress Cataloging-in-Publication Data

Homer.
[Iliad. English]
The Iliad / Homer ; translated, with an introduction and notes, by Stephen Mitchell.
p. cm.
Includes bibliographical references.
1. Epic poetry, Greek—Translations into English. 2. Achilles (Greek
mythology)—Poetry. 3. Trojan war—Poetry. I. Title.
PA4025.A2M57 2011
883'01—dc22
2010051827

ISBN 978-1-4391-6337-5
ISBN 978-1-4516-2762-6 (ebook)

To Michael Katz

Contents

The Iliad

---

*Book 10, recognized since ancient times as a later addition to the *Iliad,* has been omitted in this translation.

Book 21 336

The battle between Achilles and the river Scamander. The gods fight among themselves. Achilles drives the Trojans inside their wall.

Book 22 353

Achilles chases Hector around the wall of Troy and finally kills him, with Athena's help.

Book 23 367

The funeral of Patroclus and the funeral games. (Evening of day 20 through day 22.)

Book 24 393

Zeus commands Achilles to return Hector's body and commands Priam to go to Achilles' hut with a large ransom. Priam is led to the hut by Hermes. The encounter between Priam and Achilles. The funeral of Hector. (Evening of day 22 through day 45.)

Introduction

Reading the *Iliad*

We return to the *Iliad* because it is one of the monuments of our own magnificence. Its poetry lifts even the most devastating human events into the realm of the beautiful, and it shows us how vast and serene the mind can be even when it contemplates the horrors of war. "Every time I study this priceless work," Goethe said, "I am thrust into a state of astonishment."

It has always been a popular poem, in every sense of the word. In ancient Athens, more than twenty thousand people, as we know from Plato's *Ion,* would go to the marketplace, theater, or open hillside, the way we might attend a concert, to hear a famous rhapsode recite "The Death of Hector" or "The Meeting of Priam and Achilles." Most people in these crowds weren't educated, and they must have gone, bringing picnic baskets and the ancient Greek equivalent of popcorn, prepared to be transported by the power of the story and the gorgeousness of the language, like the groundlings at Shakespeare's Globe. This was poetry that gave pleasure to everyone—men and women, adults and children, the simple and the very sophisticated. It still has the power to move us all.

Here are two stories about its appeal: "Last week I was in Alice Springs," a friend wrote to me, "in the Australian outback, and I went into a tiny café serving kangaroo tacos. The young man behind the counter (he couldn't have been more than twenty-one) had a tattoo saying Μῆνιν. As I looked at it, he leaned over and said, 'Mēnin. It means "rage." First word of the *Iliad,* which is my favorite book. I wear this to tell people about the amazing text that's out there for them to discover.' He was so open and unembarrassed about his enthusiasm. I could tell he was ready to talk about the *Iliad* all day—if only he could find someone to listen."

Second story: In 1990 the Colombian Ministry of Culture set up a system of itinerant libraries to take books to the inhabitants of hard-to-reach rural areas. Donkey drivers would travel to these remote villages in the jungle or the sierra, leave the books for a few weeks with a teacher or a village elder, then come back and pick them up. Most of the books were technical works, agricultural handbooks, collections of sewing patterns, and the like, but there was a scattering of literary works among them. In one village all the books were returned to the donkey driver except for a single volume: a Spanish translation of the *Iliad*. The villagers refused to give it back; they said that they couldn't part with it, because the story so clearly reflected their own. "It told of a war-torn country in which insane gods mix with men and women who never know exactly what the fighting is about, or when they will be happy, or why they will be killed."

Of course, we can only perceive in the *Iliad* what we bring to it, and there are as many ways to see it as there are minds that see. Simone Weil, in a brilliant and famous essay, portrayed the *Iliad* as an indictment of war, while Alexander the Great used to sleep with it under his pillow, esteeming it as "a treasury of all military virtue." (His personal copy had been corrected by his tutor, Aristotle.) But all readers, whatever their point of view, can appreciate the sheer power of Homer's language, even in the most prosaic or mediocre translations.

That power is where I want to begin, and not so much with comments as with examples. I want to point to the pleasures we find everywhere in the poem, the bursts of delight that lie in store for us even before we are able to appreciate the glorious architecture of the whole or the subtleties of its moral insight. Here is a ship sailing to Troy:

> And as soon as the flush of dawn appeared in the heavens,
> they boarded the ship and launched her. Apollo sent them
> a favoring breeze, and they raised the mast, and they hoisted
> the white sail aloft, and it bellied out with the wind,
> and on either side of the ship's prow, the deep blue water
> sang out as the ship flew over the waves to her goal.   (1.469–74)

A Trojan archer shooting an arrow:

> And laying the arrow's notched end in the ox-gut bowstring,
> he pulled it back with his right hand as far as his nipple,
> with the iron tip of the arrow touching the bow shaft,
> and the shaft was bent back, and he aimed, and then he let go,
> and the great bow twanged, and the string sang out, and the arrow
> flew through the dense crowd, eager to find its mark.　　(4.112–17)

As the arrow is about to find its mark, the goddess Athena deflects it:

> But then, Menelaus, the blessed gods did not forget you.
> Athena stepped out before you and with her hand
> deflected the deadly arrow, brushing it off
> as a mother brushes a fly from her sleeping child.　　(4.118–21)

The Trojan army, after a day of sustained carnage, is camped out on the plain, dangerously close to the Achaean ships:

> So, with elated hearts, they sat up all night
> on the battlefield, and their watch fires blazed all around them.
> As, in the night sky, around the light of the moon,
> the stars emerge, when the air is serene and windless,
> and the stars shine bright, and the heart of the shepherd rejoices:
> so, before Ilion, the watch fires the Trojans had set
> blazed midway between the ships and the river Xanthus.
> A thousand watch fires were burning upon the plain,
> and around each, fifty men sat in the glow of the firelight,
> and the horses stood alongside the chariots, munching
> white barley and oats, and waited for dawn to arise.　　(8.487–97)

Where did this shepherd come from? He miraculously pops up out of the poet's imagination, and his joy and the glittering stars and the casual chewing of the horses give a feeling of profound awe to the scene. What an astonishing image this is, with its sense of infinite serenity that arises not from any of the characters (the Trojans are revved up with anticipation; the Achaeans are terrified) but from the poet's own peace of heart.

Here is a passage in which Homer feels his way into the very horses. It ends with a line that may at first seem chilling in its matter-of-factness and lack of sentimentality:

> . . . just so did the Trojan troops fall, and many horses
> pulled empty chariots that rattled across the plain,
> and they longed for their drivers; but these lay dead on the ground,
> far dearer now to the vultures than to their wives. (11.159–62)

As the Achaean hero Ajax is being pushed back by the Trojans, Homer superimposes a willful donkey onto him:

> And as when a donkey is led by some boys down a road—
> a stubborn beast, on whom many sticks have been broken—
> and they pass a field, and his strength is too much for the boys,
> and he willfully turns in to ravage the high-standing grain,
> and although they beat him with sticks, their strength is too feeble,
> they manage to drive him out with much effort, and only
> when he has eaten his fill: just so did the Trojans
> keep crowding Ajax and thrusting at him with their spears.
>
> (11.518–25)

Both the armies fight on, evenly balanced, and suddenly, again out of nowhere, a poor spinning-woman springs into vivid existence through the power of the simile:

> The Trojans kept trying to drive the Achaeans back;
> but both sides held on. As an honest, hardworking woman
> who spins for a living will hold the scales by the beam
> and keep adding wool to a pan till the weight is balanced,
> and thus she can earn a wretched wage for her children:
> so evenly matched were the Trojans and the Achaeans. (12.406–11)

A devastating blow by the god Apollo becomes a child's game by the seashore:

And with utter ease he knocked down the Argives' wall,
like a young child sitting and playing beside the sea
who amuses himself by building a sand castle, then
gleefully knocks it down with his hands and feet:
so you, Lord Apollo, demolished what the Achaeans
had toiled so hard to build, and drove panic among them.   (15.332–37)

Achilles' troops swarm into battle like wasps. What is most marvelous here is the presence of the mischievous little boys and of the unsuspecting passerby, all of whom, at one or two steps from the primary simile, are generated out of the pure abundance of the poet's imagination:

Meanwhile the Myrmidons, greatly exhilarated,
advanced with Patroclus leading and charged at the Trojans,
swarming out all at once like wasps on a roadside
that boys, in their childish sport, have stirred up to anger,
poking them over and over again in their nest,
the little fools, creating a public nuisance
for many people; and if a man passing by
jostles the nest and disturbs them, they all fly out
in a seething rage to attack him and fight for their young:
with a spirit like this, the Myrmidons all swarmed out
from the ships, and their furious battle cries filled the heavens.

(16.232–42)

When the Trojan warrior Euphorbus is killed, we are shown the mysteriously touching detail of his plaited hair:

. . . and the point
tore its way through the tender flesh of the neck,
and he fell with a crash, and his armor clattered upon him,
and blood soaked his hair, which was like the hair of the Graces,
the long locks plaited with spirals of silver and gold.   (17.43–47)

Achilles' slave girl Briseïs mourns for the dead Patroclus, and we are given a momentary entrance into the lives of the other slave women:

Thus she grieved, and the women joined in her wailing
for Patroclus, and each one wept for her own private sorrows.

(19.309–10)

In the boxing match during the funeral games for Patroclus, as Eurýalus looks for an opening,

... Epéüs rushed in and hit him
full on the cheek. He was lifted up off the ground
like a fish that leaps from the shallow seaweed-strewn waters
and falls back into the dark waves: just so did he leap,
and his legs collapsed underneath him, and down he fell.   (23.701–5)

Finally, Teucer, aiming an arrow at Hector, kills a young Trojan prince:

... he missed him and hit Gorgýthion in the chest,
Priam's son by a wife who came from Æsýmē,
Cástianíra, as beautiful as a goddess;
and his head drooped, like a poppy in a spring garden
weighed down with seeds and a heavy rain: so his head
leaned to one side beneath the weight of his helmet.   (8.281–86)

Is there a more poignant image than this in all of literature? Here the pathos of the young man's death arises from the precision of the simile: as we see his head droop, we also see a poppy slowly bending over beneath the weight of its own fertility and of the life-bestowing rain. This is not a prettifying of a brutal reality; it is a parallel reality; it springs, spaceless and timeless, from the poet's intense noticing. Nor is it a mere memory of the pleasures of a lost peacetime far from the battlefield of Troy. The alternative world of the spring garden isn't in the background, it is right before our eyes, presented in stereoscopic vision; the drooping poppy is just as real as the arrow-pierced body that in a moment will keel over and fall to the ground in a pool of blood. There is an immense tenderness at work here, a peacefulness of heart that infuses this great poem of war with the music of its own acceptance.

Honor and Fate

We know almost nothing about the Trojan War, which seems to have taken place around 1200 BCE, and we know very little about Homer. He was probably born around 700 BCE in one of the Greek colonies on the west coast of present-day Turkey or on one of the islands in the eastern Aegean Sea, and he almost certainly wasn't named Homer. He was trained in the ancient tradition of oral poetry, and he used a traditional language that had evolved over centuries, bearing signs of its history in its many archaic features and its mixed dialect. As an epic singer, he went from town to town, or from noble house to noble house, to find new audiences, and he sang his poems to them in partly extemporaneous performance, accompanying himself on the *phorminx* (a four-stringed lyre), like the bards described in the *Odyssey*:

> And the herald approached, leading the honored poet
> whom the Muse loved beyond all others, granting him both
> good and evil: she deprived him of sight but gave him
> the gift of sweet song. The herald, Pontónoüs,
> set out for him a large chair, studded with silver,
> in the midst of the banquet and leaned it against a tall pillar,
> and he hung the beautiful clear-toned lyre on a peg
> a little above the singer's head, and he showed him
> how to reach up and take hold of it in his hands.
> And he put on a table beside him a basket of food
> and a cup of wine to drink when he felt the urge to.
> And they all reached out for the feast that was set before them.
> And when they had had enough of eating and drinking,
> the Muse moved the poet to sing of the glorious deeds
> of heroes.   (*Odyssey,* 8.62–73)

At some point Homer wrote down or dictated his material, and in the course of years or decades he composed the vast panorama of the *Iliad,* expanding his early draft to four or five times its original length and thus creating the supreme masterpiece that has been handed down to us, amazingly intact, over more than two and a half millennia.

In the *Iliad* Homer describes a legendary past that contains elements of historical reality. The epic takes place in an age when men used bronze for their tools and weapons, rather than the iron that was common in Homer's time, and when the great cities were much wealthier and more populous than the ones he had seen, and the heroes bigger and braver—an age when gods and goddesses had human offspring and attended weddings and feasts on earth and were intimately and sometimes fatally involved in the lives of men and women. Details of this heroic past, part historical and part legendary, had been handed down to him by the epic tradition, and he himself had spent time among the ruins of the massive Trojan walls that still stood twenty feet above the ground.

Everyone in Homer's audience knew the story of the Trojan War; poets had been celebrating it, so people thought, ever since the event itself, even during the lifetime of some of its heroes. The story is simple. It begins with the folly of a handsome young Trojan prince, Paris, who seduces the famously beautiful Helen, wife of his host, King Menelaus of Lacedaemon, and takes her to Troy, along with many of her possessions. In retaliation Menelaus's brother Agamemnon, the most powerful king in Achaea (Greece), gathers a vast army from all over the land and sails across the Aegean with a fleet of a thousand ships to attack Troy. We aren't shown the end of the story in the *Iliad,* but everyone knew that after ten years of siege the Achaeans finally conquered the great city, burned it, killed the men, enslaved the women and children, and sailed back to their various destinies.

The story about Achilles' rage and its ruinous consequences is a later addition to this ancient plot, but it is at the center of the *Iliad,* and Homer wisely and elegantly restricts his story to this particular strand. It too can be easily summarized. In the tenth year of the war Agamemnon publicly dishonors Achilles, the greatest of the Achaean warriors, by taking back Briseïs, a beautiful young woman whom the army gave to Achilles as a war prize. Achilles, humiliated and enraged, withdraws to his camp and refuses to fight in the war, and as a result the Trojans gain the upper hand. Desperate, Achilles' beloved friend Patroclus gets his permission to lead the Myrmidon troops out and drive the Trojans back to their city, but in the ensuing battle he is killed by Hector, the greatest warrior of the Trojans. Achilles is devastated and furious, returns to the fighting, kills Hector, and savagely mistreats his corpse, day after day dragging it around Patroclus's funeral mound. After the elaborate funeral games for Patroclus, Priam travels to the Achaean camp and begs for the body of his eldest son. Achilles relents, as Zeus has commanded him to, agrees to a truce, and returns the body. The poem ends with the funeral rites for Hector.

The destruction of Troy may seem barbarous to us, and wildly unfair, but to Homer's Greek audience it was justified; it was the direct result of Paris' crime and thus neither arbitrary nor excessive, however much compassion they might feel for the agony of the Trojans. There were certain rules of conduct that everyone took for granted, both in Homer's time and in the dream time of the *Iliad*. One rule was that the laws of hospitality are sacred. A host is obligated to entertain his guest with the utmost generosity, to provide for his comfort and safety, and to send him off with expensive gifts, while the guest is bound to honor his host and treat him with equal respect. This mutual bond between host and guest is more than a matter of courtesy. It is, in the moral world, what the law of gravity is in the physical world: the force that holds things together and prevents society from flying apart into lawlessness and savagery. Even a man whose grandfather had been the host of an enemy's grandfather, as we see in one touching incident in the *Iliad*, would refuse to face that man in hand-to-hand combat, so sacred was the relationship of host and guest.

Another rule is that a man's reputation is more valuable than anything else, even his life. A warrior dedicates all his efforts to winning honor and glory among his peers and hopes that his fame will last forever, through the songs of endless generations of poets. "The best men choose one thing above all others," the philosopher Heraclitus said, "everlasting fame among mortals." That is the motivation and reward for the hardships he must endure, and it is why a hero always strives to be the bravest of men. It is also the basis for the loyalty that common people have for their princes and soldiers for their commanders. The hero's creed is famously expressed by the great Trojan ally Sarpedon, who says to Glaucus, his comrade-in-arms:

"Glaucus, why is it that we two are held in the greatest
esteem in Lycia and honored with pride of place,
the choicest meat, and our wine cups always refilled,
and all men look up to us both, as if we were gods,
and we each have a large estate on the banks of the Xanthus,
beautiful tracts of orchards and wheat-bearing farmland?
It is so that we may now take our stand in the front ranks
and lead our army into the thick of battle
and fight with courage, so that the soldiers will say,
'These men who rule us in Lycia are not unworthy.
They may dine on fat sheep and drink the best of the wines,
but they are strong, too, and brave, and they fight in the front ranks.'
Dear friend, if the two of us were to survive this war
and could live forever, without old age, without dying,
I wouldn't press on to fight in the front lines myself
or urge you into the battle. But as it is,
since death stands facing us all in ten thousand forms
and no mortal can ever escape it, let us go forward
and either win glory ourselves or yield it to others."   (12.289–307)

With this code of conduct in mind, consider the situation at the beginning of the war. It is clear that the Achaeans are entirely in the right. Paris has committed a reprehensible crime by seducing the wife of his host. No one disputes this: King Priam states that his son's action is the cause of the war, Paris is considered "a great curse" by Hector, his elder brother, and is "hated / by every one of the Trojans like death itself." The Achaeans have already tried to restore the honor of Menelaus by peaceful means—Menelaus and Odysseus went on an embassy to Troy before the war began—but the Trojans refused to give Helen back. The only option left, since it would be intolerable to do nothing, is to punish the whole city of Troy for its complicity in the crime.

Why don't the Trojans give Helen back? Homer doesn't address this issue, except in a few asides. He says that during the embassy to Troy a man named Antimachus had "dissuaded the Trojan assembly / from giving back Helen to Menelaus," but he doesn't tell us what Antimachus's arguments were and why the Trojans agreed. He also has the Trojan counselor Antenor, later on, warn that "no possible good / can happen to us until we have given her back." In response Paris states that he will do no such thing; and in spite of the fact that "all the Trojans / have urged him to do so," neither Priam nor Hector makes him return Helen, although Paris should have no authority in the matter. (In Act 2 of *Troilus and Cressida,* by contrast, Shakespeare, seeing the dramatic possibilities, has Paris, Troilus, and Hector offer passionate arguments for and against keeping Helen.) All that we notice in the *Iliad* is the Trojans' suicidal obtuseness. By the time Hector is faced with death at the hands of Achilles in Book 22 and considers giving Helen back as a last desperate measure, it is far too late.

The Trojans' refusal to make things right is particularly baffling since they are well aware of the consequences of an Achaean victory: the total destruction of their society. Both Hector and Priam, toward the beginning and the end of the poem, talk about the devastation of Troy, the horrible slaughter, the rape and enslavement of the women, the infants brutally tossed from the city wall. This savagery on the part of a conquering army was not considered immoral in the ancient world: it was simply what conquering armies did. Still, granted that war is insane and the most terrible of solutions, there is an at least equal insanity in the Trojans' not doing the right thing.

By the time of the poet Stesichorus, a half century or so after Homer, the failure to understand the Trojans' thinking gave rise to a story that Helen had never gone to Troy in the first place. Here is how the historian Herodotus explains it:

> The Egyptians' priests [told me that Helen stayed in Egypt throughout the war], and I myself believe their story. I reason thus: If Helen had actually been in Troy, then the Trojans would certainly have given her back to the Greeks, whether Paris agreed to or not. For neither Priam nor his kinsmen could have been so insane as to risk their own lives and their children and their whole city merely so that Paris could live with Helen. Even in the first years of the war, they would have realized this and returned her. After all, many Trojans were being killed in every battle with the Greeks, and Priam himself was losing two or three or even more of his sons in every

battle, if the poets are to be believed. And even if Priam himself had been married to Helen, I think that he would have returned her to the Greeks in order to put an end to these calamities. Paris was not even heir to the throne; if he had been, things might have been in his hands, since Priam was old. But Hector, who was his elder brother and a far better man, was first in line and heir to the kingdom on Priam's death. And it couldn't have been in his interest to support his brother's wrongdoing, especially when it brought such calamities on himself and the rest of the Trojans. So it is clear that Helen couldn't have been in Troy and therefore they couldn't give her back, and this is what they told the Greeks, but the Greeks wouldn't believe them.

The only substantial explanation in the *Iliad* occurs in Book 3, when Priam and his counselors sit on the great wall of Troy watching the battle:

And when they saw Helen climbing the stairs to the ramparts,
they nodded to one another, and softly they said,
"No wonder that both the Trojans and the Achaeans
should endure long years of sorrow for such a woman:
she is dreadfully like an immortal goddess; her beauty
pierces the heart. But let her sail back to her home
and not remain here, a curse to us and our children." (3.142–48)

In these lines we see the uncanny, awe-inspiring power of Helen's beauty, which is—almost—a justification for wanting to keep her in Troy. But it is not enough, not if they all have to die for her sake. So the puzzlement remains.

The real explanation for the Trojans' fatal insanity is the shape of the story that Homer was bound to tell. That story could be deepened and expanded and elaborated, but it had to end with the destruction of Troy. However we may feel like begging Priam or Hector to give Helen back (the way early twentieth-century audiences at the Yiddish theater in New York used to yell at King Lear, "Don't believe them! They're rotten!"), we can be sure that Priam and Hector won't listen. Heraclitus said that character is fate; in the *Iliad,* story is fate. The Trojans couldn't return Helen because they didn't return her. Troy had to fall because it did fall. Fate, which is mightier than the best intentions of the protagonists or the gods' conflicting sympathies or the will of almighty Zeus, is nothing but the story handed down to Homer, the story he had to tell.

Wretched War, Man-Glorying War

Homer inherited many epithets for war from the oral tradition, and most of them describe war as an affliction: *ainos* (dreadful), *argaleos* (gruesome, cruel, bitter), *dēios* (deadly), *dusēlegēs* (bringing much grief), *kakos* (evil), *leugaleos* (wretched), *lugros* (miserable), *olöos* (ruinous), *poludakrus* (bringing many tears), *stugeros* (loathsome), *phthisēnōr* (man-destroying), among others. It's easy for us to see why this is so. In scene after scene Homer records the death in battle of a vigorous young man, someone with a wife and children perhaps, and loving parents who will never see him again, someone who just a few moments earlier was filled with the vibrancy of young manhood, and now—with a spear in his chest or with his tongue and jaw sheared away or an arm lopped off at the shoulder or a spear pushed up through his buttock into his bladder or crushing his skull and splattering his brains inside his helmet—he topples over the rails of his chariot, already dead or bleeding to death, screaming in agony or reaching out for his comrades, with his massive bronze armor clattering upon him, his teeth chewing the dirt, his nails desperately clawing for a way back to life. The pathos of this final moment is repeated over and over with slight variations, often with biographical details that give a poignant individuality to the young man whose life has been snuffed out.

Homer's battles are described graphically, and they may seem to us like unmitigated hell. Day after day there is a constant din of men fighting, an uproar of war cries and battered shields and helmets, spears clashing against shields, shields grinding into other shields, warriors yelling for help or shouting out in agony or triumph, the whole battlefield strewn with mangled, gore-covered corpses, the air loud with the cries of killers and killed, the whole earth, it seems, drowning in blood. Panic can suddenly grip a whole army; when a hero approaches, lesser men are terrified and flee, and even the heroes themselves can be terrified or heartsick or overwhelmed with despair. Sometimes the battlefield is such a slaughter-house that it is difficult to find a spot where the ground is visible through the heaped-up corpses. Sometimes when a warrior drives his chariot, the horses gallop over bodies living and dead, and the chariot rails are splat-tered with the blood flung up by the horses' hooves and the wheel rims.

And yet there is another side to the slaughter, an aspect that is more difficult for us to comprehend, since in our culture sympathy naturally goes out toward the apparent victim. Homer inherited other kinds of epi-thets: war is also *kudianeira,* man-glorying, and both Achaeans and Tro-jans are called *philoptolemos,* war-loving. There is even a word, *charmē,* for the exhilaration that a warrior feels at the prospect of entering a battle. All this seems very strange to us. And we may be totally disoriented when we come to the moment in the famous, heartbreakingly tender scene between Hector and Andromache when the Trojan hero prays for the welfare of his infant son:

> "Zeus and you other gods who can hear my prayer,
> grant that this child, this boy of mine, may grow up
> to be as I am, outstanding among the Trojans,
> strong and brave, and rule over Troy with great power.
> And let people say of him, 'He is a better man
> than his father was,' as they see him returning from battle,
> having killed his enemy, carrying back in triumph
> the gore-stained armor to gladden his mother's heart." (6.475–82)

Who among us can read the final line of this speech, at least for the first time, without a shock of bewilderment? Here, amid all the sorrow and concern and deep husbandly love, in what both these admirable people sense may be their final meeting, at the climax of a prayer that Hector must know will never be fulfilled, is the image of a mother rejoicing at her son's return from battle with the bloody armor of the enemy he has just killed, as if she were watching him in his robe and mortarboard graduat-ing from college. There is no revulsion or squeamishness in her heart, no fear, no sympathy for the young man he has killed. She is the wife and daughter and mother of warriors, and all she feels at that moment is pride in the honor of her son. Of course, Hector's imagined Andromache is not Andromache, but we are meant to believe that he understands how his wife, or any sensible woman, will react.

It isn't easy to feel our way into the warrior culture that Homer is describing, but as we enter the rhythms of the poem we become imaginatively acclimated to that culture and perhaps even comfortable in it as we wouldn't be in real life, given the values that we have grown up with. Some readers may feel reluctant to identify themselves with men trained to be killers, as if this mode of sympathy will somehow harden their hearts and turn them into desperadoes or freebooters, eager to leave their civilized habits behind and rush out to sign up with Blackwater USA. The mind of the warrior, though, is only one side of the reality in this poem. Homer is always supremely balanced. He includes the *for* and the *against* in his boundless sympathy, the apparently tragic and the apparently comic, the friend and the enemy, the victor and the vanquished. And through this inclusion we can begin to understand a part of the human experience that may have been opaque and unavailable to us before.

The warriors of the *Iliad* are eager to win glory in battle, but even aside from that, they feel intense pleasure in the act of fighting. After Achilles has withdrawn from the war, he wants nothing more than to return; he longs for "the battle shouts and the fighting." Later, when he sends Patroclus out to push back the Trojans, he warns him not to let his attention be distracted by the sheer pleasure of killing. This pleasure is what an athlete feels in the exercise of his prowess, the total immersion in the present moment, where there is no thinking about past or future, and life keeps moving, staccato, moment by moment, into the continuous intensity of what comes next: running, leaping, driving your horses, judging the moves of the enemy, holding the spear in your hand at just the right spot to balance its weight, looking so precisely into the chaotic movements of the battle that a deeper order arises and suddenly skin flashes between the layers of bronze and as you hurl your spear you see that it has already hit its mark. "I know about fighting," Hector says.

> "I know how to kill a man;
> I know how to swing my shield to the right or left;
> I know how to charge straight into the frenzy of chariots
> attacking or fleeing in terror; and I know how
> to step in the deadly dance of hand-to-hand combat." (7.226–30)

You can feel his exhilaration especially in the last line: a heightened sense of aliveness amid the continual threat of extinction, an adrenaline-testosterone high that soldiers have testified to in wars ancient and modern. Right-thinking people are properly horrified by the thought of war, but soldiers know what athletes know, that there is a zone you can enter, a state of pure body-awareness, in which the right movement happens by itself, effortlessly, without any interference of the conscious will. A veteran from the war in Iraq told a friend of mine about flying an F-16 with a surface-to-air missile chasing her, "and you could tell," my friend said, "that she was having the time of her life." Homeric combat is, for the brave man, a superior form of competition, the gambler's ultimate high. Death, as Dr. Johnson said, concentrates the mind wonderfully. Victory over an opponent who has been trying to kill you is an exhilarating experience, as we see time after time in the battle scenes.

This intoxication of combat shows us why it is easy for a goddess like Athena to stir up an entire army so that they long to enter the fighting:

> within the heart of each soldier
> she stirred up the strength to fight on without any respite,
> and at once the desire for war became sweeter to them
> than sailing back in their ships to their own dear country. (2.434–37)

There are times during the battle when a warrior feels inspired, indestructible, alive with a vitality beyond his wildest dreams. Hector even goes berserk at one point, foams at the mouth, his eyes blaze, and in his invulnerability he rages through the enemy ranks like an unstoppable fire. And here are the two Ajaxes after meeting the great god Poseidon. "My heart has been struck by a jolt of courage," Ajax the Smaller says; "I feel / my body tingling all over, my arms and legs / surge with strength, and I long to go into battle." His namesake and comrade-in-arms, Ajax the Tall, answers,

> "I feel that too. A current runs through my hands,
> they long for a spear, my legs want to sprint, my body
> feels stronger than it has ever been, and I can't
> wait to meet Hector and fight him in all his fury."
> These were their words to each other as they exulted
> in the joy of war that the god had put in their breasts.   (13.76–81)

Homer describes war with an objectivity that can easily offend modern readers because he so obviously *isn't* offended at the violence he describes. But objectivity doesn't mean coldness or lack of involvement. His descriptions are passionate; they include both the pain of the victim and the joy of the victor, and they seem endlessly inventive. Men are pierced, stabbed, cut, carved, hacked, slashed, and severed in dozens of ways, and Homer's astonishing virtuosity makes many of these deaths fresh, surprising, even fascinating to witness. Here, for example, is a particularly vivid and gruesome example. After Agamemnon spears Hippolochus's brother through the chest, Hippolochus jumps out of the chariot and tries to run away, but Agamemnon

> cut him down with his sword,
> then sliced off his arms and his head, and he kicked the torso
> and sent it rolling away through the crowd like a log.   (11.145–47)

Even when a warrior simply falls over from a spear wound he may be given an extended simile that has him fall in slow motion with a majesty that we could never have anticipated, as when Ajax spears a young Trojan in the first great battle of the poem:

> . . . the spear drove on through his shoulder,
> and he fell to the ground in the dust like a stately poplar
> that has grown up in a broad meadow beside a marsh,

and its trunk is smooth, but small branches grow from its top;
and a wheelwright cuts it down with his gleaming iron
and bends it into a rim for a handsome car,
and it lies on the bank of a river and dries in the sunlight.   (4.452–58)

Homer's poetry always touches the defeated and the dead, but also the victorious and the living. The fallen Hector is no more poetic than the triumphant Achilles; the young man cut down like a poplar is no more worthy of our empathy than the young man who leaps onto his enemy like a lion breaking a heifer's back. When Patroclus hauls in Thestor as if he were a prize-winning marlin, we feel his pride as a sportsman, and it is clear how inappropriate any moral judgment of him would be.

Next, he rushed straight at Thestor, the son of Enops,
who was huddled up in his chariot, out of his mind
with terror; the reins had slipped from his hands, and Patroclus
came up and stabbed him on the right side of his jaw
and drove the spear through his teeth. Then, gripping the spear shaft,
he pivoted back and lifted him over the rail
like a fisherman who sits on a jutting boulder
and hauls a tremendous fish up out of the sea
at the end of his line, caught on the bright bronze hook:
just so did Patroclus haul him up out of his car,
mouth gaping around the spear point, and tossed him down
on his face, and he lay there flopping until life left him.   (16.362–73)

As we immerse ourselves in the poem, our response to passages like this is not revulsion but enjoyment, because Homer's depiction of war is as beautiful as it is terrible. "The battle scenes hardly ever, in the original, read like mere transcriptions of carnage," one critic says. "The formality of the verse form does not so much distance as heighten them, they are not less but more than usually 'there,' so that—our own powers of response enormously intensified—the narrative can blaze for hundreds of lines on end, seemingly at full stretch but with always enough energy in reserve to reach still higher and burst into almost intolerable splendor."

Achilles

Achilles is the most loved character in the *Iliad,* along with Patroclus and Hector. Like all great leaders, he inspires an extraordinary devotion in his men, and they long for him as he sits suffocating in his rage. But he also inspires a deep personal devotion among the people closest to him.

His friendship with Patroclus is marked with such passion that Greeks of later ages, when homosexuality was the norm, assumed that they were lovers, although there is not a trace of erotic feelings between them in the *Iliad.* The most moving statement of Patroclus's devotion comes in the request his ghost makes at the end of the poem: "May my bones not be buried apart from your bones, Achilles. / May they lie together, just as we grew up together." This kind of passion is something that we in our culture rarely experience in friendships; we can relate to it more in matters of sexual love. But for the ancients there was nothing more intense than the love of comrades-in-arms. We find the same passion in the friendship of David and Jonathan in the Bible, in which "the soul of Jonathan was knit with the soul of David, and Jonathan loved him as his own soul." When David mourns him, he says, "Your love for me was wonderful, passing the love of women."

In this friendship Achilles is clearly the superior; he is higher in birth, martial prowess, and every other kind of excellence, and Patroclus is happy to serve him as lieutenant, butler, and confidant. Their friendship is a privilege for him, and it was a privilege even when they were growing up together as boys; he is grateful to Achilles' father for allowing him to be his son's attendant. Patroclus knows his friend well and is skillful at not provoking his imperious nature. When Nestor asks him to sit down in his hut for a moment, Patroclus replies,

> "This is no time for sitting, my lord; he is proud
> and may take offense if I linger—the one who sent me.
>   . . . You understand
> how terrifying a man he can be, my lord;
> he might be quick to blame even one who is blameless."   (11.599–605)

For his part Achilles treats Patroclus with tenderness and a bit of gentle mockery, at one point comparing his tears of compassion at the slaughter of the Achaeans to the tears of a little girl tugging at her mother's skirts. But Patroclus doesn't hesitate to speak out about the dire situation of the Achaean army and Achilles' share in it:

> . . . But you are impossible
> to deal with, Achilles. I hope I am never seized
> with such anger as yours. What good is your excellence? How
> will it benefit others, now or in times to come,
> if you hold it back and refuse to save the Achaeans?
> Your father cannot have been Lord Peleus, nor
> can Thetis have been your mother: the rough sea bore you,
> the harsh cliffs fathered you, since your heart has no pity.　　(16.25–32)

This passionately honest response to a dangerous superior is testimony to the strength of their friendship.

The sea goddess Thetis, Achilles' mother, is equally devoted to him and even more attuned to his moods; she hears his grief from the depths of the sea and comes whenever he needs her. One of my early readers found herself weeping in a New York subway car as she read a printout of Book 1, so touching was Thetis's motherly solicitude:

> At once she arose like a mist from the gray waters
> and sat down before him and listened to him as he wept
> and stroked his hair and spoke to him softly: "Child,
> why are you weeping? What has caused you this sorrow?"　　(1.364–67)

Thetis is a tragic figure in the *Iliad*, the only one among the blessed gods who doesn't and can't live at ease. She was forced by Zeus to marry a mortal against her will, and after she suffered the pain of seeing Peleus grow old, she left him. The only person she deeply loves is her doomed son, and she is constantly devastated by his misery. What Zeus says to Achilles' immortal horses he might with equal appropriateness have said to her:

When he saw them weeping, Lord Zeus was filled with pity,
and he shook his head and said to himself, "Poor fools,
why did we give you to Peleus, a mortal man,
when you are unaging and deathless? Was it to let you
share in the wretched sorrow of humankind?
For there is nothing so miserable as humans
among all the creatures that live and breathe on the earth." (17.439–45)

Truly Thetis is the *mater dolorosa* before the fact, an immortal god-
dess who looks like a twenty-year-old, tenderly stroking the hair of her
doomed twenty-something-year-old son, like the Mary of Michelange-
lo's *Pietà*. Grief at Achilles' fate dominates her mind, to the exclusion of
everything except the desire to help him. When Zeus, at the end of the
poem, calls on her to deliver a message to Achilles, she is ashamed to
show her face on Olympus, since her sorrow contradicts the very nature
of a god. Achilles knows what the difference between men and gods is; he
says to Priam, with unconscious irony, "However we can, we [humans]
must learn to bear / misfortune like this, but *they* [the gods] live free of
all sorrow." His demeanor toward his mother is perfectly childlike, open,
and frank. But he is also aware of the sorrow he is inadvertently causing
her. At one point, in a gesture of pure love, he even wishes himself into
oblivion for the sake of her happiness:

If only you could have stayed at home with the sea nymphs
and Peleus had taken a mortal woman as bride!
But as it is, your heart will be filled with endless
grief for the death of your child.   (18.71–74)

The most striking instance of devotion to Achilles is from Briseïs,
the subject of the quarrel between Achilles and Agamemnon that is the
mainspring of the *Iliad*'s plot. We get just two glimpses of her. The longest
is her lament for the dead Patroclus, in which she mentions that Achil-
les killed her husband and her three brothers when he conquered the
city of Lyrnessus, to the southeast of Troy, and that Patroclus promised,
after the war, to make her Achilles' lawful wife. The other glimpse is in

Book 1, when Patroclus, obeying Achilles' command, hands her over to Agamemnon's heralds:

> He led out the beautiful girl, and he handed her over
> to the two men. And they walked back beside the ships,
> and Briséïs walked with a heavy heart.   (1.350–52)

The last phrase translates the Greek *aekous'*, which literally means "unwillingly, reluctantly." Is it too much to read devotion into this one word? It is remarkable that a woman whose husband and beloved brothers have been killed by an enemy should be reluctant to leave him. And from Achilles' own remarks about Briseïs—he calls her "my wife, my darling" and says, "I . . . loved this woman, with all my heart, / even though she was a captive, won by the spear"—we may reasonably infer deep feelings between them. But whatever she feels for Achilles, whether it is in fact devotion or simply the desire of a powerless slave to be comfortable and protected, she wants nothing more than to be his wife.

It's easy to see why people would be devoted to Achilles. He is tall and handsome, three times more powerful than an ordinary warrior, the best and bravest of the Achaeans, always supremely confident of his own abilities, a loyal friend, a good son. He is also the most intelligent character in the *Iliad,* if we define intelligence as subtlety and complexity of thought, and he speaks with a fierce eloquence. He is passionate and direct, is fluent with his emotions, says what he thinks, and "hate[s] like the gates of Hades / the man who says one thing and hides something else inside him." During the funeral games for Patroclus in Book 23 Achilles shows his most genial side, and his charisma and princely generosity dominate the scene.

In his enforced idleness, while the rest of the Myrmidons pass the time "amusing themselves on the seashore / with archery and with throwing the spear and the discus," we find Achilles reciting or composing poetry,

> singing and plucking a clear-toned lyre,
> a beautiful instrument with a silver crossbar
> to hold the strings; he had taken it from the spoils

when he had captured and plundered Ëétion's city;
with it he was delighting his heart, and he sang
poems about the glorious deeds of heroes.   (9.183–88)

This brief scene links Achilles to someone at the other end of the heroic
spectrum: Paris, who is the only other character said to play the lyre.
But for Achilles poetry is a mark not only of his sensitivity but also of
his love of excellence and his desire for martial greatness. We can see
the same love of excellence in his reaction to the armor that Hephaestus
has made for him: his delight in the shield, breastplate, and helmet come
partly from the fact that he knows he can now kill Hector, but also from
the god's marvelous craftsmanship; rather than back away in awe, as the
rest of the Myrmidons do, he lets himself gaze at the armor for a long
time.

And yet, in spite of all these virtues, Achilles spends almost the whole
of the *Iliad* in a circle of hell as painful as any that Dante imagined. *Mēnin*,
rage, the first word of the *Iliad* and its theme, is a word used only of the
anger of Achilles or of the gods; it indicates an elemental, cataclysmic,
indiscriminately destructive emotion. (At one point Achilles wishes that
both armies, Trojans and Achaeans alike, were annihilated.) Rage, resent-
ment, depression, the sense of being "a useless burden upon the earth,"
guilt for causing the death of his beloved friend, unassuageable grief, a
cruelty and savagery that go far beyond the bounds of acceptable heroic
behavior—all these emotions are forms of intense suffering that proceed
directly from Achilles' inflexible pride. To be choked with hatred, as Yeats
wrote, is the greatest of evils. When Achilles reenters the war he is in
such a frenzy to slaughter that he barely seems human anymore; he is
more like a force of nature, destroying whatever lies in his path. Later,
in a refinement of cruelty, he sacrifices twelve young warriors whom he
captured in the Xanthus river:

. . . and with butchery in his heart
he ordered his men to bring the dozen young Trojans,
and he slit their throats with his knife, one after the other,
and threw them onto the pyre.   (23.172–75)

The argument between Agamemnon and Achilles is the beginning of the Achaeans' grief in the *Iliad*. Given the exigencies of the heroic code of honor, there is nothing Achilles can do once the intemperate words have been spoken and Agamemnon has publicly humiliated him. When you subscribe to a code of honor, as everyone in the *Iliad* does, your freedom of action is drastically curtailed. This is not simply the barbarism of Bronze Age ethics; well into the twentieth century distinguished men were still killing each other in duels over so-called affairs of honor. But killing Agamemnon is not an option for Achilles. In one of the most riveting scenes in the poem Athena descends from heaven, seizes him by his blond hair, fixes "her terrible blazing eyes" upon him, and forbids him to draw his sword. His only options now are to accept the insult, which honor won't permit, or to withdraw from the war. Even after Zeus grants Achilles' horrifying request to pin the Achaean army close to their ships, which results in the slaughter of hundreds or thousands of his comrades-in-arms, no one disputes that he is in the right. Agamemnon himself later says so—"I was out of my mind with rage; I will not deny it"—as does Poseidon: "King Agamemnon is absolutely / at fault in this, because he dishonored Achilles." (The Greek word for what descended on Agamemnon is *atē*, which means "madness" or "moral blindness," a kind of temporary insanity in which passion overwhelms all rational considerations.)

Where Achilles is clearly in the wrong is in refusing Agamemnon's offer of reparation. The offer is magnificent and should satisfy even the most arrogant of heroes: treasures of gold, champion race horses, skilled women slaves, plus Briseïs, certified as sexually untouched; and a promise of even more lavish gifts later on, including one of Agamemnon's daughters in marriage and the kingship over seven large cities in Argos. Achilles' refusal is a breach of the heroic code, which has its time-tested mechanisms for restoring balance. Men are permitted to expiate their crimes by exile or by payment; the details may be in dispute, but the principle isn't. Ajax bluntly expresses what all the Achaeans feel:

> "I see that Achilles
> has hardened his heart. He hasn't listened. He won't
> be reasonable. He doesn't honor the friendship

we honored him with, above others. He is relentless.
And yet a man will accept due reparations
for his brother or son, even from someone who killed him,
and the killer stays on at home, having paid enough,
and the family's anger is held back once they receive
the blood-price."   (9.629–37)

However much Achilles loves Briseïs, it isn't the loss of her in itself that rankles so deeply; it is the public humiliation. Honor is his only concern. It is true that at the height of his rage there are moments when he doubts that honor is worth dying for. "Nothing is worth my life," he says, and he means it, for the moment. At one point it actually seems as if he has a conscious choice at his disposal:

"My mother, Thetis,
tells me that there are two ways I might die: if I stay here
and keep on fighting around the city of Troy,
I can never go home, but my glory will live forever;
but if I return in my ships to my own dear country,
my glory will die, but my life will be long and peaceful."   (9.412–17)

Whether this is a matter of fate or choice is irrelevant. By remaining in Troy, Achilles keeps choosing honor, as he has to, and thus keeps choosing to accomplish the will of the story.

Achilles intimately knows the seductions of even justified anger, "which, far sweeter / than trickling honey, expands in the breast like smoke." But to everything there is a season: a time to kill and a time to heal, a time to reject and a time to accept. It is clear that acceptance of Agamemnon's offer is the appropriate response now, and that it is only excessive pride that motivates Achilles to reject it. The rhetoric of his refusal is brilliant beyond any other speech in the *Iliad,* but the emotion behind it seems perilously close to that of a small child who keeps working himself into a tantrum.

The aftermath of the refusal is catastrophic for Achilles. It leads to the death of Patroclus and his own unassuageable grief. As Agamemnon says, in one of his few insightful remarks, "of all the gods, only Hades / is implacable and perverse, which is why men hate him." The Tao Te Ching states this more clearly:

> Whoever is stiff and inflexible
> is a disciple of death.
> Whoever is soft and yielding
> is a disciple of life.

In these long speeches in which he proclaims the value of life, Achilles ironically proves that he is a disciple of death. When a person will not bend, the universe eventually takes him across its knees and snaps him like a dry twig.

Helen

Helen is the loneliest character in the *Iliad*, the loneliest woman in the world. There is something uncanny about her beauty. People are either in awe of it or they shudder at it. When Homer says that she is dreadfully like an immortal goddess, the adverb isn't merely formulaic: it has the weight of desolation behind it. Beauty for her is a curse. She is the dream of every woman who looks in the mirror and finds something lacking, and the helpless desire of every man. She can do nothing to mitigate or control the intensity of their reactions. Even the old men of Troy feel their hearts pierced and their bones shaken when she passes. But what good can that do her? They are seeing only her outer form, and she has long since stopped deriving any pleasure from that.

She has also long since awakened from her infatuation with Paris. Now she feels nothing but contempt for him and for herself. She is living with a man who, however handsome and brave he may be, is a fool, someone without moral awareness or "a proper sense of the people's outrage." From her point of view there is nothing between them; no affection, no understanding, just the prospect of boredom, frustration, and loveless sex that she wants no part of. She speaks to him, and of him, with the utmost rudeness, which is a measure of her despair. All her life she, like Paris, has been the recipient of "the enchanting gifts / of Aphrodite the golden." But Aphrodite is a harsh mistress, and sexual enchantment, though one of

"the radiant gifts of the gods," turns out to be yet another form of tempo-
rary insanity. In the first flush of intoxication Helen left her whole world
behind for Paris's sake, only to discover later on that her great love story
was in reality a deadly farce, that the more she lived with his magnetic
charm, the less it meant to her, until at last it means nothing at all.

When Paris and Menelaus enter into single combat over her, with the
understanding that "whoever wins will take [her] away," she becomes, lit-
erally, the trophy wife. What does it matter to her who wins? It is a hope-
less situation, and the only way out she can think of is death. But death
isn't an option either. As she says to her father-in-law, Priam,

> "If only death had come to me when I followed
> your son here, leaving my home and my marriage bed
> and my precious daughter and all my beloved friends.
> But death didn't come, and I melt away in my weeping."   (3.161–64)

Her self-hatred would be excruciating if it weren't so morally beauti-
ful, as a first step toward regeneration. "Brother-in-law of mine," she says
to Hector, in her soft voice, "of the bitch that I am, / a cause of evil, a curse
and abomination." She blames herself and Paris for all the misery that has
descended on the Trojans and the Achaeans; it has all happened "through
my fault, bitch that I am, and through Paris's folly." Even her private med-
itation is infused with the consequences of her crime. We first see her

> in her own chambers, in front of the loom,
> making a large purple robe, in which she had woven
> many fierce combats that Trojans and Argives both
> had endured on the field of battle because of her.   (3.116–19)

Here she makes a palatable beauty out of the warriors' suffering, repeat-
ing her self-loathing in every scene she weaves, just as she knows that
someday her own suffering will be transformed into a source of beauty
for other people, as if she were feeling her way into the very moment
when future becomes present and the listener can actually see her and
hear her speak, intimately, nearer than breath, than heartbeat: "Zeus has
brought us an evil fate, so that poets / can make songs about us for all

future generations." But her awareness that "these evils are as the gods have ordained them" does nothing to relieve her permanent, crushing sense of guilt. This taking of responsibility on her part is very moving.

Helen realizes what Paris is too vain and immature to realize: the consequences of her transgression. But there is nothing she could have done about it, and nothing she can do now. She had and has no choice in the matter, as we can see from the chilling incident in which Aphrodite, in the guise of an old wool-spinner, orders her to return to the bedroom and make love with Paris. Her whole being flinches and draws back in revulsion, and for a moment she rebels:

> These were her [Aphrodite's] words, and they made Helen's heart beat
> faster.
> She knew the goddess: her luscious neck and her ravishing
> breasts and her brilliant eyes. Astonished, she said,
> "What do you want now, goddess? Why are you always
> tricking me? Will you drive me still farther on,
> to Mæónia or Phrygia and hand me over
> to another one of the pretty men you so love?
> Is it because Menelaus has beaten Paris
> and wishes to take his contemptible wife back home?
> Is that why you came here with treachery in your heart?
> *You* go to his side now; give up being a goddess;
> don't return to Olympus; forever worry
> about his welfare; pamper him and protect him
> until he makes you his wife, or perhaps his whore.
> I will not budge. It would be disgraceful to go there
> and share that man's bed; the women of Troy would be right
> to blame me for it. I have enough grief in my heart."   (3.371–87)

But in words that pulse with casual rage, Aphrodite lifts the mask of her charm to reveal the death's head underneath, and Helen has to obey, like the most abject slave in her household.

> The radiant goddess turned upon her in a fury:
> "Do not provoke me, headstrong girl, or I might

lose my temper; I might withdraw my protection
and hate you as passionately as now I adore you.
You have no idea what hatred of you I could cause
in both Trojans and Argives—how cruelly you would die."
The goddess glared, and Helen was chilled with terror.
Wrapping herself in her shining white shawl, she left
without a word, and none of the Trojan ladies
saw her go, and she followed the goddess in silence.   (3.388–97)

Hector

In her famous essay Simone Weil points to "the extraordinary impartial-
ity that breathes through the *Iliad*." This impartiality is one of the poem's
most impressive qualities and makes her judgment of it as "a miracle" not
hyperbolic but the simple truth. The *Iliad* has no equals and few succes-
sors in portraying the enemy as fully human and worthy of our deepest
compassion. Most of the young men whose deaths Homer depicts with
such exquisite pathos are Trojans. Major Trojan characters like Priam,
Paris, Andromache, and Hector are portrayed with at least as much clar-
ity and affection as the major Achaean characters. Simone Weil is also
right that Homer's impartiality is completely lacking in Hebrew and
Roman literature, and, I would add, in the Gospels as well, except for
the saying of Jesus (the authentic ones). It is as impossible to imagine the
author of 1 Samuel, for example, taking us into Gath and letting us see
Goliath at home with his wife and children, as it is to imagine Matthew
giving us more than a nasty caricature of a Pharisee or John the Evange-
list mentioning "the Jews" without a deadly hiss in his voice.

This is not to say that we aren't well aware that Homer is a Greek and
not a Trojan. He always makes it clear that the Achaeans are the supe-
rior men, both in bravery and prowess. The Trojan army is described as
relatively undisciplined; at the beginning of the first battle in the poem,
for example, they advance "with a raucous shouting, like cranes," while
the Achaeans advance in dignified silence. When a fighter turns his back
and flees, he is likely to be a Trojan. The great Hector himself, although
described as a formidable hero and at times a scourge to the Achaean
army, is defeated twice by Ajax and knocked to the ground by a spear-

cast from Diomedes, and in the end he is no match for Achilles. His only major triumph is over Patroclus, and that happens only after Apollo stuns and disarms Patroclus and Euphorbus spears him in the back.

Hector is a more complicated character than any of the Achaeans except for Achilles. He is "the one defender of Troy," the joy and glory of the people, honored by them like a god, a loving husband, father, and son, and the only man in the poem who is called gentle, besides Patroclus—though, as Andromache says, Hector is not gentle in combat. But he is also impetuous, arrogant, dismissive of good advice, and at one point, after killing Patroclus, he descends into gratuitous barbarism. In Book 12, as the Trojans are about to break through the Achaean wall, when Polydamas prudently advises him to hold back, Hector attacks his friend and counselor with withering scorn, impugning his courage and threatening his life. Occasionally he has to be rallied by other warriors. At the end of the poem he, like Achilles, unwisely sacrifices everything for the sake of his honor, although as he considers his apparent choices he shows a touching sense of his own bad judgment:

> ". . . I could back off and enter the gate,
> but Polydamas will be quick to accuse me of rashness.
> He begged me to lead the troops back inside the city
> during this last disastrous night, when Achilles
> arose again and returned to the fighting; but I
> didn't take his advice. It would have been far
> better for me if I had. And now that my own
> reckless conduct has ruined us, I feel shame
> at facing the men and the long-robed women of Troy.
> What if some lesser man were to say of me, 'Hector
> thought he could trust his own strength and destroyed his people'?"
>
> (22.96–106)

As an ancient scholiast aptly remarked, "The poet shows here how disastrous is the love of honor, for because Hector doesn't wish to be called a coward by a more cowardly man . . . he perishes. His reasoning displays a noble spirit, but also folly, since he wants to cure one evil by another."

Hector's attitude toward Paris is fascinating. He knows his brother well, has no illusions about him, is constantly aware that it is only because of Paris "that this miserable war / has flared up around sacred Ilion," and several times wishes him dead. But in spite of Hector's clear-sighted vision about the rights and wrongs of the issue, he does nothing to correct it. It is as if he is suffering from a brain injury that keeps one part of his mind from communicating with the other: he knows that something is terribly wrong, but he can't see the solution that is right in front of his nose. We can call this a blind spot in an otherwise deeply responsible man. But of course if Hector were to right the wrong, the story would end.

Hector also recognizes that whatever Paris's faults are, he is a fine warrior: "No man of any sense could ever belittle / your exploits in war, since you are such a brave fighter." This fairness echoes the impartiality of Homer, who never makes Paris a villain. Yes, he is vain, selfish, superficial, and morally blind, but he is also charming, remarkably cheerful in the face of criticism, honest in his own way, and filled with a physical grace that is numinous, like Helen's beauty. When Paris runs out to battle at the end of Book 6 Homer's delight in him is palpable, and we can only gaze in admiration at the radiant vitality of this man who has blithely brought ruin to his entire world:

> Just as a stabled horse who has fully eaten
> breaks his tether and gallops across the plain,
> eager to have a swim in the fast-flowing river,
> and exults as he runs—he holds his head high, and his mane
> streams in the wind, and he runs on, aware of his own
> magnificence, to the fields where the mares are at pasture:
> so Paris ran down from the height of Pérgamus, shining
> in his armor like sunlight, exulting, laughing out loud,
> and his swift legs carried him onward.   (6.506–14)

The most moving glimpse we are given of Hector is in the meeting between him and Andromache. Homer devotes fewer than a hundred lines to it, but their conversation feels like an entire tragic novel. In Plato's *Ion* the eponymous rhapsode describes his audience's reaction to famous passages like this one: "I look down from the stage and see them weeping and gazing up at me, filled with awe as they surrender to the amazement of the story." I myself, in my brief side job as a Homeric rhapsode, have noticed that same look of awe on people's faces as they listen to this episode. Their emotion is not sadness, they tell me, nor is it pity and terror. It is a kind of rapt identification.

The poignance, the intimacy of this scene are extraordinary, and what makes it even more extraordinary is our awareness that Hector and his wife are "the enemy." There is something beyond sorrow in the meeting of these two lovers who, in spite of themselves, know that war is about to destroy their country and everything they hold dear. Their past has been filled with suffering (Andromache, like Briseïs, has had her whole family slaughtered by Achilles and now depends on one man for her safety); their future is doomed (although Hector kindly lets himself imagine the possibility of his son growing up to rule over Troy, they both know that mass slaughter and the enslavement of the women are imminent). But as they balance so precariously on the fulcrum of the moment, the only reality is what shines through their words: the tenderness of their marriage and their concern for each other. Even apart from the words, each physical detail—Andromache taking Hector's hand in hers as she approaches him; Hector reaching out to pick up his son; the parents' laughter when the baby shrinks back, frightened by the horsehair-crested helmet; Hector taking it off and putting it on the ground; Andromache's smile with tears in her eyes, which moves Hector to stroke her face, and then her slow walk to the house, as she continually stops to look back, like a reverse Orpheus, and loses the beloved every time—brings us, ironically enough, into the grace of the present moment, for as long as it lasts (which happens to be forever, although they don't know that). Our emotion when we hear or read this scene is much more and much less than pity: it is an enormous empathy, a flowing into these characters, a feeling that all of life and death has flowed into them. We are immersed in pure presence, and the doomed man and woman stand before us with such an abundance of love that we find an infinite blessing in them and in all of life. "Nothing can explain the power of such moments over us," the critic Lionel Trilling wrote, "or nothing short of a recapitulation of the moral history of the race."

Priam and Achilles

Priam is not developed as a character until the end of the poem. He makes a few brief appearances in the earlier books, but he is mostly a vague, venerated presence, whose several wives and fifty sons give him an air of Oriental exoticism. We do see his love for Paris when he can't bear to watch the duel between him and Menelaus in Book 3. We are also shown how he, like Hector, treats Helen with kindness; after we are introduced to him and his council of old men who sit on the wall, chirping like cicadas with their lily-like voices, he gently calls to her and says, "I do not blame you—it is the gods whom I blame / for this wretched war that they inflicted upon me." He is insightful enough to know that Helen is only a puppet in the hands of the gods. On the divine level, behind the curtain, it is the implacable hatred of Hera, Poseidon, and Athena that has doomed Troy ever since "Paris committed that act of madness." In spite of Zeus's love for the city and its people's exemplary piety, the hatred of these three gods bears inexorably down on Troy.

But it is not until the death of Hector that Homer focuses our attention on the old king. His mourning is extreme—he is sure that sorrow will drag him "down to Death's house"—but his royal dignity remains intact, though he grovels in the dung before the gates of the city. It is a grief and shatteredness that may remind us of that other stricken patriarch, Jacob, who, when he recognizes Joseph's bloody coat, refuses to be comforted and says, "I will go down to my son in the grave, mourning."

When we come to Book 24, Priam becomes the central figure. It is impossible to give adequate praise to this last book of the *Iliad*. All one can do is read and admire. It is, as Tolstoy said, "inexpressibly beautiful."

Book 24 depicts a moment of grace: a moment as improbable before the fact as it would be for the wolf to dwell with the lamb and the leopard to lie down with the kid, though after the fact it is the necessary fulfillment toward which the whole epic in its intricate vicissitudes has been moving. The meeting between Priam and Achilles is narrated with great intensity; its drama unfolds in a little over two hundred lines. First, though, it has to be set up by Zeus's commands: that Achilles return Hector's body and that Priam collect it, bringing a great ransom with him in the royal mule cart. Zeus also commands the great liminal figure Hermes—messenger of the gods, inventor of the lyre, psychopomp, god of travelers, thieves, whores, and businessmen—to convey Priam safely through the dangers of the Achaean camp to Achilles' hut. Hermes hurries down to Troy, taking the form "of a handsome young prince, with the first slight traces of hair / on his lips and cheeks, in the loveliest prime of youth."

The dialogue between him and Priam is the longest in the poem, and the lightheartedness that he brings to this transitional scene makes it feel like a buoyant dream. He is obviously having a very fine time, not only as an emissary but as a trickster. Hermes may not be the father of lies, but he is a kissing cousin, and the whoppers that he tells about his just-invented persona are unnecessary for the progress of the story; they are a matter of pure enjoyment. He is the ancestor of every charming, unabashed liar in literature, from Odysseus to Huckleberry Finn to Felix Krull. Unlike Athena or Aphrodite, he delights in befriending mortals. Priam is in excellent hands.

Once Priam hears that the apparent young man is Achilles' attendant, his most urgent question is about his son's body, whether it is still intact or whether Achilles in his relentless savagery has hacked it to pieces and fed it to the wild dogs. This is the persistent anxiety of all the characters in the *Iliad.* It is not death itself that they dread, so much as lying unburied, without the proper funeral rites, being eaten by dogs and maggots and carrion birds, and thus not being able to "pass through the gates of Hades." The fact that this dread is entirely culture-bound—for contrast, think of the ceremony of Tibetan sky burial, in which monks reverently chop up the corpse of the departed, light incense, and welcome the arrival of the vultures—doesn't make it any less moving. Hermes, always the essence of courtesy, reassures the grieving father:

> "... you would be astonished to see how alive
> it seems, as it lies there: it looks as fresh as the dew.
> Every wound on the flesh has been healed completely,
> though many Achaeans stabbed it. Such is the care
> that the blessed gods have shown for your dear son, even
> for his dead body—so close is he to their hearts."   (24.410–15)

Priam enters Achilles' quarters as a suppliant—that is to say, as someone who is entirely at the mercy of a warrior and whose position is protected by the gods, though this protection is no assurance of survival. The scene is extraordinary:

> Priam walked in, unseen,
> and went to Achilles. He clasped his knees, then he kissed
> his terrible hands, the deadly hands that had slaughtered
> so many of Priam's sons. As when a man
> who is gripped by madness murders someone in his homeland
> and escapes to another country and then seeks refuge
> in the house of some lord, and all who look on are astounded:
> just so was Achilles astounded when he saw Priam,
> that godlike man. And everyone in the hut
> was astounded as well, and they looked around at each other.
>
> (24.465–74)

This is one of those skewed Homeric similes in which the surprise of the perspective takes you back at first. The point of comparison is between Priam's physical position and the murderer's, and between Achilles' astonishment and the lord's; but the moral position in the simile is reversed, since in reality Achilles is the killer, and Priam is the rich man in whose domain this scene is taking place. Everything has suffered a sea-change into something rich and strange.

Priam speaks out forthrightly and with great skill, beginning with an appeal to Achilles' feelings as a son. He has an intuitive understanding of Achilles' preference for plain speech, and when he begs for the return of Hector's body, there are no rhetorical flourishes. He speaks with his usual dignity, not only as suppliant to victor, but as father to son, and as human to human. He ends with these famous lines:

> "Respect the gods now. Have pity on me; remember
> your father. For I am more to be pitied than he is,
> since I have endured what no mortal ever endured:
> I have kissed the hands of the man who slaughtered my children."
>
> (24.494–97)

And the whole scene—the whole world, it seems—waits in breathless anticipation to see how Achilles will react. What he does is as unexpected to us as Priam's appearance is to him:

> Taking the old man's hand,
> he gently pushed him away. And each of them sat there
> remembering. Priam, crouched at Achilles' feet,
> sobbed for Hector; Achilles wept now for his father,
> now for Patroclus. And every room in the house
> rang with the sound of their mourning and lamentation.   (24.499–504)

What delicacy there is in Achilles' gesture, and how much Homer is able to express in that one adverb, "gently"! (The Greek word is *ēka*, which can also mean softly or effortlessly; it is used to describe the voices of Priam and the elders as they speak in an undertone about Helen's dreadful beauty, and the soft play of light on the glossy surface of the young men's tunics depicted on Achilles' marvelous shield.)

There is another gesture that Achilles makes toward the end of the conversation, after Priam has requested a truce to give the Trojans time to gather firewood for Hector's funeral pyre.

> "Yes. I agree, sir. This too shall be as you say.
> I will hold off the war for the time that you have requested."
> As he spoke these words, he clasped the old king's right hand
> at the wrist, so that he would have no fear in his heart.   (24.663–66)

Here too the physical movement is the embodiment of Achilles' unexpected, unhoped-for delicacy and compassion. This compassion for the father of his enemy is truly remarkable—one of the most deeply moving elements in the scene. And once more we are thrust into a state of astonishment. How in the world has Homer managed to arrive at this place of mutual understanding after beginning Book 24 with Apollo's complaint that "Achilles has lost all pity, all sense of shame" and with Hecuba's dire warning to her husband?

"Good god! Are you out of your mind? Where is your wisdom,
which once was famous all over the earth? How can
you think of going alone to stand face to face
with the man who slaughtered so many of your brave sons?
Your heart must be made of iron. If that man gets you
within his grasp—but he is a savage beast
and not a man—he will kill you without even blinking.
Please don't go. We can mourn for our son right here
as we sit in our own house. This must be what Fate spun
when I gave him birth: to be food for the wild dogs,
far from his parents. That butcher! If I could get
my hands on him, I would tear out his liver and eat it
raw! That would give me some small revenge for my son . . ."

(24.193–205)

The scene between Priam and Achilles is what lifts the poem beyond tragedy. Patroclus and Hector had to die for this grace to happen. The scene's power is self-evident, as is its subtlety and lightness of touch. There is a sense of forgiveness that breathes through it—or if forgiveness is not the right word, perhaps a sense of readiness or ripeness.

The undercurrent of violence that runs beneath Achilles' courtesy makes the ongoing moment of grace even more precious. Achilles knows himself well, perhaps for the first time, and he is aware that the slightest provocation will push him over the edge, into a violence he will be unable to control. "So do not provoke my grieving heart any further," he says, " / or else, disobeying Zeus's command, I may not / spare even you, sir—suppliant though you are." A little later he tells his handmaids to take measures that will prevent any confrontation,

to wash and anoint the dead man, but somewhere else,
in another part of the house, so that Priam would not
see his son—in case, in his anguish of heart,
he might not be able to keep from voicing his anger
and Achilles' own heart flare up into violent rage.   (24.575–79)

When we come to the point in the scene where Priam and Achilles eat together, the sense of communion between them and within us is deeper than words. The meal takes place in the vast silence after one line of verse ends and before the next one begins.

> Achilles then served the meat,
>   and they helped themselves to the food that was set before them.
>
> (24.622–23)

However long it lasts—an hour? a moment?—that silence contains everything that can't be expressed about the strength and beauty of the human heart.

> And when they had had enough of eating and drinking,
>   Priam gazed at Achilles in wonder—how tall
> he was and how handsome, like one of the blessed gods.
> And Achilles gazed at Priam in wonder, admiring
> his noble face and the brave words that he had spoken.   (24.624–28)

After supper both men go to bed, and Homer could easily have left it at that. But in his generosity he gives us and Achilles yet another gift:

> And so the herald and Priam, with many thoughts
>   in their minds, lay down to sleep outside on the porch.
> But Achilles slept in the innermost part of the hut,
> and by his side lay that beautiful girl Briséïs.   (24.667–70)

Shortly before, Thetis had told her son that it would do him good now "to make love with a woman." Of course, Briseïs is not just "a woman." Their lovemaking is one further fulfillment, another circle closed.

In Borges's story "The Secret Miracle," as the Jewish hero stands before a Nazi firing squad, God stops the physical universe and gives him a year of subjective time in a moment, so that he can complete his great unfinished task. At the end of the *Iliad* Homer gives Priam and Achilles a reprieve of infinite time. The final agony of Troy, the appalling misery that is fated to happen in the traditional account of the Trojan War, will never happen within the confines of the *Iliad*. The great city of Troy still stands, forever poised on the brink of disaster. Andromache will never become a slave, nor will her child be hurled off the wall of Troy. Hecuba will see Hector's body come home, as she desired. Priam will forever sit at the funeral feast, eating, drinking, and mourning over his fallen son to his heart's content. Achilles will sleep with his beloved Briseïs forever.

Poetry

Both the *Iliad* and the *Odyssey* know what a powerful effect poetry has. "It must give pleasure," and it does. Even the most desolating of human experiences, when raised to the level of poetry, are a joy to be savored by those who surrender to the music of the words. "It is a fine thing," Odysseus says to King Alcinous in the *Odyssey*,

> "to be listening to a poet
> such as this, who is like the immortals in speech.
> For I think that there must be no greater fulfillment
> than when joy takes over an audience in the great hall,
> and the banqueters are sitting next to each other
> listening to the poet, and beside them the tables
> are loaded with bread and meat, and the steward carries
> the drawn wine around and fills their cups to the brim.
> This seems to me the most beautiful thing in the world."
>
> (*Odyssey*, 9.3–11)

What kind of pleasure does the poetry of the *Iliad* give us? It is not simply an aesthetic pleasure; it doesn't evade or deny human suffering, but embraces it and includes it in something greater: the mind that can understand. Anyone who has been taken up into the rhythms of Homer's Greek has had the experience of being left, as one critic says, "shaken and exalted, with the sense of an abounding, transfigured reality." Everything—from cruelty to reconciliation, from the cosmic to the everyday, from the repulsive to the magnificent—is seen for what it is, compassionately, *dis*passionately, with the most exquisite attention. There is an intricate counterpoint of two voices in it, each of them independent, each essential: in one voice we hear the story of what happens, and in the other voice we hear the sound of the verse, which is always the story of the beautiful. The meter remains the same, but the rhythm is constantly changing and renewing itself with different variations of the pattern, as measured and fundamental as the breath. This music, with "its extraordinary artistic precision, calm, and purity," infuses every event in the poem; it *is* the poem; it is what we hear even before we are aware of the meaning of the words.

Many readers of the *Iliad* have felt a sustained exaltation while reading it. "I am always glad to return to the *Iliad*," Goethe wrote, "for one is always lifted up by it, as if in a hot-air balloon, above everything earthly, and one truly finds oneself in the realm where the gods soared to and fro." We have a sense of looking on from the vantage point of a mind that has thoroughly understood and therefore transcended human suffering. This state of mind is a kind of eternity in itself. Homer lets us see the actions of humans and gods in the same way that the gods see the actions of humans, but with a vision that is wider than their partial view. As characters, the gods are usually comic or contemptible; Zeus is a mere brute, Hera a harridan, and the rest of them one happy, seething, frivolous, dysfunctional family. But sometimes the father of men and gods is portrayed as above it all, the ideal spectator. Though deeply affected, he is in a condition of pure pleasure:

> "I *am* concerned: so many of them will die.
> But now I will sit here at ease on a ridge of Olympus
> where I can watch, to my heart's delight." (20.20–22)

Another way of saying this is that Homer looks at the world with a heart that is at peace; everything he says is beautiful because everything he sees is beautiful, however filled with suffering it may be. This quality may be what made Schiller say of Book 23 what could be said of the entire poem: "No matter how unhappy your life has been, if you have lived long enough to read [it], then you can have no complaints." Homer's genius transforms whatever it touches. Even slaughter and mayhem and savagery and grief become beautiful in that serene music. Everything is included in it; everything sings. We are shown the world from a point of view in which reality itself, even the most tragic reality, is perfect just as it is. We feel for the suffering of Achilles, Helen, Hector, Andromache, and Priam; we feel deeply *with* them; but we don't want that suffering to change; we don't want anything in the poem to change. Heraclitus, who disapproved of Homer, describes the Homeric vision best: "To men, some things are good and some are bad. But to God, all things are good and beautiful and just."

Homer sees everything without judgment. He is not shocked at any form of human stupidity, violence, or greed, and finds no need for consolation. He simply observes, and in the purity of that observation he can see life in death and death in life, the interpenetration of the human and the nonhuman, the equal truth of opposites, and the preciousness of even the smallest or most abject of creatures. His vision is not only an aesthetic but a moral one. I call it love.

About the Greek Text

Twentieth-century translators of the *Iliad* worked from a Greek text (the old Oxford Classical Texts edition, first published in 1902) that is far inferior to what we now have available. I was lucky enough to begin this translation after M. L. West's *Homeri Ilias* had been published. His edition, one of the great works of textual scholarship, was my daily companion for almost two and a half years. I doubt that it has ever had a less educated or a more grateful reader.

Textual scholarship is a fiercely complicated matter, and West's decisions include, among many other elements, the choice between variant readings, the minutiae of spelling, punctuation, and stanza breaks, and (though rarely) the conjectural reconstruction of a corrupted text. In addition—and this is one of the essential features of his text—he identifies many passages in the received text as probable interpolations by rhapsodes, spliced into it during the decades or centuries after it was written. Wherever West has deleted or bracketed a passage, I have omitted it from my translation. I have also omitted a number of passages whose authenticity he questions in others of his books, and very occasionally I have omitted a passage that he thinks may be an expansion by the original poet. I have also omitted five lines that West has not doubted but that other good scholars have.

Usually the interpolations are of just a line or two, but sometimes a more substantial passage has been added, to the detriment of the music and the story. The longest example is the baroque and nasty episode of Book 10, which has been recognized as an interpolation since ancient times, and by modern scholars almost unanimously: it has major inconsistencies with the rest of the *Iliad*, its style is different, and it can be excised without leaving a trace. There are more than five hundred other interpolated lines, and the cumulative effect of omitting these passages is a dramatically sharper and leaner text. I am under no illusion that I have translated the original text of the *Iliad,* as written or dictated by the anonymous poet called Homer—just the most intelligent attempt we have at getting back to an original, and a text that I could use as the basis for the most intense possible poetic experience in English.

About This Translation

"Nobody will give a damn about the meter," Ezra Pound once told an aspiring translator of the *Iliad,* "if there is FLOW." That is true, and precisely why everything depends on the choice of meter. How can you even begin to recreate the energy and simplicity, the speed, grace, and continual forward thrust and pull of the original if the meter in English isn't supple enough, generous enough, to sustain an entire epic poem?

The meter I have used is a minimally iambic five-beat line that I came to know well in the course of translating Rilke's *Duino Elegies.* The anapests and dactyls make this line longer than the pentameter of blank verse; it usually has from twelve to fourteen syllables, and occasionally eleven or fifteen. The extra syllables give it something of the sound of Greek verse, while the five-beat limit respects the tendency of English to break longer lines in two. I have worked hard to find a balance between end-stopping and enjambment; I have also worked at keeping the rhythms from becoming too regular and have varied them so that no two consecutive lines have the identical rhythm. With diction as with rhythm, I have tried to sound natural, to write in a language that felt genuine to me, neither too formal nor too colloquial. My intention throughout has been to recreate the ancient epic as a contemporary poem in the parallel universe of the English language.

Matthew Arnold's famous advice has been my guide: "The translator of Homer should above all be penetrated by a sense of four qualities of his author:—that he is eminently rapid; that he is eminently plain and direct both in the evolution of his thought and in the expression of it, that is, both in his syntax and in his words; that he is eminently plain and direct in the substance of his thought, that is, in his matter and ideas; and, finally, that he is eminently noble." Faithfulness to the Homeric style thus, paradoxically, sometimes requires a good deal of freedom from the words of the Greek. What sounds rapid, direct, and noble in ancient Greek may very well sound cluttered, literary, or phony in contemporary English. "So essentially characteristic of Homer is his plainness and naturalness of thought," Arnold wrote, "that to the preservation of this in his own version the translator must without scruple sacrifice, where it is necessary, verbal fidelity to his original, rather than run any risk of producing, by literalness, an odd and unnatural effect."

I have been quite sparing with one of the characteristic features of Homer's oral tradition, the fixed or stock epithet: "flashing-helmeted Hector," "bronze-clad Achaeans," "single-hoofed horses," and so on. In Greek these epithets elevate the style; in English they are often merely tedious. Here again Arnold's advice is helpful. "An improper share of the reader's attention [should not be] diverted to [words] which Homer never intended should receive so much notice." "Flashing-helmeted Hector," for example, means no more than "Hector"; the poet is not calling our attention to Hector's helmet. The Trojans aren't any less "bronze-clad" than the Achaeans. The "single-hoofed" horses are not being differentiated from any imaginary double-hoofed horses.

Another example: at the beginning of Book 1 Apollo shoots plague-arrows at the Achaeans. The Greek says literally, "First he attacked the mules and the swift dogs." Here Apollo is attacking *all* the dogs—the slow ones too, if there should be any, not just the swift ones. "Swift dogs" simply means "dogs"; the adjective has no significance at all, and if the Greek words had had a different metrical value the poet would have said "First he attacked the strong mules and the dogs" or "First he attacked the strong mules and the swift dogs." All of these sentences are strictly equivalent in meaning to "First he attacked the mules and the dogs."

Throughout Homeric poetry the fixed epithet simply fills out the meter and is usually irrelevant to the context, and sometimes inappropriate to it. (In *Odyssey* 16.4, for example, when Telemachus returns to Eumaeus's hut, "the loud-barking dogs did not bark.") Occasionally the epithet does have meaning, as in the deeply moving lines at the end of the poem when Achilles is astounded at seeing "godlike Priam." But usually, as the Homeric scholar Milman Parry said, they are best left untranslated. Because the reader "soon ceases . . . to seek for any active force in such single words, they too finally become for him simply epic words with no more meaning than the usual term would have." So I have omitted most of the fixed epithets. I have also omitted many of the patronymics ("Achilles, *son of Peleus*," "Agamemnon, *son of Atreus*"), except as vocatives or in introducing a character. To my ear these omissions make the English sound more natural and rapid, without any sacrifice of nobility.

The most fascinating part of the process of translation was after I had done all my homework, looked up all the Greek words I didn't know, pored over West's textual apparatus, studied the commentaries, and was left with a bramble of possibilities on the right-hand page of my notebook and a blank page on the left. At this point I began to listen for the rhythm, and line by line, sometimes after a minute, sometimes after ten—magically, it seemed—the words began to configure themselves, my hearing created what I wanted to hear, the pen started to write, and I got to witness it all. And (even if twenty or fifty further drafts were necessary to fine-tune the passage) from that point on, as with Chuang-tzu's master woodworker Ch'ing, the real work was done.

On the Pronunciation of Greek Names

For the pronunciation of the names of major and secondary characters, peoples, and places, see the Pronouncing Glossary (pp. 457–62). Here are a few helpful rules: The consonant *ch* is pronounced like *k*. The consonants *c* and *g* are hard before *a, o, u,* and other consonants, and soft before *e, i,* and *y*. Initial *Eu-* is pronounced *yoo,* final *-cia* is pronounced *sha, -gia* is pronounced *ja, -cius* and *-tius* are pronounced *shus* unless otherwise marked, and *-eus* is pronounced *yoos* unless otherwise marked.

To make scansion easier in the text, I have marked the principal accents of secondary and minor characters, peoples, and places, except for two-syllable names, which are always accented on the first syllable. The principal accents of major characters, peoples, and places are as follows: Achǽans (the usual name for the Greeks in the *Iliad;* "Argives" and "Danäans" are synonyms), Achílles, Aenéas, Andrómachē, Antílochus, Apóllo, Athéna, Aphrodítē, Autómedon, Dánäans, Diomédes, Hécuba, Hephǽstus, Idómeneus, Ílion, Meneláüs, Meríones, Mýrmidons, Odýsseus, Patróclus, Polýdamas, Sarpédon, and Scamánder.

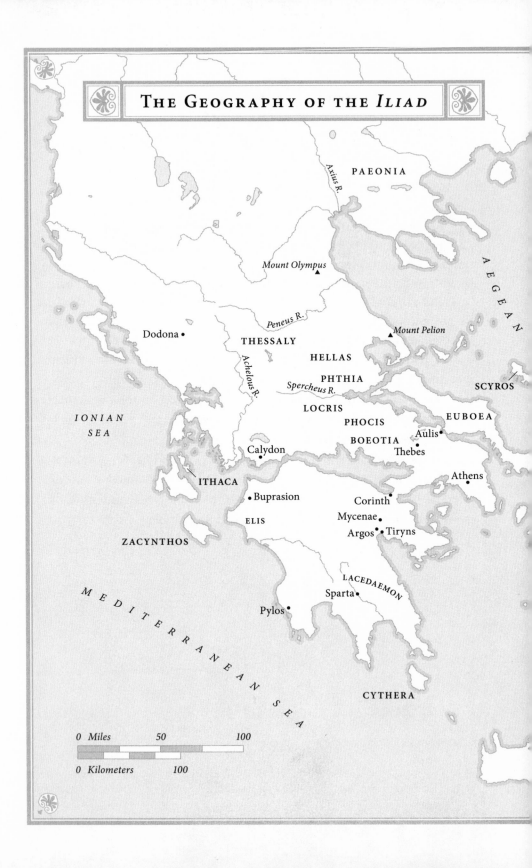

THE GEOGRAPHY OF THE *ILIAD*

PAEONIA

Axius R.

Mount Olympus ▲

A E G E A N

Peneus R.

Dodona •

THESSALY

Mount Pelion ▲

HELLAS

Achelous R.

PHTHIA

Spercheus R.

SCYROS

LOCRIS

IONIAN
SEA

PHOCIS

EUBOEA

BOEOTIA

Aulis •

Calydon •

Thebes

ITHACA

Athens

• Buprasion

Corinth

ELIS

Mycenae •

ZACYNTHOS

Argos • • Tiryns

LACEDAEMON

Sparta •

Pylos •

M E D I T E R R A N E A N   S E A

CYTHERA

0 Miles	50	100

0 Kilometers	100

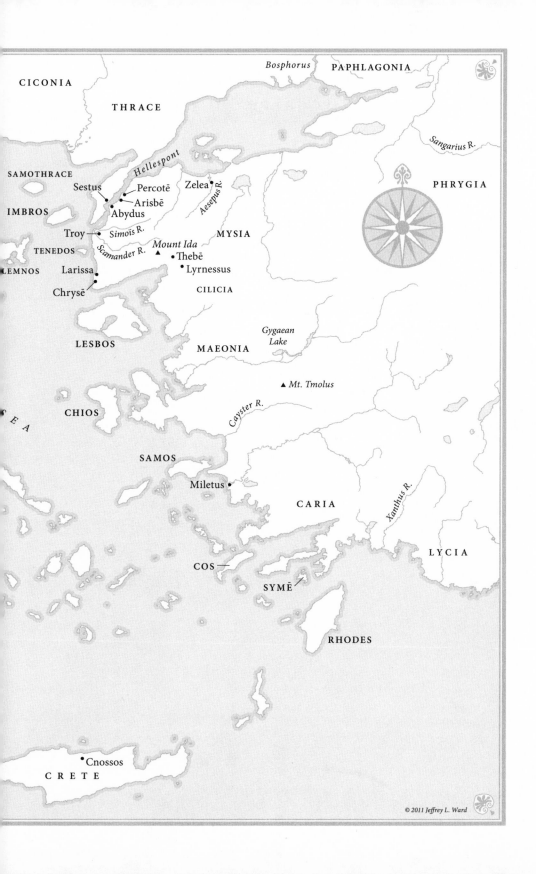

CICONIA

THRACE

SAMOTHRACE

IMBROS

TENEDOS

LEMNOS

Bosphorus

Hellespont

Sestus

Percotē

Arisbē

Abydus

Troy

Simoïs R.

Scamander R.

Larissa

Chrysē

PAPHLAGONIA

Sangarius R.

PHRYGIA

Zelea

Aesepus R.

MYSIA

Mount Ida

Thebē

Lyrnessus

CILICIA

Gygaean
Lake

LESBOS

MAEONIA

Mt. Tmolus

CHIOS

S E A

SAMOS

Cayster R.

Miletus

CARIA

Xanthus R.

LYCIA

COS

SYMĒ

RHODES

Cnossos

CRETE

© 2011 Jeffrey L. Ward

The symbol * indicates a space between verse paragraphs whenever such spaces are lost in pagination. Bracketed line numbers at the top of each page of the translation refer to the Greek text.

The Iliad

Book 1

The rage of Achilles—sing it now, goddess, sing *through* me
the deadly rage that caused the Achaeans such grief
and hurled down to Hades the souls of so many fighters,
leaving their naked flesh to be eaten by dogs
and carrion birds, as the will of Zeus was accomplished.
Begin at the time when bitter words first divided
that king of men, Agamemnon, and godlike Achilles.

What god was it who caused the two men to clash?
Apollo, who took offense at the king and sent
a deadly plague to the camp, and many were dying,   10
because he had dishonored the god's priest, Chryses,
who had come with a splendid ransom to the beached ships
to beg for his daughter's freedom. Holding the god's
golden staff adorned with his sacred ribbons,
he addressed the Achaean army, and most of all
the commanders Agamemnon and Menelaus:
"Sons of Atreus, and all you Achaean soldiers,
may the gods allow you to plunder Priam's great city,
then grant you a safe homecoming. But hear my plea.
Give me back my dear child; accept this ransom,   20
in reverence for Apollo, who strikes from afar."

Then all the Achaeans shouted out their assent
to honor the priest and accept the glorious ransom.
But this did not please Agamemnon, and he refused,
frowning, and sent him off with a harsh command:
"Get out of here now, old man, and don't let me find you
loitering by our ships or sneaking back later,
for then not even the staff of the god will save you.
As for your daughter: No—I will not return her.
She will grow old in Argos, far from her own dear country,   30
working the loom and coming to bed when I call her.
Go, before I get angry . . . while you still can."

*

The old priest, recoiling in terror, obeyed his words
and departed, then silently walked back along the shore
of the loud-roaring sea. And when he had gone some distance,
he fervently prayed aloud to the lord Apollo:
"God of the silver bow, all-glorious ruler
of the isle of Ténedos, lord of the holy cities
of Chrysē and Cilla, O Mouse-god, god of the plague,
hear me now. If ever you have been pleased   40
when I built a temple for you or burned in your honor
the fragrant fat-wrapped thighbones of goats and oxen,
grant me this prayer, and let your terrible arrows
take vengeance upon the Danäans for my tears."

He ended his prayer, and Apollo was swift to answer,
striding to Earth from the pinnacles of Olympus,
filled with fury. His bow and his quiver were slung
on his shoulder. The arrows rattled with every step.
Down he strode, and his coming was like the night.
He dropped to one knee and drew back a deadly arrow,   50
and a dreadful twang rang out from the silver bow.
First he attacked the mules and the dogs, but soon
he shifted his aim and struck down the men themselves.
And the close-packed pyres of the dead kept burning, burning,
beside the Achaean ships, all day and all night.

For nine days the deadly arrows rained down on the camp.
On the tenth day Achilles called all the men to assemble
(the goddess Hera had put this into his mind
because she was pained to see the Achaeans dying).
And when they had all come together for the assembly,   60
Achilles stood up and said to Lord Agamemnon,
"Son of Atreus, this plague is killing our men,
and if it continues, we will be driven back
and forced to return home—*if* we escape death at all.
So let us consult some soothsayer or prophet
or dream-interpreter (dreams too are sent by Zeus)
who can explain why Apollo has grown so angry—

whether because we have broken some solemn vow
or failed to perform some sacrifice in his honor.
Perhaps with the savor of burning lamb flesh or goat flesh   70
he will change his mind and call off this devastation."

When Achilles had finished speaking, he took his seat,
and Calchas, the son of Thestor, stood up—by far
the wisest of those who scan the flight patterns of birds;
he knew all things of the present, the past, and the future
and had guided the Argive fleet to the shores of Troy
by his power of divination, a gift of the god.
With confidence in his judgment, he spoke to the men:
"You ask me, sir, to interpret Apollo's rage.
This I can do. But first you must swear, on your honor,   80
that you will defend me, not only in words but in action,
because I think that I am about to offend
a man who has great authority over the Argives.
Whenever a king is enraged at a lesser man,
even if he should swallow his wrath for the moment
he will nurse his grievance until he can take revenge.
So before I speak out, promise that you will protect me."

Then in reply Achilles stood up and said,
"Have no fear, Calchas; tell us what you have seen.
I swear by Apollo, to whom you pray when you show   90
the will of the gods to the Argives, that no man shall harm you
as long as I am alive—not one of us here,
not even if it is Lord Agamemnon you mean,
who boasts that he is the greatest man in the army."

When he heard these words, the prophet took heart and said,
"It is not because of a solemn vow that was broken
or a sacrifice unperformed that the god has done this,
but because his priest was dishonored by Agamemnon,
who would not release the girl or accept the ransom.
That is why Lord Apollo has sent us these evils,   100
and if we do nothing, he will continue. Nor will he
stop this terrible plague from destroying our men

until we give back the dark-eyed girl to her father
without accepting a ransom, and offer the god
a hundred oxen and goats in the city of Chrysē.
Only then can we change his mind and appease him."

After he finished speaking, Calchas sat down,
and the warrior son of Atreus stood up, the king
of many lands, Agamemnon; his heart brimmed over,
black with rage, and his eyes were blazing like fire.   110
He shot a murderous glance at Calchas and said,
"Prophet of evil, not once have you ever spoken
in my favor; you always love to foretell what brings harm;
no good have you ever seen or brought to fulfillment.
Now you declare that the god has caused us this evil
because of me, since I wouldn't accept the ransom
for the girl Chrysēïs. And yes, I do want to keep her;
I like her better than Clytemnéstra, my wife,
whom she more than equals in beauty of face and figure,
in intelligence, wit, and all the womanly skills.   120
Still, I am willing to give her up now, if that
is the best way to keep my army alive and not dying.
But if I do, you must give me another girl
at once, so that I am not the only commander
without a prize, since that is against our custom."

In answer to Agamemnon, Achilles said,
"Son of Atreus, of all men most honored, most greedy,
how can the army award you another prize?
Do you think that we keep a stockpile of prizes lying
around, in case they are needed? No: what we won   130
from the cities we took and plundered we have already
divided fairly, and it is against our custom
to reclaim a prize from our captains. Give back the girl
as the god demands, and we will see that you get
three or four times as much, if ever Lord Zeus
allows us to plunder the thick-walled city of Troy."

Then, in response, Lord Agamemnon addressed him:

"You are great as a fighter, Achilles, but do not try
to outwit me or win me over with your fine words.
What kind of justice is it that you are proposing?   140
That *you* get to keep your own prize, yet I am forced
to give up the girl, and must sit here, meekly, with nothing?
No: let the army give me another prize,
a girl whom I like just as much, who is equal in value.
Or else I myself will come and take away *your* prize
or the prize of Odysseus or Ajax. The man I come to,
I assure you, will not be pleased. But let us discuss this
later. For now, I will pick a suitable crew,
and load a ship with a hundred oxen and goats
for the sacrifice, and send off the girl Chryséïs.   150
Let someone who is a wise leader be placed in charge—
Ajax perhaps, Lord Idómeneus, or Odysseus,
or you, Achilles, the most wonderful of all men,
so that we may placate the god and win back his favor."

Achilles glowered at Agamemnon and said,
"Clothed as you are in shamelessness and deceit,
how can any Achaean follow your orders
to go on a mission or risk his life in this war?
I didn't come here to Troy because of the Trojans.
I have no quarrel with them; they have done me no harm.   160
They have never ridden off with my horses or cattle,
nor on the rich plains of Phthia, my native country,
have they cut down and stolen my harvests; too many miles
stretch out between us—high mountains and thundering sea.
We followed you here for *your* sake, not for our own;
we all came to win back Menelaus's honor
and yours too, dog-face. You don't even mention that.
And now you threaten to carry away my prize,
which I worked for so hard and which the whole army gave me.
My prizes are never like yours whenever we take   170
and plunder one of the Trojans' richly stocked towns;
although it is *my* strong hands that have won the battles,
when it comes to dividing the spoils, *you* always get
the biggest prize, while the prize that I take to my ships,

having worn myself out in the fighting, is small, though precious.
Now I will sail home to Phthia; there is no point
in staying here with my ships. I refuse to keep on
piling up riches for *your* sake, while I am dishonored."

Then Agamemnon answered him with these words:
"Fine—go home, if that is the way you feel.   180
I will not beg you to stay. There are many others
who will help me regain my honor, especially Zeus.
And to tell the truth, no man, of all the commanders
gathered here, is as hateful to me as you are,
because you are steeped in strife and contention and fighting.
If you *are* a great warrior, that is the gift of a god.
Go home, and take all your ships and your precious companions,
and lord it over the Myrmidons, back in your province.
I care nothing for you; your anger cannot affect me.
But I promise you this: When the god takes Chryséïs from me,   190
I will come to your hut in person and take *your* prize,
that girl Briséïs. And then you will understand
how much greater I am than you are—and anyone else
will think twice before he challenges me as an equal."

He stood there, glaring. Fury came over Achilles.
He could not move. His mind was paralyzed: should he
draw his sword and plow through the ranks and plunge it
into the king's heart? Or should he try to choke off
his own rage? And while he pondered this, slowly drawing
the sword from its sheath, Athena came down from heaven,   200
sent by Hera, who loved and cared for them both.
She stood right behind him and seized him by his blond hair.
In deep amazement, Achilles wheeled round, and at once
he knew the goddess: her terrible blazing eyes.
(No one else, among the assembly, could see her.)

When Achilles was able to speak, he said, "Why now,
daughter of Zeus, have you come here? Is it to see
the intolerable contempt of King Agamemnon?
I am telling you, and I promise that it will happen:

Soon he will pay for this insolence with his life."   210

To this, the goddess, gray-eyed Athena, answered,
"I have come to hold back your blind rage. Hera sent me.
Enough: abandon this quarrel; put up your sword.
Attack him with words instead; and I promise that someday
because of this insult, three times as many gifts
will be granted to you. But hold back now, and obey us."

Achilles answered her, "Goddess, a man must do
what you two require, though his heart is seething with fury.
Whoever obeys the gods, the gods will favor."
So, with his massive hand on the silver pommel,   220
he thrust the great sword back into its sheath, as Athena
had commanded him to. But she had already left
to join the other immortals, in Zeus's palace.

Achilles once again spoke to Lord Agamemnon
with violent words, and he did not soften his anger:
"Drunkard, dog-face, quivering deer-hearted coward,
you have never dared to arm with your soldiers for battle
or go on a raid where only the bravest survive—
oh no, you avoid that like death; you would much rather stay
safe, right here in the camp and direct your efforts   230
to stealing the prize of whoever might contradict you.
You parasite king of the nobodies, if there were even
one real man here, this outrage would be your last.
But hear me. I swear a solemn oath to you now:
that by this staff, which has never grown leaves or branches
since the day it was cut down, deep in the mountains, and never
will blossom again, for the bronze axe has stripped it bare;
by this staff, which the leaders among us hold in their hands
when they give their judgments and safeguard the laws of Zeus,
I swear that a day will come when every Achaean—   240
every last soldier among you—will long for my presence,
and I swear that you, sir, will not be able to help them,
however heartsick you are about all your men
being massacred at the hands of man-killing Hector.

That day, you will gnaw your own heart as you keep recalling
how you dishonored the best of all the Achaeans."
When Achilles had finished speaking, he flung to the ground
the great staff studded with golden nails, and sat down.
Across from him, Agamemnon smoldered with fury.

Then Nestor stood up, the eloquent lord of Pylos,   250
a man from whose smooth tongue words flowed sweeter than honey.
He had seen two generations pass on in sacred Pylos
during his lifetime, and now he ruled over the third.
With confidence in his judgment, he spoke to the men:
"Dear god, what a wretched day this is for us all!
King Priam would surely rejoice, and the sons of Priam,
and the rest of the Trojans would probably laugh out loud
to hear the news about the two of you brawling—
the best of all the Achaeans in war and in council.
Listen to me. You both are younger than I am;   260
in my time, I fought beside men who were even greater
than you two are. Never since have I seen,
and never shall see, such men as Perítho̊ü̈s, Dryas,
Polyphémus, Cǽneus, Exádius, men like the gods,
the strongest warriors ever to live on earth,
and their enemies too were the strongest—the mighty centaurs,
mountain-dwelling, whom terribly they destroyed.
These were my comrades-in-arms, and I came to join them
from faraway Pylos, when they called for my help.
No one today could fight against such great men.   270
These heroes listened to me and took my advice,
and you would do well to listen to me as they did.
You, son of Atreus, powerful though you are—
don't take the girl. Give her up; let him keep her,
since the army already granted her as a prize.
And you, Achilles, you mustn't defy the king
or try to match him in dignity or in power.
A king is entitled to honor above all men,
since Zeus grants his kingship. You may be the stronger man,
and your mother, we know, is a goddess. Yet Agamemnon   280
is your superior; *his* realm is greater than yours.

Son of Atreus, hold back your rage, I beg you;
stop this fight with Achilles, who for our soldiers
is a mighty bulwark against the horrors of war."

Then Agamemnon answered him with these words:
"Everything that you said, sir, is true enough.
But this man wishes to be above all the others;
he wishes to have his way over all men, to order
us all around at his own good pleasure, to lord it
over us all; and I, for one, will not have it.   290
Although the gods have made him a great man in war,
that doesn't give him the right to heap me with insults."

Achilles interrupted him: "People would call me
a nobody, a coward, if I gave in
to your desire each time you opened your mouth.
Push others around, but don't you try to tell *me*
what to do! And one thing more: I will not
put up a fight because of that girl—not with you
or with anyone else. Our soldiers gave her to me
and now they can take her back. But don't imagine   300
that you can come and walk off with anything else
that is mine. Just try, and let the whole army witness
how quickly your dark blood will spurt out around my spear."

When these two had hurled the last of their violent words,
they stood up, and soon the whole assembly dissolved.
Achilles went back to his huts and ships, with Patroclus
and all their comrades, while Agamemnon prepared
one of *his* ships, picked twenty rowers, and had it
pulled to the water, loaded it with a hundred
oxen and goats for the sacrifice to the god,   310
then led Chryséïs on board. And he put Odysseus
in charge of the mission, to serve as the ship's commander.

So they set sail; and in the camp Agamemnon
ordered the men to do ritual purification.
They washed themselves clean, then threw the polluted water

into the sea, and they offered up to Apollo
hundreds of oxen and goats, and they skinned them and burned them
on the shore of the restless sea, and the broiled fat's savor
rose with the black smoke, spiraling up to heaven.

Meanwhile Lord Agamemnon did not forget   320
the threats he had made to Achilles. He summoned the heralds,
Talthýbius and Eurýbates, his attendants,
and gave them instructions: "Go to Achilles now
and take that beautiful girl he was given, Briséïs.
Take her hand and bring her back to me here.
And if he doesn't surrender her, I myself
will go to his camp, with a few armed men at my side,
and take her by force. And I promise you, he will regret it."

They had to obey, but with heavy hearts the two men
left him and walked on the shore of the restless sea   330
until they arrived at the camp of the Myrmidons. There
they found Achilles, sitting beside his hut,
and he was not happy to see them. The heralds, frightened
and in awe of the great man, stood there, unable to speak.
But Achilles knew exactly why they had come.
"Welcome," he said, "heralds of Zeus and of men.
Don't be afraid to approach; I do not blame you.
My quarrel is not with you, but with Agamemnon,
who sent you here to take back the girl, Briséïs.
Go, Patroclus, bring her out, hand her over,   340
and let them witness this solemn oath: Before men,
before the immortal gods, and before that harsh
king, I swear that if ever again he needs me
to save his army from ruin, I will not come.
He is crazed with anger and doesn't know how to look
forward and backward at once, so that he can safeguard
the lives of his men, as they battle beside their black ships."

Immediately Patroclus went into the hut
to do as his beloved companion had told him.
He led out the beautiful girl, and he handed her over   350

to the two men. And they walked back beside the ships,
and Briséïs walked with a heavy heart. Then Achilles,
in tears, moved far away from his comrades, and sat down
on the shore, and gazed out over the wine-dark sea.
And he prayed to Thetis, his mother, with outstretched hands:
"Mother, listen to me. Since you are a goddess,
surely Zeus owes me respect, especially since
my life span will be so short. But he hasn't shown me
even the slightest honor. Now Agamemnon
has used his power to dishonor me; he himself   360
has taken my prize and robbed me of what is mine."

His tears kept flowing, and in the depths Thetis heard him
as she sat beside the Old Man of the Sea, her father.
At once she arose like a mist from the gray waters
and sat down before him and listened to him as he wept
and stroked his hair and spoke to him softly: "Child,
why are you weeping? What has caused you this sorrow?
Tell me. Don't keep it hidden; let me know too."

Then, with a deep groan, Achilles answered, "You know it.
Why do I need to tell you? You know what happened.   370
We sailed to Thebē, Ëétion's sacred city,
and plundered it and brought the spoils back to Troy.
The Achaeans divided the prizes among themselves, fairly,
and for Agamemnon they chose a girl named Chryséïs.
Then Chryses, the priest of Apollo who strikes from afar,
came with a splendid ransom to the beached ships,
to beg for his daughter's freedom. Holding the god's
golden staff adorned with his sacred ribbons,
he addressed the Achaean army, and most of all
the commanders Agamemnon and Menelaus.   380
Then all the Achaeans shouted out their assent
to honor the priest and accept the glorious ransom.
But this didn't please Agamemnon, and he refused,
frowning, and sent him off with a harsh command.
And the old priest withdrew in anger, and Lord Apollo
heard his prayer, since he was dear to the god,

and he sent a horrible plague against the Achaeans,
and hosts of our men began to die, and the god's
deadly arrows fell everywhere through the camp.
A clear-eyed prophet explained why Apollo was angry,   390
and I was the first to urge that the god be appeased.
But anger seized Agamemnon. He jumped to his feet
and threatened me. Now he has carried out what he said.
The men are sailing his girl to Chrysē, with gifts
for the god, and two heralds from Agamemnon just took
my girl, Brisēïs, the prize that the army gave me.
Hear me now, mother; help me in this, if you can.
Go to Olympus and plead with Zeus for my sake;
clasp his knees and remind him of all the times
when by word or action you brought delight to his heart.   400
Beg him to help the Trojans, to pin the Achaeans
close to their ships, on the seashore. Let them be slaughtered
and learn how fine it is to have such a king.
And may Agamemnon come to regret his madness
in refusing to honor the best of all the Achaeans."

Then, weeping, the goddess answered, "Alas, my child,
why did I bring you up to so harsh a fate?
If only you could have stayed by the ships, without tears,
without pain, since your life is destined to be so short.
Not only must you die young, but your fleeting days   410
are doomed to be full of sorrow beyond all others.
Of course I will go, as you ask, to snow-capped Olympus
and will speak to Zeus and see if I can persuade him.
Stay here for now. Keep raging at the Achaeans,
and hold back from any fighting till I return.
Yesterday Zeus went off to the Ocean, to feast
with the Ethiopians, and the immortals went too.
Twelve days from now they will all return to Olympus,
and then I will speak with him in his bronze-paved palace
and clasp his knees. And I think he will do what I ask."   420

With these words she left him: angry and sick at heart
because of the beautiful woman whom they had seized

against his will. Meanwhile Odysseus arrived
at the city of Chrysē. The ship sailed into the harbor,
and they took down the sail, and stowed it, and lowered the mast
by the forestays and brought it down smoothly into the mast-crutch
and rowed the ship to a mooring place close to shore
and dropped the anchor-stones from the bow and fastened
the stern-cables and stepped out into the surf.
Then, when they had unloaded the goats and oxen,   430
Chrysēïs came out of the ship, and Odysseus led her
to the altar and placed her in her dear father's arms
and said to him, "Chryses, I come here from Agamemnon.
He returns your child and offers to Lord Apollo
a sacrifice from the Danäans. May this appease
the god who has given us so much grief and affliction."

He handed her to her father, who joyfully
embraced his beloved child. Then quickly they brought in
the oxen and goats and arranged them around the altar
and washed their hands and scooped up the barley grains.   440
And Chryses lifted his arms and prayed in a loud voice:
"God of the silver bow, all-glorious ruler
of the isle of Ténedos, lord of the holy cities
of Chrysē and Cilla, hear me. Just as you did
when I prayed before, and you honored me and attacked
the Achaean army and caused them grievous affliction,
hear me and lift this terrible plague from the Argives."

Apollo did what he asked for. And when they had prayed
and sprinkled the goats and oxen with grains of barley,
they pulled back their heads and cut their throats, and they skinned them 450
and carved out the thighbones and wrapped these in layers of fat
for the god, with strips of lean meat on top. The old priest
burned them over the fire and poured wine upon them,
and the young men stood near him, holding the five-pronged spits.
When the thighbones were burned and the men had tasted the entrails,
they carved the rest of the meat and skewered the pieces
and roasted them and lifted them off the flames.
Then, when their work had been done and the food was ready,

they feasted, and all of them had their fair share and were happy.
And when they had had enough of eating and drinking,   460
the attendants filled the mixing bowls to the brim,
and passed them around, first pouring a few drops of wine
into the cups for each man to make a libation.
For the rest of the day they sought to appease the god
with singing and dancing and beautiful hymns of praise.
And Apollo heard them and took deep joy in their song.

After the sun had set and darkness had fallen,
they lay down and slept on the beach by the ship's stern-cables.
And as soon as the flush of dawn appeared in the heavens,
they boarded the ship and launched her. Apollo sent them   470
a favoring breeze, and they raised the mast, and they hoisted
the white sail aloft, and it bellied out with the wind,
and on either side of the ship's prow, the deep blue water
sang out as the ship flew over the waves to her goal.
And when they arrived at the Danäan camp, they hauled her
onto the shore and drew her high up on the sand
and set the long props beneath her to hold her upright.
And then they scattered, and each man went to his hut.

Meanwhile Achilles remained by the black ships, raging.
He never appeared at the place of assembly, never   480
went into battle, but gnawed on his heart as he sat there.
And he longed for the war: for the battle shouts and the fighting.

And when the twelfth dawn had come, the immortal gods
returned to Olympus, all together, with Zeus
leading the way. And Thetis had not forgotten
her promise to see him; she rose from the depths of the sea
at daybreak, and she ascended the sky to Olympus.
There she found Zeus; he was sitting apart from the others
on the topmost peak. And she sat down and clasped his knees
with her left hand, and with her right hand she touched his chin,   490
and she said "Zeus, Father, if ever among the immortals
by word or deed I was able to serve you, hear me.
Do what I ask you; honor my son, Achilles,

who is doomed to an early death. But King Agamemnon
has dishonored him now and robbed him of what is his.
So you, Lord, show him the honor that he deserves.
Grant victory to the Trojans, until the Achaeans
honor my son, and pay him due compensation."

Zeus did not answer. He sat for a long time in silence.
And Thetis stayed there beside him, clasping his knees   500
and holding him closely, then asked him a second time:
"Bow your head, Lord, and promise that you will do this,
or refuse me now—it is in your power—and show me
that I am the least respected of all the gods."

Greatly troubled by what she had said, Zeus answered,
"A bad business, this, since it is bound to involve me
in a quarrel with Hera; it certainly will inflame her.
Even now, she constantly tries to provoke me
and blames me and says that I always favor the Trojans.
But be off now, go home, in case she notices something.   510
I will take care of all this and see that it happens.
Look: I am bowing my head, so that you can believe me.
This is my solemn pledge. Once I have made it,
I never revoke it or fail to do what I say."
Thus Zeus decreed, and he bowed his dark brow in assent,
and the glistening blue-black locks of immortal hair
rippled on down, and all Olympus was shaken.

After the two had reached this agreement they parted.
Thetis dived into the sea from the heights of Olympus,
and Zeus went into his palace. All the gods stood up   520
as their father entered the hall; not one of them dared
to stay seated; they all arose to greet him, and stood
until he sat down on his throne. But Hera had seen him
and knew that Thetis was plotting with him and had begged
an important favor and somehow won his assent.
Quickly she spoke to her husband with heart-wounding words:
"You schemer—which god has crept in *this* time to see you?
You always do things behind my back; you keep secrets

and have never been willing to tell me of your intentions."

To this the father of men and gods replied,   530
"Hera, you shouldn't expect to know all my plans,
though you are my wife. Whenever I think it is fitting
for you to be told, I assure you that neither god
nor human will hear about it till you do first.
But when I intend to keep a plan to myself,
you must not start prying or nagging me for an answer."

Then Hera responded, "Dread Lord, what are you saying?
When have I ever pried or nagged you for answers?
I have always let you have your own way—you always
do what you want, without me. But now I am greatly   540
afraid that Thetis has tricked you and won you over.
Early this morning I saw her beside you, clasping
your knees, and you bowed your head, and I think that you promised
to honor Achilles by hemming in the Achaeans
and slaughtering them on the sand beside their black ships."

Lord Zeus said in response, "How absurd you are!
You are always imagining things; I can never escape you.
Yet the only thing you accomplish with such suspicions
is to distance yourself from my heart, to your own undoing.
If what you just said is true, it is how I want it.   550
So sit down and hold your tongue, and do what I tell you.
No one among the gods will come to your aid
if I get up and lay my invincible hands upon you."

He glared at her, and Hera was seized with terror
and sat down. She said no more, and she stifled her rage.
And throughout the room, the heavenly gods were chilled.
Hephaestus, the master craftsman, was first to speak,
choosing his words to quiet the heart of his mother:
"It would be a disgrace, an intolerable thing,
if you two keep quarreling for the sake of mortals   560
and bring discord among the gods. We would have no joy
at our glorious feasts, but anger and pain would rule.

So please, Mother—and I know that you understand this—
make peace with our father, Zeus, so that he will no longer
scold you and trouble the happiness of our feasting.
He can hurl the lightning down from on high, and if ever
he blasted us from our seats, we would all be helpless.
Go to him now, caress him with gentle words,
and soon he will be gracious to us again."

With these words he rose and put the two-handled cup   570
into his mother's hands, then said to her, "Patience.
Be strong now, Mother, and put aside your resentment.
I love you, and it would be painful to see you thrashed
in front of me, but I wouldn't be able to help you.
No one can stand up to Zeus, the lord of Olympus.
Remember what happened the last time I tried to save you?
He picked me up by one foot and flung me from heaven,
and all day long I plunged through the air, and at sunset
I fell to Earth on Lemnos and barely survived
until the Síntians found me and helped me recover."   580

As she heard the words of Hephaestus, the goddess smiled,
and smiling, she reached out and took the cup he had brought her.
And he poured out sweet nectar to her and to all the others
around the table, moving from left to right.
Then from the gods rose an inexhaustible laughter
as they watched him limping and bustling about the hall.

The feast went on for the rest of the day, until sunset,
and all of them ate and drank their fair share and were happy,
and they listened, entranced, to the sound of Apollo's lyre,
and the Muses sang, voices responding to lovely voices.   590
And when the glorious light of the sun had faded,
they went home to sleep in the houses expertly built
by Hephaestus, the master craftsman, the crippled god.
And Zeus climbed into his bed, where he had always
taken his rest when he felt sweet sleep overcome him.
And there he slept, and Hera his queen slept beside him.

Book 2

Now all the other immortals and all the humans
slept through the night, but sweet sleep fled from Lord Zeus;
he lay and thought about how he could honor Achilles
by slaughtering the Achaeans beside their ships.
And, in the end, he decided that the best way
was to send a malicious dream to King Agamemnon.
So he summoned the dream. It came to him, and he said,
"Go now, dream, to the army of the Achaeans,
and when you have slipped in to King Agamemnon's hut,
repeat these words, exactly as I command you.   10
Tell him to arm the Achaeans, quickly, and have them
attack, since now he can seize the great city of Troy.
Now the Olympian gods are no longer divided
among themselves, because Hera has swayed their minds
by her endless appeals—and they grant Agamemnon the glory."

When it heard Lord Zeus's instructions, the dream flew off.
Soon it arrived at the army of the Achaeans,
and it looked for King Agamemnon. At last it found him
asleep in his hut. It came up beside him and stood there
above his head and assumed the likeness of Nestor,   20
whom the king respected more than all others, and said,
"Son of Atreus, how can you still be sleeping?
A commander to whom an army has been entrusted,
a king who is weighed down with so many cares, must not
sleep through the night. I bring you a message from Zeus,
who pities and loves you, although he is far away.
He bids you to arm the Achaeans, quickly, and have them
attack, since now you can take the great city of Troy.
The gods are no longer divided among themselves.
Hera has won them all over and swayed their minds   30
by her endless appeals; so grief is ordained for the Trojans
by the will of Zeus. Remember this and don't let
forgetfulness grip you, once honey-sweet sleep lets you go."

*

And the dream flew off into the night and left him
pondering things that were fated never to happen.
He really thought he would capture Troy on that day—
fool that he was, blind to what Zeus was planning,
so much heartache and pain that were still to come
on Trojans and Danäans both, in their fierce struggle.

Then he awoke, with the dream's voice swirling around him.   40
He sat up, got out of bed, put on a tunic,
threw his great cloak around him, fastened his sandals
onto his feet and slung his silver-bossed sword
over his shoulder, took his ancestral staff,
and stepped out to walk alongside the Achaean ships.

As dawn spread out and arrived at the peak of Olympus,
announcing the light to Zeus and the other gods,
King Agamemnon commanded his clear-voiced heralds
to summon all the Achaeans to an assembly.
And as the heralds called out, the men quickly gathered.   50

But first Agamemnon arranged for his senior commanders
to come together in council, by Nestor's ship.
And when they had gathered, he told them the plan he had made:
"Listen, my friends. A dream that was sent by the gods
from heaven appeared to me in the dead of night,
and it looked like Nestor and stood beside me and said,
'Son of Atreus, how can you still be sleeping?
A commander to whom an army has been entrusted,
a king who is weighed down with so many cares, must not
sleep through the night. I bring you a message from Zeus,   60
who pities and loves you, although he is far away.
He bids you to arm the Achaeans, quickly, and have them
attack, since now you can seize the great city of Troy.
The gods are no longer divided among themselves;
Hera has won them all over and swayed their minds
by her endless appeals; so grief is ordained for the Trojans
by the will of Zeus. Remember this.' Then the dream

flew off into the night, and sweet sleep left me.
Now let us arm our troops for the coming battle.
But first I will test them with false words, as custom dictates,   70
and command them to flee in their ships, while you, on all sides,
hold them back from carrying out my command."

When he had said this, Agamemnon sat down,
and Nestor stood up, the ruler of sand-swept Pylos.
With confidence in his judgment, he spoke to the men:
"My friends, commanders and captains of the Achaeans,
if it were anyone else who told us this dream,
we would call him a liar and turn our backs in disdain.
But the man who saw the dream is precisely the man
who claims that he is the best of all the Achaeans.   80
So let us now arm our troops for the coming battle."

With these words he moved off and led the way out of the council,
and all the senior commanders stood up and followed,
and the men rushed forward to listen to Agamemnon.
As thick-bunched troops of bees from some hollow rock
swarm out, throng after throng, and clouds of them fly off
filling the air, now wheeling this way, now that,
to cluster around the flowers in the spring meadows:
just so did the troops rush out from the ships and huts
to the meeting-place. And Rumor went blazing among them,   90
Zeus's messenger, urging them on; and they gathered,
and the meeting-place heaved into turmoil, and the earth groaned
beneath the men as they moved in a tumult of voices.
Nine heralds kept shouting, trying to hold back the uproar
and settle the crowd. Finally, after great effort,
when the last of the troops were seated, the noise died down.
And Lord Agamemnon stood up amid the assembly,
holding the staff that the gods' master craftsman had made.
(Hephaestus gave it to Lord Zeus, and Zeus to Hermes,
and Hermes to Pelops, and Pelops in turn to his son   100
Atreus, and on his deathbed Atreus left it
to his brother Thyéstes, who left it to Agamemnon,
to rule over many islands and over all Argos.)

Leaning upon this staff, he addressed the troops:
"My dear friends, Danäan soldiers, companions in battle,
Zeus has tangled me up in a heartbreaking madness.
He swore once that I would capture Troy and sail home
with its riches. But now he has cruelly broken his word.
He commands me to leave, to return in disgrace to Argos,
though so many men have died here. Such is the will,   110
it seems, of almighty Zeus, who has broken the walls
of many proud cities, and still will break many more.
But what a disgrace when generations to come
hear that so vast an army, of such brave men,
battled in vain against men far fewer than they were!
For if both Achaeans and Trojans agreed to a truce
and numbered themselves, all Trojans who live in the city
and all Achaeans, counted in groups of ten,
and if each of our groups chose a Trojan to pour its wine—
many groups would be left with no one to pour,   120
so greatly do we outnumber the Trojans, the ones
who live in the city. But then there are all those allies
from many cities, good soldiers, who hold me back
and defeat the best of my efforts to conquer Troy.
Already nine years of this war have gone by, and now
the planks of our ships have rotted, the ropes have frayed,
and across the wide sea our wives and our little children
sit in our houses, pining for us to return;
yet the task that we all embarked for remains unfinished.
So listen now, and let us all do as I say.   130
Launch the ships and sail back to our own dear country."

With this, Agamemnon aroused the hearts in the breasts
of every man who had not attended the council.
The whole assembly surged back and forth like the long
waves that the east and the south winds churn up upon
the Icárian Sea as they hurtle down from the heavens.
And as the west wind sweeps through the high-standing grain
with its violent blast, and the ears all shudder and bow:
just so was the army shaken, and in the uproar
men rushed toward the shore, and the dust from beneath their feet   140

rose high and hung in the air. And they called out briskly,
"Take hold of the ships, boys!" "Drag them down to the sea!"
And they set about clearing the launch ways and pulling the props
out from beneath the hulls, and the din of their shouting
ascended to heaven—the shouts of men longing for home.

And beyond what was fated, the Argives would have set sail
if Hera had not then turned to Athena and said,
"Athena, daughter of Zeus, this must not happen.
The Argives have fled and will sail home across the sea,
and they will leave Priam and all of Troy to exult   150
at keeping Helen, for whose sake so many Achaeans
have died here at Troy, far from the homes they love.
Go now throughout the army, talk to the men,
encourage the captains, and stop them from launching their ships."

When she heard the command of Hera, Athena was quick
to do her bidding. Down from the peaks of Olympus
she flew, and she found Odysseus beside his ships,
motionless, doing nothing, since disappointment
at the army's flight weighed heavy upon his heart.
And Athena walked up and stood beside him and said,   160
"Noble son of Laértes, resourceful Odysseus,
are you going to let your men rush off to the ships
like this, so ignobly, and flee to their own dear country?
And will you leave Priam and all of Troy to exult
at keeping Helen, for whose sake so many Achaeans
have died here at Troy, far from the homes that they love?
Go now throughout the army, talk to the men,
with your gentle words hold back the ones who are fleeing,
encourage the captains, and stop them from launching their ships."

Odysseus knew that it was a goddess speaking.   170
He started to run and threw off his cloak, which his herald,
Eurýbates, picked up. He ran to King Agamemnon
and he took from his hands the ancient staff of the gods,
and with it he walked on through the Achaean army.
Whenever he met with one of the prominent captains,

he would turn him back with gentle words such as these:
"What is wrong with you, friend? It wouldn't be proper
to threaten you, since you aren't a coward, but please
stop this mad flight, and make your soldiers stop too.
You don't know King Agamemnon's intention in giving   180
these orders; not all of us heard him speak in the council.
He is testing us now, but soon his patience will end,
and if he is angry, his measures will be severe.
The heart of a king is proud, since he knows that his honor
is given by Zeus and that Zeus's power supports him."
But whenever he met with one of the common soldiers
shouting or causing a row, he would raise the staff
and beat him with it, admonishing him with harsh words:
"What is wrong with you, fellow? Stop now! Go back!
Obey the command of those who are better than you are,   190
you nobody! Do you think that every Achaean
can be in charge? No good can come from the rule
of the common mob. There is only one man who rules us,
and Lord Zeus has given him power over us all."
Odysseus thus brought the army under control,
and they hurried back from the ships to the place of assembly
with much noise, as when a wave of the loud-roaring sea
crashes upon a beach and the surf keeps resounding.

All the troops took their seats and were ready to listen.
Only a man named Thersítes still shouted; his mind   200
was filled with disorderly thoughts, and he spewed out discord,
reckless and insubordinate, railing at leaders,
spouting whatever nonsense might make the troops laugh.
The ugliest man in the army that came to Troy,
he was bowlegged and lame in one foot, and his shoulders hunched
over his chest; his head was pointed; upon it
sprouted a few sparse patches of scraggly hair.
Achilles despised him deeply, and so did Odysseus.
He had reviled them many times; now he was shouting
shrill words at Agamemnon, as every soldier   210
listened with mounting anger and indignation.
"Son of Atreus, why are you blaming us *this* time?

What more do you want? Your huts spill over with bronze
and are stocked with women to serve you, whom we Achaeans
gave you as prizes whenever we plundered a town.
Do you want more gold, which some terrified Trojan father
will bring from the city as ransom to save his son
when I or another soldier has dragged him here—
or one more beautiful girl to screw in your hut?
It isn't right that you lead the Achaean army   220
back to this wretched war, for your own selfish goals.
And as for the rest of you weaklings—women, not men—
let us launch our ships and sail home and leave this fellow
to enjoy his prizes, and let him find out if we soldiers
have helped him at all, this hero who robbed Achilles,
giving offense to a man far better than he is.
But it seems quite clear that Achilles must feel no resentment,
he has been so submissive. If he were truly angry,
son of Atreus, this outrage would be your last."

With these insults Thersítes railed at King Agamemnon.   230
Quickly Odysseus walked up and stood beside him
and rebuked him, glaring at him with an angry scowl:
"What drivel you talk, Thersítes! Now hold your tongue,
and don't speak another word. Of all those who came here
to Troy with Atreus's sons, there is no man, I think,
as abominable as you are. So go sit down
and don't presume to criticize those above you
or stir up the men with your cowardly talk of homecoming.
Nobody knows how all these things will turn out,
whether or not we Argives will make it home safely;   240
yet you sit here hurling abuse at Lord Agamemnon
because our courageous soldiers chose to reward him
so generously with their gifts, and you keep on mocking.
But I swear to you now—and if I don't do what I say,
may somebody come and cut my head from my shoulders—
that if ever I catch you spewing such nonsense again
I will strip you naked and whip your ass out of here
and send you back to the ships, howling and bawling."

*

He lifted the staff and brought it down hard, across
Thersítes' back, who doubled over in pain.   250
Tears streamed from his eyes, and a large bloody welt appeared
on his flesh, from the golden staff. He sat down, frightened,
and with a dazed look, he wiped away some of the tears.
And the soldiers broke into gales of laughter, forgetting
their disappointment, and turned to their neighbors and said,
"Isn't this fine? Leave it to old Odysseus!
He has done so many good things in council and war,
but this is the best—to make this insolent windbag
choke on his words. The next time he won't be quite
so eager to open his trap and mouth off at our leaders."   260

And Odysseus stood up, holding his staff. At his side,
in the form of a herald, Athena commanded silence,
so that everyone—even those who were farthest back—
would be able to hear him and profit from his advice.
With confidence in his judgment, he spoke to the men:
"Son of Atreus, it seems that the army wishes
to make you the most contemptible of all kings
by not fulfilling the solemn pledge that they made you
when they came here from Argos: never to sail back till
they had plundered Troy. Like widows or little children   270
they are whining to one another, 'We want to go home.'
True, it has been an enormous hardship to stay here.
A sailor becomes impatient when winter blasts
and high-raging seas delay him and pen him in
and keep him away from his wife for a single month;
but for us Achaeans, nine long years have gone by
and we are still here. So I cannot blame you at all
for being discouraged. Still, it would be a disgrace
to fight for so long in front of Troy, then go home
empty-handed. Therefore be patient, my friends,   280
and stay for a little while longer, until we find out
if Calchas's words of vision come true or not.
We all know what happened at Aulis—you yourselves
witnessed it, all of you, each man whom death has spared
since that great day—when our vast armies were gathered

with ships from across Achaea, ready to bring
swift destruction to Priam and all the Trojans.
Around a spring we sacrificed goats and oxen
to the blessed gods, on the altars beneath a plane tree
from which a stream of shimmering water flowed.   290
And then an omen appeared. A huge snake, with blood-red
stains on its back—it was terrifying; Lord Zeus
himself had sent it up to us into the light—
slid from beneath the altar and up the tree,
up to the topmost branch, where there was a nest
of baby sparrows cowering under the leaves—
eight of them, and the mother who hatched them made nine.
And the snake devoured the chicks as they cheeped in terror;
the mother flitted around them, shrieking, wailing,
but the snake coiled up and caught her as well, by the wing.   300
And when it had eaten the sparrow's chicks and herself,
the god who had made it appear, at once made it vanish.
We stood there, awestruck, and marveled at what we had seen
when the dreadful monster had cut the sacrifice short.
Then Calchas began to prophesy with these words:
'Why are you standing here speechless, men of Achaea?
This, I swear, is a mighty portent from Zeus,
late in arrival and late in fulfillment, whose fame
will never die. And here is its meaning: Just as
the snake devoured the sparrow's chicks and herself—   310
eight of them, and the mother who hatched them made nine,
so we will wage harsh war for as many years,
but in the tenth, we will seize Troy, with all its riches.'
These were his words, and now they are coming true.
So patience, all of you; trust what the prophet said,
and stay here until we conquer Priam's great city."

After he finished, the soldiers roared their approval,
and the ships beside them rang out with the sound of the shouting.
Then Nestor stood up and said these words to the army:
"Shame on you all! Up to now you have sat here   320
like silly boys, who have no idea what a war is.
If we waste our time like this with these childish disputes,

what will become of our solemn oaths and our compacts?
We will have to toss all our war plans into the fire,
with our oblations of wine and our sacred hand clasps.
Enough of these foolish words—they bring us no closer
to winning the war, though we talk here for hours on end.
Son of Atreus, hold to your purpose, unshaken,
as you did before, and lead the men into battle.
If there are one or two sniveling cowards among us   330
who are plotting to set sail for home, even before
we have learned if the promise of Zeus is a lie or not,
they can go to hell—they will certainly not succeed.
The very day when we boarded our ships to bring slaughter
and death to the Trojans, Zeus flashed a bolt of lightning
to the right of us, a sign that all would be well.
So we shouldn't be in a hurry to leave for home
until every man has slept with the wife of some Trojan
and takes his revenge for our struggles and groans over Helen.
And if any soldier is desperately eager to leave,   340
let him just try to enter his ship: right now,
in front of us all, he will meet his appointed death.
But you, my lord, must be prudent. Listen to me;
the words that I speak are not to be valued lightly.
Divide the soldiers by tribes and by clans, Agamemnon,
so that each man fights for the sake of his closest comrades.
If you take my advice, and if the Achaeans obey,
you will know which leaders and common soldiers are cowards
and which ones are brave, since they will be fighting in units.
And you will know also if it is by heaven's will   350
that you haven't taken the city or if the real cause
is the cowardice and incompetence of your men."

Lord Agamemnon answered him with these words:
"Once again, you surpass all Achaeans in counsel.
By Father Zeus and Athena and Lord Apollo,
if only I had ten counselors with your wisdom,
then right away the city of Priam would fall
to our powerful hands, and we would plunder its riches.
But instead of that, Zeus has given me grief and ensnared me

in useless strife that has torn our army apart,   360
when I and Achilles quarreled over a girl
with violent insults, and I was the first to get angry.
If the two of us ever again could see eye to eye,
Troy's destruction would not be postponed, not even
for a little while. But go now, each to your hut;
go eat your meal and gather strength for the battle.
All of you, sharpen your spears and get your shields ready
and feed your horses; make sure that your chariots
are in good order; prepare for the grueling combat,
since all day long we will have no respite, not even   370
for a little while, till night comes to pause our frenzy.
Drenched with sweat will your shield-strap be on your chest,
and around your spear your hand will ache with exhaustion,
and drenched with sweat will your horses be, straining to pull
their polished car. And if I should see any man
hanging back from the battle or skulking around
beside the ships, I swear it: that man will have
no hope of escaping the wild dogs and carrion birds."

After he finished, the soldiers roared their approval,
with a sound like high breakers crashing against a cliff   380
when the south wind flings them upon it, wave after wave,
and they never stop pounding and battering it from all sides.
And they all rushed back and scattered among the ships
and made fires in the huts, and every man ate his dinner,
and every man sacrificed to one of the gods
and prayed to escape from death in the chaos of battle.

Then Agamemnon sacrificed a plump ox,
five years old, to almighty Zeus. And he summoned
the chief commanders, the bravest of the Achaeans.
First of all Nestor, and next Idómeneus came,   390
and then the two Ajaxes, and Diomedes,
and the sixth was Odysseus; and Menelaus, unasked,
came also, knowing how burdened his brother was.
They gathered around the ox, and they scooped up the barley,
and Lord Agamemnon stood among them and prayed:

"Zeus, most glorious king, O sky-dweller, lord
of the black clouds, keep night away and the sun from setting
until I have pulled down the smoke-charred palace of Priam
to its last stone and torched its gates with all-ravaging fire
and pierced Hector's heart and ripped his tunic to shreds   400
with my spear point and watched, exulting, as all his comrades
fall down headlong and chew the black dirt beneath them."
This was his prayer, but Zeus did not yet fulfill it;
he accepted the gift, but deepened the toils of war.

When they had prayed and sprinkled the young ox with barley,
they pulled back its head and cut its throat, and they skinned it
and carved out the thighbones and wrapped these in layers of fat
for the god, with strips of lean meat on top, and they burned them
and spitted the entrails and held them over the fire.
When the thighbones were burned and the men had tasted the entrails, 410
they carved the rest of the meat and skewered the pieces
and roasted them and lifted them off the flames.
Then, when their work had been done and the food was ready,
they feasted, and all of them had their fair share and were happy.

And when they had had enough of eating and drinking,
Nestor stood up and was first among them to speak.
"Most glorious son of Atreus, king of men,
we must no longer waste our time in talking, or further
delay the task that the god has placed in our hands.
Command the heralds to summon the troops to battle,   420
and let us go, all together, through the wide camp
and wherever we go arouse the fierce spirit of battle."

When he heard these words, Agamemnon did as he said.
Immediately he commanded the clear-voiced heralds
to summon the whole Achaean army to battle.
And as the heralds called out, the men gathered quickly.
Then Agamemnon and all the commanders with him
rushed out to marshal the troops, and the goddess Athena
was beside them, holding the shield of almighty Zeus,
awe-inspiring, unaging, deathless, from which   430

a hundred tassels of solid gold waved in the air,
skillfully braided, each worth a hundred oxen.
With it, she darted in and out through the army,
urging them on, and within the heart of each soldier
she stirred up the strength to fight on, without any respite,
and at once the desire for war became sweeter to them
than sailing back in their ships to their own dear country.

And as a fire burns through a boundless forest
on the mountain crests, and from far off the glare can be seen:
just so did the gleam from the polished bronze of their armor   440
flash through the whole sky, up to the very heavens.
And as the great flocks on the Asian wetlands—wild geese
or cranes or long-throated swans—by the streams of Cäÿster
wheel this way and that way, glorying in their wings,
and with loud cries keep settling, and the whole marshland resounds:
just so did the troops pour forth from the ships and huts
onto the plain of Scamander, and the earth rumbled
beneath the feet of the men and the hooves of the horses,
and they stood there massed in Scamander's flowery meadow
as measureless as the leaves and flowers in their season.   450
And just as great hordes of flies keep swarming around
a sheepfold in spring, when milk overflows the buckets:
in such vast numbers the Argives stood massed on the plain
against the Trojans, eager to tear them to pieces.

And as easily as goatherds can separate out
their wide-ranging herds when they become mixed in the pasture:
just so did the leaders gather their troops for battle,
sorting them out, and among them was Agamemnon,
his splendid eyes and head like almighty Zeus's,
his thighs like the thighs of Ares, his chest like Poseidon's.   460
As a bull stands out in a herd above all the others,
sovereign among the cows as they graze in a field:
just so, on that day, did Lord Zeus make Agamemnon
supreme over all the warriors massed before Troy.

Tell me now, Muses, who have your homes on Olympus—

since you are divine, and present, and know all things,
while *we* hear only a rumor, and we know nothing—
who were the lords and commanders of the Achaeans?
As for the common soldiers, they were so many
that I could not name them even if I had ten tongues,   470
even if I had ten mouths, an unwearying voice,
and my heart were of bronze. And now I will tell the names
of all the captains, and how many ships came with them.

The Bœótians were led by Penéleos, Léïtus,
Clónius, Árcesiláus, and Próthoénor.
These were the men who lived in Hýria, Aulis,
the highlands of Eteónus, in Schœnus and Scolus,
Thespía, Græa, wide Mycaléssus, and Harma;
they lived in Ilésion, in Erýthrae and Hylē,
Ocaléa, Éleon, Péteon, Médeon, Copæ,   480
Coronéa, Eutrésis, and Thisbē, teeming with doves,
the pastures of Haliártus, Platæa, and Glisas,
the city of lower Thebes, and sacred Onchéstus,
the bright grove of Poseidon, and Arnē, abundant in vineyards,
Midéa, Nisa, Anthédon upon the seashore.
With them came fifty ships, and aboard each one
a hundred and twenty young Bœótians set sail.

And the men who lived in Orchómenus and Asplédon,
the realm of the Minyans, were led by Ascálaphus
and Ĭálmenus, whom the virgin Astýochē   490
had borne in the house of Actor after she went
upstairs into her room and Ares in secret
made love to her. And with them came thirty ships.

And Epístrophus and Schédius led the Phócians—
sons of Íphitus, grandsons of Náıbolus.
These were the men who held Cyparíssus and Crisa,
rocky Pytho and Pánopeus and Daulis,
who lived in Hyámpolis and in Ánemoréa
and beside the river Cephísus and in Lilǽa
by the springs of the river. With them came forty ships.   500

*

And Ajax the Smaller, son of Öíleus, led
the Lócrians. Far from being huge like his namesake,
Ajax the son of Télamon, he was a short man,
with a breastplate of linen; and yet in throwing the spear
he surpassed all the Hellenes and all the other Achaeans.
His men lived in Ópoïs, Cynus, Callíarus, Bessa,
in Scarphē and lovely Augéæ, Tarphē, and Thrónion
beside the Boágrius. With him came forty ships.

And the raging Abántes were led by the lord Elephénor,
the son of Chalcódon, descended from the god Ares.   510
They held Eubœa, Erétria, and Chalcis,
Histiǽa, abundant in vineyards, and lovely Cerínthus
beside the sea, and the hilltop city of Dion;
with them were also the men of Carýstus and Styra.
They were fierce warriors and grew their hair long in back,
and with their strong ashen spears they would try to tear open
their enemies' breastplates. With them came forty ships.

And the men who held Athens, its citadel and strong walls,
were led by Menéstheus, the son of Péteos.
No man on earth was as good as he was in marshaling   520
chariots and soldiers. Only Nestor could match him,
since he was older. With him came fifty ships.

And from Sálamis Ajax came, and he brought twelve ships.

And the men who held Argos and Tiryns, famed for its walls,
and Hermíone, and Ásinē on the gulf,
Ëíonæ, Trœzen, the vineyards of Epidáιrus,
and the young Achaeans who held Aegína and Mases—
these men were led by the great fighter Diomedes,
and also by Sthénelus, Cápaneus's son,
and Eurýalus, son of Mecísteus, was the third   530
in command. But over all of them, Diomedes
was chief commander. With them came eighty ships.

*

And the men who held the citadel of Mycénæ,
Orníæ, and wealthy Corinth, and strong Cleónæ,
Áræthyréa, and those in Hyperésia,
Pellénē, and steep Gonoéssa, and those who lived
in Ægion, Hélicē, and along the coast,
were led by the son of Atreus, Agamemnon,
who came with a hundred ships and the largest army,
the best and the bravest men; and he stood in their midst,   540
preeminent, splendid in armor of gleaming bronze,
the greatest of leaders, with by far the most troops.

And the men who held Lacedæmon, famed for its valleys,
Pharis, and Sparta, and Messē, teeming with doves,
and who lived in Brysíæ, Augéæ, and in Amýclæ,
and in Œtylus, Láas, and Helos beside the sea,—
of these, Agamemnon's brother, Lord Menelaus,
was the commander. With them came sixty ships,
which were stationed apart from the army of Agamemnon.
Menelaus was striding among them, eager for battle,   550
urging his men to fight; and above all others
he longed to avenge his struggles and groans over Helen.

And the men who lived in Pylos and lovely Arénē,
and Thryon, the ford of the river Alphéüs, and Æpy,
Cýparissëïs, Ámphigenía, and Helos,
in Ptéleos and in Dórion, where the Muses
met Thámyris the Thracian as he was coming
from King EÚrytus in Œchália, and stopped his music
forever, since he had boasted that he would surpass
even the Muses, daughters of Zeus, if they sang   560
in a competition; and so in anger they maimed him
and took away his divinely sweet power of song
and made him forget how to play the lyre. These men
were led by Nestor, and with him came ninety ships.

And the men of Arcadia, living beneath Mount Cyllénē,
by the tomb of Æpytus, where good soldiers are trained,
and the men who held Phéneos, Strátia, Rhipē, Tegéa,

Orchómenus, rich in flocks, and windswept Eníspē,
and Mántinéa, Parrhásia, and Stymphálus
were led by Lord Agapénor, the son of Ancǽus,   570
and with them came sixty ships, and aboard each one
were many Arcadian warriors skilled in battle.
Lord Agamemnon had given them all these ships
to cross the sea, because they had none of their own:
a people who normally traveled only by land.

And the men who lived in Buprásion and bright Elis,
as much of it as is enclosed between Hyrmínē,
Mýrsinus on the shore, the Olénian rock,
and Alésion—they came under four commanders,
who each had ten ships, with many Epéans on board.   580
They were led by the grandsons of Actor, Amphímachus, son
of Ctéatus, and the son of EÚrytus, Thálpius,
and by Dióres, Ámarýnceus's son,
and by Pólyxínus, the son of Agásthenes.

And the men who lived in Dulíchion and the Echínæ,
the sacred islands across the wide sea from Elis,
were led by Meges, the son of Phyleus—who long
before, enraged at *his* father, had left his home
to settle Dulíchion. With him came forty ships.

And Odysseus commanded the Céphallénians,   590
the men who held Íthaca, those of Nériton, thick
with forests, of steep Crocylía and Ægilips,
Zacýnthus and Samos and the land facing the islands.
All these were led by Odysseus, the equal of Zeus
in wisdom. He brought twelve ships with vermilion prows.

And the men of Ætólia, living in Ólenus, Pleuron,
Pylénē, the shores of Chalcis, and Cálydon—
these men were led by Thoas, the son of Andrǽmon,
since Œneus was dead, and all his sons were as well,
and the great hero Meleáger. And so the lordship   600
had been given to Thoas. And with him came forty ships.

*

And Idómeneus, that great fighter, commanded the Cretans,
the men who held Cnossus, the strong-walled city of Gortyn,
Lyctos, Milétus, Lycástus, its cliffs white with chalk,
the populous cities of Phæstos and Rhýtion;
and the others who lived in the hundred cities of Crete.
All these were led by Idómeneus and his attendant
Meriones. And with them came eighty ships.

And Tlepólemus, a huge and powerful man,
brought nine ships filled with the bravest soldiers from Rhodes,   610
who lived on that island divided into three groups—
in Ïálysus, Lindos, Camírus, its cliffs white with chalk.
Their commander was Héracles' son by Ástyochéa;
he had carried her off from Éphyra, on the Selléïs,
after plundering many cities and slaughtering men.
But once Tlepólemus grew up, he killed Licýmnius,
his father's uncle, a famous warrior once,
who was then growing old. Tlepólemus quickly built ships,
and he gathered men, and he sailed off across the sea,
being threatened by Héracles' other sons and his grandsons.   620
As he wandered about, he suffered many great hardships,
but he finally came to Rhodes, where his people settled
in three divisions, according to their three tribes,
and there the people were loved by Zeus, the ruler
of gods and men, and he poured great riches upon them.

And Nireus brought three ships from the island of Symē.
He was the son of King Cháropus and of Aglǽa,
and the handsomest man of all those who sailed to Troy,
but he was a weakling, and just a few men came with him.

And the men of Nisýrus, Crápathus, Casus, and Cos,   630
who held the Calýdnean islands, were led by Phidíppus
and Ántiphus, the two sons of Théssalus, who
was the son of Héracles. With them came thirty ships.

Now all those who held Pelásgian Argos and Alus,

Álopē, Trachis, and all the soldiers who came
from Phthia and Hellas, the land of beautiful women,
and were known as Hellenes, Myrmidons, and Achaeans—
had fifty ships, and Achilles was their commander.
But they took no thought of the war now, since there was no one
to lead them, because Achilles was lying idle   640
beside his black ships, furious over Briséïs,
that beautiful girl from Lyrnéssus whom he had captured
after much toil, when he had plundered Lyrnéssus
and Thebē, and cut down Epístrophus and Mynes,
Euénus's sons, fierce warriors. Grieving for her,
Achilles lay idle. But soon he was to arise.

And the men who held Phýlacē and the grove of Deméter,
flowery Pýrasus, Iton with ample flocks,
Ptéleos, and Antron beside the sea,
had been led by Protesiláüs while he was alive.   650
But by then the dark earth already held him beneath it,
and his wife had been left behind to lament and wail
and tear her cheeks, and his house was only half built;
a Dardánian soldier had killed him as he was leaping
out of his ship, the first one to land in Troy.
Podárces, the son of Íphiclus, now was their leader;
he was the younger brother of Protesiláüs,
who was not just the elder but also the braver man.
So the men did not lack a commander, although they longed for
the one they had lost. With him came forty ships.   660

And the men who lived in Pheræ beside lake Bœbéïs,
and in Bœbē, Gláphyræ, and the walled town of Ïólcus—
they came with eleven ships and were led by Eumélus,
son of Admétus; that radiant woman Alcéstis,
the most beautiful daughter of Pélias, was his mother.

And the men who lived in Methónē and in Thaumácia,
and those who held Melibœa and rugged Olízon,
were commanded by Philoctétes, the great archer;
their seven ships were each manned with fifty skilled bowmen.

But their captain lay in great pain on the island of Lemnos,   670
where the Argives had left him suffering with a wound
from a poisonous water snake, and he lay there in anguish;
but the Argives beside their black ships would soon recall him.
Yet although they missed him, his men had a second commander:
they were led by Medon, Öïleus's bastard son.

And the men of Ithómē, with its steep hills, and Tricca,
and Œchália, city of EÚrytus, were commanded
by Asclépius's sons, who were skilled in the art of healing,
Podalírius and Macháon, with thirty ships.

And the men who held Orménion and the fountain   680
of Hypería, Astérion, and the white cliffs
of Mount Títanus—Eurýpylus led these men,
the son of Euǽmon. And with him came forty ships.

And Polypœtes, the son of Piríthoüs,
whose father was Zeus, commanded the men of Argíssa,
Gyrtónē, Orthē, Elónē, and the white town
of Olöósson. Leónteus also came with them
as their second commander. He was a scion of Ares
and son of Corónus. With them came forty ships.

And Guneus came out of Cyphus with twenty-two ships,   690
and with him the brave Peræbians and Æniénēs,
whose homes could withstand the bitter storms of Dodóna,
and who lived in the plowlands around the Titarésius;
though it joins the river Penéüs, its lovely waters
never mix with Penéüs's silvery eddies
but flow on the surface like oil, since the Titarésius
is a branch of the river Styx, the dread river of oaths.

And Próthoüs, son of Tenthrédon, led the Magnésians.
They were the men who lived by the river Penéüs
and forested Pélion. With him came forty ships.   700

These were the lords and commanders of the Achaeans.

Tell me now, Muse: who were the best among them,
of the men and horses that came with Atreus's sons?
Of the horses, the best by far were the mares of Admétus,
Pheres' son, which his own son Eumélus drove.
They were as fast as birds, in age and in color
a perfect match, and their backs were as perfectly even
as if the two had been made with a leveling line.
Apollo had bred these enormous mares in Peréa,
and their charge spread panic throughout the enemy's ranks. 710
Of the men, the best was Ajax, Télamon's son,
while Achilles raged. Achilles by far was the greatest,
as were his horses; but he was holding aloof now
beside his ships, still raging at Agamemnon,
and his men passed the time amusing themselves on the seashore
with archery and with throwing the spear and discus,
and their horses stood idle, each one untied from its yoke,
eating the clover and parsley that grow in marshland,
while the chariots lay covered and idle inside the huts.
And longing for him, the men of Achilles wandered 720
throughout the wide camp, and did not take part in the fighting.

But the rest of the army marched forward, as if the land
were being consumed by fire, and the earth groaned beneath them,
as when Zeus in his anger lashes the land in Aríma,
where they say Typhœus lies captive beneath the ground:
just so did the earth groan under the feet of the army
as they marched from the ships at great speed across the plain.

And Iris, swift as the wind, was sent now by Zeus
with a message to warn the Trojans, who had all gathered
in assembly at Priam's gates, both the young and the old. 730
Iris came up to Priam and spoke with the voice
of Polítes, one of his sons, a very fast runner,
who was stationed on Æsÿétes' tomb to keep watch
for the moment when the Achaeans would move from their ships.
In his likeness she said, "My lord, you are always fond
of unceasing words, as before, in the time of peace.
But we are at war now. I have seen many battles,

but never before have I seen an army as vast
as the one that is now advancing; they are as countless
as leaves or as grains of sand, and they are marching   740
across the plain to attack our city. Lord Hector,
I call upon *you* now. Do as I say. There are many
allies throughout the city, and many lands
have many languages. Make sure that every commander
gives orders to his own people, and let each one
prepare his own men and lead them out into battle."

When Hector heard her, he knew that she was a goddess,
and at once he broke up the assembly. All of them ran
to arm themselves, and the gates were opened, and out rushed
soldiers and charioteers, and a great din arose.   750
There is a high mound in front of the city, far out
in the plain, with an open space on all sides around it.
It is called Batiéa by humans, but the immortals
have named it the tomb of Myrína, the peerless dancer.
There the Trojans and allies gathered their forces.

The Trojans were led by Priam's son, glorious Hector,
and his were the most and the best men, eager for battle.

Next, the Dardánian troops were led by Aeneas,
whom Aphrodite bore to Anchíses, when she,
a goddess, made love with a man on the slopes of Mount Ida.   760
Aeneas was not their only commander; with him
were Archélochus and Ácamas, sons of Anténor,
both of them skilled in warfare of every kind.

And the men who lived in Zeléa at Ida's foot,
wealthy men, Trojans by race, who drank the dark water
of the river Æsépus—Pándarus led these men,
Lycáon's son, whose bow was a gift from Apollo.

And the men who held Adrestía, the land of Apæsus,
Pitÿéa, and the region of steep Teréa
were led by Adréstus and by Amphíus, whose breastplate   770

was made of linen. They were the sons of Merops,
an excellent prophet, who had forbidden his sons
to go to the war. But they would not listen to him,
because the spirits of death were driving them onward.

And the men who lived in Percótē and in Abýdus,
Práctius, Sestus, and bright Arísbē were led
by the son of Hýrtacus, Ásius; his huge horses
had brought him to Troy from Arísbē and the Selléïs.

And Hippóthoüs led the tribes of Pelásgian fighters,
fierce men, who lived in Laríssa—Hippóthoüs   780
and Pylǽus led them, the sons of Pelásgian Lethus.

And Ácamas and Píroüs led the Thracians;
they came from beyond the Héllespont's mighty stream.

And Euphémus, the son of Céas's son Trœzénus,
came as commander with the Cicónian troops.

And Pyrǽchmes led the Pæónians, with their curved bows;
they came from the far west in Ámydon, by the broad waters
of the Áxius, the most beautiful river on earth.

And Pylǽmenes led the Páphlagónians
from the land where the wild mules breed, among the Enéti.   790
These were the men who held the town of Cytórus,
who lived around Sésamus, by the Parthénius river,
in Ægialus and Cromna and Erithíni.

And the Hálizónians, led by Epístrophus
and Ódius, came from Álybē, birthplace of silver.

And the Mysians were led by Chromis and Énnomus,
who was a prophet; but prophecies did not save him
from death, for Achilles cut him down in the river,
as he rampaged, slaughtering other Trojans as well.

*

And Ascánius and Phorcys commanded the Phrygians   800
from distant Ascánia; both were eager to fight.

And Mesthles and Ántiphus led the Mæónians—
Talǽmenes' sons, who were born by the Gygǽan Lake.
These led the Mæónians, who lived under Mount Tmolus.

And Nastes commanded the Cárians, wild of speech,
who held Milétus and thickly forested Phthires
and the streams of Mæánder and the high peaks of Mycálē.
These men were led by Amphímachus and by Nastes—
Nastes and Amphímachus, sons of Nomíon.
And Nastes went into battle decked out in gold   810
like a girl—fool that he was. But the gold could not save him
from a wretched death, when Achilles, there in the river,
killed him, stripped him, and carried his gold away.

And Sarpedon and Glaucus commanded the Lycians, who came
from their distant land by the swirling waters of Xanthus.

Book 3

When the armies were ready, each company with its leader,
the Trojans advanced with a raucous shouting, like cranes
whose shrieks fill the sky as they flee from the storms of winter
and the endless rain, and fly toward the river Ocean,
bringing swift death through the air to the Pygmy troops.
But the Argives advanced in silence, breathing out fury,
eager to fight and stand by each other in battle.
As when the south wind pours mist on the peaks of the mountains—
feared by all shepherds, but better than night for a thief,
and a man can see only as far as a rock can be thrown: 10
just so did a dust cloud arise from beneath their feet
as the troops marched forward at full speed across the plain.

When they had come within range and were facing each other,
Paris stepped out in front of the Trojan army,
a leopard skin on his shoulders and a curved bow
and a sword; and shaking two bronze-tipped spears, he challenged
the best and the bravest of the Achaeans to come
out from the crowd and face him in single combat.
Lord Menelaus caught sight of him as he strutted,
and as a hungry lion is filled with joy   20
when he finds a large carcass, a wild goat or a huge stag,
and at once he begins to devour it, though dogs and hunters
keep rushing at him and trying to drive him off:
just so Menelaus rejoiced at the sight of Paris;
he thought that now, at last, he would have his revenge.
And he leaped to the ground from his chariot, in full armor.

But when Paris saw Menelaus come out from the ranks,
his heart shook, and he recoiled to avoid destruction.
And as a man sees a snake in some mountain valley
and jumps back with trembling legs and cheeks drained of color: 30
just so did Paris shrink, terrified, into the crowd.

*

Then Hector rebuked his brother with shaming words:
"You miserable disgrace, most handsome of men
but woman-crazed, a seducer, a selfish fool,
I wish you had never been born, or had died unmarried—
that would have been far better than to become
a cause of contempt like this, whom good men despise.
The Achaeans must now be mocking us, laughing out loud
and saying, 'Some champion they have! Just a pretty face,
a man without any strength, without any courage.'   40
Do you save your courage for stealing men's wives? You gathered
your faithful comrades and sailed off to distant lands
and mingled with strangers and brought back a beautiful woman
by marriage linked to a warrior race; in all this
you have been a great curse to your father, your city, your people—
to the Argives a joy, but a boundless shame to yourself.
And now you refuse to stand against Menelaus?
If you fought, you would soon learn what kind of man you offended.
The lyre won't help you then, nor will Aphrodite's
gift of good looks, when you lie face down in the dirt.   50
The Trojans are cowards; they should have stoned you to death
a long time ago, for all the harm you have done them."

And Paris answered him, "Hector, you are entirely
right to rebuke me, and you have said nothing unfair,
though your heart is always unyielding, just like an axe
that a shipwright holds in his right hand to cut through a beam,
and it adds to his force: so resolute is your spirit.
But please don't throw in my face the enchanting gifts
of Aphrodite the golden. Not to be scoffed at
are the radiant gifts of the gods; they offer them freely   60
to whomever they wish, and a man wouldn't willingly choose them.
But now, since you want me to fight against Menelaus,
tell all the Trojans to sit down, and all the Achaeans,
and put me with Menelaus between the two armies
to fight to the death for Helen and her possessions.
Whoever can prove that he is the better man
will be given the wealth and will carry the woman home.
And all the soldiers will swear solemn oaths of friendship

that let us remain in our city and let the others
return in their ships to Argos and to Achaea."   70

Hector greatly rejoiced at his brother's proposal,
and he stepped out into the open and held back the Trojans.
The Achaeans began to aim at him, and they tried
to hit him with stones and arrows, till Agamemnon
shouted out a command at the top of his voice:
"Hold back, Achaeans! Hold back the shooting—now!
Be quiet! It looks as though Hector has something to tell us."

At once they were all silent and stopped the shooting.
And Hector spoke out in the space between the two armies:
"Hear me, you Trojans and you Achaeans. I bring you   80
the words of Paris, through whom this war has arisen.
He asks that all you brave warriors, on both sides,
lay your bright weapons down on the bountiful earth
while he, between the two armies, fights to the death
with Menelaus for Helen and her possessions.
Whoever can prove that he is the better man
will be given the wealth and will carry the woman home,
and the rest of us all will swear solemn oaths of friendship."

After he finished, everyone there was silent.
Then from the ranks Menelaus stepped out and said,   90
"Hear me now too: since my heart, more than all others,
is weighed down by sorrow. I want both Argives and Trojans
to part in peace, since we all have suffered much harm
because of my quarrel and Paris's, who began it.
Whichever one of us meets his appointed death,
may he die, and may the rest of you part in peace.
You Trojans—bring two lambs, a white male and a black female,
for Earth and Sun; and for Zeus we will bring another.
And let mighty Priam come also to swear an oath
himself—since his sons are reckless and not to be trusted—   100
so that no man may violate oaths sworn in Zeus's name."

When they heard these words, Achaeans and Trojans rejoiced,

hoping that now the horrors of war were over.
So they pulled their chariots back, and the captains stepped out,
and they took off their armor and put it down on the ground,
and there was hardly a space between the two armies.
Hector sent off two heralds to go to the city
to get the lambs and request that King Priam come;
and Agamemnon sent Talthýbius down
to the Argive ships and told him to bring back a lamb,   110
and at once the herald did what his lord had commanded.

Meanwhile Iris flew with a message to Helen
in the likeness of Paris's sister Laódicē,
her sister-in-law, the most lovely of Priam's daughters,
who was married to Helicáon, Anténor's son.
She found her in her own chambers, in front of the loom,
making a large purple robe in which she had woven
many fierce combats that Trojans and Argives both
had endured on the field of battle because of her.
Iris came up and stood beside her and said,   120
"Quickly, my dear—come look at the wonderful thing
that is happening on the plain. Achaeans and Trojans
are no longer killing and dying. Look: they have halted
this dreadful war; they have stopped their fighting; they stand
and lean on their shields, with their long spears stuck in the ground.
They are all waiting for Paris and Menelaus
to fight for you, to the death, in single combat.
Whoever wins will take you away as his wife."

And the goddess filled Helen's heart with a sweet longing
for her former husband, her parents, and for the city   130
she had left. She covered herself with a shawl of white linen
and with tears streaming down her cheeks, walked out of the room,
and two of her handmaids followed closely behind her.

Quickly they came to the place where the Scaean Gates stood.
There, Priam and his companions—Thymœtes, Pánthoüs,
Hicetáon, Clýtius, Lampus, brothers of Priam,
Anténor, Ucálegon, both of them clear-minded men—

sat as the elders of Troy. Because of their age
they had long ceased from fighting, but still they were eloquent speakers.
They sat on the wall like cicadas that in a forest   140
sit on a tree and call with their lily-like voices.
And when they saw Helen climbing the stair to the ramparts,
they nodded to one another, and softly they said,
"No wonder that both the Trojans and the Achaeans
should endure long years of sorrow for such a woman:
she is dreadfully like an immortal goddess; her beauty
pierces the heart. But let her sail back to her home
and not remain here, a curse to us and our children."

When Helen approached, King Priam called out to greet her:
"Come here, dear child; sit down in front of me. Look,   150
you can see your former husband and kinsmen and friends.
I do not blame you—it is the gods whom I blame
for this wretched war that they have inflicted upon me.
Tell me now, what is the name of that splendid man
who is standing down there, so powerful and so tall.
To be sure, there are other men who are even taller,
but never before have I seen a man so majestic,
so splendid in form and bearing. He must be a king."

Helen looked down at the army, and then she answered,
"Dear father-in-law, with all my heart I revere you.   160
If only death had come to me when I followed
your son here, leaving my home and my marriage bed
and my precious daughter and all my beloved friends.
But death didn't come, and I melt away in my weeping.
As to your question: That man is Atreus's son,
Lord Agamemnon, commander of the Achaeans,
not only a mighty soldier: a noble king.
And he was my brother-in-law once, bitch that I am—
if the life I seem to have lived then was ever real."

The old king gazed down and marveled. At last he said,   170
"Fortunate son of Atreus, blessed by the gods,
how vast is this army of young men that you command!

A long time ago, I traveled to Phrygia, where
I saw the great Phrygian armies, the tens of thousands
of men assembled for war under Otreus and Mygdon,
encamped on the banks of the river Sangérius—
being their ally, I too was numbered among them
when the Amazons struck us, women as fierce as men.
But not even that was as vast an army as this is."

Next, catching sight of Odysseus, Priam said,   180
"Now tell me about that man over there, dear child.
He is shorter than Agamemnon but, truly, he looks
more muscular, and broader in chest and shoulders.
His weapons and armor lie on the bountiful earth,
and he himself strides about through the ranks of soldiers
like a thick-fleeced ram through a flock of silvery ewes."

Then Helen, daughter of Zeus, looked down and said,
"That is Laértes' son, resourceful Odysseus,
who knows all kinds of tricks and cunning maneuvers."

To this, Anténor, that clear-minded man, responded,   190
"What you just said, my lady, is very true.
Once, long ago, Odysseus came here on a mission
concerning yourself, together with Menelaus.
They were my honored guests; they stayed at my palace,
and I came to know the character of them both.
And when they stood up to speak in our great assembly,
Menelaus surpassed him in height, with his broad shoulders,
but when they sat down, Odysseus was more majestic.
And when they delivered their message before us all,
Menelaus spoke freely, with few words, but very clear ones,   200
right to the point, though he was the younger man.
But whenever Odysseus stood up to speak among us,
he would first fix his gaze on the ground, without ever moving
the speaker's staff that he held, either backward or forward,
but would keep it stiff and straight, like a man unpracticed
in the orator's art—like a lowbred fellow, a fool.
But when he hurled forth that stupendous voice from his chest

and his words began falling fast like snowflakes in winter,
then no other man on earth could compete with Odysseus."

Third, as he caught sight of Ajax, the old king said,   210
"Who is that man, so powerful and so tall,
who stands head and shoulders above the other Achaeans?"

When Helen saw whom he was looking down at, she answered,
"That is gigantic Ajax, the Danäans bulwark.
And next to him stands Idómeneus, like a god,
surrounded by all the Cretan commanders. Often
he visited us as our honored guest; Menelaus
would entertain him whenever he came from Crete.
And there, below, are the other Achaean captains—
I recognize them and could tell you the names of them all.   220
But two commanders I look for and I don't see:
Castor and Pollux, my mother's sons, my dear brothers.
Either they didn't come here from Lacedæmon,
or else, though they came, they haven't entered the fighting
because of the insults and shame I have brought upon them."
So she thought. But already the life-giving earth
lay piled up over them in their beloved country.

Meanwhile the heralds were carrying through the city
the sacrifices: two lambs and a goatskin bottle
of wine that gladdens the heart; and the herald Idæus   230
carried the gleaming bowl and the golden wine cups.
When he came to King Priam's side, he delivered the message:
"Arise, great son of Laómedon—the commanders
of both the armies request that you come to the plain
so that you yourself may seal the oaths that they take.
Soon Paris and Menelaus will fight to the death.
Whoever wins takes the woman and her possessions;
and the rest of us all will swear solemn oaths of friendship
that let us remain in our city and let the others
return in their ships to Argos and to Achaea."   240

At these words, the old man shuddered, then told his companions

to yoke the horses, and speedily they obeyed.
Priam climbed up on the splendid chariot and took
the reins in his hands as Anténor climbed up beside him.
They drove through the Scaean Gates and onto the plain;
and when they reached the place where the armies were standing,
they stopped and dismounted, and with unhurried steps
the old men walked to the space between the two armies.
At once Agamemnon stepped up, and Odysseus also;
and both sides' heralds brought out the victims whose death   250
would bind the oath for the gods, and they mixed the wine,
and they poured clear water over the hands of the kings.
Lord Agamemnon quickly drew out the knife
that always hung beside the great sheath of his sword,
and he cut off hairs from the heads of the lambs, and the heralds
passed them around to the Trojan and Argive commanders.
And Agamemnon lifted his arms and prayed:
"Zeus, our father, you who rule from Mount Ida,
most glorious king; and you, Lord Hélios, Sun,
who behold all things and hear all things under heaven;   260
and you rivers, you earth, you gods of the world below
that punish the dead who have broken their solemn vows—
be witnesses now; make sure that these oaths are binding.
If, on the one hand, Paris kills Menelaus,
he shall go on holding Helen and her possessions,
and at once we Achaeans will launch our ships and sail home.
But if, on the other hand, Menelaus kills Paris,
the Trojans shall give back Helen and her possessions
and pay us the kind of penalty that is fitting
and will be remembered for generations to come.   270
If Priam and Priam's sons are unwilling to pay me
a penalty that is fair, once Paris has fallen,
I will fight against Troy for the sake of my retribution
and stay here until I have brought this war to an end."

As he finished, he slit the lambs' throats with the pitiless bronze,
then laid them down on the ground as they quivered and gasped
for breath and their life poured out, cut short by his blade.
The men drew wine from the mixing bowl into their wine cups,

spilled it as a libation, then prayed to the gods.
And this is what someone would say, Achaean or Trojan: 280
"Zeus, most glorious king, and you other immortals—
whichever army is first to betray this oath
by breaking the truce, may their brains be spilled on the ground
as this wine is spilled—their brains and the brains of their children;
and may their dear wives be other men's slaves and whores."
This was their prayer; but Zeus would not yet fulfill it.

Then Priam, beside his chariot, addressed the troops:
"Listen to me, you Trojans and you Achaeans.
I am going back now to Troy, since I cannot bear
to see my beloved son in a fight to the death   290
with Menelaus, though Zeus and the other immortals
must already know which one is fated to die."
And once he had had the lambs put onto his car,
the godlike old man climbed up himself, and he took
the reins in his hands, as Anténor climbed up beside him,
and together the two of them drove back to windswept Troy.

Odysseus and Hector measured a space for the combat,
and they took two stones and put them into a helmet
to decide which man would be first to throw his bright spear.
And the soldiers lifted their hands to the gods and prayed;   300
and this is what someone would say, Achaean or Trojan:
"Zeus, our father, most glorious king, now hear us—
whichever man brought these troubles upon both sides,
let him be killed and descend to the realm of Hades
while the rest of us live in peace and abide by our oath."
Then Hector took hold of the helmet and shook the lots,
looking away; and out jumped the lot of Paris.

The men in both armies sat down in rows, at the place
where each man's battle gear lay by his high-stepping horses.
And Paris quickly put on his resplendent armor.   310
First, he strapped the bronze greaves to his lower legs
and fastened them onto his ankles with silver clasps.
Next, on his chest he put the finely wrought breastplate

of his brother Lycáon, which fitted his body too.
Over his shoulder he slung his silver-bossed sword
and above it his massive shield. And last he put on
his bronze helmet with its blood-chilling horsehair crest,
then chose a powerful spear that fitted his hand.
In just the same way, Menelaus prepared for battle.

And when the two men had armed and taken their weapons,   320
they strode out into the space between the two armies,
glaring fiercely. Excitement seized all who watched
as the warriors took their stands on the combat ground,
raising their spears, caught up in the fury of battle.

Paris was first to throw his long-shadowed spear,
and he hit Menelaus's shield, right in the center,
but the spearhead did not break through; its point was bent back
by the shield's great mass. Then Menelaus got ready
to throw his spear, first praying to Father Zeus:
"Lord Zeus, grant me revenge on the man who wronged me,   330
Paris, and let me kill him with my own hands,
so that for all generations a man may shudder
at doing harm to the host who offered him friendship."
And lifting his own spear up, he hurled it at Paris.
It tore through his shield and through his finely wrought breastplate
and slit his tunic and grazed him under his ribs;
but Paris had leaned to one side and escaped destruction.
Then Menelaus drew his great silver-bossed sword
and brought it down on the ridge of Paris's helmet;
but when the sword struck, it shattered and fell from his hand.   340
He looked up to heaven, and bitterly he cried out,
"Lord Zeus, truly no god is more spiteful than you are.
I thought that at last I would have my revenge on Paris
for the harm he has done me; but look here: my sword lies shattered,
and the spear has flown from my hand, and I haven't killed him."
With these words he rushed at Paris and, seizing his helmet,
he spun him around and dragged him toward the Achaeans,
strangling him by the richly embroidered strap
beneath his chin, which was being pulled tighter and tighter.

*

And now Menelaus would surely have dragged him away   350
and won for himself imperishable glory
if Aphrodite had not been so quick to notice.
At once she rushed out and broke the strap, and the helmet
came away empty in Menelaus's hands.
He whirled it around and flung it to the Achaeans
and charged back, holding his spear, in a frenzy to kill.
But Aphrodite swept Paris away with ease,
as a god can do; she shrouded him in dense mist
and set him down in his own sweet-smelling bedroom.
Next, she went off to summon Helen. She found her   360
in the midst of a crowd of ladies on the high ramparts.
And taking the form of a wool-spinner—an old woman
whom Helen loved, who had woven her beautiful things
in the days when she was her servant in Lacedæmon—
she tugged at the edge of her fragrant robe, and she said,
"Come with me, ma'am. Prince Paris wants you back home.
He is waiting for you; he is sitting there in his bedroom
dressed in the finest of clothes and gleaming with beauty.
No one would think he came from a battle. He looks
as fresh as if he were on his way to a dance."   370

These were her words, and they made Helen's heart beat faster.
She knew the goddess: her luscious neck and her ravishing
breasts and her brilliant eyes. Astonished, she said,
"What do you want now, goddess? Why are you always
tricking me? Will you drive me still farther on,
to Mæónia or Phrygia and hand me over
to another one of the pretty men you so love?
Is it because Menelaus has beaten Paris
and wishes to take his contemptible wife back home?
Is that why you came here with treachery in your heart?   380
You go to his side now; give up being a goddess;
don't go back to Olympus; forever worry
about his welfare; pamper him and protect him
until he makes you his wife, or perhaps his whore.
I will not budge. It would be disgraceful to go there

and share that man's bed; the women of Troy would be right
to blame me for it. I have enough grief in my heart."

The radiant goddess turned upon her in a fury:
"Do not provoke me, headstrong girl, or I might
lose my temper; I might withdraw my protection   390
and hate you as passionately as now I adore you.
You have no idea what hatred of you I could cause
in both Trojans and Argives—how cruelly you would die."
The goddess glared, and Helen was chilled with terror.
Wrapping herself in her shining white shawl, she left
without a word, and none of the Trojan ladies
saw her go, and she followed the goddess in silence.

And when they arrived at the sumptuous house of Paris,
the handmaids quickly turned to their tasks, and she,
the most beautiful of all women, went to the bedroom.   400
And Aphrodite went too and brought her a chair
and set it in front of Paris. Helen sat down
and with eyes turned away began to rebuke her husband:
"So: you are back from the fight. I wish you had died there,
killed by that warrior who was my husband once.
You used to boast that you were a better man
than Menelaus, stronger, a finer spearman,
so return to the plain and challenge him one more time
to a combat—although, on second thought, I would advise you
not to do that. It might be a little reckless;   410
you might end up as a corpse on the point of his spear."

Paris looked at her, then he answered, "My love,
don't rebuke me so harshly. This time Menelaus
defeated me, with Athena's help; but next time
I will win, since we too have gods on our side.
But come, let us go to bed and be joined in pleasure.
Never before has desire so mastered my heart—
not even when I first met you and carried you off
from Lacedæmon and sailed you away on my ships
and we stopped at a rocky island to make sweet love—   420

even that time, what I felt for you was less strong
than now, when this desire has overwhelmed me."
He stood up and moved toward the bed, and his wife followed.

So the two of them lay together. But Menelaus
prowled through the crowd of Trojans like a wild beast,
looking for Paris everywhere. No one could see him
or point him out; and surely, if he had been there,
the men would not have concealed him, since he was hated
by every one of the Trojans like death itself.
And that king of men, Agamemnon, stepped forth and said,   430
"Hear me, Trojans, Dardánians, and brave allies.
Victory clearly belongs to Lord Menelaus.
Surrender Helen of Argos and her possessions
and pay us the kind of penalty that is fitting
and will be remembered for generations to come."
Thus Agamemnon; and all the Achaeans cheered.

Book 4

At Zeus's side the gods were sitting in council
in the golden courtyard. Among them the cupbearer Hēbē
poured nectar into their golden cups, and they drank
and toasted each other, gazing down upon Troy.
And before long, Zeus began to provoke his wife,
taunting her with these heart-stinging, devious words:
"Menelaus may have Athena and you to help him;
but while you sit here and merely look at the war,
Aphrodite protects that other one, warding off danger.
Just now she saved him; he thought he was going to die.   10
The victory clearly belongs to Lord Menelaus,
so let us consider how this affair should proceed.
Shall we go ahead and once again stir up the war
or shall oaths of friendship be made between the two armies?
If all of us here agree to the latter outcome,
then Priam's city can still be a place men live in,
and Menelaus, with Helen, can sail back home."

These words caused Athena and Hera to seethe with fury
as they sat together devising grief for the Trojans.
Athena was silent; though angry at Zeus, her father,   20
and though a fierce passion gripped her, she held her tongue.
But Hera could not contain herself, and she cried out,
"Dread Lord, what are you saying? How can you wish
to make my incessant labors pointless and vain,
the sweat I have poured out, the efforts of my two horses
grown bone-tired as I assembled Achaea's armies
to bring boundless sorrow on Priam and on his sons.
Do as you wish; but not all the gods will approve."

Greatly annoyed by what she had said, Zeus answered,
"How absurd you are! What harm has King Priam done you,   30
or the sons of Priam, to make you so wildly rage
and wish to tear down the mighty ramparts of Troy?

If you could walk through the gates and into the city
and eat Priam raw and devour his children as well
and the other Trojans besides—would *that* heal your fury?
But have it your own way; so small a quarrel as this
must never become a cause of discord between us.
And one thing more: The next time *I* have an urge
to smash a city where people dear to *you* live,
don't oppose me, but let me act as I want to,   40
because I have given in to you on this matter,
not under compulsion, but sorely against my will.
Of cities under the sun and the starry heavens,
I honored Ilion most, and it had a place
deep in my heart, with Priam and Priam's people,
who never withheld the abundant feast from my altar,
the wine spilled for me, the savor of burning fat—
oblations that are the honors due to us gods."

Then Hera said, "These are the cities that I love best:
Argos, Sparta, Mycénæ. Topple all three   50
if you wish—destroy them if they should incur your hatred;
I won't defend them or grudge you in any way.
And even if I objected and tried to stop you,
it would do no good, since you are the stronger by far.
Still, you should never undermine what I have done.
I too am a god, and I come from the same stock as you do;
Cronus fathered me also, the first of his daughters.
But let us give way to each other in this affair,
and all the immortals will follow us. Quickly now,
command Athena to go to the battlefield   60
so that she can arrange for the Trojans to be the first
to break the truce, in spite of their sacred oaths."

The father of men and gods did what she had asked for;
he turned at once to Athena, with this command:
"Quickly, Athena, go to the battlefield
so that you can arrange for the Trojans to be the first
to break the truce, in spite of their sacred oaths."

*

This made Athena glad; she was eager to act,
and down from the topmost peak of Olympus she flew.
As Zeus hurls a shooting star across the wide heavens   70
and it blazes forth with a stream of sparks in its wake—
an omen for sailors or for an army encamped:
just so did Athena plummet, flashing, to Earth
and into their midst. Amazement seized all who saw her,
both the Trojans and the Achaeans. And the men turned
to their neighbors, awestruck, and said, "Does this omen mean
that the war will continue? Or does it mean that the oaths
of friendship between the two armies are now assured
by Zeus, who is for us all the decider of battle?"

This is what the men said as they saw her streak down.   80
And Athena entered the Trojan ranks in the likeness
of Laódocus, son of Anténor, a mighty captain,
and she looked for Pándarus. When she found him at last,
flanked by the many rows of shield-bearing soldiers
who had followed him out to Troy from the river Æsépus,
she went up and said, "Good friend, do you have the daring
to take Menelaus down with a single shot?
Imagine what fame you would win among all the Trojans,
what gratitude, and especially from Prince Paris,
who would certainly grace you with all kinds of splendid gifts   90
if he saw Menelaus, who just now faced him in combat,
killed by your arrow and laid on his funeral pyre.
Go ahead—shoot. But first you must vow to Apollo
to sacrifice a hundred fat lambs in his honor
once you return to your city, sacred Zeléa."

With these words Athena led him into great folly.
He quickly uncased his bow, which was made from the horns
of an ibex he once had shot as he lay in ambush
(it sprang from behind a crag, and his arrow hit it
right in the chest, and it fell back among the rocks;   100
its horns were each four feet long, and the craftsman inset them
in long strips on wooden staves and bound them together,
and at both its tips he put golden hooks for the bowstring).

He braced it against the ground and bent it and strung it,
and his comrades held up their shields, in case the Achaeans
saw him and rushed in before Menelaus had fallen.
He raised the lid of his quiver and took out an arrow
and fitted it to the bowstring. Before he shot it
he made a vow to Apollo, who strikes from afar,
to sacrifice a hundred fat lambs in his honor   110
once he returned to his city, sacred Zeléa.
And laying the arrow's notched end in the ox-gut bowstring,
he pulled it back with his right hand as far as his nipple,
with the iron tip of the arrow touching the bow shaft,
and the shaft was bent back, and he aimed, and then he let go,
and the great bow twanged, and the string sang out, and the arrow
flew through the dense crowd, eager to find its mark.

But then, Menelaus, the blessed gods did not forget you.
Athena stepped out before you and with her hand
deflected the deadly arrow, brushing it off   120
as a mother brushes a fly from her sleeping child.
She guided it to the place where your golden belt-clasps
were fastened and where your breastplate was doubled over;
the arrow tore through the belt, through the finely wrought breastplate,
and through the bronze kilt that protected you against missiles;
through all these defenses it drove, and its point grazed your skin,
and at once the dark blood came flowing out from the wound.
As when some Cárian or Mæónian woman
stains ivory with a dazzling scarlet dye
to make a cheek guard for horses, and it is treasured   130
and for years it lies in a storeroom; though many horsemen
long to possess it, it lies there, a joy to the king,
an ornament for his horse, for its rider a glory:
just so, Menelaus, your strong thighs were stained with blood,
and your handsome legs, and the shapely ankles beneath them.

Lord Agamemnon shuddered to see the blood
flow from the wound, and so did Lord Menelaus;
but when he saw that the arrow's barbs and the sinew
that bound its head to its shaft were outside the wound,

his spirit revived, and courage returned to his breast.   140
And Agamemnon sighed deeply—his comrades did too—
as he held Menelaus's hand, and he said, "Dear brother,
I have been the death of you, letting this truce be made
and sending you out as our champion, alone, to do battle
with the Trojans, since now they have shot you and trampled upon
the oaths of friendship that all of us swore to uphold.
But oaths are not sworn in vain with the blood of lambs;
even if Zeus is slow to take action, surely
he will bring our oaths to fulfillment sooner or later,
and the Trojans will pay—with their heads, their wives, and their children. 150
I am certain of this; deep in my heart I know
that a day will come when the sacred city of Troy
will be devastated, and Priam, and Priam's people;
and Lord Zeus himself will shake his dark storm shield upon them
in anger at their bad faith. These things will happen.
Yet I will feel heart-wrenching grief for you, my dear brother,
if you die now and come to the end of your fated life span,
and I will go home as the most despised of all men.
At once the Achaeans will want to sail back to their country,
and they will leave Priam and all of Troy to exult   160
at keeping Helen, while your bones rot in the ground
as you lie in the land of Troy with your task unfinished.
And before long, one of the arrogant Trojans will say,
'So this is how Agamemnon fulfills his anger.
He led the Achaean army to Troy for nothing,
and now, with ships that are empty, he has sailed home,
leaving his brother here dead.' Thus they will gloat.
On that day, may the earth gape open and swallow me up."

But Menelaus answered to reassure him:
"Take courage, brother, and please don't alarm our soldiers;   170
the arrow didn't get lodged in a vital spot.
My glittering belt-clasps stopped it, and the thick loin-guard,
and the plaited kilt underneath, which the bronze-smiths made."

And he answered him, "Dear Menelaus, I hope it is so.
But a healer will come to examine the wound and treat it

with soothing herbs that will quickly relieve the dark pain."
And he said to the herald Talthýbius, "Quickly, go now,
as fast as you can, and find our excellent healer
Macháon, son of Asclépius. Bring him at once
to see Menelaus. Some Trojan or Lycian archer   180
has wounded him—to his own glory, but to our grief."

The herald obeyed; he went through the army, trying
to find Macháon, and after a while he saw him
standing there flanked by rows of shield-bearing soldiers
who had followed him out to Troy from the grasslands of Tricca.
He approached and called to him, "Son of Asclépius, come
as fast as you can. Lord Agamemnon commands you
to treat Menelaus. Some Trojan or Lycian archer
has wounded him—to his own glory, but to our grief."

When he heard these words, Macháon was touched to the core,   190
and they rushed through the crowds of soldiers and ran on till
they came to the spot where Menelaus lay wounded.
Around him the chief commanders stood in a circle,
and Macháon walked to the center. He stooped and deftly
pulled out the arrow from Menelaus's belt,
and as it came out, its barbs were broken off backward.
He loosened the glittering belt and the thick loin-guard,
and the plaited kilt underneath, which the bronze-smiths had made;
then he examined the wound where the arrow had entered,
and he sucked out the blood, and he put soothing herbs upon it,   200
which the centaur Chiron had given his father in friendship.

But while they were all attending to Menelaus,
the Trojan army moved forward, and the Achaeans
put on their armor again and got ready to fight.
And then you would not have seen Agamemnon relaxing
or lagging behind, but fired up with zeal for battle.
He stepped down from his magnificent, inlaid car—
his attendant, Eurýmedon, reined in the snorting horses—
and he told him to keep them close by, in case exhaustion
came over his limbs as he gave commands to so many;   210

and he set out on foot to inspect the ranks. And whenever
he came to troops who were getting ready for battle,
he would try to stir up their courage with words like these:
"Now is the time to remember your fighting spirit.
Zeus won't support these Trojan liars and cheats
who attacked us and trampled their sacred oaths. I tell you:
vultures will dine on their delicate flesh—I swear it,
and we will carry their wives and their little children
home in our swift ships, once we have plundered Troy."

But whenever he came to troops who were holding back,   220
he would shout at them and rebuke them with angry words:
"You pitiful cowards—don't you have any shame?
Why are you standing around like this in a stupor,
like fawns exhausted from running across a plain
who stand still, panting, with hearts that are dazed by fear?
That is what *you* are like, standing here. Are you waiting
until the Trojans push all the way to our ships
so that you can see if Zeus will come to your rescue?"

In this way he strode through the warriors' ranks, commending
and rebuking, until he arrived at the Cretan troops.   230
They were arming around Idómeneus, their commander,
who stood in the front lines, fierce as a wild boar,
while Meriones, far back, urged on the rear battalions.
When he saw them so eager, Lord Agamemnon rejoiced,
and at once he spoke to their leader with admiration:
"Idómeneus, you are a man whom I greatly honor,
more than all others, in war and on other missions—
in our banquets as well, when the chief men among the Achaeans
are served in their turn from the great bowl of glistening wine.
The other commanders drink their allotted portion,   240
but your cup, along with mine, is always kept full
so that you can drink whenever your heart desires.
Go now, and show us how great a man you still are."

Idómeneus nodded to Agamemnon and answered,
"Son of Atreus, you can depend on my fighting,

as I promised you from the first when you asked me to come.
But urge on the other Achaeans, and let us prepare
to attack these Trojans, who have so vilely betrayed us.
Death and sorrow will be their lot in the future,
since they were the first to shatter the sacred oath."   250

Leaving him, Agamemnon went on, rejoicing,
and he walked through the crowd and came to Ajax and Teucer,
half-brothers, as both men were getting ready for battle,
and a mass of foot soldiers followed. As when from some mountain
a goatherd watches a cloud speed over the sea,
driven before the furious blast of the west wind,
and far in the distance it seems to him blacker than pitch
as it comes ever closer, bringing a mighty storm,
and he shudders and drives his goats on into a cave:
just so, beside the two men, did the dark battalions   260
of densely packed soldiers keep moving forward to join
the deadly battle, bristling with shields and spears.
When he saw them, Lord Agamemnon rèjoiced and said,
"Ajax and Teucer, commanders of the Achaeans,
to either of you there is nothing I need to say,
since your very presence inspires your troops to fight boldly.
By Father Zeus and Athena and Lord Apollo,
if only such hearts could be found within all my soldiers,
then right away the city of Priam would fall
to our powerful hands, and we would plunder its riches."   270

Leaving them, Agamemnon went on to others,
and soon he found Nestor, the eloquent lord of Pylos,
setting his troops in order and urging them on,
around the commanders Pélagon, Chrómius, Hæmon,
Alástor, and Bias. He stationed the charioteers
in front, with their horses and chariots; then, behind them,
he placed his foot soldiers, many of them, as a bulwark;
and into the army's middle he drove the cowards,
so that, even unwilling, a man would be forced to fight.
He first instructed the charioteers, and he told them   280
not to drive recklessly forward into the crowd:

"Let no man, trusting his horsemanship and his courage,
go charging ahead of the others and fight alone;
and let none fall back, since his absence will weaken the line.
But when you get within reach of an enemy's horses,
stay in your chariot; *thrust* with your spear—don't throw it.
That is the way the ancients conquered great cities,
with strength and purpose immovable in their hearts."

When he heard the old warrior urge them on, from his long
experience, Agamemnon rejoiced and said,   290
"Sir, I wish that your body had stayed as strong
as the heart in your breast; but old age lies heavy upon you.
If only this frailty had happened to someone else
and you remained at the height of your youthful vigor!"

And Nestor said, "Son of Atreus, I as well
wish that I were the man that I used to be
on the day that I killed Ereuthálion hand to hand.
But the gods don't give us mortals all things at one time.
Then I was young; now age has taken me over.
But even so, I will be with the charioteers   300
and urge them on and give them my best advice.
That is the job of the old; the thrusting of spears
I leave to men who are younger and stronger than I am."

Hearing this, Agamemnon walked on, rejoicing,
and he soon found Menéstheus, and with him the men of Athens,
and Odysseus was standing nearby, and all around him
the ranks of the Céphallénians also were standing.
None of their troops had yet heard the call to battle,
because both the Trojan and the Achaean armies
were just now beginning to move out against each other,   310
so these men were waiting until some other battalion
advanced to attack the Trojans and start the fighting.
When he saw them standing there, Agamemnon rebuked them:
"Shame on you, son of Péteos! You too, Odysseus,
whose mind is skilled in all kinds of subtle deceits—
why are you hanging back now and waiting for others?

You, of all men, should take your stand in the front ranks,
not cringing, but charging into the thick of battle.
You both are always the first to come when you hear me
announce a feast prepared for the senior commanders;   320
you are glad enough then to fill your mouths with roast meat
and drink cups of honey-sweet wine to your heart's content.
But now you would look on, even if ten battalions
of our troops were fighting here right in front of your eyes."

Odysseus answered him then, with an angry scowl,
"Son of Atreus, how can you say such a thing
or even think that we have hung back from battle?
Whenever Achaean troops advance, you will see—
if you dare to come close and take a good look at the fighting—
that Telémachus's father fights hand to hand   330
in the foremost ranks. So your words are absolute nonsense."

When he heard this reply, Agamemnon turned to him, smiling,
aware of his anger, and took back what he had said:
"Noble son of Laértes, resourceful Odysseus,
let us not quarrel. I have no orders to give you.
I know how loyal you are to me deep in your heart
and how you support me; the two of us think alike.
But enough. Later on, I will make these things right. If harsh
words have been uttered, may the gods help me correct them."

After he finished, he left and went on to others,   340
and soon he found Diomedes, Tydeus's son,
standing there in his chariot behind his horses,
and Sthénelus, son of Cápaneus, stood at his side.
When he saw him idle, Lord Agamemnon rebuked him:
"Shame on you, son of Tydeus! Why do you cringe
and cower like this, just eyeing the lanes of battle?
It wasn't your father's way to hang back; he would always
charge ahead of his comrades—so people say.
I never met him, but those who did see him in battle
agree that he was the best of his generation.   350
Once, he came to Mycénæ with Polyníces

to gather troops; they were marching against the walls
of Thebes, to drive out Etéocles, and they begged us
to help them recruit an army of seasoned men.
And our people agreed and granted them their request,
but Zeus changed our minds abruptly with evil omens.
Afterward, when they had left us and gone some distance
and had come to the grassy, reed-thick river Asópus,
the Achaeans sent him ahead of them with a message,
and he entered the city and found a great crowd of Thebans   360
at a feast in Etéocles' palace. But though a stranger
and alone with so many Thebans, he had no fear;
he challenged them all to tests of strength, and he won
every event, such help did Athena give him.
The Thebans were furious. After Tydeus had gone,
they laid an ambush for him, of fifty strong men,
who were commanded by Mæon and Lycophóntes.
But Tydeus killed them all in a hideous slaughter,
except for Mæon; he let him escape with his life
in obedience to the omens sent by the gods.   370
That is the man that Tydeus was; but his son,
though he talks more smoothly, cannot match him in fighting."

After he finished, Diomedes said nothing,
out of respect for Lord Agamemnon's rebuke.
But Sthénelus answered, "Son of Atreus, don't
tell such lies when you know how to speak the truth.
I say that we are much better men than our fathers.
We did conquer Thebes, the city of seven gates,
though its wall was stronger, our soldiers fewer than theirs were;
we trusted in the gods' omens and Zeus's help.   380
But our fathers were cut down through their own reckless folly.
So don't pretend that their honor can equal our own."

Diomedes answered him then, with an angry scowl,
"Be quiet, my friend, and listen to what I say.
I don't blame Lord Agamemnon for urging us on
to fight our best in this war. The glory is his
if we kill the Trojans and conquer their sacred city,

and, likewise, the grief is his if we should be slaughtered.
But come, let us both remember our fighting spirit."
He leaped to the ground from his chariot; as he landed   390
his bronze armor clattered with so unearthly a sound
that fear would have seized the heart of even a brave man.

As when the sea's swell keeps pounding against the shore,
wave after wave, hard driven before the west wind—
far out, it rises into a crest, then it breaks
on the land with a thundering roar, and around the headlands
it arches and comes to a peak and spits out the salt foam:
just so, on that day, did the Argive battalions move,
row after row, unceasingly, into battle.
Each captain issued commands, and his soldiers followed   400
silently; you would think that in all those vast
multitudes not one man had a voice in his mouth,
so quiet were they in obedience to their captains;
and on every man the armor flashed in the sun.
But the Trojans cried out like countless ewes in a rich man's
sheepfold, who wait to be milked and incessantly bleat
as they hear their lambs crying: so did the Trojan war shouts
arise with great uproar throughout the whole breadth of the army,
because their soldiers had no common language among them,
but the different tongues of people from many lands.   410

And the Trojans were urged on by Ares, and the Achaeans
by Athena, and also by Terror and Panic and Strife,
the insatiable goddess, sister of man-killing Ares.
When Strife first appears, she is small, but she keeps on growing
till her forehead touches the sky while her feet walk the earth.
Into the hearts of both sides she spread fierce hatred
and swept on, multiplying the death groans of men.

And when the two armies met, spear clashed against shield
in the fury of battle, and bronze armor rang, and shields
ground into other shields, and a great din arose;   420
and the moans and the shouts of triumph were mingled together,
the cries of killers and killed, and the earth ran with blood.

Just as when two winter torrents rush from their springs
and hurl themselves down to the place where the valleys meet,
and the massive waters are joined in a deep ravine,
and far off in the mountains the shepherd can hear their thunder:
such was the deafening noise of the armies clashing.

Antilochus was the first among the Achaeans
to kill a man—a noble Trojan who fought
in the front, Echepólus, son of Thalýsias.   430
The long spear flew, and it hit the ridge of his helmet,
and the point drove into his forehead and through the bone,
and darkness covered his eyes, and he fell like a tower.
Then Lord Elephénor, the leader of the Abántes,
Chalcódon's son, took hold of him by the feet,
and quickly he tried to drag him out of the way
of the spears and arrows, eager to strip off his armor
as soon as he could. But his efforts were soon cut short.
As he pulled the body, Agénor saw him, and where
his side was exposed beneath the shield as he bent down,   440
he thrust his spear; Elephénor crumpled to earth,
and the spirit left him. And there was a savage struggle
over his body; Achaeans and Trojans, like wolves,
rushed at each other's throats, man tearing at man.

Then Ajax speared Simöísius, a young man,
the son of Anthémion, whom his mother had borne
by the Símoïs river as she came down from tending
her flocks on Mount Ida. He never repaid his dear parents
the debt that he owed them for bringing him up; his life
was ended abruptly by Ajax's bronze-tipped spear.   450
As he moved along the front lines, he was hit in the chest
beside his right nipple; the spear drove on through his shoulder,
and he fell to the ground in the dust like a stately poplar
that has grown up in a broad meadow beside a marsh,
and its trunk is smooth, but small branches grow from its top;
and a wheelwright cuts it down with his gleaming iron
and bends it into a rim for a handsome car,
and it lies on the bank of a river and dries in the sunlight:

that is how Ajax cut down this young man. And at once
Priam's son Ántiphus hurled his spear through the crowd 460
at Ajax. He missed his mark, but his spear hit Leucus,
one of Odysseus's comrades, full in the groin,
as he tried to drag Simöísius's corpse to one side;
the body slipped from his hands, and he crashed down on top.
Odysseus, enraged at the death of his dear companion,
strode through the front ranks, armored in fiery bronze.
He stood in front of the Trojans and, glaring around him,
he aimed his spear, and the Trojans pulled back, and it hit
a bastard son of King Priam, Demócoön,
who had come from Abýdus, where he bred racing horses; 470
the bronze point drove through one temple and then came out
through the other temple, and darkness covered his eyes.

Hector and the front ranks of the Trojans retreated,
and the Argives gave a loud shout and dragged off the bodies
and pushed far ahead. And Apollo looked on, indignant,
from Pérgamus, and he shouted down to the Trojans,
"Courage now, Trojans! Don't give way to the Argives!
Their skin is like yours; it is *not* made of stone or iron
and will not deflect the flesh-tearing bronze when you spear them.
And Achilles is no longer fighting beside them; far back 480
among the black ships he nurses his heart-wrenching anger."
So from the city the dread god spoke. At the same time,
Athena strode through the Achaean ranks to encourage
and urge them on, whenever she saw a man falter.

And Dióres, Amarýnceus's son, was cut down;
he was hit by a jagged rock on the right leg, above
the ankle. The Thracian commander, Píroüs,
son of Ímbrasus, who had come there from Ænus,
had hurled it with all his might. The pitiless rock
utterly crushed the bones and the two tendons, 490
and he fell on his back, gasping, stretching his arms
to his comrades, and Píroüs ran up and speared his belly,
and his innards gushed out, and darkness covered his eyes.

*

As Píroüs dashed back, the Ætólian leader,
Thoas, hit him above the nipple; the spear point
drove through his lung. And Thoas ran up beside him
and pulled the spear out of his chest, then drew his sword
and plunged it into his belly and ended his life.
But he could not strip off his armor; the Thracian soldiers,
men with long hair in topknots, ran up to surround him,   500
raising their spears; and though he was tall and strong,
they drove him back and, staggering, he gave way.
And the two men lay stretched out, side by side, in the dirt,
the Thracian chief and the leader of the Epéans;
and around them many others were killed that day.

And no one who entered the battle could take it lightly,
not even a man unwounded by spear or sword
who roamed at the fighting's center—not even a man
whom Athena led by the hand through the thick of battle,
protecting him from the onslaught of hurtling spears.   510
And by nightfall many Trojans and many Achaeans
lay stretched out beside one another, face down in the dirt.

Book 5

Meanwhile Pallas Athena infused Diomedes
with strength and bravery, so that he might surpass
all the Achaeans and win himself glorious fame.
She caused a bright light to flare from his shield and helmet,
like the star of late summer that rises out of the Ocean
to shine in the night sky, most brilliant of all the stars.
Such was the light that blazed from his head and shoulders
as she sent him into the fighting where men pressed thickest.

Among the Trojans was one wealthy man named Dares,
a priest of Hephaestus; his two sons were equally skilled   10
in all kinds of fighting; their names were Idæus and Phegeus.
The two of them broke from the line, and they charged Diomedes,
driving their chariot as *he* charged forward on foot.
And when they had come close, Phegeus hurled his long spear,
and it missed Diomedes, sailing above his left shoulder.
But Diomedes charged forward and hurled *his* spear,
and it hit the young man in the chest, between his nipples,
and it knocked him out of the chariot into the dust.
And Idæus jumped off and, terrified, ran for his life,
not daring to stand there straddling his brother's body;   20
nor would he himself have escaped from the grip of death
if Hephaestus had not noticed and wrapped him in darkness
to spare the old man from absolute devastation.
And Diomedes took hold of the two strong horses
and gave them to his companions to drive to the ships.

And when the Trojans saw one son of Dares fleeing
and the other son lying face down, dead in the dirt
alongside his chariot, they were all filled with panic.
And Athena took Ares' hand and said, "Murderous Ares,
butcher of men, bloodstained destroyer of cities,   30
let us now leave the Trojans and the Achaeans
to fight on their own, so that Father Zeus may award

the victory to whichever army he wishes,
while we two withdraw far away from his terrible rage."
After she said this, she led him away from the battle
and made him sit down on the high bank of the Scamander.
And the Danäans pushed back the Trojans, and each of the captains
cut down his man. The first was King Agamemnon,
who killed Ódius, the Hálizónian leader,
as he turned to flee; he thrust his spear with such force   40
that the huge man was knocked from his chariot; the bronze tip
plunged in between his shoulders and out through his chest.

Idómeneus then killed Phæstus, the son of Borus,
from Mæónian Tarnē. Idómeneus stabbed him through
his right shoulder as he was trying to mount his car,
and he fell in the dirt, and hideous darkness seized him.
And Idómeneus's attendants stripped off his armor.

And Scamándrius, son of Stróphius, was brought down
by Menelaus. The young man was a great hunter;
the goddess Ártemis had herself taught him to shoot   50
every wild creature bred in the mountain forests.
Yet there was no way that the goddess could save him now,
nor all his skill as an archer. As he was fleeing,
Menelaus caught up and punched a spear through his back,
and he fell face down, and his armor clattered upon him.

And Meriones killed Pheréclus, Harmónides' son—
the father a craftsman whose hands were skilled in creating
all kinds of beautiful things, since Athena loved him.
He was the man who had built Lord Paris the ships
that caused so much evil and brought such disaster to Troy   60
and to Paris himself, who was blind to the gods' decrees.
Meriones ran him down, and as he drew close
he hit him in the right buttock, and the bronze spear point
pushed up under the pubic bone into his bladder,
and he fell to his knees, screaming, and death embraced him.

And Meges cut down Pedæus, Anténor's son—

a bastard son, but Theáno had brought him up
as one of her own, so much did she love her husband.
Meges' spear hit the back of his neck, then cut
right through his jaw, and sliced off his tongue at the root.   70
He fell in the dirt, and his teeth closed around the cold bronze.

And Eurýpylus, son of Euǽmon, cut down Hypsénor,
the son of a priest of Scamander named Dolopíon
whom the people revered as a god. As Hypsénor fled,
Eurýpylus overtook him, and bringing his sword
down on his shoulder he sheared off his massive arm;
the arm fell blood-soaked onto the ground, and death
seized him, veiling his eyes in a purple mist.

And so the two armies toiled in the fury of combat,
and you could not tell which side Diomedes was on,   80
so far did he range among both Achaeans and Trojans.
He swept across the wide plain like a winter torrent
whose rushing water has burst its embankments; the thick-built
dikes cannot hold it back, nor can it be halted
by the walls of the flourishing vineyards, when heavy rains
suddenly make it spill over, and farmers watch
as their beautiful fields of grain are destroyed beneath it:
just so, before Diomedes, the densely packed
Trojan battalions were driven off in confusion;
vast as they were, they buckled before his attack.   90

When Pándarus saw him storming across the plain
and driving entire battalions in rout, he quickly
drew an arrow and aimed it at Diomedes
as he charged forward, and hit him on the right shoulder
on the front of his breastplate; the arrow drove through, and the armor
was splattered with blood. And Pándarus gave a great shout:
"Onward, Trojans! The bravest of all the Achaeans
has been hit, and I think he will die—I am as sure
as I am that it was Apollo, the son of Zeus,
who called me from Lycia and granted me his protection."   100

*

This was his boast. But he had not killed Diomedes,
who drew back until he came to his horses and car,
and he said to Sthénelus, "Quickly, dear friend, get down;
take hold of this arrow and pull it out through my shoulder."
Sthénelus jumped to the ground and, grasping the point
of the arrow, he pulled it right through the back of the breastplate,
and the dark-red blood rushed out from the linen tunic.

Then Diomedes looked up and prayed to Athena:
"Hear me now, daughter of Zeus, great warrior goddess.
If ever you loved my father and stood beside him   110
in the fury of battle, now show your love for me too.
Grant that I kill this man, that I come within spear's range
of the one who shot me before I could see him, and now
must be boasting about his glorious triumph and saying
that I will not see the light of the sun for much longer."

This is the prayer that he spoke, and Athena heard him
and gave him fresh power and quickened his hands and feet,
and she stood beside him and said, "Son of Tydeus, courage.
Go now, attack the Trojans; into your breast
I have put the inexhaustible strength of your father.   120
I have also taken the human mist from your eyes
so that you can clearly discern a god from a mortal.
If any god comes here and challenges you to a combat,
refuse to fight—unless it is Aphrodite.
If *she* comes, feel free to cut her up with your spear."

With these words she left him, and Diomedes went back
to rejoin the foremost ranks of Achaean fighters.
And although, before, his heart had been fierce to kill Trojans,
three times that fierceness took hold of him now, like a lion
that a shepherd out in the wilds, guarding his sheep,   130
has wounded after it jumped the wall of the sheepfold,
but the wound does not stop it; instead, it arouses its fury,
and the shepherd no longer tries to defend his flock
but hides in a shelter, the sheep run in panic, deserted,
and their bloody carcasses pile upon one another,

and the lion, still furious, leaps out over the wall:
just so Diomedes rampaged among the Trojans.

He killed Astýnoüs and the commander Hypéron,
his long spear hitting the first man above the nipple,
and the other he slashed with his sword, where the collarbone is,   140
hacking his shoulder off from his neck and back.
He turned then and ran after Abas and Polyídus,
sons of Eurýdamas, famous reader of dreams;
but he had not interpreted dreams for them as they left
for the war, and Diomedes slaughtered them both.
And he went after Xanthus and Thoön, the two sons of Phænops,
who, worn out with age, could no longer father a son
to inherit his wealth. Diomedes took both their lives,
and he left the old man with an inconsolable sorrow;
never again would he welcome them home alive,   150
and the next of kin would inherit all his possessions.
Then he took down two of the sons of King Priam,
Echémmon and Chrómius, caught in one chariot.
As a lion charges into a herd of grazing
cattle, and leaping onto one, breaks its neck:
just so Diomedes knocked them out of their car
brutally; then he stripped off their armor and handed
their horses to his companions to drive to the ships.

When Aeneas saw the great havoc that Diomedes
had wrought on the Trojans, he strode through the rain of spears   160
in search of Pándarus. When he found him at last,
among the spearmen, he rushed to his side and said,
"Pándarus, where have you put your bow and your arrows?
Your fame as an archer is so great that no man here
can compete with you or claim to be better than you are.
So pray to Zeus and shoot a death-dealing arrow
at this man, whoever he is, who has done us so much
harm and has killed so many of our brave men—
unless it is some god, angry at us for omitting
a sacrifice, and a god's rage lies heavy upon us."   170

*

Then Pándarus answered, "Aeneas, counselor, friend,
to me it seems that the man must be Diomedes—
I think that I know his shield and his visored helmet
and his chariot horses; yet possibly he is a god.
If he is a man, the one who I think he is,
he has certainly not been raging like this on his own;
one of the blessed gods has been standing beside him,
shrouded in mist, invisible, and has turned
my arrow away as it was about to kill him.
A moment ago, I shot an arrow that hit   180
his shoulder and pierced straight through the front of his breastplate,
and I thought I had sent him to Hades. And yet, despite that,
he isn't dead. Some god must be fighting against us.
And furthermore, there is no chariot I can ride in,
although, at home, eleven new chariots wait
with cloths spread upon them, and by the side of each one
a pair of horses stand, munching their oats and barley.
As I was leaving, my father, the hero Lycáon,
urged me to take many chariots, so that, mounted,
I could ride into battle leading the Trojan forces.   190
But I didn't take his advice—it would have been far
better for me if I had—but I spared the horses;
they were used to eating their fill, and I was afraid
that they might go hungry here, where so many people
are under siege. So I left them and came on foot,
trusting my bow, which seems to have done me no good,
since I have already shot at two of their best men,
Diomedes and Menelaus, and with them both
I scored perfect hits, drew visible blood, but I didn't
kill them; I only managed to stir up their fury.   200
Fate was against me that day when I took my bow
from its peg and I led my soldiers to Troy, out of friendship
for Hector. If I should ever return to see
my beloved country again, my wife, and my home,
may some stranger come and chop my head from my body
if I do not smash this damned bow into pieces and toss it
onto the fire—so utterly useless it is."

*

Aeneas answered him, "No more speeches like that.
Nothing will get any better till you and I
mount my chariot and face this strong man in combat.   210
Come with me now, and see for yourself the power
of these horses, bred by my ancestor Tros—how incredibly
fast they can run, in either attack or retreat.
And if Zeus once again gives the triumph to Diomedes,
they will bring the two of us safely back to the city.
So come up beside me; take the whip and the reins,
and I will dismount from the car and fight him—or else
you go face him, and I will take charge of the horses."

Then Pándarus answered, "Aeneas, you keep the reins
and drive your own horses; if we are forced to retreat,   220
they will pull us better beneath a driver they know.
If they miss the sound of your voice when they expect it,
they may panic and bolt and not take us out of the battle,
and that rampaging Diomedes could charge ahead
and slaughter us both and ride away with the horses.
So go ahead, manage the car and horses yourself,
and when he comes, I will take him on with my spear."

They mounted and charged ahead against Diomedes
at breakneck speed. And when Sthénelus saw them coming,
he quickly said, "Son of Tydeus, joy of my heart,   230
I see two warriors rushing toward you in fury,
both of them men of infinite courage and strength:
Pándarus, the great archer, Lycáon's son,
and Aeneas, the son of Anchíses and Aphrodite.
So let us mount and give way to them. Don't keep raging
along the front lines of war. It may cost you your life."

Diomedes answered him then, with an angry scowl,
"There is no chance that I will retreat; you shall not persuade me.
It is not in my blood to back down or flee; my courage
never falters. I will not climb up in the car;   240
I will go out to face them, just as I am. Athena
gives me the strength; there is no man I will retreat from.

And even if one of these warriors should escape,
their horses will never take them both back to the city.
And one thing more: If Athena grants me the glory
of killing these two, you must leave our own horses here—
you can tie their reins to the rail—and go out and seize
Aeneas's horses and drive them down to the ships.
They descend from the stock that Zeus once gave to King Tros
in return for his dear son Gánymede; they are the finest   250
of all horses under the sun and the sweet light of day.
This is the famous stock that Anchíses stole from,
mating his mares with them slyly, without the knowledge
of Laómedon. From them six foals were born in his stables;
four foals he kept, and these two he gave to Aeneas.
If we could take them, we would both win great glory."

As they were speaking, the two Trojans galloped up
in their chariot. Pándarus called out to Diomedes:
"Son of Tydeus, the arrow I shot before
failed to kill you. Now I have come again;   260
we will see if I can bring you down this time for good."
And drawing his spear back, he hurled it at Diomedes,
and it hit his shield, and the spear point drove through the hides,
but it did not have enough force to puncture his breastplate.
And when the spear struck him, Pándarus shouted loudly:
"A hit! Clean through to your belly, and I don't think
you will hold out much longer. What a great triumph this is!"

Then, with no hint of fear, Diomedes said,
"You missed me, friend. But before this combat is over,
one of you two will be stretched face down in the dirt,   270
gorging mad Ares with blood." And he aimed and threw,
and Athena guided his spear, and it hit the Trojan
on his nose, near the eye, and thrust down and drove through his teeth,
and the sharp bronze spear point sliced off his tongue at the root
and came out the base of his chin. He fell from the car
into the dirt, and his massive, glittering armor
clattered upon him, and the two horses panicked
and swerved aside, and the soul slipped out of his body.

*

Aeneas jumped down from the chariot, seized with fear
that the Argives would capture the body and drag it off.   280
He straddled it like a lion sure of its strength,
and in front of him he held out his spear and his shield,
determined to cut down anyone who approached him,
and he uttered a blood-chilling war shout. But Diomedes
picked up a boulder that no two men of today
would be able to lift, and he held it above his head
and threw it. It hit Aeneas full on the hip
where the thighbone turns in the pelvis; it crushed the joint
and broke both the tendons and tore away all the flesh;
and Aeneas fell to his knees, and he stayed there, propped up   290
with one hand on the ground, and darkness covered his eyes.
And now Aeneas would surely have lost his life
if Aphrodite had not been so quick to notice.
She threw her arms around her beloved son
and in front of him held out a fold of her shining garment
to shield him from harm, so that no Danäan soldier
might drive a spear point into his chest and kill him.

As she carried Aeneas out of there, Sthénelus
did not forget what Diomedes had told him;
he took his own horses out of the thick of the battle,   300
tying their reins to the chariot rail, and proceeded
to fling himself on Aeneas's famous horses,
and he drove them away and into the Argive lines.
He handed them to Deípylus, his dear comrade,
whom he valued beyond all men of his generation
because their minds were alike; and he told him to drive them
down to the ships. Then he mounted behind his own horses
and drove out, eagerly searching for Diomedes.

But Diomedes had gone after Aphrodite,
his spear in his hand, knowing that she was fragile   310
and not a goddess triumphant in human warfare
like Athena or like Enýo, destroyer of cities.
And at last when he had caught up with her through the crowd,

he charged ahead and, thrusting at her with his spear,
he stabbed her delicate wrist, and the point pierced her skin
above the base of her palm, and the blood of the gods
flowed out—the ichor that runs in the blessed gods' veins
(they eat no food nor do they drink wine, and so
they do not have human blood and are therefore deathless).
The goddess cried out and dropped her son, and Apollo   320
caught him and took him up in his arms and hid him
inside a dark cloud, so that no Danäan soldier
might drive a spear point into his chest and kill him.
Then Diomedes shouted to Aphrodite:
"Keep away, daughter of Zeus. Haven't you caused
damage enough by seducing the hearts of weak women?
If you keep on meddling with war, you will come to hate it
so much that you will shudder when it is mentioned."

Then she withdrew, in terrible pain, distraught;
and Iris took her and led her out of the tumult   330
whimpering, and her beautiful skin grew dark.
Soon she found Ares, who sat to the left of the battle;
his long spear leaned on a cloud. She fell to her knees
and begged him for his celestial, gold-bridled horses,
who were standing beside him. "Save me, dear brother; give me
your horses so that they can take me up to Olympus.
I am in pain from a wound that a mortal dealt me—
Diomedes, a man who would fight with Lord Zeus himself."

Ares allowed her to take the gold-bridled horses,
and she mounted his chariot; Iris mounted beside her,   340
and she touched her whip to the backs of the horses, and gladly
they flew off, and soon they reached the heights of Olympus.
Iris reined in the horses, then she unyoked them
and spread before them a mound of celestial fodder.

Then Aphrodite flung herself onto the lap
of her mother, Dióne, who took her into her arms
and stroked her hair, and spoke to her softly: "Child,
which of the gods did this terrible thing to hurt you,

as if you had done something wicked in front of us all?"

And Aphrodite said, "It was Diomedes;   350
he is the one who stabbed me, because I was moving
Aeneas out of the battle, my own dear son,
who of all mortal men is the one I love best by far.
This war is no longer between Achaeans and Trojans;
the Argives are fighting even against the gods."

Diónē answered, "Be strong now, my child, and bear up
under this hardship. Many of us on Olympus
have suffered at men's hands, as we have hurt one another.
Ares suffered when Otus and Ephiáltes,
the sons of Alœus, caught him and put him in chains,   360
and for thirteen months he was bound up inside a bronze jar,
and he would have died if their stepmother, Eribœa,
hadn't told Hermes, who came and stole him away
when his strength failed and his life force was flickering out.
And Hera suffered when Héracles hit her right breast
with a three-barbed arrow; nothing could heal that pain.
Hades suffered as well, when an arrow hit him
shot by this same man, the powerful son of Zeus,
in Pylos among the dead; and he was in anguish.
That hard-hearted brute thought nothing of the great harm   370
that his arrows did to the gods who live on Olympus.
And now Athena has sent *this* man to attack you—
fool that he is, not realizing that whoever
fights against the immortals will not live long
and will not return from the horrid combats of war
to see his children climb onto his lap calling, 'Daddy!'
So let Diomedes, however mighty he is,
be careful that no god stronger than you attacks him—
or Ægialía, his wife, Adrástus's daughter,
will rouse her dear servants from sleep with her long laments   380
as she wails for her husband, the bravest of the Achaeans."
And gently, with both hands, she wiped off the oozing ichor,
and the wrist was healed, and the terrible pain went away.

*

Athena and Hera were looking on, and they started
to provoke Zeus with taunts. Athena was first to speak:
"Dear Father, please don't be angry at what I say,
but Aphrodite, it seems, has been trying to coax
some other Achaean girl to run off with one of
those Trojans whom she so passionately adores,
and while she was caressing this new girl, she must have   390
scratched her delicate hand on a golden dress pin."

Thus she mocked, and the father of men and gods
smiled and called Aphrodite before him and said,
"It is not your business, my child, to mix in the fighting.
Rather, attend to the lovely secrets of marriage
and leave all matters of war to Athena and Ares."

Meanwhile Diomedes charged at Aeneas.
Though he knew that Apollo himself was standing right there,
he was not afraid of that mighty god, but kept trying
to kill Aeneas and strip off his glorious armor.   400
Three times he charged, in a frenzy to bring him down;
three times Apollo beat back his massive shield.
But when for the fourth time he rushed at him in a frenzy,
Apollo shouted at him with a deafening voice:
"Stop, son of Tydeus! Right now! Stay where you are!
Do not presume yourself equal to the immortals,
since there is nothing alike between the two races—
the deathless gods and mere humans who walk on the earth."
At this, Diomedes gave ground, but only a little,
avoiding Apollo's wrath. And the god took Aeneas   410
out of the crowd and set him apart from the fighting
on Pérgamus, where his glorious temple stood.
There Leto and Ártemis, inside the great inner sanctum,
healed his wound and made him even more splendid.

And Apollo said to the war god, "Murderous Ares,
butcher of men, bloodstained destroyer of cities,
can't you go back and drag that man from the fighting?
He stabbed Aphrodite and wounded her, and he even

dared to keep on attacking me in a frenzy."
With these words Apollo sat down on Pérgamus, high up,   420
and Ares entered the Trojan ranks to inspire them.

Sarpedon rebuked Lord Hector: "Great son of Priam,
where is the fighting spirit that you once had?
You used to say you could hold this city alone
without any help from your people or from your allies,
just you and your brothers and brothers-in-law. But now
when I look around, I don't see one of them here;
they have slunk back, cringing like dogs in front of a lion,
while we, your allies, bear the whole brunt of the fighting.
I have come a great distance to help you, from far-off Lycia   430
by the swirling waters of Xanthus, with many troops,
and I left my beloved wife and my baby son
and all my possessions, the envy of every man.
But even so, I urge on my Lycian soldiers,
and I stand my ground fiercely, although I have nothing here,
not one thing the Argives could carry or drive away.
But you just stand around idly; you don't even urge
your men to dig in and fight to defend their women.
All this should be your one concern, night and day,
and you should be begging the leaders of your brave allies   440
to hold firm. Thus you will clear yourself from reproach."

These words of Sarpedon bit into Hector's heart,
and he leaped to the ground from his chariot in full armor
and, holding a pair of spears, he ranged through the army
spurring the men on, arousing their spirit for battle,
and they rallied and turned to fight against the Achaeans.
But the Argives stood firm, in dense ranks, and did not retreat.

And as the breeze blows the chaff on the threshing floors
when the farmers winnow, the golden-haired goddess Deméter
separates grain and chaff in the rush of the wind,   450
and the chaff piles up and turns white: just so did the Argives
turn white from the cloud of dust that settled upon them,
kicked up to the bronze-colored sky by the horses' hooves

as their drivers wheeled them around and they stormed back to battle.
And the warriors fought in hand-to-hand combat, and Ares,
ranging everywhere, covered the battle in darkness
as a help to the Trojans, thus carrying out the command
of Apollo, who said that as soon as he saw Athena
leaving the fight he should rouse the hearts of the Trojans,
since she was the goddess who helped the Achaeans most.   460
And Apollo himself, on Pérgamus, brought Aeneas
out of his temple and poured strength into his breast;
and Aeneas returned to his comrades, and they rejoiced
to see him alive, unhurt, and glowing with vigor.
But they did not ask what had happened; they were too focused
on the battle stirred up by the god of the silver bow
and man-killing Ares and Strife, the insatiable goddess.

On the other side, the two Ajaxes and Odysseus
and Diomedes were rousing the Argives to battle.
But the men needed no encouragement; they were undaunted   470
facing the Trojans' ferocious assault. They stood
as motionless as the clouds that Zeus in clear weather
sets on the mountain tops when the fierce north wind
sleeps, along with the other tumultuous winds
that scatter the clouds and drive them with their shrill blasts:
just so did the Argives stand firm at the Trojan attack.

And everywhere Agamemnon exhorted the soldiers:
"Dear friends, be men now. Put courage into your hearts
and act honorably in the sight of your comrades in battle.
When men act with honor, more are saved than are killed,   480
but when they take flight, there is neither glory nor refuge."
He hurled his long spear, and brought down Deícoön,
the son of Pérgasus, one of Aeneas's comrades,
whom the Trojans honored no less than they did Priam's sons,
a man who had always fought in the foremost ranks;
the spear hit his shield with such force that it passed right through it
and drove through his belt and into his abdomen.

And Aeneas cut down two champions of the Achaeans,

Crethon and Ortílochus, Díocles' sons,
a wealthy man who lived in the city of Pheræ;   490
his ancestor was the god of the river Alphéüs,
whose broad waters flow through the country of the Pylíans;
it fathered Ortílochus, ruler of many men,
and Ortílochus was the father of Díocles,
and Díocles, in his turn, was the father of twins,
Crethon and Ortílochus, skilled in all fighting.
And when they had grown to manhood, they both set sail
for Troy with the Argives, in their black ships, to regain
the honor of Agamemnon and Menelaus;
but in Troy death came and put an end to them both.   500
They were like a pair of young lions reared by their mother
on the mountaintops, in the thickets of a deep forest;
they ravage the homesteads and carry off sheep and cattle
until they are caught and killed by the spears of men:
such were these two, cut down at the hands of Aeneas;
and when they were hit, they fell to earth like tall pine trees.

As he saw them cut down, Menelaus was filled with pity,
and he strode through the front ranks, armored in fiery bronze,
shaking his spear; and Ares aroused his courage,
intending for him to be killed by Aeneas's spear.   510
But Antilochus, son of Nestor, happened to see him
and strode through the front ranks, fearing that the commander
would come to great harm and bring all their efforts to nothing.
So when Menelaus was standing there facing Aeneas,
both aiming their spears, both eager to start the fight,
Antilochus came up and stood beside Menelaus.
When Aeneas saw the two of them facing him, side
by side, he gave ground, bold warrior though he was.
And when they had dragged the dead bodies back to the army,
they put the unlucky twins in the hands of their comrades,   520
and then they themselves returned to the front line of battle.

And they killed Pylæmenes, the courageous leader
of the Páphlagonians, when he climbed down from his car;
Menelaus stabbed him; his spear broke his collarbone,

while his comrade killed Mydon, Pylæmenes' charioteer,
as he was turning the horses around to flee.
He hit him with an enormous rock on the elbow;
the reins, white with ivory, fell down into the dust,
and Antilochus rushed up and plunged his sword through his temple.
Gasping, he fell from the chariot, head and shoulders   530
sinking into deep sand. For some time the body
stood, feet in the air, till the horses trampled it over.
And Antilochus whipped them and drove them on back to the camp.

Hector caught sight of the two through the ranks, and he charged
with a blood-chilling shout, and the mighty Trojan battalions
followed him, led by Ares and fierce Enýo,
who always comes with the ruthless carnage of war,
while Ares, holding aloft a gigantic spear,
now strode in front of Hector and now behind him.
At the sight of the god, Diomedes stopped fighting and shuddered.   540
And as a man who is walking across a wide plain
helplessly stands at the edge of a fast-flowing river
and looks at it rushing and seething with foam, then turns back:
just so Diomedes gave ground, and he said to his men,
"Dear friends, we are right to marvel at Hector, and how
bold and deadly he is in the thick of battle.
There is always some god at his side to ward off destruction.
Keep facing the Trojans, but give way, little by little;
we mustn't move forward or try to attack the gods."

And as he was speaking, the Trojans came very close.   550
Hector slaughtered two men who were skilled in war,
both in one car, Anchíalus and Menésthes.
As he saw them cut down, Ajax was filled with pity,
and he moved in as close as he could and hurled his spear,
and he hit Amphíus, the son of Sélegus, who
had traveled from Pæsus; he owned much wheatland, but fate
had brought him to Troy to fight as an ally of Priam.
The shining spear hit his belt, and it drove deep into
his abdomen, and he fell to the ground with a crash.
Ajax ran forward to strip him of his fine armor,   560

but the Trojans rained spears upon him, which in the air
glittered and fell, and many spears hit his shield.
He braced his foot on the corpse, and he pulled out *his* spear
but, rained on by missiles, he could not strip off the armor.
And he was afraid of the fierce assault that the Trojans
would make to defend the body. Now many men came,
raising their spears; and though Ajax was tall and strong,
they drove him back and, staggering, he gave way.
And so the two armies toiled in the fury of combat.
And Tlepólemus, Héracles' son, a strong and brave man,   570
was impelled by resistless fate to attack Sarpedon.
When the two of them had advanced to within close range—
one man the son of Zeus, the other his grandson—
Tlepólemus was the first one to speak: "Sarpedon,
what are you doing here, slinking and skulking around
among warriors—a man with no knowledge of fighting?
They lie when they say that you are a son of Zeus,
since you are by far inferior to the men
who were born to the god in earlier generations.
How different you are from the way men describe my father,   580
Héracles, fearless in war, with the heart of a lion,
who once came here to claim Laómedon's horses,
and with only six ships and quite a small force of men
he laid waste to Troy and desolated its streets.
But yours is a coward's heart, and your men are dying,
and I do not think that your coming from far-off Lycia
will help the Trojans. However mighty you are,
you will fall to me now and pass through the gates of Death."

Sarpedon answered, "Tlepólemus, it is true
that your father destroyed sacred Ilion—but it was only   590
through Laómedon's folly, that proud, irresponsible man,
who rewarded your father's good service with insults, refusing
to give him what he had come for, from so far away.
But I promise that you won't profit from what *I* give you;
you will soon be cut down by my spear and will grant me the triumph
and will have to give up your soul to Death, the pale horseman."
As Sarpedon finished, Tlepólemus raised his arm,

and both spears flew from their hands at the very same moment.
Sarpedon's spear hit his throat, and the point passed through,
and black night covered his eyes. But *his* spear went deep   600
into Sarpedon's left thigh, and the spear point drove
eagerly through the flesh, and it grazed the bone;
but his father, Zeus, for the moment kept off destruction.

As his comrades carried Sarpedon out of the battle,
the spear dragged and weighed him down, but in their great haste
none of them noticed or thought of pulling the spear point
out of his thigh, to let him stand: so intently
were they concentrated on getting him safely out.
On the other side, the Achaeans carried away
Tlepólemus. And Odysseus raged when he saw it;   610
he pondered whether to go in pursuit of Sarpedon
or to slaughter more Lycians. But since it was not ordained
for him to cut down the son of Lord Zeus, Athena
directed his anger out toward the Lycian captains.
And he cut down Cœranus, Chrómius, and Alástor,
Alcánder, Prýtanis, Hálius, and Noémon;
and he would have slaughtered even more Lycians if Hector
had not been quick to notice. He strode through the front ranks,
armored in fiery bronze and bringing great terror
to the Danäans; and Sarpedon rejoiced at his coming   620
and begged him to stop there: "Son of Priam, protect me.
Don't leave me to fall into Argive hands now; permit me
to die in your city, since it turns out that I was not
destined to see my beloved country again
or gladden the hearts of my dear wife and baby son."

Hector did not respond but hurried on past him.
His heart was on fire to push back the Argive troops
and slaughter them—as many of them as he could.
And Sarpedon's faithful companions set him down gently
under a beautiful oak tree sacred to Zeus,   630
and one comrade, Pélagon, pulled the spear from his thigh;
and his spirit left him, and dark mist covered his eyes.
But soon he came to; the breath of the north wind revived him

after he had gasped out his spirit in pain.

Meanwhile the Argives, though pressed by Ares and Hector,
did not panic and flee toward the ships or counterattack,
but little by little, step by step, they gave ground
when they learned that Ares was in the front lines of the Trojans.

Who was the first and who the last to be slaughtered
by Hector, the son of Priam, and brazen Ares?   640
Teuthras was first, then Oréstes, the famous horseman,
Trechus, who came from Ætólia, Œnomáüs,
Hélenus, son of Œnops, Orésbius,
who lived in Hylē on the wide shores of Cephísus,
where he spent his time farming his vast estate, and around him
lived other Bœótians with land in that fertile country.

When Hera realized that in the fury of battle
the Argives were being slaughtered, she said to Athena,
"Shame on us, daughter of Zeus! If Ares keeps raging
unimpeded, what will become of the promise   650
we made to Lord Menelaus when we assured him
that he wouldn't return until he had plundered Troy?
Let us go arm now and call up our fighting spirit."
At these words, Athena nodded her head in agreement.
Then Hera yoked the celestial, gold-bridled horses,
and Hēbē fitted the bronze wheels, each with eight spokes,
to the chariot frame at both ends of the iron axle.
These wheels have rims of imperishable gold,
with tires of bronze, a marvel of craftsmanship,
and the hubs that revolve on either side are of silver;   660
and the body itself is made of a network of straps
of gold and silver stretched tight, with two rails around it.
From it extends a long silver pole; at its tip
she bound the beautiful golden yoke and attached
golden breast-straps; and Hera brought the swift horses
under the yoke and was eager to enter the battle.

Athena then took off the richly embroidered robe

that her own hands had made, and she put on Lord Zeus's armor.
Around her shoulders she threw the terrible gold-tasseled
storm shield, crowned with the figures of Strife and Panic   670
and inset with all the heart-chilling horrors of war
and the monstrous head of the Gorgon, which strikes terror
in all who see it, a dreadful portent from Zeus.
And upon her head she put the great golden helmet
adorned with two ridges and four golden plates and engraved
with the forms of foot soldiers drawn from a hundred cities;
and she mounted her fiery chariot, and she grasped
the huge, heavy spear that she uses to overpower
ranks of brave soldiers when she is stirred up to fury.

Hera then touched the whip to the backs of the horses,   680
and of their own will, the gates of Olympus groaned open;
they are kept by the Seasons, who are in charge of the sky,
to roll the thick cloudbanks away or to roll them back.
Through these the goddesses urged on their speeding horses.
They found Zeus sitting apart from the other gods,
gazing down from the topmost peak of Olympus.
And Hera said to the father of men and gods,
"Dread Lord, how can you not be angry at Ares
for killing so many noble Achaean soldiers—
a brutal, indecent slaughter; it breaks my heart—   690
while Apollo and Aphrodite look down at the fighting,
happy that they have let this maniac loose?
Will you be angry at me if I go and wound Ares
badly enough to force him out of the fighting?"

Then Zeus said, "Go ahead; send Athena against him;
she, more than anyone, knows how to cause him pain."
At these words, Hera went off to fulfill his command;
she touched her whip to the backs of the horses, and gladly
they flew midway between earth and the starry heavens.
As far as a man sees into the hazy distance   700
from a mountaintop, looking out onto the wine-dark sea:
that far the gods' proud horses can leap at one bound.
And when they arrived at Troy and its two great rivers,

Hera reined in the horses, unfastened their yoke,
set them free, and poured thick mist all around them,
and a field of ambrosia sprang up for them to graze on.

Then the two goddesses walked out, stepping like doves,
eager to come to the aid of the Danäan army.
And when they reached the place where the best of the troops
crowded around Diomedes like ravenous lions,   710
Hera yelled out, in the likeness of Stentor, whose brazen
shout was as loud as the voice of fifty strong men:
"Shame on you, Argives—disgraces, pretty-boys, frauds!
At the time when Achilles was fighting, the Trojans wouldn't
have dared to go even beyond the Dardánian Gates,
so much did they dread that man and his deadly spear.
Yet now they are fighting their way right up to our ships."
With these words she stirred up the courage of every man.

At once Athena rushed off toward Diomedes,
and she found him beside his horses and chariot, airing   720
the painful wound that the arrow of Pándarus
had caused. Beneath the broad strap of his shield, the sweat
was making the wound very sore, and his right arm ached
from lifting the strap and wiping away the blood.
The goddess took hold of the horses' yoke, and she said,
"Tydeus fathered a son unworthy of him.
He was a small man, but what an amazing fighter!
Even when I forbade him to fight or to be
conspicuous when he went as an envoy to Thebes,
a single Achaean among the people of Cadmus—   730
I had told him not to speak out at the palace banquet—
he, with the daring spirit he always had, challenged
the Thebans to feats of strength, and he won every contest.
And now I am standing at your side too, to protect you,
and I urge you to fight the Trojans without holding back.
Yet either these long assaults have exhausted your body
or cowardly fear has seized you and stunned your spirit.
So how can it be that you are your father's son?"

*

Then Diomedes nodded to her and said,
"I recognize you, great goddess, daughter of Zeus,   740
so I will speak plainly and not hide anything from you.
No exhaustion has taken me over, no cowardly fear;
I have only followed the orders that you yourself gave me.
You commanded me not to fight with the blessed gods;
that is why I have given ground and have ordered
the rest of the Argives to move here and mass around me,
since I see that Ares is dominating the field."

Athena answered him, "Joy of my heart, Diomedes,
son of Tydeus, do not fear Ares or any
other immortal, since I have come here to help you.   750
Get up, drive straight at Ares, close in and hit him.
Don't be awed by this raging madman, a monster
of violence, a brazen and two-faced liar
who a while ago made a promise to me and Hera
that he would stand by the Argives and fight the Trojans,
yet now he is fighting on *their* side, forgetting his pledge."

She picked up Sthénelus, tossed him over the rail,
and he leaped clear and was suddenly on the ground.
And she mounted the car and stood beside Diomedes,
eager to fight; and the oaken axle creaked loudly   760
under the weight of the man and the dreadful goddess.
Athena seized the whip and the reins, and she drove
straight at the god, who was busy stripping the armor
from Périphas, the son of Ochésius,
a huge man who was the bravest Ætólian fighter.
And while he was stripping it, splattered with blood, Athena
put on the cap of Hades, which makes its wearer
invisible. But when Ares saw Diomedes,
he left the huge man lying where he had killed him
and hurried toward Diomedes, tamer of horses.   770

When the two of them had advanced to within close range,
Ares lunged over the yoke and reins in his fury
to kill Diomedes. Athena, though, caught the spear

and pushed it aside, and it flew past the chariot, harmless.
Then Diomedes thrust with his spear, and Athena
guided it, and it plunged into Ares' belly
at the place where his bronze kilt was fastened, and after it tore
into his flesh, she pulled the spear out again.
And Ares bellowed; his roar was as loud as the shout
of ten thousand men as they join in the tumult of battle.   780
Achaeans and Trojans were seized with trembling, such terror
did the roar of Ares strike into each man's heart.
And as a spout of black air appears from the clouds
when the weather is hot and a violent wind arises:
just so did the war god whirl up before the eyes
of Diomedes and vanish into the heavens.

Quickly Ares arrived on the heights of Olympus,
and he sat down by Zeus, anguished and in great pain,
and pointed to the immortal blood that was flowing
from his deep wound, and in tears for himself, he said,   790
"How can you not be angry, Father, at seeing
such savagery? We gods have had to endure
terrible pain whenever we favor men.
And we hold it against you that you are so damned indulgent
with your crazy daughter, who always commits some outrage.
All the other immortal gods on Olympus
are subject to you, and all of us bow to your will;
but *she* does whatever she wants, and you don't scold her
or punish her, ever; you even encourage her,
because you yourself gave birth to this violent girl.   800
Now she has stirred up that reckless man Diomedes
to lash out wildly against the blessed immortals.
First he stabbed Aphrodite and wounded her wrist,
and now he has dared to charge at me in a frenzy.
If I had been slow on my feet, I would still be lying
in torment, among the ghastly piles of the dead."

Lord Zeus answered him then, with an angry scowl,
"How dare you sit whining to me, you two-faced liar!
No god here is as hateful to me as *you* are,

Liar.

because you are steeped in strife and contention and fighting.   810
You have the same headstrong, ungovernable spirit
that possesses your mother, Hera; however I try,
I can barely control her. It is her scheming that got you
into this trouble. Still, I cannot permit
such dreadful pain to continue, since you are my child.
But if any other immortal had given birth
to a killer like you, you would long ago have been buried
far below Hades, deeper than any Titan."
Then Zeus commanded Pæéon to heal his wound,
and the god of healing spread pain-killing herbs upon it.   820
As wild-fig sap is added to milk, and it thickens,
and quickly the liquid curdles as it is stirred:
just so, right away, the deep wound of Ares was healed.
Hēbē washed him and clothed him in lovely garments,
and he sat down by Lord Zeus, glorying in his splendor.

And Athena and Hera went back to Zeus's halls,
having put a stop to Ares' murderous rampage.

Book 6

And so the terrible fighting was left to itself.
And the battle across the plain veered this way and that,
many times, as they hurled their spears at each other
in the wide space between the Xanthus and Símoïs rivers.

Ajax, Télamon's son, the Achaeans' bulwark,
shattered the Trojan front line, bringing his comrades
breathing space and killing the bravest Thracian,
the tall and powerful Ácamas, son of Eussórus.
The bright spear flew, and it hit the ridge of his helmet
by the horsehair crest, and the point drove into his forehead,   10
straight through the bone, and darkness covered his eyes.

Then Diomedes cut down the son of Teuthras,
Axýlus, who came from the strong-walled town of Arísbē,
a wealthy and generous man—he lived by the main road
and would open his house to any stranger who passed.
But none of his friends came to fight for him on this day
or ward off a wretched death. Diomedes slaughtered
both him and his faithful attendant, Calésius,
his charioteer, and both sank under the earth.

Then Eurýalus cut down Ophéltius and Dresus,   20
and he went in pursuit of Pédasus and Æsépus,
whom Abárbaréa, a nymph of the river, had borne
to Bucólion, Laómedon's eldest son,
though illegitimate; he had made love with the naiad
while tending his flocks, and she gave birth to twin sons.
Eurýalus snuffed out the strength of the shining bodies
of both young men and proceeded to strip off their armor.

Next, Polypœtes rushed in to put an end
to Astýalus, and Odysseus brought down Pidýtes,
a man from Percótē, and Teucer killed Aretáon,   30

and Ablérus fell to the spear of Antilochus,
and Élatus to that king of men, Agamemnon
(he lived in steep Pédasus, by the Satníoïs river).
And Léïtus cut down Phýlacus as he turned
to flee, and Eurýpylus laid Melánthius low.

But Lord Menelaus took Adréstus alive.
His horses had bolted across the wide plain and charged
into the shoots of a tamarisk bush and shattered
the chariot at the pole's end, then ran by themselves
toward Troy, where the other horses were fleeing in panic,   40
and he was flung headlong, over the wheel, and lay
face down in the dirt. And Menelaus strode forward
and stood above him, holding his long-shadowed spear.
Adréstus got up and clasped his knees and implored him:
"Son of Atreus, take me alive. I promise
a worthy ransom. My father is rich; there are treasures,
many of them, that lie there stored in his house,
bronze and gold and iron skillfully worked.
From these my father will give you a huge ransom
if he learns that I am alive by the Danäan ships."   50

Menelaus's heart was touched, and he was about
to have his attendant take him back to the camp
when Agamemnon came running over, indignant:
"Menelaus, you simpleton, how can you show such tender
concern for a Trojan life? Did the Trojans treat you
so generously when they were your honored guests
at your own palace? No, we must leave not a single
Trojan alive, not even the baby boy
that his mother still holds in her womb—not even one
must slip from our hands now. All the males must be slaughtered,   60
every last male in Troy, unmourned, unburied."

With this he persuaded his brother, pointing his mind
to what was proper and fated; and Menelaus
pushed Adréstus away, and Lord Agamemnon
lifted his spear and stabbed him below the ribs,

and he fell back, face upward, and Agamemnon walked over,
braced his foot on his chest, and pulled out the spear.

Then Nestor, with a great shout, addressed the Achaeans:
"My dear friends, Danäan soldiers, companions in battle,
no looting, no hanging back in the hope of returning   70
to the ships with your arms full of bronze. Now is the time
for killing Trojans. Afterward, at your leisure,
you can scour the plain and strip the dead bodies naked."
With these words he stirred up the courage of every man.

And then the Trojans would soon have been driven back
inside the walls of Ilion, overcome
by their own weakness, if Hélenus, son of Priam,
the wisest of those who scan the flight patterns of birds,
had not approached Aeneas and Hector and said,
"Dear comrades, on you two lies the grave burden of war,   80
more than on any other Trojan or Lycian,
for in every action you are the best of them all.
So make a stand here; go everywhere through the army
and rally the men in front of the gates, before
they run home and throw themselves into the arms of their women
and bring joy to our enemies. When you have roused their spirits,
we will stand our ground here and fight against the Achaeans,
worn out as we are; for necessity bears down upon us.
And Hector, you go to the city, speak to our mother,
tell her to gather the elders among the women   90
and to go to the city heights, to Athena's temple,
unlock the doors of the holy shrine, and inside it
place a fine robe on the goddess's knees, choosing
the largest and loveliest robe in her house, the one
that she herself has taken the most delight in,
and vow to offer twelve heifers outside the temple,
yearlings untouched by the goad, so that Athena
may pity Troy and our wives and our little children,
and hold Diomedes back from our sacred walls.
He fights like a maniac, filling men's hearts with terror,   100
and is now, I think, the most powerful of the Achaeans.

Not even Achilles ever aroused such panic,
who they say was born of a goddess; but this man rages
beyond all measure, and no one can match his fury."

Hector proceeded to do what his brother had asked for.
He leaped to the ground from his chariot in full armor,
and, holding a pair of spears, he ranged through the army,
spurring the men on, arousing their spirit for battle.
And they rallied and turned to stand against the Achaeans,
who stopped their murderous onslaught now and gave ground;   110
they thought that some god had come from the starry heavens
to help the Trojans, so fast had their spirits been rallied.

Then Hector, in a loud voice, addressed the army:
"You great-hearted Trojans, and you, our heroic allies,
be vigorous fighters. Defend the city from outrage
while I go to Troy and tell our elders and wives
to pray to the gods and promise them sacrifices."
And Hector went off toward Troy, and the dark rim of oxhide
that ran all around the edge of his shield kept tapping
against his ankles and neck as he strode along.   120

Then Glaucus and Diomedes entered the space
between the two armies. Both men were eager to fight;
and when their chariots had driven within close range,
Diomedes was first to speak, and he said in a loud voice:
"Who among mortal men are you, my good friend?
I have never seen you in battle until today,
but now you have far surpassed all other Trojans
in courage, since you have stood up to me and my spear.
Unhappy are those whose sons have stepped out to face me.
But if you are one of the gods and have come down from heaven,   130
I will not fight you. Even the son of Dryas,
mighty Lycúrgus, didn't flourish for long
after the time when he clashed with the heavenly gods.
He once chased the nymphs who were nursemaids of Dionýsus
down from Mount Nysa; they all dropped their sacred branches
as that murderous man kept beating them with his ox goad;

and Dionýsus, the child-god, terrified, plunged
under the waves of the sea, and Thetis embraced him
and comforted him on her breast, he was so frightened;
trembling had seized him at the man's menacing shouts.   140
The gods who live at their ease were incensed at Lycúrgus,
and Zeus struck him blind; and he didn't live long after that,
since he had incurred the hatred of all the immortals.
So I wouldn't presume to fight with the blessed gods.
But if you are a mortal and eat what the earth produces,
come closer now, the sooner to meet your death."

Then Glaucus spoke out in answer to Diomedes,
"Son of Tydeus, why do you ask who I am?
Men come and go, just like the leaves in their seasons.
The wind scatters one year's leaves on the ground, but the forest   150
bursts with new buds as soon as springtime arrives,
and it is the same with men: one generation
comes to life while another one passes away.
But if you insist on my lineage—many men know it—
listen now. There is a city, Éphyra, set
in a corner of Argos. The son of Æolus lived there,
Sísyphus, the most cunning of all mankind,
and he fathered a son named Glaucus, and Glaucus fathered
Bellérophon, whom the blessed gods graced with beauty
and all that is lovely in manhood. But Prœtus, the king,   160
bore him ill will and plotted against him and drove him
from the land of the Argives; he was by far the stronger,
since Zeus had subjected all Argos beneath his rule.
The wife of King Prœtus, Antéa, fell madly in love
with Bellérophon, and she longed to lure him to bed;
but he was a virtuous man, and she couldn't seduce him.
So she went to her husband, the king, with this noxious lie:
'Bellérophon tried to rape me, Prœtus. Beware.
If you do not kill him, you will be killed yourself.'
When he heard these words, the king was shaken by fury,   170
yet he shrank from killing him outright; he could not do that,
so he sent him away to Lycia, and with him he sent
fatal tokens, a folded tablet inscribed

with many murderous symbols, and told him to show these
to Antéa's father, the king, to ensure his own death.
So he went to Lycia—the gods brought him safely there—
and when he arrived and came to the river Xanthus,
the king received him and treated him with all honor;
he entertained him for nine days with lavish feasts,
and each day he slaughtered an ox. And on the tenth day,   180
as soon as the flush of dawn appeared in the heavens,
he questioned him, and he asked to be shown the message
that Prœtus, his son-in-law, must have told him to bring.
And when he had understood Prœtus's evil token,
he commanded him first to kill the raging Chimæra,
born of the gods, inhuman, a monster who had
the head of a lion, a serpent's tail, and the body
of a goat, and whose every breath was a blaze of fire;
but Bellérophon killed her, obeying signs from the gods.
Next, he attacked the Sólymi, and this battle   190
was the hardest he ever fought, he said. And thirdly,
he slaughtered the Amazons, women as fierce as men.
And as he returned, the king planned one final trap.
He picked out the strongest men from all over Lycia
and set them in ambush. But none of these men came back;
Bellérophon cut them all down, every last one.
And when the king realized that he must be a god's offspring,
he kept him there and gave him the hand of his daughter,
and much wealth besides, and half of his royal honors;
and the Lycians marked out their best land and gave it to him,   200
a beautiful tract of vineyards and fertile fields.
And in time his wife, the king's daughter, bore him three children:
Isánder, Hippólochus, and Laodamía,
who slept with Zeus and bore him godlike Sarpedon.
But Bellérophon came to be hated by all the gods,
and he wandered alone across the plain of Aléa,
gnawing his heart and avoiding the paths of men;
and his son Isánder was killed by Ares while fighting
the Sólymi, and Ártemis killed his daughter.
But Hippólochus, I am proud to say, was my father.   210
And when he sent me to Troy, he gave me instructions

always to be the bravest, above all others,
and not to bring shame on my fathers, who were by far
the bravest men in Éphyra and in all Lycia.
That is the lineage I am proud to descend from."

When he heard this, Diomedes was overjoyed.
He stuck his spear in the ground, and he said to Glaucus,
"Amazing! You are a guest-friend of mine, from far back
in our grandfathers' time, since my own grandfather, Œneus,
once entertained yours, Bellérophon, in his palace   220
and kept him for twenty days, and they also exchanged
magnificent gifts of friendship. Œneus's gift
was a sword-belt brilliant with scarlet, Bellérophon's
a two-handled golden cup; I left it at home
when I set out for Troy. (I cannot remember my father,
Tydeus; he left us when I was a little child,
that time the Achaean army was slaughtered at Thebes.)
So now I will be your dear host in the center of Argos,
and you will be mine in Lycia, whenever I visit.
We must keep away from each other's spears in the fighting.   230
There are many Trojans and allies for me to cut down—
whomever a god may send and my feet overtake—
and *you* will find many Achaeans to kill, if you can.
Now let us exchange our armor, so all can see
that our grandfathers' friendship has made guest-friends of us also."

After he finished, both jumped down from their cars
and clasped hands and made a solemn promise of friendship.
Then Zeus took Glaucus's wits away: he exchanged
armor with Diomedes, golden for bronze,
a hundred oxen's worth for the worth of nine oxen.   240

When Hector came to the Scaean Gates and the tower,
the Trojan daughters and wives came running to meet him,
asking about their sons and brothers and friends
and husbands. Hector was silent, then told each to offer
prayers to the gods (though for many it was too late).

*

Then he arrived at the glorious palace of Priam.
It was fashioned with stone colonnades, and in it were fifty
high-ceilinged bedrooms of polished marble, built close
to one another. In them the sons of Priam
slept, along with their wives; and opposite these,   250
for his daughters, across, on the other side of the courtyard,
there were twelve more high-ceilinged bedrooms of polished marble,
built close to one another, and in these rooms
the sons-in-law slept, along with their wives. His mother
came to meet him as she was escorting home
Laódicē, the most beautiful of her daughters.
And she said to Hector, taking his hand in hers,
"Why have you left the fighting and come here, my child?
Because the cursed Achaeans are wearing you down
as they press on toward Troy? Your heart has moved you to come   260
and lift up your hands to Zeus from the city's heights.
But wait here, and I will bring you some heart-cheering wine.
You can pour a libation to Zeus and the other immortals,
and then you yourself can drink, and you will feel better.
Wine renews a man's strength when he is exhausted,
and you have tired yourself out defending your people."

Then Hector said, "Please don't offer me wine, dear Mother;
it may rob me of strength and weaken my will to fight.
And I dare not pour a libation to the immortals
with unwashed hands, nor may anyone offer prayers   270
to Lord Zeus when he is filthy with blood and gore.
But go now. Gather the elders among the women,
and with your offerings go to Athena's temple.
Place a fine robe on the goddess's knees, choosing
the largest and loveliest robe in your house, the one
that you yourself have taken the most delight in,
and vow to offer twelve heifers outside the temple,
yearlings untouched by the goad, so that Athena
may pity Troy and our wives and our little children
and hold Diomedes back from our sacred walls.   280
He fights like a maniac, filling men's hearts with terror.
So go to the goddess's temple, and I myself

will look for Paris and summon him back to the fighting,
and I hope he will listen to me. If only the earth
would gape open and swallow him up! The Olympian raised him
to be a great curse and cause of unending grief
to the Trojans and to King Priam and all his sons.
If I could see him gone to realm of Hades,
my heart would be eased, and I would forget my sorrow."

He left, and his mother the queen walked into the palace   290
and instructed her handmaids; and they went out through the city
to find and gather the elders among the women.
She herself went down into the fragrant storeroom
where her robes were kept, brilliant and richly embroidered,
the work of Sidónian women, whom Paris himself
had abducted from Sidon after his ships had stopped there
on the voyage when he had carried Helen to Troy.
Hecuba picked up one of these robes and took it
as a gift for Athena, the robe that in its design
was the loveliest and the largest; it lay beneath   300
all the others and shone like a star. And she left,
and a great crowd of women elders hurried behind her.

When they came to Athena's shrine on the city heights,
Theáno opened the doors for them; she was the daughter
of Cisses and wife of Anténor, and had been appointed
Athena's priestess. With ritual trilling and arms
held high, they prayed to the goddess, and then Theáno
placed the magnificent robe on the knees of the statue
and said this prayer to the daughter of mighty Zeus:
"Lady Athena, bright goddess who guards our city,   310
break Diomedes' spear and let him be hurled
face down in the dirt in front of the Scaean Gates.
And we will be glad to sacrifice outside your temple
twelve fine heifers, all yearlings untouched by the goad,
if you pity Troy, and the Trojans' wives and their children."
When she heard this, Athena shook her head in refusal.

And while the women said their prayers to the goddess,

Hector went to his brother's beautiful palace,
which Paris himself had built with the finest craftsmen
in all of Troy; they had made him a bedroom, a great hall,   320
and a spacious courtyard, close to the palaces
where Priam and Hector lived on the city's heights.
Hector strode into the palace, holding a spear
sixteen feet long; in front of him glittered its bronze point,
fixed to the spear's oak shaft by a ring of gold.
He found Paris there in the bedroom, cleaning his gorgeous
armor, his shield and his breastplate, and handling his bow,
and Helen of Argos was sitting among her women,
directing their handiwork and their famous weaving.
And Hector rebuked his brother with shaming words: 330
"Why are you acting like this? You are wrong to sulk
and steep your heart in such anger. Our people are dying
as they fight the Achaeans close to the city wall,
and it is your fault that this miserable war
has flared up around sacred Ilion. You yourself
would tear into anyone else who hung back from the fighting.
So come out, or soon the whole city will go up in flames."

Paris answered him, "You are right to rebuke me,
Hector, and it is not more than what I deserve.
But not because I am angry now at the Trojans   340
have I been sitting like this in my room, but because
I wanted to yield to my grief at losing the combat.
Just now my wife was gently urging me back
to the fighting, and I too think that this would be better;
victory shifts, after all, from one man to the next.
But wait here a little, and I will put on my armor . . .
or else you go first—I think that I can catch up."

Hector said nothing. Then Helen spoke with her soft voice:
"Brother-in-law of mine—of the bitch that I am,
a cause of evil, a curse and abomination—   350
it would have been better that when my mother first bore me
some evil storm wind had suddenly whirled me off
to the mountains or into the swell of the loud-roaring sea

where the waves would have swept me away before all this happened.
But since these evils are as the gods have ordained them,
I wish I had been the wife of a better man,
who could feel a proper sense of the people's outrage.
This one will never be sensible. He is a fool,
and he always *will* be, though he will pay for it someday,
if I am right. But come in, dear brother-in-law,   360
sit down on this chair and rest yourself for a while,
since the burden falls upon you more than the others,
through my fault, bitch that I am, and through Paris's folly.
Zeus has brought us an evil fate, so that poets
can make songs about us for all future generations."

Then Hector said, "Please don't ask me to sit down, Helen;
I know your intention is kind, but you won't persuade me.
Already I feel impatient to help our men,
who miss me greatly when I am not fighting beside them.
But see that this fellow leaves the house soon and hurries   370
to catch up with me while I am inside the walls.
I am going home now; I want to pay a short visit
to my family, to my dear wife and my baby son.
I do not know if I will be able to see them
ever again, or if soon the gods will destroy me."

With these words he left, and quickly he reached his own palace.
But he did not find Andromache there; she had gone
with her child and one of her handmaids up to the tower,
and she stood looking down at the battlefield, weeping and mourning.
When Hector found that his wife was not there, he stopped   380
at the door to the women's quarters and said to the maids,
"Tell me exactly where Andromache went
when she left the house. Did she go to one of my sisters
or one of my brothers' wives or Athena's temple,
where the women seek to propitiate the dread goddess?"

And his chief housekeeper came to the threshold and answered,
"Sir, you asked us to tell you the truth. I know
that she hasn't gone to visit one of your sisters

or one of your brothers' wives, or Athena's temple.
She went to the tower as soon as she heard the news   390
that our army was overwhelmed. She was in a total
frenzy and rushed off—it seemed as if she was out of
her mind—and the nurse went with her, holding the baby."

At these words, Hector ran from the house, back along
the route he had taken, through the broad streets of Troy.
He had crossed the city and come to the Scaean Gates,
where soon he would make his way out onto the plain,
when breathlessly his wife came running to meet him,
Andromache, King Ëétion's noble daughter
(he had ruled the Cilícians in Thebē under the wooded   400
slopes of Mount Placus). Now she ran up to meet him,
and behind her a handmaid came who was holding the child
in her arms, an infant, cooing and gurgling, Hector's
beloved son, as beautiful as a star.
Though Hector had named him Scamándrius, everyone called him
Astýanax, "Lord of the City," because his father
seemed to them all the one defender of Troy.
Hector smiled as he looked at the boy in silence.
Andromache came even closer and stood beside him
weeping and said to him, taking his hand in hers,   410
"My dearest, this reckless courage of yours will destroy you.
Have pity now on your little boy and on me,
your unfortunate wife, who before long will be your widow.
Soon the Achaeans will kill you, and when you are gone,
it will be far better for me to die and sink down
under the earth, since once you have met your fate
I will have no comfort—only unending sorrow.
I have no one else. My father and mother are dead.
Achilles cut down my father when he took Thebē,
though he didn't strip off his armor—respect touched his heart   420
and he couldn't do that—he burned his body with all
his beautiful war gear and heaped a mound over his ashes,
and the nymphs of the mountain planted elm trees around it.
I had seven brothers, who lived in my father's palace,
and all of them, on the very same day, went down

to the realm of Hades; Achilles slaughtered them all
while they were tending their sheep and their lumbering oxen.
As for my mother, the queen of our proud city,
he carried her here along with the rest of his spoils,
then set her free, in exchange for a huge ransom;   430
but Ártemis shot her down in her father's halls.
Hector, you are my everything now: my father,
my mother, my brother—and my beloved husband.
Have pity on me. Stay with me here on the tower.
Don't make your child an orphan, your wife a widow."

Hector answered her, "Dearest, what you have said
troubles me too. Yet I would feel terrible shame
at facing the men and the long-robed women of Troy
if, like a coward, I shrank from the fighting. Nor *can* I:
my heart would never allow that; it is my place   440
to be brave and scorn danger and always fight in the front line,
winning great fame for my father and for myself.
But however it is, deep in my heart I know
that a day will come when the sacred city of Troy
will be devastated, and Priam, and Priam's people.
And yet it is not their anguish that troubles me so,
nor Hecuba's, nor even my father, King Priam's,
nor the blood of the many brave brothers of mine who will fall
in the dirt at the hands of their enemies—that is nothing
compared to your grief, when I picture you being caught   450
by some bronze-armored Achaean who claims you and takes
your freedom away and carries you off in tears.
Then, all your life, in the Argives' land, you will work
long days, bent over the loom of some stern mistress
or carrying water up from her well—hating it
but having no choice, for harsh fate will press down upon you.
And someone will say, as he sees you toiling and weeping,
'That is the wife of Hector, bravest of all
the Trojans, tamers of horses, when the great war
raged around Troy.' And then a fresh grief will flood   460
your heart, and you will start sobbing again at the thought
of the only man who was able to ward off your bondage.

But may I be dead, with the cold earth piled up upon me,
before I can hear you wail as they drag you away."

Then Hector reached out to take his son, but the child
shrank back, screaming, into his nurse's arms,
scared by the flashing bronze and the terrible horsehair
crest that kept shaking at him from the peak of the helmet.
At this, his father and mother both burst out laughing;
and right away Hector took off his helmet and laid it,   470
glittering, on the ground. And he picked up the child,
dandled him in his arms and stroked him and kissed him
and said this prayer to Zeus and the other immortals:
"Zeus and you other gods who can hear my prayer,
grant that this child, this boy of mine, may grow up
to be as I am, outstanding among the Trojans,
strong and brave, and rule over Troy with great power.
And let people say of him, 'He is a better man
than his father was,' as they see him returning from battle,
having killed his enemy, carrying back in triumph   480
the gore-stained armor to gladden his mother's heart."

He handed the child to his wife then, and she took him
to her fragrant breast and smiled with tears in her eyes.
And looking at her, her husband was touched with pity,
and he stroked her face, and he said, "My foolish darling,
please do not take these things so greatly to heart.
No man shall send me to Hades before my time,
and no man, I promise, has ever escaped his fate
from the moment that he was born, whether brave man or coward.
Go now, return to our house and your daily work   490
at loom and spindle; command your women as well
to go about *their* work. The men must take care of the fighting—
all men of Troy, but I more than any other."

As he said this, Hector picked up his gleaming helmet
with its horsehair crest. Andromache walked home, slowly,
and she stopped many times, turning around to look back
and bitterly weeping. And when she came to the palace

of man-killing Hector, she found all her handmaids inside,
and they burst into lamentation. So, in his own house,
they mourned for Hector even though he was alive,   500
for they thought that he would never return from the fighting
or escape from the deadly hands of the Achaeans.

Paris did not remain in his palace for long.
Once he had put on his beautiful inlaid armor
he rushed through the city, confident of his swift legs.
Just as a stabled horse who has fully eaten
breaks his tether and gallops across the plain,
eager to have a swim in the fast-flowing river,
and exults as he runs—he holds his head high, and his mane
streams in the wind, and he runs on, aware of his own   510
magnificence, to the fields where the mares are at pasture:
so Paris ran down from the height of Pérgamus, shining
in his armor like sunlight, exulting, laughing out loud,
and his swift legs carried him onward. And right away
he caught up with Hector, as he was leaving the spot
where he just had been speaking so tenderly with his wife.

Paris said, "Here I am, Brother; I must have delayed you
by taking so long and not coming as fast as you wished."

And Hector answered, "What kind of warrior are you?
No man of any sense could ever belittle   520
your exploits in war, since you are such a brave fighter;
but then you slack off and willfully hang back from battle
and my heart is grieved when I hear the contemptuous words
of our men, who endure such hardship because of you.
But come. Later on, we will make these things right, if someday
Zeus grants that we celebrate, drinking wine in our halls
in thanks to the gods for our freedom—if we should ever
manage to drive the Achaeans away from Troy."

Book 7

After he said this, Hector rushed out through the gates,
and with him went Paris; both men could hardly wait now
to return to the battle and enter the front lines of fighting.
And like a fair breeze that a god sends to longing sailors
when they are worn out from striking the sea with their oars
of polished fir and their arms are weak with exhaustion:
so welcome did these two seem to the longing Trojans.

Then Paris slaughtered Menésthius, from Arnē,
the son of King Areíthoüs, Lord of the Mace,
and lovely Phýlomedúsa. And Hector cut down   10
Ëíoneus with his spear; it went through his neck,
beneath his helmet's bronze rim, and he crumpled to earth.
And the Lycian commander Glaucus's bright spear hit
Iphínoüs, son of Déxius, on the shoulder
as he was mounting his chariot behind his mares,
and he fell off the edge, and his body crumpled to earth.

And when Athena began to notice how many
Argives were being killed in the fury of battle,
down from Olympus she swooped, to the walls of Troy.
And Apollo strode down from Pérgamus in the city   20
to stop her; he wanted a victory for the Trojans.
And so the two of them met in front of the oak tree.
Apollo spoke first: "Daughter of mighty Zeus,
why have you come this time from the heights of Olympus,
flying so eagerly? What is your mission now?
Do you want to change the course of this battle and give
victory to the Danäans, having no pity
for the Trojan troops who are dying? But take a moment
and listen to my suggestion. This would be better:
for us to arrange a halt in the battle for one day.   30
Afterward they can resume their fighting, until
Troy is consumed, since it is the heart's desire

of you and Hera to utterly tear down this city."

Athena answered, "So be it. That was my thought
when I came down here from Olympus. But what should we do?
How do you think we should put a stop to the fighting?"

Then Lord Apollo said, "Let us stir up the spirit
of Hector, tamer of horses, and have him challenge
one of the Argives to face him in single combat.
When he does, the pride of the army will be affected,   40
and they will send out some champion to fight against him."
Athena agreed with his words and did as he said.

Now Hélenus, Priam's son, had divined the plan
that the two gods had settled upon as they were meeting.
He went up to Hector and stood beside him and said,
"Son of Priam, peer of the gods in wisdom,
brother of mine, please listen to what I suggest.
Tell the Achaeans to sit down, and also the Trojans,
and challenge whoever is bravest among the Achaeans
to step forward now and face you in single combat.   50
There is no risk: it is not yet your time to die.
This is what the immortals say—I have heard it."

Hector greatly rejoiced at his brother's proposal.
He stepped out into the open and pushed back the Trojans,
grasping his spear by the middle. They all sat down,
and Agamemnon made the Achaeans sit too.
And Athena and Lord Apollo, taking the form
of vultures, sat on an oak tree sacred to Zeus,
delighting to see the warriors packed together,
dense and bristling with shields and helmets and spears.   60
And as the west wind, whenever it springs up, ripples
the face of the sea, and the water grows dark beneath it:
just so did the ranks of Achaeans and Trojans ripple
as they sat on the plain. And Hector stood forth and spoke:
"Listen to me, you Trojans and you Achaeans,
while I say the things that the heart within me compels.

Zeus didn't bring our solemn oaths to fulfillment
but is planning evil for both sides until the time comes
when either you conquer the mighty ramparts of Troy
or else you yourselves are slaughtered beside your black ships.   70
You are here with the bravest men of all the Achaeans,
so let some hero whose heart commands him to fight
step out in front to act as your champion against me.
Here are the rules of the contest, and may Lord Zeus
be witness to them: If the Achaean kills me,
he can strip off my armor and carry it to your camp;
but he must allow our people to take home my corpse,
so that the men and women of Troy can give me,
once I am dead, the burning that is my due.
And if I kill him—if Apollo grants me that glory—   80
I will strip off his armor and take it to sacred Troy
and hang it aloft at Apollo's shrine, in his honor;
but the corpse I will let you take back to the Argive camp,
where you can give him all his due rites and place him
under a funeral mound by the Hellespont.
And someone will say, in a generation far distant,
as he sails in his swift ship over the wine-dark sea:
'This is the funeral mound of some great man
who in ancient times was killed by glorious Hector.'
Thus he will speak, and my honor will never die."   90
No one stood up to answer him. They were all
ashamed to refuse, but afraid to take up his challenge.

Finally, Menelaus stepped forth to rebuke them,
his heart oppressed by humiliation and shame:
"You braggarts, you pitiful cowards—not men, but women—
how can you let such bitter disgrace come upon us
if not one man here stands up to fight against Hector?
May all of you rot and turn into water and dirt,
each man who sits here, gutless, in such dishonor!
Now I myself will go fight him. As to who triumphs—   100
such things are ordained on high by the deathless gods."

With this he began to put on his armor and helmet.

And soon, Menelaus, your life would have come to an end
if the leaders of the Achaeans had not leaped up
and taken hold of you. Agamemnon himself
ran over to you and grasped your right hand and said,
"Are you out of your mind, Menelaus? What possible need
could there be for this madness? Step back, distraught as you are,
and don't even think of fighting a man like Hector,
a warrior who is so much more powerful   110
than you, and whom all others dread. Even Achilles
shudders to meet this man in battle, and he
is far braver than you are. Be sensible now. Sit down,
and let the army send someone else as our champion.
Even if Hector is fearless and yearns for bloodshed,
I think that he will be glad to rest if he ever
manages to escape with his life from this combat."

With this he persuaded his brother, pointing his mind
to what was proper, and Menelaus obeyed.
Then, joyfully, his attendants took off his armor,   120
and Nestor stood up among the Achaeans and said,
"What a disgraceful day this is for us all!
How loudly the noble old warrior Peleus would groan—
the Myrmidons' wise advisor, who took such delight,
when I stayed with him once, in learning from me about
the lineage of all the Achaean commanders.
If he were to hear that these men are cowering in fear
before Hector, he would pray to the gods that his soul
might leave his body right now and descend to Hades.
By Father Zeus and Athena and Lord Apollo,   130
if only I were as young as I was at the battle
on the swift-flowing Céladon's banks, when the men of Pylos
gathered to face the ferocious Arcádians!
In that battle the great Ereuthálion stood forth
wearing the armor of King Areíthoüs,
whom his countrymen and their wives called the Lord of the Mace
since he never fought with a bow or spear but would use
an iron mace to smash through the enemy ranks.
Lycúrgus had killed him, by cunning rather than strength,

in a narrow pass where his iron mace couldn't swing;   140
before he could use it, Lycúrgus leaped forward and speared him
in the belly, and he fell backward and crashed to the ground.
And Lycúrgus stripped off his armor, a gift from Ares;
from then on he wore it himself when he went into battle.
Afterward, when he was growing old in his palace,
he gave it to Ereuthálion, his attendant,
who in this same armor challenged the best of our men.
They trembled with dread; not one man dared to come forward;
but *my* bold heart compelled me to take him on,
though I was the youngest of all. The fighting was fierce,   150
but Athena gave me the triumph. He was by far
the tallest and strongest man that I ever killed.
If only I were as powerful as I was then,
Hector would soon find someone to meet him in combat.
But what a disgrace that among the bravest Achaeans
not one of you has the courage to face this man!"

When they heard the old hero's rebuke, nine men arose.
The very first on his feet was Lord Agamemnon,
then Diomedes stood up, then Ajax and Teucer,
filled with the spirit of war, then Idómeneus   160
along with Meriones, his comrade-in-arms,
then Eurýpylus stood up, and Thoas, and then Odysseus.
Each was prepared to enter the combat with Hector.

Then Nestor said to them, "Now you must all draw lots.
Whoever is chosen will benefit not just the Argives
but himself as well and will win great fame, if he ever
escapes with his life and defeats great Hector today."

Then each of the warriors scratched his mark on a stone
and dropped it into the helmet of Agamemnon.
The soldiers lifted their hands to the gods and prayed;   170
and this is what someone would say as he looked up to heaven:
"Zeus, let the lot fall on Ajax (or Diomedes
or Agamemnon, the king of golden Mycénæ)."

                                *

This was their prayer, and Nestor then shook the helmet
and out jumped the very lot that most men had hoped for:
Ajax's. And the herald took it and showed it,
moving from left to right, to each of the leaders,
and they saw that the lot was not theirs, so each one denied it.
At last he came to the man who had scratched his mark
on the white stone and had dropped it into the helmet.   180
Ajax put out his hand, and the herald came
and gave him the lot, and Ajax knew at a glance
that the lot was his, and, beside himself with excitement,
he flung it down on the ground at his feet and said,
"Friends, it is mine, this lot! And I too rejoice,
because I am certain that I will overcome Hector.
But help me now, as I put on my armor for battle.
Make your prayers to Lord Zeus, but make them in silence,
so that no Trojan is able to overhear you."

After he finished, all the men prayed to Lord Zeus;   190
and this is what someone would say as he looked up to heaven:
"Zeus our father, you who rule from Mount Ida,
most glorious king, give victory now to Ajax,
and may his triumph be huge. But if you love Hector
also, then grant the two of them equal glory."

As they prayed for him, Ajax put on his glittering armor;
and when he was ready, he strode like gigantic Ares
as he moves into battle among the soldiers whom Zeus
brings together to fight in heart-crushing combat:
just so, gigantic Ajax, the Danäans' bulwark,   200
strode from the ranks with a savage smile on his face,
and he walked ahead with long strides, gripping his spear.
The Achaeans rejoiced as they watched, but a terrible trembling
seized the limbs of every Trojan who stood there.
Even Hector could feel his heart pound in his chest;
but it was too late for him to retreat and enter
the ranks, since he was the one who had issued the challenge.

Ajax drew near, with his body shield like a tower;

it was made of bronze and had seven layers of oxhide.
Týchius of Hylē had made it, the best   210
master craftsman of leather in all Achaea;
he had made it with seven tough hides and had overlaid them
with an outer layer that he had hammered of bronze.
Holding this huge shield in front of him, Ajax strode up
and stood close to Hector and threatened him with these words:
"Hector, now you will find out, one against one,
what kind of champions fight for the Danäans, even
without lion-hearted Achilles, smasher of men.
He is holding aloof from the fighting now, sitting idle
beside his black ships, still raging at Agamemnon,   220
but among us are other men who can stand up against you—
many of them. So go ahead; take the first throw."

Hector stepped up and answered, "Achaean, don't
try to frighten me like some untested boy
or a woman who doesn't know the first thing about warfare.
I know about fighting. I know how to kill a man;
I know how to swing my shield to the right or left;
I know how to charge straight into the frenzy of chariots
attacking or fleeing in terror; and I know how
to step in the deadly dance of hand-to-hand combat.   230
On guard now; seeing the man that you are, I won't
sneak a shot, but will openly cut you down."

And drawing back his long spear, he hurled it at Ajax
and hit his enormous seven-hide-thick shield
on the outermost layer, the eighth, which was made of bronze.
Through six thick layers of leather the spear head tore,
but the seventh hide stopped and held it. Then, in his turn,
Ajax hurled his long-shadowed spear at Hector.
It tore through his shield and through his finely wrought breastplate
and slit his tunic and grazed the flesh under his ribs;   240
but Hector had leaned to one side and escaped destruction.

Then, at the same time, both pulled the spears from their shields
and flung themselves onto each other like ravenous lions

or like wild boars in their inexhaustible fury.
And Hector's spear stabbed at the center of Ajax's shield,
but the spear head did not break through; its point was bent back.
Then Ajax lunged forward at Hector's shield, and the spear
drove right through it and stunned him and pushed him back,
and the point cut his neck, and the dark blood began to flow.

Yet though he was wounded, Hector did not stop fighting,   250
but stepping back, with one hand he picked up a huge
jagged black rock that lay on the plain, and with it
he hit the enormous seven-hide-thick shield
right on the knob in the center, and the bronze clanged.
Then Ajax picked up a rock as huge as a millstone,
held it above him, then threw it with all his might,
and it smashed Hector's shield and buckled his knees; he was flung
onto his back, with the massive shield pressing upon him;
but quickly Apollo set him again on his feet.

And now they would have been slashing with swords, in close combat,   260
if the heralds from each of the armies had not stepped in,
Talthýbius and Idǽus, both men of good sense.
They held out their staffs between the two fighters to part them,
and the herald Idǽus spoke these sensible words:
"You must stop right now, dear children, and end this combat,
for almighty Zeus loves both of you. It is clear
that you both are great fighters; all of us know that by now.
But night is falling, and we must give way to night."

Then Ajax answered, "Idǽus, you should ask Hector
to decide this matter, since he was the one who challenged   270
the best of our men to fight him in single combat.
Let him speak first, and I will accept his decision."

Then Hector said to him, "Ajax, the gods have given
a huge body to you, great strength, and excellent sense,
and you are by far the best spearman of all the Achaeans.
But let us now put a halt to this for today.
Later, our troops will resume the fighting until

the gods decide between the two armies and grant
the victory to one side or to the other.
Night is now falling, and we must give way to night   280
and bring joy to the Achaeans back at the ships,
and most of all to your kinsmen and your companions.
And I will bring joy, throughout the great city of Priam,
to the Trojan men and the long-robed women of Troy,
who will enter the sacred assembly with prayers of thanksgiving
for my sake. But let us first exchange gifts of great value,
so that all the people, both Argives and Trojans, will say,
'These two great warriors fought with heart-crushing fury,
but then they were reconciled, and they parted friends.' "
And he gave him a sword, its handle studded with silver,   290
along with its sheath and a sword-strap of figured leather;
and Ajax gave him a sword-belt brilliant with scarlet.

When they parted, Ajax went back to join the Achaeans
and Hector to join the Trojans; and these rejoiced
to see him returning to them alive and unhurt
from Ajax's deadly hands, and they brought him back
to the city, hardly believing that he was safe.
On the other side, Ajax was led by the Achaeans
to the son of Atreus, flushed with the joy of triumph.
And when they had come to his hut, Lord Agamemnon   300
slaughtered an ox, and they flayed the carcass and dressed it
and dismembered it and divided it into joints
and expertly carved it into small pieces and skewered
and roasted them and lifted them off the flames.
Then, when their work had been done and the food was ready,
they feasted, and all of them had their fair share and were happy,
and then, as a special honor, Lord Agamemnon
gave Ajax the long, succulent cut of the backbone.

And when they had had enough of eating and drinking,
Nestor stood up and began to give his advice,   310
which often before had proved to be best for the army.
With confidence in his judgment, he spoke to the men:
"Son of Atreus, and all you Achaean commanders,

many men of Achaea have died before Troy;
their dark blood has stained the banks of the lovely Scamander,
and their souls have gone down to Hades. Therefore at dawn
you should stop the fighting; then we can gather the bodies,
and wheel them back here with oxen and mules and burn them.
Around the pyre we should heap up a single mound,
a communal grave that stretches across the plain;   320
and against it we should build a high, towered wall,
a protection for us and our ships, with close-fitting gates
that are large enough for our chariots to drive through them.
And just outside, we should dig a deep trench around it
that will keep back their chariots and foot soldiers, in case
the Trojan army should ever press hard against us."
When they heard his suggestions, all the leaders assented.

Meanwhile the Trojans held an assembly; the men
were very upset, and they gathered at Priam's doors.
The first to speak was Anténor, a clear-minded man: 330
"Hear me, Trojans, Dardánians, and brave allies,
while I say the things that the heart within me compels.
We must now give Helen of Argos and her possessions
to the sons of Atreus. Let them take her away.
We have broken our solemn oaths, and no possible good
can happen to us until we have given her back."

After he finished, he sat down; and in the assembly
Prince Paris stood up, the husband of beautiful Helen,
and he answered, "I do not care for your speech, Anténor;
you could have come up with better advice than this.   340
But if indeed you mean what you say, then it simply
proves that the gods themselves have addled your brains.
Now listen to me, you Trojans. I absolutely
refuse to return the woman. But I am willing
to give back all the possessions I brought here from Argos,
and to these things I will add some wealth of my own."

When he had spoken, he sat down, and in the assembly
King Priam stood up, whose wisdom was like the gods'.

With confidence in his judgment, he spoke to the men:
"Have supper inside the walls, as you normally do;   350
and when the sun rises, Idǽus will go to the ships
and declare to Lord Agamemnon and Menelaus
the words of Paris, through whom this war has arisen.
He will also propose a further sensible plan:
He will ask if they would be willing to stop the fighting
long enough so that both sides can burn their dead.
Later on, we will resume our fighting until
the heavenly powers decide between us, and grant
the victory to one side or to the other."

They listened to him with attention, and all agreed,   360
and before the sun rose, Idǽus went to the ships.
When he got there, he found the Achaean army assembled
by the stern of Lord Agamemnon's ship; and the herald
took his position among them and spoke to them all:
"Son of Atreus, and all you Achaean leaders,
King Priam and the Trojan princes command me
to declare to you, in the hope that this meets your approval,
an offer from Paris, through whom this war has arisen.
All the possessions that Paris brought along with him
in his ships to Troy—how we wish he had died before that!—   370
he agrees to return and will add some wealth of his own.
But as for the wife of glorious Menelaus,
he says he will not return her, though all the Trojans
have urged him to do so. They told me also to ask
if you Danäans would be willing to stop the fighting
long enough so that both sides can burn their dead.
Later on, we will resume our fighting until
the heavenly powers decide between us, and grant
the victory to one side or to the other."
After he finished, everyone there was silent.   380

Finally, Diomedes stood up and spoke:
"Let no man agree to accept these possessions from Paris
or take back Helen. Even a fool can see
that the Trojans are doomed." He sat down, and all the Achaeans

clapped their hands and shouted out their approval
for the plain words of Diomedes, tamer of horses.

Then Agamemnon turned to the herald and said,
"Idǽus, you have heard the Achaeans' reaction,
and that is how I feel too. But as for the dead,
if you want to gather them now, I have no objection;   390
on both sides there is no shortage of corpses to burn.
Let Zeus, the lord of the thunder, now witness our oaths."
And he held up his staff to heaven, to all the gods.
Idǽus left and went back to Troy, where the Trojans
and Dardánians sat in assembly. They were all waiting
for him to return; he took his position among them
and delivered the message. Then they all quickly prepared
for both these labors, some to bring in the dead,
others to search for firewood. And for their part,
the Achaeans hurried out of their black ships, some   400
to bring in the dead, others to search for firewood.

The sun was just now beginning to light up the fields
as it rose from the slow, deep-flowing stream of Ocean
to climb the sky, when the armies met on the plain.
It was hard to know whom the corpses belonged to, covered
with gore as they were and mangled, until the soldiers
with buckets of water washed off the clotted blood;
and they lifted them onto the wagons, shedding hot tears.
But Priam had told the Trojans not to lament,
so they heaped their dead on the pyre, inwardly   410
grieving, and when they had burned the bodies, went back
to sacred Troy. And also on their side, the Argives
heaped their dead on the pyre, inwardly grieving,
and when they had burned the bodies, went back to their ships.

The next day, before it was dawn, between light and darkness,
a group of Achaeans gathered about the pyre,
and all around it they heaped up a single mound,
a communal grave that stretched out across the plain;
and against it they built a wall and a high tower,

a protection for them and their ships, with close-fitting gates.   420
And they dug a deep trench outside it, both long and broad,
and they hammered a row of sharp stakes along the trench.

Thus the Achaeans labored at their defenses.
Meanwhile the gods were sitting at Zeus's side
and marveling at the great wall the Argives were building.
And the first one to stand among them and speak was Poseidon:
"Zeus, is there no man left on the boundless earth
who thinks of informing the gods about his intentions?
Don't you see that the Argives have gone ahead
without us, building a wall to defend their ships   430
with a deep trench around it, and yet have completely neglected
to offer appropriate sacrifices to us?
Its fame will spread on the earth as far as the dawn spreads,
and men will forget the wall that I and Apollo
built for Laómedon, painfully, with such effort."

Greatly troubled by what he had said, Zeus answered,
"Earthshaker, how can you talk in this way? A lesser
god might be anxious, concerned for his prestige or power;
but *your* wall's fame will keep spreading as far as the dawn spreads.
Besides, when the war is over and the Achaeans   440
launch their ships and return to their own dear country,
you can break down the wall and sweep it into the sea
and once again cover the long, wide beaches with sand,
and so the great wall of the Argives will be demolished."

Thus they spoke. And by sunset, the work was completed,
and the men went to bed and received the blessing of sleep.

Book 8

As dawn spread its saffron glow over all the earth,
Zeus called the gods to a council upon the topmost
peak of rugged Olympus. They all sat down,
and when he began to speak, they paid close attention.
"Listen to me, you gods and you goddesses.
I want to bring this affair to a speedy conclusion,
so all of you must agree; none must oppose me.
And if I discover that one of you has slipped off
to bring help to either the Danäans or the Trojans,
I will blast him with lightning, and he will return to Olympus   10
howling with pain; or else I will seize him and hurl him
all the way down to the gloom of Tártarus, far
under the earth, straight down to the deepest abyss,
where the massive gate is of iron, the threshold of bronze—
as far below Hades as heaven is above earth—
and then you will know my supremacy over you others.
Just try me and let me prove it once and for all.
Go hang a golden cord from heaven and pull it,
you gods and you goddesses; pull as hard as you can,
you will never drag Zeus down from heaven to Earth, however   20
hard you may try. Yet if I were to pull, from *my* side,
I could pull you all up, and the sea and the earth as well,
and could wrap the cord around some peak of Olympus,
and there you would all stay, dangling in empty space.
So far superior am I to gods and men."

After he finished, everyone there was silent,
stunned by his words, so forcefully had he spoken.
Finally, Athena stood up and said,
"Son of Cronus, father and lord of us all,
we know very well that you are invincible; no one   30
can stand up against you. Some of us, though, feel pity
for the Danäan troops, who now must wretchedly die.
But we will keep out of the fighting, as you command;

we will just give helpful advice to the Argive leaders
so that not all their men will die because of your anger."

Zeus smiled and said, "All right. Don't worry, dear child;
I didn't mean what I said. You can have your own way."

With this he got up and left; and he harnessed two horses,
bronze-hoofed and swift as the wind, with long golden manes,
and he strapped on his golden armor and picked up his splendid   40
golden whip and mounted his golden car,
and he touched the whip to the backs of the horses, and gladly
they flew midway between earth and the starry heavens.
And when he came to Mount Ida, abundant in springs
and mother of many wild creatures, to Gárgarus
where he has his domain and his sacrifice-fragrant altar,
the father of men and gods reined in the horses,
set them free, and poured dense mist all around them;
and he sat on the mountain, enjoying his splendor, looking
out over Troy and the warships of the Achaeans.   50

The Achaeans meanwhile hastily took their meal
in their huts, and after they ate they put on their armor,
and inside the city the Trojans armed themselves too;
they were fewer, but even so, they were eager to fight,
through necessity, to protect their wives and their children.
The gates were all opened, the Trojan army rushed out,
and when the two armies met, spear clashed against shield
in the fury of battle, and bronze armor rang, and shields
ground into other shields, and a great din arose,
and the moans and the shouts of triumph were mingled together,   60
the cries of killers and killed, and the earth ran with blood.

While it was morning, as long as the sun climbed higher,
the weapons of both sides pierced, and the men kept dying.
But once the sun stood bestriding the top of the sky,
the Father held out his golden scales, and upon them
he put two portions of death—one for the Trojans,
the other for the Achaeans—and lifted the scales

by the middle, and the Achaeans' portion sank downward.
And he thundered loudly from Ida and hurled down a blazing
lightning bolt into the army of the Achaeans.   70
They were stunned at the sight, and pale fear gripped every heart.

Idómeneus drew back; so did Lord Agamemnon;
not even the two Ajaxes dared to remain.
Nestor alone stood firm—not that he wished to,
but one of his horses was wounded. Paris had shot it;
the arrow had pierced the top of its head, where the first hairs
of the mane begin, the deadliest spot. The trace horse
reared up in the throes of death, as the arrow bit
into its brain; and its agonized writhing panicked
the two yoke horses. And while the old warrior hacked   80
at the traces that held the dying horse to the car,
Hector's horses drew near. And now the Achaean
counselor would surely have lost his life
if Diomedes had not been so quick to notice.
He called to Odysseus with a tremendous shout:
"Stop, Odysseus! Why are you running away
into the ranks like a coward? You should be careful
or someone will stick a spear in your back! Come here now;
help me defend the old man from Hector's fierce onslaught."
But Odysseus went rushing past him; he did not hear   90
but kept on running, straight toward the ships on the beach.
And Diomedes, alone though he was, strode forward
and flung himself into the thick of the fight. He stood firm
in front of the old king's horses and said to him, "Sir,
it is clear that these young fighters are wearing you down.
Your strength is gone, since old age lies heavy upon you;
your charioteer is useless; your horses are slow.
But come with me now, and see for yourself the power
of these horses, from Tros's stock—how incredibly fast
they run on the plain in either attack or retreat.   100
I captured them from Aeneas; they can strike panic
into men's hearts. Our attendants will see to your own pair,
and we can drive these two straight ahead at the Trojans,
so that Hector may learn how fiercely *my* spear can rage."

*

The old warrior listened to him and did as he said.
Sthénelus and Eurýmedon, the attendants,
took charge of Nestor's horses, while the two men
quickly mounted the chariot of Diomedes.
When he had climbed in, Nestor took hold of the reins
and touched the whip to the backs of the horses. Soon   110
they came close to Hector, who charged toward them at full speed,
and Diomedes threw his long spear. He missed Hector
but hit his driver, Thebæus's son, Eniópeus,
in the chest, near his nipple, as he was holding the reins;
the horses swerved, and he fell from the chariot headlong.
Hector's mind was darkened with wrenching grief,
yet as much as he grieved for his comrade, he let him lie there,
and he went off to find another charioteer.
And his horses did not have to wait very long; quickly
he found Archeptólemus, Íphitus's brave son,   120
and he had him climb up beside him and take the reins.

There would have been inescapable grief for the Trojans,
who would have been driven to Troy and penned in like lambs
if Father Zeus had not been so quick to notice.
He boomed out his terrible thunder and hurled down a flashing
bolt of white fire before Diomedes' team;
it flared up and blazed with sulfur, and the two horses
shied and shrank back against the chariot. The reins
dropped out of Nestor's hands, and his heart went cold,
and he said to Diomedes, "Let us turn back—   130
can't you see that the hand of Zeus is against you?
He has granted Hector the victory for today.
Another time, if he wants, he will give it to us.
No man, not even the bravest, can thwart the intention
of Zeus, since his might is so much greater than ours."

Then Diomedes answered, "What you just said
is true and fitting. But one thought troubles my heart:
that someday Hector will say as he speaks to the Trojans,
'When Diomedes saw me, he lost his nerve

and fled to the black ships.' This is how he will gloat.   140
On that day, may the earth gape open and swallow me up."

Then Nestor said, "Son of Tydeus, that thought is nonsense.
Even if Hector called you a coward or weakling,
the Trojans and the Dardánians wouldn't believe him,
nor would the widows whose men you flung in the dirt."

With these words he turned the horses around and fled
toward the Achaean ranks, and the Trojans and Hector,
with a deafening roar, rained hundreds of spears upon them.
And Hector shouted out to him, "Son of Tydeus,
the Danäans used to honor you greatly; they gave you   150
pride of place, the choicest meat, and a wine cup
always refilled. But now they will all despise you;
it turns out that you are as cowardly as a woman.
Go ahead, sissy, run! I will never let you
set foot on our walls or carry our women off.
I will send you to Hades before that can ever happen."

At this, Diomedes' mind was paralyzed: should he
turn his horses around and go back to fight him?
Three times he wavered and made up his mind to go;
three times Zeus thundered down from the peaks of Mount Ida   160
to give the Trojans a sign that the battle was theirs.
Then Hector shouted out and addressed the army:
"Trojan, Lycian, Dardánian soldiers and friends,
be men now. Onward; remember your fighting spirit.
Zeus has promised me victory and great glory,
and has massive destruction in store for the Achaeans.
Fools that they are, they think that their flimsy wall
will protect them, but it will never withstand our onslaught;
our horses will leap right over their trench. And once
I get as far as their black ships, bring me some torches,   170
and I will set them on fire and slaughter the men."

After he finished, Hector called out to his horses:
"Now you can pay me back for all the provisions

served to you by Andromache, your kind mistress,
who has given you luscious wheat in such great abundance.
Hurry now, run as fast as you can; we will capture
Nestor's great shield, whose fame soars up to the heavens—
it is fashioned of gold, both hand-grips and shield itself—
and then we can take from the shoulders of Diomedes
his finely wrought breastplate, made in Hephaestus's smithy.   180
If we could manage to capture these two, then perhaps
we can make the Achaeans sail off, this very night."

When she heard his boasting, Hera became enraged,
and she said to the great god Poseidon, "Earthshaker, doesn't
even your heart feel pity for the Achaeans
as they are cut down? Yet they bring generous gifts
to your famous shrines in Hélicē and in Ægæ,
and you used to want victory for them. If we all wished,
we who support the Argives, to drive back the Trojans
and keep away far-seeing Zeus, then we could do it,   190
and he would sit brooding on Ida, all by himself."

Greatly annoyed by these words, Poseidon answered,
"Hera, what are you saying? Such reckless talk!
I would never want the rest of us to be fighting
Lord Zeus, since his strength is so much greater than ours."

This was their conversation. Meanwhile the whole space
between the wall and the trench was filled with Achaeans
falling back, horses and shield-bearing soldiers alike.
Hector was penning them in with a savage fury,
since Zeus had decided to grant him glory this day.   200

And he would have set fire to the ships if Hera had not
noticed it and inspired Lord Agamemnon
to stir up the fighting spirit of the Achaeans.
He strode along by the huts and the beached ships, holding
his great purple cloak in his massive hand, and he stopped
beside Odysseus's huge black ship, in the middle
of the Danäan camp, where his voice could reach to both ends.

And he called with a mighty shout that moved all who heard him:
"Shame on you, Argives—disgraces, pretty-boys, frauds!
What happened to all our boasts about being the bravest   210
of men, and to all the fine words that you uttered at Lemnos
as you gorged yourselves on portions of roasted oxen
and tossed down beakers of wine that were filled to the brim,
claiming that each of you in the heat of battle
could slaughter a hundred Trojans—or was it two hundred?
But we are not even a match for one single man,
Hector, who soon will set fire to our ships. O Zeus,
has there ever before been any great king that you struck
with such delusion as this and robbed of such glory?
Yet not once, I swear, has there been an altar of yours   220
that my ship ever passed while I made my ill-omened way here,
but on each one I burned the fat and thighbones of oxen
as I sailed to plunder the thick-walled city of Troy.
Now grant me this one prayer: Let us escape with our lives
and not all be wretchedly slaughtered here by the Trojans."
He was in tears as he prayed, and the Father took pity
and nodded to show that the Argives would not be destroyed.
And quickly he sent an eagle, the surest omen
among all birds; in its talons there was a fawn,
and it put the fawn down right next to the splendid altar   230
where the Danäans made their sacrifices to Zeus.
And when they saw that the bird had been sent from heaven,
they rushed at the Trojans more fiercely, with freshened spirits.

Among the many commanders, there was no man
who could boast that he had driven across the trench
to fight in close combat sooner than Diomedes.
Long before anyone else, he cut down a Trojan,
Ageláüs, the son of Phradmon, who had just turned
his horses around to flee. Diomedes stabbed him
between his shoulders; the spear drove on through his chest,   240
and he fell to the ground, and his armor clattered upon him.
After him came Agamemnon and Menelaus,
then the two Ajaxes, filled with the spirit of war,
and Idómeneus, along with his comrade-in-arms

Meriones, then Eurýpylus. Ninth came Teucer,
drawing his supple bow as he took his position
behind the shield of his brother, Ajax the Tall.
Then Ajax would move his shield to one side, slightly,
and Teucer would look around, would pick out some Trojan,
shoot an arrow, and when the Trojan fell dead,   250
he would dive back down, like a child running back to its mother,
and Ajax would hide him again behind his huge shield.

Tell me now, which of the Trojans did Teucer kill first?
Orsílochus first, Órmenus, Opheléstes,
Dætor and Chrómius and Lycophóntes,
Melaníppus and Polyǽmon's son Amopáon.
And when he saw him, Lord Agamemnon rejoiced
as his mighty bow devastated the ranks of the Trojans.
Then he approached and stood beside him and said,
"Teucer, dear heart, brave leader of the Achaeans,   260
keep shooting like this, and be a great light to the army
and an honor and joy to Télamon also, your father,
who brought you up in his house, though you were a bastard.
Bring glory to him, as far away as he is.
I promise you this: If Zeus and Athena let me
someday break through the mighty ramparts of Troy,
you will be first to be given the prize of honor
(of course, after me)—either a precious tripod
or a pair of splendid horses along with their car
or a beautiful young woman to share your bed."   270

Teucer replied, "Most glorious son of Atreus,
you need not encourage me; I am already eager.
I have been fighting with all the strength that is in me,
since the moment when we began to drive them toward Troy,
looking for chances to shoot down men with my bow.
I have shot eight long-barbed arrows, and every one
has buried itself in the flesh of some brave young Trojan.
This one alone I cannot hit—this mad dog."
As he spoke, he aimed and let fly another arrow
straight at Hector. His heart was longing to kill him,   280

but he missed him and hit Gorgýthion in the chest,
Priam's son by a wife who came from Æsýmē,
Cástianíra, as beautiful as a goddess;
and his head drooped, like a poppy in a spring garden
weighed down with seeds and a heavy rain: so his head
leaned to one side beneath the weight of his helmet.

Again Teucer aimed, and he let fly another arrow
straight at Hector, longing to bring him down.
But once more he missed—Apollo deflected the shot,
and it hit Archeptólemus, Hector's charioteer,   290
in the chest, by his nipple, as he was charging forward,
and the horses swerved as he fell from the chariot headlong.
Then Hector's mind was darkened with wrenching grief,
yet as much as he grieved for his comrade, he left him there,
and he told his brother Cebríones, who was nearby,
to take up the horses' reins, and Cebríones did it.
He himself leaped to the ground from his shining car
with a blood-chilling war shout, took a huge rock in his hands,
and went straight for Teucer; his heart was on fire to kill him.
Teucer had just pulled an arrow out of his quiver   300
and had fitted it to the bowstring. But as he took aim,
drawing it back to his shoulder, Hector rushed up
and hurled the rock, and it smashed down onto the deadly
place where the collarbone separates neck from chest.
The bowstring broke, and his fingers and wrist went numb,
and he dropped to his knees, and the great bow fell from his hand.
But when Ajax saw that his brother had fallen, he ran up
and straddled him, and he covered him with his shield.
And two loyal comrades picked him up on their shoulders—
Mecísteus, son of Échius, and Alástor—   310
and carried him, groaning, back to the Argive ships.

Then Zeus once again breathed power into the Trojans,
and they drove the Achaeans back, straight toward the trench,
and Hector charged in the front ranks, fiercely elated.
As when a hunting dog chases a wild boar or lion
and snaps from behind at its flanks or at its hindquarters

and follows it as it twists and turns to escape:
just so did Hector follow and keep on killing
the men in the rear as they ran back, stricken with panic.
And when the Achaeans had fled past the stakes and the trench   320
and many of them had died at the hands of the Trojans,
they came to a halt alongside the ships. And they called out
to one another and prayed to the gods with raised arms.
But Hector kept wheeling his horses, and his eyes glared
like the eyes of the Gorgon or of man-murdering Ares.

When she saw them fleeing in terror, Hera felt pity,
and at once she spoke to Athena: "Daughter of Zeus,
do we no longer care if the Danäans live or die?
Is there no way to help them, even at this last moment,
to prevent them from being slaughtered and pushed to their doom   330
by the raging of one man? Look at the terrible havoc
this Hector has wrought in his irresistible fury."

Athena answered, "Nothing would please me better
than to see his onslaught stopped right now in its tracks.
But my father is raging too, with a mind turned to evil,
hard-hearted, ill-willed, always wrecking my plans.
He has forgotten the times when I rescued his son
Héracles—when he was overwhelmed by the tasks
of Eurýstheus and he kept crying aloud to heaven
and Zeus kept sending me down from Olympus to help him.   340
If only I had foreseen all this at the time
when Eurýstheus sent him down to the underworld
to bring back the dog of Hades, I would have made sure
that he never recrossed the steep-flowing waters of Styx.
But now Zeus hates me and does what Thetis requested
when she kissed his knees and took his chin in her hand
and wept and implored him to honor her son, Achilles—
though I know that someday he will call me 'dear child' again.
Meanwhile harness the horses, while I myself enter
the palace of Zeus and arm for the coming battle.   350
I want to see whether Hector is pleased when we two
appear on the field of war, or whether the Trojans

begin to fall in the dirt by the ships of the Argives
to feed the wild dogs and birds with their delicate flesh."

At these words, Hera nodded her head in agreement,
and she went to yoke the celestial, gold-bridled team.
Athena armed herself for the coming battle,
mounted the fiery chariot, grasped her spear,
and Hera touched the whip to the backs of the horses.

When Lord Zeus saw them from Ida, he was enraged,   360
and he sent down golden-winged Iris to take them a message:
"Hurry now, Iris, turn them back; don't allow them
to proceed any further. They would regret it, deeply.
For if they keep daring to interfere, I assure you
I will cripple their team with a powerful blast of lightning
that will hurl them both from the car and smash it to pieces,
and not even after ten circling years have gone by
will they be healed of the wounds that my thunderbolt causes,
and Athena will learn what it means to oppose her father.
But as for Hera, I am less angry at her,   370
since I know that she always undermines what I plan."

Swift as the storm wind, Iris rushed to obey.
She flew to the outer gates of Olympus and stopped them
and delivered the message, speaking with Zeus's own words:
"Where are you off to? Have you both lost your minds?
The great son of Cronus forbade you to help the Argives.
If you keep daring to interfere, he assures you
he will cripple your team with a powerful blast of lightning
that will hurl you both from the car and smash it to pieces,
and not even after ten circling years have gone by   380
will you be healed of the wounds that his thunderbolt causes.
Thus you will learn what it means to oppose your father."

After she had delivered the message, she left them.
Then Hera said to Athena, "Daughter of Zeus,
I have changed my mind. We shouldn't be waging war
against Lord Zeus for the sake of these paltry mortals.

Let one of them live and another die, just as fortune
dictates, and let Zeus ponder these things in his mind
and decide between Trojans and Argives however he wishes."
With these words she turned the team around and drove back.   390
And the Seasons touched the beautiful manes of the horses,
unyoked and tethered them at their celestial stalls,
and leaned the chariot against the bright wall of the courtyard.
And the goddesses both sat down on their golden chairs
among the other gods, pained and angry at heart.

Meanwhile Zeus drove his chariot from Mount Ida
to Mount Olympus and reached the place where the gods
had all assembled. Poseidon, the great Earthshaker,
unyoked his horses and took the chariot and set it
on its golden stand and covered it with a cloth.   400
Then Zeus sat down on his golden throne, and the whole
of Olympus began to tremble beneath his feet.
Athena and Hera were sitting alone, apart,
and neither one said a word. But Zeus knew exactly
what they were thinking and said to them, "Why are you pained?
Surely you haven't grown tired of destroying Trojans,
whom you hate with such deadly passion. As for myself,
my strength is so irresistible that no god—
not even all the gods on Olympus—could turn me
from what I want. But both you goddesses trembled   410
and terror sent chills through your glorious arms and legs
before you could get to the battle and all its slaughter.
I tell you this, and I swear that it would have happened:
My lightning bolt would have blasted you from your seats,
and your chariot wouldn't have brought you back to Olympus."

His words caused Athena and Hera to seethe with fury.
Athena was silent; though angry at Zeus, her father,
and though a fierce passion gripped her, she held her tongue.
But Hera could not contain herself, and she cried out,
"Dread Lord, what are you saying? We know very well   420
how invincible is your power; yet even so,
we pity the Danäan warriors, doomed as they are."

*

Zeus answered, "Wait until morning, Hera. At that time,
if you are curious, you will see more of my power
as I attack the Achaean army and slaughter
great multitudes. Hector will not draw back from the battle
until Achilles is stirred to action again
on the day that they fight by the sterns of the beached ships,
in grim confinement, over the corpse of Patroclus.
That is decreed. I do not care in the least   430
about your anger. Go to the uttermost ends
of the earth and the sea, where Ïápetus and Cronus
sit, uncheered by a single glimmer of sunlight
or a single breeze, with the black abyss all around them—
not even then will I care about your resentment,
since there is not a more insolent bitch than you are."
He glared at her, and Hera seethed but said nothing.

And the glorious light of the sun sank into the Ocean,
drawing the night down over the grain-giving earth.
The Trojans were sorry that daylight had left, but the Argives   440
welcomed night as an answer to all their prayers.

Then Hector held an assembly, leading the Trojans
away from the ships to a place by the swirling river
where the ground could be seen through the corpses. Each of the men
dismounted and listened to him. He was holding a spear
sixteen feet long; in front of him glittered its bronze point,
fixed to the spear's oak shaft by a ring of gold.
Leaning upon this spear, he addressed the troops:
"Hear me, Trojans, Dardánians, and brave allies.
I thought that today, before I returned to the city,   450
I would surely destroy the ships and all the Achaeans.
But darkness came on too soon; it was only darkness
that saved the Achaeans' lives and rescued their ships.
So let us give way to night and prepare our supper.
Unyoke your horses and feed them, and from the city
bring oxen and sheep and heart-cheering wine and bread
from your houses, and also gather great piles of firewood.

All night long, until dawn appears, we can burn
many fires and their glare will rise to the heavens,
in case the Achaean troops, in spite of the darkness,   460
try to escape across the broad back of the sea.
Don't allow them to board without a fierce struggle;
let most of them leave with wounds that they will be nursing
at their own sweet leisure, an arrow or spear in the back
as they scurry onto their ships, so that others think twice
before they bring war and its misery to the Trojans.
And let the heralds proclaim that those who have stayed back—
the boys and the gray-haired men, who are too old to fight—
should camp on the god-built walls that surround the city.
As for the women, let each of them light a great fire   470
in her house, and let an unceasing vigil be kept
so that no Achaeans slip in while our troops are away.
These are my orders, great-hearted men of Troy;
carry them out now. That is all, for the moment.
Tomorrow, when dawn appears, I will speak again.
I hope and pray to Zeus and the other immortals
to drive these fate-cursed dogs away from our city.
So, for tonight, we must firmly guard our position;
but early tomorrow, at daybreak, let us all arm
and fight our fiercest beside the Achaean ships."   480

So Hector spoke to the men, and they roared their approval.
They all loosed the sweating horses from under their yokes,
and tied them with straps, each man beside his own car.
And they went to bring oxen and sheep and heart-cheering wine
and bread from their houses, and also gathered much firewood.
And soon the winds took the savor of burned flesh to heaven.

So, with elated hearts, they sat up all night
on the battlefield, and their watch fires blazed all around them.
As, in the night sky, around the light of the moon,
the stars emerge, when the air is serene and windless,   490
and the stars shine bright, and the heart of the shepherd rejoices:
just so, before Ilion, the watch fires the Trojans had set
blazed midway between the ships and the river Xanthus.

A thousand watch fires were burning upon the plain,
and around each, fifty men sat in the glow of the firelight,
and the horses stood alongside the chariots, munching
white barley and oats, and waited for dawn to arise.

Book 9

While the Trojans kept their night vigil, all the Achaeans
were gripped by panic, the comrade of bone-chilling fear,
and their leaders were overwhelmed with a desperate sorrow.
As when the north and the west wind that blow from Thrace
suddenly spring up and roil the fish-teeming waters
and in a moment the dark waves surge to the heavens
and strew the seaweed in thick piles along the shore:
just so stirred up was the heart of every Achaean.

And Lord Agamemnon, heartsick and deeply troubled,
went up and down, commanding the heralds to summon   10
everyone, man by man, to quickly assemble,
but not to shout out, and he himself hurried among them.
The men sat down, despondent, and Agamemnon
stood up to speak, in tears, like a spring of water
that pours its dark stream down over some goat-steep cliff:
thus, weeping, with many sighs, he addressed the Achaeans.
"My dear friends, Danäan soldiers, companions in battle,
Zeus has tangled me up in a heartbreaking madness.
He swore once that I would capture Troy and sail home
with its riches. But now he has cruelly broken his word;   20
he commands me to leave, to return in disgrace to Argos,
though so many brave men have died here. Such is the will,
it seems, of almighty Zeus, who has broken the walls
of many proud cities, and still will break many more.
So listen now, and let us all do as I say.
Launch the ships and sail back to our own country,
since no hope remains of ever capturing Troy."

After he finished, everyone sat there speechless.
A long time passed. Nobody said a word.
Finally, Diomedes stood up and spoke: 30
"Are you such a fool as to really consider the Argives
cowards and weaklings, as you have just proclaimed?

137

If you are so eager to go back to Argos—well, go then;
you know the way, and all the ships that you brought
stand on the shore in front of us, ready to sail.
But the rest of the Argive commanders are going to stay here
until we have plundered Troy. And if *they* flee as well,
then the two of us, I and Sthénelus, will fight on
and conquer Troy, since we know that the gods are with us."
After he finished, he sat down, and all the Achaeans   40
clapped their hands and shouted out their approval
for the plain words of Diomedes, tamer of horses.

Next, the old hero Nestor stood up and spoke:
"Son of Tydeus, in war you are a great fighter,
and in speaking you have no rival of your own age.
Not one of us here will find fault with what you just said
or contradict it. But it was beside the point.
You have spoken sensible words to the Argive leaders
and have said what is appropriate for your age;
but of course, you are young—you could easily be my own boy,   50
my youngest-born. And since I am so much older
than you, I will cover all points, nor will any man here
dishonor my words, not even Lord Agamemnon.
The man who arouses conflict in his own people
is clanless, lawless, and homeless among all men.
But let us give way to night and prepare our supper,
and let sentinels camp out along the trench that we dug
outside the wall. The men must be quick to perform this.
Then you, son of Atreus, must lead us, since you are clearly
the most powerful king of us all. You must offer a banquet   60
for the senior commanders. That would be right and proper;
your huts are filled with the wine that the Argive ships
bring you each day from Thrace across the wide waters.
You have the resources to entertain all of them, richly,
and you rule over many; if many can come together,
you will hear their thoughts and can then choose the best advice.
The Achaeans desperately need a sensible plan,
since our enemies have advanced and are burning their watch fires
so close to our ships. Which one of us isn't appalled?

This night will either destroy our army or save it."   70
All of them listened carefully; all agreed.
The sentinels armed and hurried off with their weapons,
commanded by Thrasymédes, the son of Nestor,
by Ascálaphus too and Ïálmenus, sons of Ares,
and Meriones and Deípyrus and Apháreus,
and last of all Lycomédes, the son of Creon.
These were the seven captains. A hundred young men
marched behind each of them, holding their bronze-tipped spears,
and took their posts midway between the trench and the wall.
There they lit fires, and each man prepared his supper.   80

And Lord Agamemnon led the senior commanders
into his hut and served them a glorious banquet,
and they helped themselves to the food that was set before them.
And when they had had enough of eating and drinking,
Nestor stood up and began to give his advice,
which often before had proved to be best for the army.
"Most glorious son of Atreus, Agamemnon,
with you my speech will begin, and with you it will end,
since you are king over many, and Zeus has bestowed
the scepter on you and the long-established traditions,   90
so that the people may profit from your sound judgment.
You, more than anyone here, must not only speak well
but listen well, and act when another man's heart
prompts him to give advice for the good of us all;
the words may be his, but the credit will go to you.
Now I will speak out and tell you what I think best.
No one will put forth a better idea than this one,
which I have long had in mind, since the day when you,
great king, infuriated Achilles by going
and taking that girl Briséïs away from his hut.   100
We were all against it. I, for one, did my best
to dissuade you, but you would not listen to me; you gave in
to your reckless pride and dishonored the greatest of men,
whom the very immortals honor; you took his prize
and have kept it. But even now, as late as it is,
we have to consider how we can make amends

and win him over with soothing gifts and kind words."

And the king of men, Lord Agamemnon, responded,
"Sir, you are telling the truth when you speak of my madness.
I was out of my mind with rage; I will not deny it.   110
A man who is loved by Zeus is worth whole battalions,
and Zeus has shown that he honors this one by almost
destroying our army. But since I was out of my mind
when I did this thing and gave in to my wretched passion,
I am willing to make amends and offer him boundless
compensation. With all of you gathered here,
I will state the magnificent gifts I am ready to send him:
seven tripods untouched by fire, and ten
solid gold bars, and twenty glittering cauldrons,
and twelve fast horses, all champions—a man who owned   120
nothing more than the prizes that they have won
would not be lacking in gold. I will also give him
seven women, each of them highly skilled
in spinning and weaving, each of surpassing beauty;
when he captured Lesbos, I chose them myself from the spoils.
These I will give him, and also the one I took,
Briseus's daughter, and with her my solemn oath
that I never entered her bed to make love to her, as
would be natural for a man to do with a woman.
These will be his, immediately. Then later,   130
if the gods allow us to plunder Priam's great city,
he may come when we Achaeans divide the spoils
and heap his ship high with as much gold and bronze as he wishes;
and he may choose twenty Trojan women, the ones
that seem to him the most beautiful, after Helen.
And if we ever reach Argos, I promise to make him
my son-in-law and treat him with all the honor
I give to my own beloved boy, young Orestes,
who is growing up there amid the greatest abundance.
I also have three daughters at home in my palace: 140
Chrysóthemis, Laódicē, Íphianássa;
he may choose for his own whichever one he likes best
and may take her home without the usual bride-price;

indeed, I will grant her a glorious dowry, far more
than any man has ever bestowed on his daughter.
I will give him seven populous cities: Anthéa
with its deep meadows, Cardámylē, grass-rich Hirē,
sacred Pheræ, Énopē, lovely Æpéa,
and Pédasus, covered with vineyards. Each of these seven
is near the sea, on the borders of sandy Pylos;   150
the men who live there are rich in cattle and sheep
and will honor him like a god, with abundant tribute,
and will live in peace, obedient to his laws.
All this I promise if he abandons his anger.
So let him give in—of all the gods only Hades
is implacable and perverse, which is why men hate him—
and let him submit to my authority, seeing
that I am the greater king and much older than he is."

Then Nestor answered, "Most glorious son of Atreus,
no one could say that your offer to Lord Achilles   160
is less than generous. Now, right away, we must send
a delegation to speak with him in his hut.
I will choose them myself, and they mustn't refuse the duty.
Phoenix should lead the way, and following him
Odysseus and Ajax the Tall, along with two heralds,
Ódius and Eurýbates. Now bring water
to wash our hands with, and everyone should be silent
so that we can pray to Zeus and ask for his mercy."

These were his words, and everyone there approved.
The heralds quickly poured water over their hands,   170
the attendants filled the mixing bowls to the brim
and passed them around, first pouring a few drops of wine
into the cups for each man to make a libation.
And after they had all done so and drunk the wine
to their hearts' content, the chosen envoys set out.
And Nestor looked at each of these men in turn
and gave them each instructions—above all, Odysseus—
to do everything that they could to persuade Achilles.

*

They walked along the shore of the loud-roaring sea
and prayed to the god who encircles the earth and shakes it   180
that he grant them a way to persuade Achilles' proud heart.
At last they arrived at the camp of the Myrmidons. There
they found him singing and plucking a clear-toned lyre,
a beautiful instrument with a silver crossbar
to hold the strings; he had taken it from the spoils
after he captured and plundered Ëétion's city.
With it he was delighting his heart, and he sang
poems about the glorious deeds of heroes.
Patroclus, alone, sat opposite him, in silence,
and listened and waited for him to leave off his singing.   190
The envoys drew near, with Odysseus leading the way,
and they stopped before him. Achilles stood up, astonished,
from the chair he sat on, still holding onto the lyre,
and Patroclus too got up as soon as he saw them.
Achilles reached out his hand to them, and he said,
"Welcome, dear friends. I am happy that you have come—
there must be some urgent need. Of all the Achaeans
I love you the best, even when I am so angry."
With these words, Achilles invited them to sit down
on chairs that had been spread with fine purple covers;   200
and quickly he spoke to Patroclus, who was nearby:
"Bring out a larger mixing bowl, son of Menœtius.
Mix the wine with less water, to make the drink strong,
and serve it to each of my friends, here under my roof."

Patroclus did what his dear companion had asked for.
He put down a chopping block in front of the fire pit;
on it he placed the backs of a sheep and a plump goat
and the ribs of a full-grown hog, edged thick with fat.
And Automedon held the meat while Achilles carved it
and cut it into small pieces and put them on spits.   210
Patroclus stirred up the fire, and when it had died down,
he spread out the embers and laid the spits on the spit racks
over them, sprinkling the pieces with holy salt.
Then, when the meat was roasted, he heaped it on platters
and took loaves of bread and passed them around the table

in fine wicker baskets. Achilles then served the meat
and sat by the opposite wall, facing Odysseus.
He told his companion to sacrifice to the immortals,
and Patroclus threw the gods' portions into the flames.

And when they had had enough of eating and drinking,   220
Ajax noded to Phoenix. Odysseus saw it
and took his cup and raised it and drank to Achilles:
"Your health, Achilles. We haven't gone hungry this evening,
in Lord Agamemnon's hut or here now with you—
a feast to our hearts' content. But of course we have come here
not for the splendid food you have served us. My lord,
we are facing a great disaster, and we are afraid.
Unless you return to the fighting, it is in doubt
whether our ships will be saved or destroyed. The Trojans
have taken positions close to our ships and wall   230
and have lit many watch fires throughout their camp, and they think
that nothing can hold their assault back now or prevent them
from hurling themselves on the ships, and Zeus shows them favor
with lightning bolts on their right, and Hector has gone
berserk, like a mad dog. Trusting that Zeus is with him,
he fears neither men nor gods; an incredible fury
has entered him. He is praying for dawn to appear,
and he threatens to hack off our stern-posts and burn our ships
and smoke us out and slaughter us by the hulls.
I fear that the gods will fulfill his threats and that we will   240
die here in Ilion, far from the homes we love.
So enter the fighting, I beg you. Rescue the Argives,
who are crumbling before the Trojans' savage attack.
If you do not, you will surely come to regret it
when disaster has struck, since then it will be too late
to undo the terrible slaughter. Before that happens,
think about how you can save us from mass destruction.
Dear friend, on the day that Peleus sent you from Phthia
to Agamemnon, he gave you this piece of advice:
'My child,' he said, 'Athena and Hera will grant you   250
strength if they wish, but you must keep your heart's passion
within your breast; good fellowship is much better.

And do not pursue a quarrel; in this way the Argives,
both young men and old, will honor you even more.'
That was your father's advice, which you have forgotten.
So stop; let go of this rage that consumes your heart.
It isn't too late. Agamemnon is willing to give you
full compensation if you will abandon your anger.
Listen to me, and I will tell you the many
splendid gifts that Agamemnon has promised: 260
seven tripods untouched by fire, and ten
solid gold bars, and twenty glittering cauldrons,
and twelve fast horses, all champions—a man who owned
nothing more than the prizes that they have won
would not be lacking in gold. He will also give you
seven women, each of them highly skilled
in spinning and weaving, each of surpassing beauty;
when you captured Lesbos, he chose them himself from the spoils.
These he will give you, and also the one he took,
Briseus's daughter, and with her his solemn oath   270
that he never entered her bed to make love to her, as
would be natural for a man to do with a woman.
These will be yours, immediately. Then later,
if the gods allow us to plunder Priam's great city,
you may come when we Achaeans divide the spoils
and heap your ship high with as much gold and bronze as you wish;
and you may choose twenty Trojan women, the ones
that seem to you the most beautiful, after Helen.
And if we ever reach Argos, he says he will make you
his son-in-law and treat you with all the honor   280
he gives to his own beloved boy, young Orestes,
who is growing up there amid the greatest abundance.
He also has three daughters at home in his palace:
Chrysóthemis, Laódicē, Íphianássa;
you may choose for your own whichever one you like best
and may take her home without the usual bride-price;
indeed, he will grant her a glorious dowry, far more
than any man has ever bestowed on his daughter.
He will give you seven populous cities: Anthéa
with its deep meadows, Cardámylē, grass-rich Hirē,   290

sacred Pheræ, Énopē, lovely Æpéa,
and Pédasus, covered with vineyards. Each of these seven
is near the sea, on the borders of sandy Pylos;
the men who live there are rich in cattle and sheep
and will honor you like a god, with abundant tribute,
and will live in peace, obedient to your laws.
All this he will give you if you abandon your anger.
But if you hate Agamemnon too much and despise
his glorious gifts—still, pity the other Achaeans,
who are crumbling, and who will honor you like a god.   300
You would win great glory with them; you might even kill
Hector now, who would probably come very close
in his mad-dog rage, since he thinks that he has no equal
among the Danäans whom the black ships have brought here."

In response to what he had just heard, Achilles said,
"Noble son of Laértes, resourceful Odysseus,
I am going to speak plain words and tell you exactly
what I am thinking and what I am going to do,
so that you won't sit here cooing and trying to coax me
into agreement. I hate like the gates of Hades   310
the man who says one thing and hides another inside him.
So, when I speak, I will say what is on my mind.
I will never be brought around by Lord Agamemnon
or by anyone else. A man gets no thanks for his tireless
struggle against the enemy, day in, day out.
We all get just the same portion, whether we hang back
or fight on with all our strength in the front lines of battle;
cowards and brave men are treated with equal respect.
I have had not the slightest profit from all the pain
I have suffered in battle, constantly risking my life.   320
Like a mother bird that brings to her unfledged nestlings
any morsel she finds, and herself goes hungry,
I have spent many sleepless nights, and my days have been bloody
battling men who fought for the sake of their sweethearts.
From my ships I conquered twelve cities surrounding Troy
and eleven more cities by land across the rich Troad.
All these I plundered and took away many treasures

and brought them here and gave them to Agamemnon,
who had stayed put beside the ships; a small part of these
he distributed to the army, but most he kept.   330
Every prize that he gave to the other leaders
remains with them still. I am the only Achaean
he has robbed. He has taken my wife, my darling. Well, let him
sleep with her, and let him enjoy it. But why
should we fight the Trojans? Why did this Agamemnon
gather an army and bring it here? Was it not
for the sake of Helen? Are Atreus's sons the only
men in the world who love their wives? But whoever
is decent and sensible loves his wife, as I too
loved this beautiful woman with all my heart,   340
even though she was a captive, won by the spear.
But now that this man has cheated me of my prize,
he had better not try to lure me back—I know him
too well; he will never persuade me to join the fighting.
He can figure out for himself with you and the others
how to defend our ships from the enemy's fire.
After all, he has had such astounding success without me;
he has built a fine wall and dug a fine trench beside it—
which won't do a thing to hold back man-killing Hector.
In the days when I was fighting beside the Achaeans,   350
Hector would never have dared to move from the walls
but would come out only as far as the Scaean Gates
and the oak tree, where he once faced me alone, and he barely
escaped me that time. But now I am not in the mood
to fight against Hector. Tomorrow—after I make
sacrifices to Zeus and the other immortals—
I will load my ships and launch them; at dawn you will see
(if you have an interest in looking) all my ships sail
over the fish-teeming Hellespont, with my men rowing,
eager to be on their way. And if the Earthshaker   360
grants me good winds, I will reach my own country, Phthia,
in three days. I have many possessions there,
which I left behind on my ill-omened journey to Troy,
and from here I will take back even more gold and bronze,
along with some lovely women and precious iron—

the spoil allotted as my share, however meager.
But as for my prize: the man who gave it, that great king
Agamemnon, has taken it back and shamed me.
Be sure to tell him everything I have said,
and tell him in public; the rest of the men should hear it   370
so that they can act to stop him in case he intends
to go and cheat anyone else. He is completely
without shame; yet the insolent son of a bitch
would not even come here and look me straight in the eye.
I will never do anything, ever again, to help him.
He cheated and wronged me. Once is enough. To hell
with that man, since Zeus has taken away his senses.
I despise his gifts, and I don't give a damn about him.
Not even if he were to offer me ten or twenty
times as much as he has, or all he can get   380
from other kings, or all the fabulous treasures
of Orchómenos or of Egyptian Thebes,
where the palaces are piled high with gold and silver
and the walls have a hundred gates and through every gate
two hundred warriors ride out with horses and cars—
not even if he were to offer me gifts as countless
as the grains of sand on the seashore or as the specks
of dust on the plain of Troy, not even then
would Agamemnon win over my heart, not till
he has paid me the full price for this heart-grieving insult.   390
I will never marry a daughter of his, not even
if she were as lovely as golden-haired Aphrodite
and as skilled as gray-eyed Athena in women's work—
not even if that were true would I marry the girl.
He can choose some other leader of the Achaeans,
a great man like him, a king as mighty as he is.
If the gods allow me to live and come safely home,
my father, Peleus, will find me a wife, I am sure.
There are many suitable girls throughout Hellas and Phthia,
the daughters of all the chief men who rule over cities;   400
whichever of these I want, I will make my wife.
It has often been my heart's desire to get married
and enjoy the wealth that my father, Peleus, has gained.

Nothing is worth my life—not all the treasures
that people say the great city of Troy possessed
in the time of peace, before our army arrived,
nor all the treasures piled up on the marble floor
of Apollo's temple beneath the high cliffs of Pytho.
Cattle and sheep can be captured during a raid;
tripods and noble horses can be acquired;   410
but a man's life cannot be gained again or recovered
once it has flown from his mouth. My mother, Thetis,
tells me that there are two ways I might die. If I stay here
and keep on fighting around the city of Troy,
I can never go home, but my glory will live forever;
but if I return in my ships to my own dear country,
my glory will die, but my life will be long and peaceful.
And one more thing: My advice to the rest of you leaders
is to sail back home, since now there is not a chance
of capturing Ilion. Zeus is shielding the city   420
with his own hand, and its people have gained back their courage.
Go now; deliver this message to all the leaders;
speak plainly, for that is a senior counselor's right.
Tell them that they must come up with a better plan
to defend their ships and save the Achaean army.
But Phoenix can spend the night in my hut, and tomorrow
he can sail with me on my ship to our own dear country
if he wishes to, although I won't force him to come."

After he finished, everyone sat there in silence,
stunned by his words and the fierceness of his refusal.   430
At last the old hero Phoenix stood up to address them;
he was weeping in his distress for the Argive ships.
"If you are truly intent on sailing back home,
Achilles, and have no desire to save our ships
from being burned, since anger consumes your heart,
how then, dear child, could I be left here without you,
alone? Your father asked me to be your companion
on the day that he sent you from Phthia to Agamemnon,
a mere boy, with hardly any knowledge of war
or of assemblies, where speech can win great distinction.   440

He sent me with you to train you in these things, so that
your words would be excellent, and so would your deeds.
And that is why I wouldn't want to be left here,
dear child, not even if some god promised to scrape off
old age from these limbs and make me as energetic
as I was when I first left Hellas, fleeing the wrath
of my father, Amýntor, son of Órmenus, who
was infuriated at me because of his mistress,
a beautiful slave girl. He lusted for her and dishonored
his wife, my mother, so she kept clasping my knees   450
and imploring me to sleep with the girl and thus make her
despise the old man. I obeyed her and did the deed.
But my father found out and cursed me, invoking the dire
Furies, praying that I would never have children
to set on his lap; and the gods of the underworld,
Perséphonē and grim Hades, fulfilled his curse.
I could no longer bear to live in my father's palace
while he was so angry; but all my cousins and kinsmen
came at once, and they begged me not to leave home.
They slaughtered many plump sheep and lumbering oxen,   460
and many hogs, rich in fat, were stretched out to singe
on the flames, and much wine was drunk from the old man's jars.
For nine days they camped beside me and stayed up all night,
each taking his turn to guard me, and kept two fires
that never went out—one fire in the colonnade
of the outside courtyard, and one inside, on the porch
in front of my bedroom door. But on the tenth night,
I broke the lock and burst through the door and escaped,
easily jumping over the wall of the courtyard,
unseen by the men on guard or the servant women.   470
I fled across the whole width of Hellas until
I came to Phthia, where Peleus took me in
and treated me kindly. He loved me the way a father
loves his own son, his only child, who will someday
inherit the land he rules and all his possessions,
and he made me rich and the lord over many people,
the Dolópians, who live on the border of Phthia.
And my upbringing made you the godlike man that you are,

Achilles; I taught you and loved you with all my heart.
You would never want to go out with anyone else   480
to a banquet, and even at home you refused to eat
until you sat on my lap and I cut your food
into small pieces and held the wine to your lips,
and many a time you soaked the front of my tunic
with the wine you spat up. I took a great deal of care
and worked very hard over you, since I knew that the gods
were never going to grant me a child of my own.
So I tried to make *you* my son, Achilles, and hoped
that you would be there to care for me in old age.
Listen to me. Conquer your pride; do not   490
have such a pitiless heart. Even the gods
will sometimes bend, though they are far greater than we are
in excellence, honor, and strength; and yet when someone
has gone too far and done wrong, that person can move them
and turn their anger aside through his humble prayers,
his libations, and the sweet savor of burning flesh.
Prayers of repentance are daughters of mighty Zeus;
they are lame and wrinkled, their eyes are always averted,
and they make it their business to follow the steps of Madness.
Now Madness is strong and fast, and so she outruns them,   500
and she damages men in every country on earth;
but Prayers come hobbling behind and bring healing with them.
When a man, though offended, shows the proper respect
to these daughters of Zeus when they draw near, they help him greatly;
but when a man hardens his heart and turns them away,
they go to their father and beg him to order Madness
to follow that man, and he pays for it with his sorrow.
Therefore, Achilles, give these daughters of Zeus
the kind of respect that causes even the strongest
of minds to relent. If Lord Agamemnon hadn't   510
offered you gifts and promised still more to come,
but kept on being vindictive, I wouldn't ask you
to abandon your rage and come to defend the Achaeans,
no matter how dire their need. But as we have said,
he has offered you great restitution now and has promised
many gifts later and sent the chief men in the army

to plead with you, your best friends among the Argives.
So do not scorn the message that we have brought here.
Haven't you heard the tales of old, when great heroes
were possessed by violent anger and nevertheless   520
they were open to gifts, and persuasion could win them over?
Here is a story that shows this, from long ago;
you are all good friends, and I will tell you what happened.
The Curétēs and the Ætólians once were fighting
around the city of Cálydon; many men died.
The Ætólians were defending it, and the Curétēs
were determined that they would utterly lay it waste.
Ártemis was the one who had started the conflict,
infuriated that Œneus hadn't remembered
to offer her the first fruits from the hill in his orchard.   530
The other gods were enjoying their sacrifices,
and the daughter of Zeus was the only one he neglected;
whether on purpose or not, this was great madness.
In her fury, the goddess sent a monster against him,
a gigantic, murderous boar, with immense white tusks,
and it did much damage in Œneus's orchard lands,
uprooting many tall trees and flinging them over
with their roots sticking up in the air. But Œneus's son
Meleáger gathered a large band of huntsmen and hounds
from many cities, and hunted it down and killed it.   540
It was so enormous that more than a few were needed
to dispatch it, and not before it had laid many men
on the funeral pyre. But Ártemis raised an uproar
over the boar's huge head and its bristly hide;
the Curétēs and the Ætólians bitterly
argued about their portions, then went to war.
And as long as Meleáger was fighting against them,
the Curétēs lost, and they were even unable
to hold their position outside the walls of the city,
however many they were. But when anger took hold   550
of Meleáger, anger that swells the heart
in others as well, even in sensible men,
then he, overcome with fury at his own mother,
Althǽa, withdrew and stayed at home with his wife,

Cleopátra, the daughter of Marpéssa and Idas,
who was the strongest man on earth at the time
and who even took up his bow against Lord Apollo
for the sake of his wife, that girl with the lovely ankles;
the god had snatched her away, and Marpéssa was mourning
for her husband with the inconsolable cries   560
of the halcyon bird, the kingfisher—which is why
Cleopátra's father and mother would often call her
Hálcyon, because of her mother's grief.
Anyway, Meleáger stayed home with his wife,
nursing his heart-wrenching fury at his own mother,
who had bitterly cursed him, beseeching the gods in her pain
when Meleáger had killed her brother; she fell down
and pounded the earth, screaming and sobbing until
her bosom was soaked with tears, and she called on Hades
and Perséphonē, queen of the dead, to come kill her son,   570
and the Fury who walks in darkness, whose heart is brutal
and implacable, heard her prayer from the underworld.
Well, soon the enemy's war cries surged toward the city,
and their missiles came whizzing and crashing against the walls,
and the elders of the Ætólians begged Meleáger
to come out and help them, and so did the high priests;
they told him that he could choose the most fertile land
around the city and make it his own estate—
fifty acres, the richest plot he could mark off,
half of it to be vineyards and half open plowland.   580
His father as well, the old warrior Œneus, implored him
and stood at the bedroom's threshold and pounded the door.
His sisters and mother begged him, but he refused;
his comrades-in-arms and dearest friends begged him too;
but none of them could persuade him to change his mind
till rocks and spears were bombarding his very bedroom
and the fierce Curétēs were swarming over the walls
and their torches were setting fire to the great city.
Then Cleopátra, sobbing, begged Meleáger
to come out, and she reminded him of the horrors   590
that happen to those whose city falls, how the men
are slaughtered and the whole city is burned to the ground

and the women and children are carried away by strangers.
When he heard her say this, his heart was touched, and he armed
and went out to fight, and he saved the Ætólians
from destruction, after succumbing to his own anger.
But nobody gave him the great reward he was promised;
although he had rescued them all, he got nothing for it.
Dear boy, don't think like that; don't let some malignant
spirit turn you that way. When the ships are burning,   600
it will be much harder to save them. So take the gifts
while they are still being offered, and the Achaeans
will honor you like a god. But if you keep waiting
and enter the battle without the gifts, then your honor
won't be as great, though you drive off the whole Trojan army."

Then, in response to these words, Achilles said,
"Phoenix, old friend, dear father, whom I respect
with all my heart, I have no need of this honor.
I already possess the greatest honor, I think,
by the will of Zeus. That honor will always be with me,   610
as long as the breath of life remains in my chest
and the strength in my legs. And there is another thing:
Don't attempt to weaken my resolution
with your groans and tears, which are only serving the purpose
of Agamemnon, that hero. You never should take
his side, or you run the risk that my love for you
will turn into hatred. Rather, you ought to join me
in hurting the man who hurts *me*. Odysseus and Ajax
can deliver my message to Agamemnon; but you
stay here and sleep in a soft bed. When dawn arises,   620
we will think about whether to sail home or stay on in Troy."

And with his eyebrows, he gave a sign to Patroclus
to make up a bed for Phoenix, so that the others
would leave the hut right away. Then Ajax spoke up:
"Noble son of Laértes, resourceful Odysseus,
come. It is clear that our mission hasn't succeeded,
on this trip at least. We must quickly report the news
to the Argive commanders, however unwelcome it is;

they are sitting and waiting for us. I see that Achilles
has hardened his heart. He hasn't listened. He won't   630
be reasonable. He doesn't honor the friendship
we honored him with, above others. He is relentless.
And yet a man will accept due reparations
for his brother or son, even from someone who killed him,
and the killer stays on at home, having paid enough,
and the family's anger is held back once they receive
the blood-price. But not you. The gods have put in your breast
a perverse, implacable spirit, and all because
of a girl—one girl—though now we offer you seven
outstandingly fine ones, and much more into the bargain.   640
So be gracious to us, and remember the welcome you owe us.
We have come here representing the Danäan army,
and we are not only your guests but your best friends too."

In response to what he had just heard, Achilles said,
"Ajax, my friend, great leader of the Achaeans,
I agree with every point that you have just made.
And yet my heart swells with anger whenever I think
of the way Agamemnon treated me with contempt
in front of the army, as if I were some filthy
tramp or some outcast who has no rights. So go back now   650
and deliver this message: Say that I will not fight
till Hector slaughters his way through the Argives and hurls
fire on the ships and reaches the Myrmidons' camp.
But when he gets anywhere near my hut and my black ship,
I think that he will be stopped, however he rages."

At these words, each of them took a two-handled cup
and poured a libation. Then they walked back to the ships
with Odysseus leading the way. Meanwhile Patroclus
gave commands to his comrades and to the slave girls
to quickly prepare a comfortable bed for Phoenix.   660
They obeyed and set out a bed for him, just as he told them,
with sheepskins, covers, and sheets of the finest linen.
Then the old man lay down and waited for morning.
And Achilles slept in the innermost part of the hut;

by his side lay a woman whom he had taken from Lesbos,
Phorbas's daughter, beautiful Diomédē.
Patroclus lay near the opposite wall, and he too
had a woman lying beside him, the lovely Iphis,
a gift from Achilles after he captured Scyros.

When the envoys arrived at the hut of Lord Agamemnon,   670
the Achaean commanders stood up and from all sides
they drank to their health from golden cups, then began
to question them. Agamemnon was first to speak:
"Tell me, Odysseus, great glory of the Achaeans,
is he willing to save our ships from the enemy's fire?
Or does he refuse, because rage still grips his proud heart?"

Then Odysseus stood before Agamemnon and said,
"Most glorious son of Atreus, king of men,
that man is not willing to quench his rage. He is filled
with even more rage and rejects both you and your gifts.   680
'Figure it out for yourself,' he says, 'with the others—
how you can save the ships and the whole army.'
As for himself, he threatens that in the morning
he will load his ships and launch them upon the sea.
And he said that his advice to the rest of the leaders
is to sail back home, since now there is not a chance
of capturing Ilion; Zeus is shielding the city
with his own hand, and its people have gained back their courage.
That was his message, and these men here, who were with me,
will tell you the same thing—Ajax and the two heralds,   690
both sensible men. But Phoenix is spending the night there,
since Achilles commanded it, so that early tomorrow
he can sail with him on his ships to their own dear country
if he wishes to, although he won't force him to come."

After he finished, everyone sat there in silence
for a long time, despondent. Nobody said a word.
Finally, Diomedes stood up and spoke:
"Most glorious son of Atreus, Lord Agamemnon,
you should never have begged Achilles to fight, or offered

such generous gifts. He was arrogant even before this,   700
but now you have driven him deeper into his pride.
He will do what he wants; he will go or stay, and will fight
in his own sweet time, whenever the heart in his breast
urges him on and some god compels him to do it.
So listen now, and let us all do as I say.
You can go to bed, since you have gladdened your hearts
with food and wine, which give a man strength and courage.
And as soon as the flush of dawn appears in the heavens,
you, Agamemnon, should quickly deploy our forces,
in front of the ships, both soldiers and charioteers,   710
then urge them on, and fight in the front ranks yourself."

When they heard this, all the leaders assented and marveled
at the plain words of Diomedes, tamer of horses,
and they poured a libation. Then each man walked to his hut
and went to bed and received the blessing of sleep.

Book 11

When Dawn arose from her bed beside Lord Tithónus
to bring light to the immortal gods and to men,
Zeus sent Strife to the army of the Achaeans,
the cruel goddess, holding a symbol of war.
She stood beside Odysseus's huge black ship
in the midst of the camp, where a shout could reach to both ends,
to Ajax's huts and the huts of Achilles (each man
had trusted enough in his bravery to draw up
his ships on the beach at either end of the line).
The goddess stood there and let loose a hair-raising war cry   10
to urge the troops on, and within the heart of each soldier
she stirred up the strength to fight without any respite,
and at once the desire for war became sweeter to them
than sailing back in the ships to their own dear country.
And Agamemnon commanded them to get ready
for battle, and then he put on his glittering armor.
First, he strapped the bronze greaves to his lower legs
and fastened them onto his ankles with silver clasps.
Next, on his chest he put the finely wrought breastplate
that Cínyras once had given him when the great   20
report had reached distant Cyprus, that the Achaeans
were going to sail a fleet of warships to Troy,
and so he had made him a gift of the splendid breastplate.
It was inlaid with ten strips of dark-blue enamel, twelve
of gold, and twenty of tin; and some dark-blue snakes
stretched toward the neck, three on each side, like the rainbow
that Lord Zeus sets in the clouds as a sign for mortals.
Over his shoulders he slung his great gold-studded sword
and its silver scabbard, attached to its strap with gold rings.
And he took up his massive, finely wrought, furious shield,   30
a beautiful thing to behold, with its ten circles
of inlaid bronze and its twenty knobs of white tin
and, at the center, one knob of dark-blue enamel;
and the shield was crowned with the horrible face of the Gorgon,

whose glare makes men's blood run cold, and on either side
Terror and Panic were standing, her grim companions.
The shield-strap was made of silver, and all along it
slithered a dark-blue snake with three intertwined
heads growing out of a single neck, one of them facing
upward, the others turned to the right and the left.   40
And upon his head he put his bronze helmet, adorned
with two ridges, four plates, and a frightening horsehair crest.
He took two spears, with points of flesh-piercing bronze,
and his armor glittered far out and up to the heavens.
And Athena and Hera caused thunder to roll above him
in honor of the great king of golden Mycénæ.

Each fighter instructed his charioteer to hold
the horses in proper formation there at the trench,
and then they all swarmed across it, in their full armor,
and an irrepressible cry rose up in the dawn air.   50
Across the trench they gathered their ranks in advance
of the charioteers, who followed a little while after.
And Zeus stirred up a great panic among them and rained
drops of blood, because it was his intention
to hurl down to Hades the souls of many fighters.

At the rise of the plain the Trojan troops were arrayed
around Hector and Polydamas and Aeneas
and Anténor's three sons, Pólybus and Agénor
and young Ácamas. And Hector carried his shield
in the foremost ranks. He was just like the evening star   60
that suddenly glows through the dark clouds in all its splendor,
then sinks back behind them: so Hector would sometimes appear
among the front ranks and sometimes among the back ones,
exhorting the men to fight, and his whole body
glittered in bronze like the lightning of Father Zeus.

As reapers move toward each other from opposite sides
of a rich man's field that is thick with barley or wheat,
cutting down swaths, and the sheaves fall under their blades:
just so did the Trojans and Argives rush at each other,

cutting down men, and neither side would give way;   70
they were pressed close, head against head, raging like wolves.
And Strife, the grief-causing goddess, looked on with joy,
the only one of the gods who was there; all the others
were sitting at home with no part in the fighting, at ease
in their beautiful houses built on the folds of Olympus,
though they seethed with resentment, blaming their father, Zeus,
for wanting to give the victory to the Trojans.
But Zeus did not care. He drew away from the others
and sat down apart, enjoying his splendor, looking
out over Troy and the warships of the Achaeans   80
at the flash of bronze, at the killers and at the killed.

While it was morning, as long as the sun climbed higher,
the weapons of both sides pierced, and the men kept dying.
But at the hour when a woodcutter has his meal
in some mountain valley—it is midday, and his arms
ache from cutting the trees, and weariness weighs down
his muscles, and a desire for food overwhelms him—
the Danäans, with a cry that echoed to heaven,
broke through the lines. And Lord Agamemnon was first
to kill a man; he quickly cut down Biénor,   90
and then his companion, the charioteer Öíleus,
who had leaped from his car, but as he was rushing straight at him
Lord Agamemnon stabbed him between the eyes,
and the spear was not stopped by the heavy bronze of his helmet
but tore right through it and through the bone, and his brains
splattered inside the bronze, and he fell in the dust.

And Agamemnon left them there lying face upward,
their bare chests gleaming, once he had stripped off their tunics,
and he went on to cut down Isus and Ántiphus,
one Priam's bastard and one his legitimate son,   100
who were riding together, Isus holding the reins
and Ántiphus fighting beside him. They had been caught
by Achilles as they were tending their flocks; he had bound them
with willow shoots on one of the spurs of Mount Ida
and had set them free for a ransom. But now Agamemnon

hurled his spear and hit Isus above the nipple,
and his sword sliced into Ántiphus close to the ear
and knocked him out of the chariot. Then he stripped off
their armor and recognized them, for he had been
beside the ships when Achilles had brought them from Ida.   110
Just as a lion seizes two fawns in a thicket
and rips them to pieces, crushing their delicate bones
in his mighty jaws; their mother may be nearby,
but she herself shivers with dread and takes off, dashing
away through the forest, through the dense undergrowth,
drenched in sweat as she flies from the terrible beast:
so none of the Trojans could save these two from destruction
since they were panicked and running away themselves.

Then he cut down Hippólochus and Pisánder,
the sons of Antímachus, who, expecting much gold   120
from Paris, had once dissuaded the Trojan assembly
from giving back Helen to Menelaus. His sons
were the young men that Agamemnon now met. Having lost
control of their car, they frantically tried to pull back
their rearing horses; the reins had dropped from their hands,
and the horses were panic-stricken. Lord Agamemnon
rushed at them like a lion, and the two brothers,
trapped inside their chariot, begged him for mercy:
"Son of Atreus, take us alive. We promise
a worthy ransom. Antímachus has great treasures,   130
many of them, that lie there stored in his house,
of bronze and gold and iron skillfully worked.
From these our father will give you a huge ransom
if he learns that we are alive by the Danäan ships."

Thus, in tears, they begged the king for their lives
with pitiful words. But the answer they got had no pity.
"If you indeed are the sons of Antímachus,
who once in the assembly, when Menelaus
came to Troy on an embassy with Odysseus,
urged the Trojans to murder him on the spot,   140
now you will pay in full for your father's offense."

With this he knocked Pisánder out of the car,
hitting him in the chest with his spear, and he fell
backward and crashed to the ground. Hippólochus jumped out
and tried to flee, but he cut him down with his sword,
then sliced off his arms and his head, and he kicked the torso
and sent it rolling away through the crowd like a log.

He charged ahead, and the other Achaeans followed,
wherever most Trojans were running away in panic.
Foot soldiers cut down foot soldiers, charioteers   150
killed charioteers—a dust cloud rose from them, churned
into the air by the horses' thundering hooves—
and everywhere there was slaughter, bronze against bronze.
And Lord Agamemnon kept charging ahead and killing
wherever he went and urging the Argives to follow.
And as a fire spreads through the thick dry woodland,
and the high winds carry it everywhere, and the bushes
blaze up and fall as the ravaging flames overwhelm them:
just so did the Trojan troops fall, and many horses
pulled empty chariots that rattled across the plain,   160
and they longed for their drivers; but these lay dead on the ground,
far dearer now to the vultures than to their wives.
And Zeus drew Hector away from the missiles and dust,
from the slaughter and bloody mayhem and deafening uproar,
while Agamemnon pressed on with his piercing war cries.

The Trojans ran back, over the plain, past the tomb
of Ilus and past the fig tree, desperate to reach
the city; and Agamemnon was at their heels,
bellowing, and his hands were dripping with gore.
But when they came to the Scaean Gates and the oak tree,   170
they stopped and waited until the stragglers caught up,
for some were still being driven across the plain,
stampeding like cows when a lion attacks at night
and the whole herd panics; he chases one down and leaps
onto her back and cracks her neck in his jaws,
then laps up her blood and gorges himself on her entrails:
just so Agamemnon pursued them and kept on killing

the men in the rear as, panic-stricken, they fled.
And many were flung from their chariots, headlong, sprawling,
by Lord Agamemnon's spear as he raged through the ranks.   180

But when he approached the city and its steep wall,
the father of men and gods descended from heaven
and, holding a thunderbolt, took his seat on Mount Ida.
And he ordered golden-winged Iris to go down to Troy:
"Hurry now, Iris, and give this message to Hector:
As long as he sees Agamemnon in the front ranks,
raging and wreaking havoc among the Trojans,
I want him to keep back and tell the rest of the army
to bear the brunt of the fighting. But when Agamemnon
is hit by a spear or an arrow and mounts his car,   190
I will then grant Hector the power to kill and to keep on
killing until he reaches the Danäan ships
and the sun sinks down and holy darkness arrives."

Iris obeyed his words, and as swift as the wind
she flew from the heights of Ida to sacred Troy.
There she found Hector standing among the horses
and inlaid chariots, and she came up and said,
"Son of Priam, peer of the gods in wisdom,
Father Zeus has sent me to you with this message:
As long as you see Agamemnon in the front ranks,   200
raging and wreaking havoc among the Trojans,
he wants you to keep back and tell the rest of the army
to bear the brunt of the fighting. But when Agamemnon
is hit by a spear or an arrow and mounts his car,
Zeus will grant you the power to kill and to keep on
killing until you reach the Danäan ships
and the sun sinks down and holy darkness arrives."
And swift as the wind, the goddess left him. Then Hector
leaped to the ground from his chariot in full armor
and, holding a pair of spears, he ranged through the army,   210
spurring the men on, arousing their spirit for battle.
And they rallied and turned to stand against the Achaeans,
who on their side, opposite, reinforced their battalions.

As the armies stood facing each other, Lord Agamemnon
was the first man to charge, and rushed in ahead of the rest.

Tell me now, Muses, who have your homes on Olympus,
who was the first to come out and face Agamemnon?
Iphídamas, son of Anténor, a huge man
who had grown up in Thrace, the land of abundant flocks.
His grandfather Cisses, his mother Theáno's father,   220
had raised him in his own palace, and when the boy
was a young man, his grandfather tried to keep him at home
by offering him his daughter's hand. But as soon
as he married, he set out, straight from the bridal chamber
in pursuit of fame when he heard that the Argives were coming,
and he sailed to the war, accompanied by twelve ships,
which he left at Percóté, and traveled on foot to Troy;
and now, from the ranks, he strode out to face Agamemnon.
When the two of them had advanced to within close range,
Lord Agamemnon hurled his spear, but it missed him;   230
and Iphídamas stabbed him, inches below his breastplate,
leaning into the spear thrust with all his might.
But he did not pierce the glittering belt, and the spear point
bent like a piece of lead when it hit the silver.
And Agamemnon grabbed hold of the spear shaft and pulled it
with a lion's fury and wrenched it out of his hands,
then slashed his neck with his sword, and he crumpled to earth.
And so he lay down and entered the sleep of bronze,
poor fellow, trying to help his countrymen, far
from his new bride, who gave him no joy, although he had given   240
a hundred cows for her hand and had promised a thousand
goats and sheep as well from his numberless flocks.
And Agamemnon stripped him and left him there naked
and carried his armor into the Danäan ranks.

When Coön, the eldest son of Anténor, saw
his dear brother fall, an overpowering sorrow
clouded his eyes. He came up, unseen, to one side
of Lord Agamemnon and stabbed him below the elbow
on his forearm. The spear point drove through the flesh, and he shuddered

with agony; yet he did not stop fighting or pull back,   250
but holding his wind-toughened spear, he charged straight at Coön,
who was dragging his brother's corpse back into the ranks
by the feet and shouting for help; but as he pulled it,
Agamemnon stabbed him, thrusting under his shield.
The spear drove into his flesh, and he crumpled to earth,
and Agamemnon cut off his head, and it fell
onto his brother. In this way, Anténor's sons
filled out their fated span and went down to Hades.

As long as the warm blood gushed from his wound, Agamemnon
kept on attacking with spear and sword and huge rocks.   260
But when the wound started to dry and the blood hardened,
sharp pains came over him, just like the pains that stab
a woman in labor, sent by the spirits of childbirth,
the daughters of Hera in charge of those violent pangs.
He mounted his car and told his charioteer
to drive to the ships, for his agony was intense.
And he called with a mighty shout that moved all who heard him:
"My friends, commanders and captains of the Achaeans,
you are the ones who must keep the fight from our ships,
since Zeus in his wisdom obliges me to withdraw now."   270
At these words, the charioteer whipped the horses; they turned
and made for the camp, and eagerly they flew onward.
Their chests were covered with foam, and dust caked their bellies
as they carried the wounded king away from the plain.

When Hector saw that Agamemnon was leaving,
he called out to the army in a loud voice:
"Trojan, Lycian, Dardánian soldiers and friends,
be men now. Forward; remember your fighting spirit.
The best of their leaders is gone, and Zeus will now give me
victory. Drive your horses straight at the Achaeans   280
so that by tonight you may win even greater glory."
With these words he stirred up the courage of every man.
As a hunter sets his hounds on a boar or a lion:
just so did Hector set the Trojan commanders
on the Argives, and he himself was in the front ranks,

exhilarated. He fell on the enemy like
a rampaging storm that swoops down onto the sea
and lashes the dark-blue waters into a fury,
and many huge waves shoot up, and high in the air
the spray is flung in the howl of the wandering wind: 290
so thick and fast did the men fall in Hector's attack.

There would have been havoc and inescapable slaughter
and the Argives would have been hurled back onto their ships
if Odysseus had not called out to Diomedes,
"Son of Tydeus, where is our fighting spirit?
Come here and take your stand by my side. It would be
an unbearable shame if Hector set fire to our ships."

And Diomedes answered him, "I will come,
but it will not do us much good, since Zeus has decided
to give victory to the Trojans and not to us."   300
With this he knocked Thymbræus out of his car,
hitting him with a spear thrust on the left nipple,
and Odysseus cut down Molíon, his charioteer,
and they left them lying there—neither would fight again.
And they moved through the enemy ranks, spreading great havoc,
as when a pair of wild boars wheel round in a fury
and with knife-sharp tusks tear into the dogs that pursue them:
just so did they cut down the Trojans, and the Achaeans
were given a moment of rest in their flight before Hector.

And then they captured a chariot with its riders,   310
the bravest men from Percóte, the two sons of Merops,
an excellent prophet; he had forbidden his sons
to go to the war. But they would not listen to him,
because the spirits of death were driving them onward.
And Diomedes killed them and stripped off their armor,
while Hippódamus and Hypírochus fell to Odysseus.

Then Zeus, looking down from Mount Ida, intensified
the slaughter, and the two sides kept killing each other.
Diomedes wounded Agástrophus, son of Pæon,

on the hip with his spear. He could not escape; his car   320
was nowhere near him—this was a terrible madness;
his attendant was holding the horses somewhere at a distance,
and he fought in the front ranks on foot, and it cost him his life.

But Hector caught sight of them through the ranks, and he charged
with a blood-chilling shout, and the mighty Trojan battalions
followed. And Diomedes shuddered to see him,
and he turned to Odysseus, who was nearby, and he said,
"Look, Hector is bearing down on us like a huge wave.
We must stand our ground and drive him off." And he drew
his long spear back and aimed and threw it at Hector,   330
and he hit the top of his helmet, but bronze glanced off bronze,
and the spear did not reach his flesh; it was stopped by the massive
hollow-eyed helmet Apollo had given him once.
Hector fell to his knees, and he stayed there, propped up
with one hand on the ground, and darkness covered his eyes.
But while Diomedes was following his spear's flight
through the front lines to the place where he saw it falling,
Hector revived; he climbed up onto his car
and drove back into the crowd to escape destruction.
And Diomedes ran after him and called out,   340
"Once again you have escaped, you cowardly dog,
though death came close; but your precious Apollo saved you.
Do you pray to him very meekly before you venture
to walk out amid the hum of our hurtling spears?
I will make sure to finish you off the next time I meet you
if I too have a god helping me. But for now
I will see what other Trojans I can bring down."

As Diomedes proceeded to strip off the armor
from the corpse of Agástrophus—the glittering breastplate,
the many-plied shield, and the massive helmet—Prince Paris   350
drew back his bowstring, leaning against a pillar
on the burial mound of the son of Dárdanus, Ilus.
He carefully aimed, and the arrow flew from his bow,
and it pierced the instep of Diomedes' right foot,
went through it, and stuck in the ground. And with a laugh

Paris jumped out from his hiding place and exulted:
"My arrow flew straight! You are wounded! I only wish
I had pierced your heart or your guts and taken you down,
so that we, who shudder before you like bleating goats
in front of a lion, could have a brief rest from this slaughter."   360

Then, with no hint of fear, Diomedes said,
"You weakling, you girl-crazed seducer, you perfumed sissy,
why don't you step out and fight me now man to man,
directly, without the help of your cowardly arrows?
You are boasting in vain. You have barely scratched me. Your shot
is no more painful than if a woman had hit me
or a child; a half-wit's arrow has a dull point.
When *I* wound a man, it is fatal. Even a slight
touch of my spear can strike a man dead on the spot,
and his widow's nails tear her cheeks in her desolation,   370
and his children are orphans; he reddens the ground with his blood
and rots there; and carrion birds, not women, surround him."
As he finished speaking, Odysseus came up and stood
covering him, and Diomedes sat down
and pulled out the arrow, and fierce pain shot through his flesh.
And he mounted his car and told his charioteer
to drive to the ships, for his agony was intense.

Odysseus was left alone; not one of the Argives
stood by him, since all of them had panicked and fled.
"What should I do?" he thought. "It would be a disgrace   380
to flee because I am so outnumbered, but worse
to be trapped alone, since Zeus has scattered my comrades.
But why do I need to debate these things with myself?
I know that only a coward retreats from the fighting;
a brave man must stand firm, ready to kill or be killed."
And while he pondered, the ranks of the Trojans advanced
and surrounded him, but soon they came to regret it.
As dogs and hunters crowd a wild boar from all sides
when he charges out of a thicket, whetting his tusks,
and as they rush to surround him they hear his tusks gnashing,   390
but they stand firm before him, dangerous though he is:

just so did the Trojans come crowding around Odysseus.
But *he* charged first, at Déïopítes, and hit him
with a downward thrust of his spear, which went through his shoulder.
And then he killed Thoön and Énnomus; after these
he stabbed Chersídamas under his shield, in the crotch,
at the moment when he was jumping down from his car;
and he fell in the dust, clawing the earth with his nails.

He left them there, and then with his spear he wounded
Charops, the son of Híppasus, Socus's brother.   400
And Socus ran up to shield him, taking a stand
in front of his fallen brother, and said, "Odysseus,
we know of your fame, and we know of your endless cunning,
but today you will have to kill me along with my brother
if you want to boast, or else you will die by my hand."
After he finished, he lunged at Odysseus; the spear point
tore through his shield and through his finely wrought breastplate
and cut off a chunk of flesh from his side, but Athena
kept it from going further on, through his organs.

And when he saw that the spear had not penetrated   410
a vital place, he stepped back and said to Socus,
"You poor fool, headlong fate is about to seize you.
Although you have wounded me now and stopped me from fighting,
I promise you that today is your last day on earth;
you will soon be cut down by my spear and grant me the triumph
and will have to give up your soul to Death, the pale horseman."
When he heard this, Socus was frightened and turned to run,
but just as he turned, Odysseus thrust his long spear
through his back, between the shoulders, and out through his chest,
and he fell with a crash, and Odysseus shouted in triumph: 420
"Death was too quick for you, Socus; you haven't escaped it.
Poor fool, your father and mother are far away
and won't come to Troy to close your eyes, and the vultures
will hack at your flesh as they sit on you, flapping their wings.
But I, when I die, will be burned with all the due honors."
With these words Odysseus began to pull out the spear
from his own side and then from his shield, and the blood gushed

out from the wound so fast that he was appalled.

As soon as the Trojans saw that Odysseus was bleeding,
they gave a tremendous battle cry and moved closer;   430
but he took a step backward and called for his comrades to help.
Three times he shouted, as loudly as lungs can call out;
three times Menelaus heard him and knew his voice.
And quickly he said to Ajax, who stood beside him:
"Ajax, my friend, I hear the shouts of Odysseus;
it sounds as though he is cut off and overwhelmed.
Quickly now, we must charge through the mass of fighters
and save him, or else the Trojans will bring him down.
Brave man though he is, he is stranded, and I am afraid;
if he dies, it will be a great loss for the Achaeans."   440
With these words he led the way forward, and Ajax went with him.
They found Odysseus, and all around him the Trojans
were swarming, like jackals who close in around a huge stag
that a hunter's arrow has wounded; the stag has escaped,
running as long as the warm blood flows and his legs
can carry him; but at last his strength is depleted,
and he falls in a shadowy grove in the mountains, and soon
the jackals tear him to pieces; but some god sends
a marauding lion; the jackals scatter in fear,
and the lion stands there, feasting upon the carcass: 450
just so did the Trojans close in on Odysseus from all sides
as, constantly lunging and feinting, he kept death at bay;
but when Ajax came up, his body-shield like a tower,
and stood beside him, the Trojans took fright and scattered.
And Menelaus grabbed hold of Odysseus's arm
and led him out of the fighting, while his attendant
drove up his chariot. Ajax rushed forward and killed
Dóryclus, one of King Priam's bastards, then stabbed
Lysánder, Pándocus, Pýrasus, and Pylártes.
Just as a river swollen by winter rains   460
hurtles down from the mountains, its headlong current
tearing up mighty oak and pine trees and sweeping
huge piles of driftwood out to the sea: so Ajax
swept through the wide plain slaughtering men and horses.

But Hector was unaware of this, since he was fighting
on the far left by the banks of the river Scamander
where the carnage was thickest and where an immense, unceasing
uproar arose near Idómeneus and Nestor.
In this place Hector was causing great devastation
with his spear and chariot, cutting down many young men.   470
Still, the Achaeans would never have yielded before him
had Paris not put an end to Macháon's brave feats
with a three-barbed arrow that hit him in his right shoulder.
Then the Achaeans were frightened, because they thought
that the battle might shift and he would surely be killed.
And quickly Idómeneus turned to Nestor and said,
"Son of Neleus, glory of the Achaeans,
mount your chariot at once, so that Macháon
can climb up beside you, and drive to the ships, right away.
A healer is worth a battalion of men, for his skill   480
in cutting out arrows and for his knowledge of herbs."
Nestor hurried to follow his comrade's instructions.
He mounted his car and carefully helped Macháon,
the Argives' great healer, up into it by his side,
then touched his whip to the backs of the horses, and gladly
they flew to the ships, for their hearts were eager to be there.

Cebríones, as he stood in the car with Hector,
saw that their troops were being cut down, and he said,
"Hector, while we are fighting on the far edge
of the battle, the rest of our army is panicking; Ajax   490
is pushing them back; I know him from the huge shield
that he is carrying. Hurry: we need to drive
to the battle's center, where most men are killing and dying
and where an unceasing uproar fills the whole sky."
After he finished speaking, he lashed the horses
with his whistling whip, and on hearing the crack, the pair
galloped ahead through the thick of the battle, trampling
over the bodies and shields of those who had fallen;
and the axle below and the chariot rails were splattered
with the blood flung up by the horses' hooves and the wheel rims.   500
And Hector tore through the mass of soldiers and plunged

into the fighting and caused a terrible panic
among the Achaeans and slaughtered many brave men.

Now Zeus instilled a great dread in the heart of Ajax,
and he stood in a daze and slung his huge oxhide shield
over his back and, glancing around like a wild beast,
began to retreat, constantly looking backward
and moving little by little, step by short step.
Just as a lion is driven off from a stockyard
by dogs and farmers, who stay up all night to prevent him   510
from killing the pick of the herd; now, greedy for flesh,
he charges ahead, but in vain—a volley of spears
falls all around him, blazing torches approach,
and he backs off, frightened, although he still longs to break in,
and at dawn he goes slinking away with a sullen heart:
so Ajax backed off from the Trojans, sullen at heart
and against his will, since he feared for the Argive ships.
And as when a donkey is led by some boys down a road—
a stubborn beast, on whom many sticks have been broken—
and they pass a field, and his strength is too much for the boys,   520
and he willfully turns in to ravage the high-standing grain,
and although they beat him with sticks, their strength is too feeble,
they manage to drive him out with much effort, and only
when he has eaten his fill: just so did the Trojans
keep crowding Ajax and thrusting at him with their spears.
He would sometimes resist and, with a tremendous effort,
wheel around and keep all the soldiers at bay,
and then, once more, he would turn in retreat. Thus, standing
midway between the Trojans and the Achaeans,
he single-handedly stopped the advance to the ships.   530
Some of the enemy spears bit into his shield,
but many spears, hungry to glut themselves on his flesh,
stuck in the ground before they could ever reach him.

And when Eurýpylus saw him attacked by the thick
barrage of missiles, he came up and stood beside him
and aimed his bright spear and let it fly; and it hit
Apisáon, son of Phásius, in the belly

and pierced his liver. At once he crumpled to earth,
and Eurýpylus charged and began to strip off his armor.
But when Paris saw him, he hit him in the right thigh   540
with an arrow; the shaft snapped off, and great pain shot through him,
and he moved back into the crowd to escape destruction
and called with a mighty shout that moved all who heard him:
"My friends, commanders and captains of the Achaeans,
quickly now, make a stand; help me save Ajax.
He is fighting alone. Spears and arrows are raining
upon him; I do not think that he can survive
like this. So hurry, come to his rescue and save him."
And when they heard Eurýpylus say this, they came
and rallied around him, leaning their shields on their shoulders   550
and holding their spears out. Ajax made his way toward them,
then turned and took a firm stand when he reached his comrades.
And so they continued to fight, like a blazing fire.

Meanwhile the mares of Neleus, drenched with sweat,
brought Nestor out of the battle along with Macháon.
Achilles saw them come in as he stood on the stern
of his huge ship, watching the slaughter and the retreat,
and quickly he said to his dear companion Patroclus,
"Noble son of Menœ́tius, joy of my heart,
now the Achaeans will have to come here and beg me   560
to return to the fighting—look how dire their need is.
But hurry and go to Nestor and ask him who
this man is that he is bringing out of the battle.
From behind, he looks just like the healer Macháon,
but I am not sure; the horses were galloping past me
at such a great speed that I couldn't see the man's face."
Patroclus was quick to do what his comrade had asked
and set out running briskly alongside the ships.

When those two at last arrived at the hut of Nestor,
they stepped from the chariot onto the bountiful earth,   570
and Nestor's attendant Eurýmedon unyoked the horses,
and the two men stood in the breeze by the seashore, drying
the sweat from their tunics. Then they went into the hut,

and a beautiful woman named Hecamédē prepared
a drink for them; Nestor had won her at Ténedos
when Achilles took and plundered it; she was the daughter
of Arsínoüs; the Achaeans had singled her out
as a prize for the old hero, since he was always
the most astute among them at planning their battles.
First she pushed up a beautiful polished table   580
with feet of dark-blue enamel, and on it she placed
a bronze dish with an onion as spice for the drink,
and golden honey and barley cakes, and beside them
a glorious cup that Nestor had brought from home;
it was studded with golden rivets and had four handles,
and on top of each of them, two golden doves were feeding.
Most other men would not have been able to lift it
when it was full, but Nestor, old as he was,
could easily pick it up. In this cup the woman
poured them some Prámnian wine, upon which she grated   590
goat cheese with a bronze grater and sprinkled white barley,
and when the mixture was ready, she urged them to drink.
Once they had drunk and quenched their extreme thirst
and after they had begun to speak to each other,
Patroclus appeared in the doorway, a godlike man.
Nestor saw him and rose from his chair and led him
in by the hand and invited him to sit down,
but Patroclus stood there, declining the invitation:
"This is no time for sitting, my lord; he is proud
and may take offense if I linger—the one who sent me.   600
He told me to find out whom you have brought here wounded;
but now I can see for myself that it is Macháon.
I will go back and tell Achilles. You understand
how terrifying a man he can be, my lord;
he might be quick to blame even one who is blameless."

Then Nestor responded, "Why is Achilles suddenly
concerned about who has been wounded? He can't imagine
the grief that we are all feeling now. Our best men
are lying in pain inside their huts: Diomedes
has been shot by an arrow, Odysseus and Agamemnon   610

have been stabbed, and this man, whom I just brought in from the fighting—
he too has been shot by a Trojan or Lycian arrow.
Yet Achilles, great warrior though he is, has no pity
for the Danäans. Is he waiting till we are helpless
and our ships have begun to light up with enemy flames
and all of us are cut down, one after the other?
And what can I do? I am not what I used to be.
If only I were as young and strong as I was
when a quarrel broke out between the Epéans and us
over a raid; I killed Itýmoneus then,   620
the son of Hypírochus, from the city of Elis.
I was riding off with the herds we had seized in reprisal,
and when he attempted to stop me, I threw a spear
and hit him as he was galloping up with his men.
He fell to the ground, and his comrades rode off in terror.
We rounded up a magnificent haul—fifty
herds of cattle, and that many flocks of sheep,
and that many droves of pigs, and that many wide-ranging
herds of goats, and a hundred and fifty bay horses,
all of them mares, many with foals still suckling.   630
At night we drove them into the city of Pylos,
and Neleus rejoiced that I had taken so much,
though I was a young man out on my first campaign.
The next day at dawn, the heralds proclaimed that any
man who was owed a debt in Elis should come;
and the leaders of the Pýlians gathered together
and divided the spoils. (The Epéans owed a great deal
to many of us, since we in Pylos were few
and greatly weakened—Héracles, years before,
had sapped our strength by killing all our best men.   640
Neleus had had twelve sons, and I was the only
one who was left; my eleven brothers had died.
Emboldened by this, the Epéans began to plunder
our farmlands, and they grew constantly more aggressive.)
Now, from the spoils, Neleus, my father, chose
a herd of cows and a large flock of sheep—three hundred,
with their shepherds as well. For he too was owed a great debt:
four swift prize-winning horses along with their car,

which had gone to the games at Elis to run in a race
with a tripod as prize; but Augéas, king of men,   650
had kept them there and sent back their driver, heartsick
for his horses, and also sent an insulting message.
Neleus, still angry, took many spoils for himself,
but he gave the rest to the people, to be divided
so that none of them left unhappy, without his fair share.
And as we were dealing with this, and throughout the city
we were offering sacrifices to all the gods,
on the third day the Epéans attacked with a large force,
galloping in with great speed, among them the twins
Ctéatus and EÚrytus, sons of Actor,   660
who, in those days, were still boys, untested in battle.
There is a steep hill-town called Thryoéssa
above the river Alphéüs, at the far edge
of Pylos. This town they besieged; they were eager to take it,
and they ravaged the plain. But Athena came down to warn us,
hurrying in the night from Olympus, proclaiming
that we must prepare for war, and she raised an army
of Pýlians who were eager to fight. My father
forbade me to go into battle; he hid my horses
and said that I was too inexperienced in warfare.   670
Nevertheless, with Athena's help I surpassed
all the charioteers, though I was on foot.
The stream Minÿéos empties into the sea
near Arénē; here the Pýlian horsemen and I
waited for dawn, when the ranks of foot soldiers flowed in.
From there we marched with all speed, in our full armor,
and by midday we reached the Alphéüs. There we offered
a magnificent sacrifice to almighty Zeus,
and then a bull to Alphéüs and one to Poseidon
and to Athena a cow that had never been yoked;   680
and we all ate the sacred meal in our battalions,
then lay down to sleep by the river, with every man
wearing his war gear. Meanwhile the Epéans
had surrounded the city, determined to overrun it;
but before they could, we forced them into a battle.
When the sun came up and shone above the horizon,

we prayed to Zeus and Athena, then we attacked.
I was the first to kill a man in the fighting
and take his horses: Múlius, son-in-law
to King Augéas, wed to his eldest daughter,   690
golden-haired Agaméde, who knew the secrets
of every healing herb that the wide earth bears.
As he was charging, I brought him down with a spear thrust;
he fell to the ground, and I jumped up onto his car
and took my place in the front ranks, and the Epéans
panicked and fled, scattering every which way
when they saw him fall, their captain and bravest man.
I charged at them in my fury like a black whirlwind,
and I captured fifty chariots, and from each one
two warriors bit the earth, cut down by my spear.   700
And now I would even have killed the twin sons of Actor
if their true father, Poseidon the Earthshaker, hadn't
veiled them in mist and carried them out of the battle.
Well, Lord Zeus gave us the victory on that day,
and we chased them across the plain, and we killed the men
and gathered their armor, till we had driven our horses
to Buprásion and the Olénian rock and the hill
of Alésion, where Athena turned back our army.
And after I killed my last man and left him, our troops
drove their chariots back to Pylos, where all   710
gave glory to Zeus among gods; among men, to Nestor.
That is who I once used to be—if that life
was ever real. But Achilles' bravery, far
from profiting others, profits only himself,
and soon, I think, he will shed bitter tears, when his comrades
have been cut to pieces and it is too late to save them.
Dear friend, Menœtius gave you some good advice
on the day that he sent you from Phthia to Agamemnon.
Odysseus and I were present then, and we heard it;
we had come to the house of Peleus on our journey   720
to gather an army all through the land of Achaea.
There we found Menœtius, your honored father,
and you and Achilles; and the old warrior Peleus
was burning to Zeus a bull's thighbones, wrapped in its fat,

out in the courtyard, holding a golden cup
and pouring out drops of wine as the sacrifice blazed.
You two were carving the meat, and when we arrived
and stood in the gateway, Achilles leaped up, astonished,
and led us in by the hand and told us to sit,
and he set before us all that a guest could wish for.   730
And when we had taken our pleasure in eating and drinking,
I spoke to you both and urged you to come to the war.
You were both eager to go, and your fathers gave you
much good advice. Old Peleus told Achilles
always to be the bravest, above all others,
and your father, Menœtius, gave you these wise instructions:
'My child, Achilles is nobler than you by birth,
and he is far stronger than you are, but you are the elder,
and your role is to advise him with sensible words,
and he will listen and profit from what you tell him.'   740
That was your father's message, which you have forgotten.
But even now, you might speak like this to Achilles
in the hope that you might get him to change. Who knows?—
if all goes well, you might move his heart with your words,
since a dear friend's advice can be a powerful thing.
But if some heavenly sign has been holding him back,
some prophecy from Zeus that his mother has brought him,
then let him at least send *you* out, and let the rest
of the Myrmidons follow, and you can be a great light
to all the Argives. And let him give you his armor   750
to wear into battle. The Trojans will take you for him
and hold off from fighting, and then we can catch our breath,
worn down as we all are. You and your men are fresh
and the Trojans exhausted—you could soon drive them back
to the walls of their city, away from our ships and huts."

These were his words, and they made Patroclus's heart
beat faster, and he went running along the shore
to Achilles. But when he came to Odysseus's ships,
where the place of assembly was and the public tribunal
and the altars built to the gods, Eurýpylus met him.   760
He was limping out of the battle; the sweat streamed down

from his head and shoulders, and out of his painful wound
the dark blood gushed, though his spirit was firm. Patroclus
felt pity for him and said with tears in his eyes,
"You wretched commanders and captains of the Achaeans,
you are fated, it seems, to feed the wild dogs of Troy
with your white flesh, far from your friends and your own dear country.
But tell me, Eurýpylus, is there a chance that we
will still be able to hold back Hector's fierce onslaught,
or will we be slaughtered today by his terrible spear?"   770

Eurýpylus said, "No longer, my lord Patroclus,
does our army have any hope of avoiding that fate.
There is no choice now but to die beside the black ships.
All those who, before this, have been our best fighters
are lying inside their huts in great pain, wounded
by arrows or spears, and Hector's power keeps growing.
But at least you can help *me*. Take me back to my ship;
cut the arrowhead out of my thigh, and wash off
the blood with warm water, and spread herbs onto the wound.
They say you have learned the use of them from Achilles,   780
who was taught by Chiron, the most humane of the centaurs.
As for Macháon and Podalírius,
our healers—the first is lying in pain in his hut,
in desperate need himself of a capable healer,
while the other is still on the battlefield, under attack."

And Patroclus said to Eurýpylus, "How did we get
caught in such a position? What should we do?
I have been sent to deliver an urgent message
from Nestor, our eminent counselor, to Achilles.
Still, I won't abandon you here in your trouble."   790

With these words he grasped his comrade around the waist
and walked him back to his hut. And when his attendant
saw him, he spread some oxhides for him on the ground,
and Patroclus had him lie down, and with a sharp knife
he cut the arrowhead out of his thigh, and he washed off
the blood with warm water, and taking a bitter root,

he crushed it between his hands, and then he applied it
to the gashed flesh, and it took away all his pain,
and the wound began to dry up, and the blood stopped flowing.

Book 12

As Patroclus, inside the hut, was tending the wound
of Eurýpylus, all the others, Argives and Trojans,
fought on ferociously. And the Achaean trench,
it seemed, would not hold the enemy back much longer,
or the wall in front of it, which they had built to defend
their ships and the massive plunder that they had collected.
They had built it without the permission of the immortals;
therefore it was not fated to last for long.
While Hector was still alive and Achilles clung
to his rage and the city of Priam remained untaken,   10
the great wall of the Achaeans also stood firm.
But after the bravest Trojans had died in battle
and Troy had been plundered in the tenth year of the siege
and the Argives had all sailed back to their own dear country,
Poseidon and Lord Apollo destroyed the wall,
smashing it down with the power of all the rivers
that flow from the mountains of Ida into the sea—
Rhesus and Rhódius, Grénicus and Carésus,
Heptáporus and Æsépus and holy Scamander
and Símoïs, where so many thick oxhide shields   20
and helmets fell in the dirt, with a whole generation
of men who seemed half-divine. Lord Apollo turned
the course of these rivers to join at a single mouth,
and for nine days he drove their fury against the great wall,
while Zeus made it rain unceasingly, so that the earthwork
was washed out to sea the more quickly. And the Earthshaker,
holding his trident, himself directed things, sweeping
out on the waves the foundation of logs and stones
that the Argives had toiled to build. He leveled it all,
everything that had once stood by the Hellespont,   30
and when he had swept it away, once again he covered
the long, wide beaches with sand and returned the rivers
to the same channels their streams had flowed in before.

*

These are the actions Poseidon and Lord Apollo
would take later on. But for now, the Achaean wall
stood firm as the battle raged, and the beams of the towers
thundered as they were struck; and the Argives, whipped
back by the lash of Zeus, were penned in between
the wall and the black ships, dreading the onslaught of Hector,
who fought, as he had before, with the force of a whirlwind.   40
As when a wild boar or a lion suddenly wheels
to attack a party of dogs and hunters—the men
close ranks into a solid mass, and they stand
facing him and let fly a volley of spears,
but his noble heart feels no fear, though his courage will kill him,
and he constantly wheels around to attack his pursuers,
and wherever he charges, the ranks of hunters fall back:
just so did Hector keep turning around and exhorting
his comrades to cross the trench. But his horses refused;
they stopped at the edge, whinnying loudly, frightened   50
by the trench's width. They could not leap over or drive through;
sheer banks of piled earth rose up on both sides along
its length, and on top it was fitted with close-set stakes,
long and sharp, a defense against all attackers.
There was no easy way for a car to cross; but the Trojan
army was massed and eager to cross it on foot.

Polydamas then went up to Hector and said,
"Hector, and all you Trojan and allied commanders,
it is madness for us to attempt to drive through the trench,
which is hard to cross and studded with close-set stakes   60
on the edge of it, and behind it there is the wall.
And even if we did cross, we couldn't dismount there
and fight our best, since the space on the other side
is too narrow, and I am afraid we would suffer great losses.
If Zeus really wants to help and intends the destruction
of our enemies, I am eager for that to happen,
to have the Achaeans die here ingloriously,
far from Argos. But what if they rally? What if
they counterattack, and we are pushed back from the ships
and get caught in the trench? I doubt then that even one man   70

would escape the slaughter and make his way back to the city
to tell the tale. So let us all do what I say.
The attendants should hold our chariots at the edge
of the trench, and we will cross it on foot in one body,
following Hector. And if it is the Achaeans'
fate to die now, their army will not withstand us."

Hector was pleased at the good advice of his comrade.
He leaped to the ground from his chariot, in full armor,
and the other Trojan commanders followed his lead.
And they all instructed their charioteers to hold   80
the horses in proper formation there at the trench;
and they grouped into five companies, and each one
followed behind its commander. The troops who went
with Hector and Polydamas were the bravest
and the greatest in number, also the most determined
to break through the wall and carry the fight to the ships,
and Cebríones was there as the third in command.
(Hector had left another soldier to guard
his chariot, one who was not so able a fighter.)
Paris was in command of the second division,   90
along with Alcáthoüs and Agénor. The third
had Hélenus and Deíphobus as their leaders,
two sons of Priam, and Ásius also led them,
the son of Hýrtacus; his huge sorrel horses
had carried him from Arísbē and the Selléïs.
The fourth was led by Aeneas, and also with him
were Archélochus and Ácamas, sons of Anténor,
both of them skilled in warfare of every kind.
And Sarpedon was in command of the allies; he chose
Glaucus and Asteropǽus to come with him,   100
since he thought that they were the bravest men of the allies
after himself (since he was the bravest of all).
They stood side by side, close-packed, with their shields touching,
then charged straight at the Danäans, and they thought
that nothing could keep them from hurling themselves on the ships.

The other Trojans and allies took the advice

of Polydamas. Only Ásius was unwilling
to leave his horses and charioteer behind.
He drove straight on toward the ships—fool that he was,
since he would not escape destruction, and he would never   110
return from the ships in triumph to windswept Troy;
before long, hovering doom would overtake him
by the spear of Idómeneus. Toward the left wing of the ships
where the Argives returned from the plain with their cars and horses
he drove, and when he came to the gateway, he found
that the two doors had not been shut, with their massive crossbar,
but the gatemen held them wide open so that those comrades
who were fleeing could still return to the Argive camp.
Ásius drove toward the gateway, and his men followed
with piercing shouts, and they were convinced that the Argives   120
could not prevent them from hurling themselves on the ships—
fools that they were, for standing in front of the gates
they found two men, the bravest of Lapith fighters:
Polypœtes, son of Piríthoüs, and Leónteus.
These stood in front of the gates like two tall oak trees
that year after year stand firm against wind and rain,
held strongly in place by their deep, wide-spreading roots:
just so did these brave men wait for the Trojans' onslaught,
confident in their strength and without any fear.
The Trojans kept charging with their ferocious war cries,   130
holding their thick shields above their heads as they followed
Lord Ásius, Ĭámenus, and Oréstes,
and Thoön and Ádamas and Œnomáüs.
The two had been standing inside the wall, exhorting
the men around them to fight in defense of the ships.
But as soon as they saw the Trojans attack, while the Argives
with panicked shouts were turning and running away,
the two rushed out and fought in front of the gates
like a pair of wild boars in the mountains, which face the attack
of a rabble of dogs and farmers coming straight at them,   140
and they countercharge, swinging their huge heads from side to side,
shattering bushes and tearing them up by the roots,
and amid the uproar, the gnashing of tusks rings out
until the javelins hit and their lives are ended:

just so did the two men's breastplates ring out as the weapons
hit them while they fought on with tremendous fury.
And the men on the towers above them kept hurling boulders
at the enemy, in defense of their lives and ships.
The boulders fell to the ground as thickly as snowflakes
that some fierce storm wind, driving the dark clouds, scatters   150
onto the earth: just so did the missiles stream
from Achaeans and Trojans alike, and helmets and shields
clanged as the immense boulders kept falling upon them.
Then Ásius, in frustration and disappointment,
pounded his thighs with his fists and shouted to heaven:
"So, Father Zeus, you too, it seems, are a liar.
I never thought that the Argives would hold out against us
in our fury. But now, like flickering wasps or bees
that have built their home by the side of a rocky pathway
and refuse to leave it behind when the honey hunters   160
find it, but stay and fight to defend their young:
just so these two men refuse to be driven back
from the gates, but stand firm, ready to kill or be killed."
These were his words, but they did not change Zeus's mind;
he still intended to give all the glory to Hector.

Then Polypœtes hit Dámasus with his spear;
it found its mark and drove through his bronze-cheeked helmet,
which could not withstand the force of it, and the spear point
tore right through it and right through the bone, and his brains
splattered inside the bronze, and he fell in the dirt.   170
Next, Polypœtes killed Pylon and Órmenus;
and Leónteus hurled his spear at Hippómachus,
and it hit him below the navel and went through his belt.
And quickly he drew his sword from its scabbard and, charging
into the crowd, ran up to Antíphates
and stabbed him, and he fell backward and crashed to the ground.
Then he stabbed Menon, Ĭámenus, and Oréstes;
and one by one they lay down on the bountiful earth.

While these two warriors stripped off the shining armor
from the men they had killed, the young Trojans following Hector   180

and Polydamas—the soldiers who were the bravest
and the greatest in number, and also the most determined
to break through the Argive wall and set fire to the ships—
were hesitating along the edge of the trench.
An omen had appeared to them as they stood there,
an eagle that flew across the front of the army
from right to left and held in his talons a monstrous
blood-red snake, still struggling to get free;
it had not yet given up, and it twisted backward
and struck at its captor, biting him on the breast   190
right near the throat, and the eagle, in agony, let
the huge snake fall to the ground in the midst of the army,
then, shrieking, he flew away on a current of wind.
The Trojans shuddered to see the wriggling monster
as it lay among them, a mighty portent from Zeus.
Polydamas went up to Hector then, and he said,
"You always find fault with me, Hector, in our assemblies,
though I give good advice; you think that it isn't proper
for someone to speak out against you, either in council
or in war, and that we should always support your opinion.   200
But now I have to speak out as seems to me best.
We mustn't press on and take this fight to the ships;
once we do, it can only cause us great damage,
if indeed the omen was meant for us, that great bird
who held in his talons a blood-red snake, still struggling
to get free; but then, before he could reach his nest,
he dropped it and failed to bring it home to his young ones.
Thus it will turn out. Even if, with a huge
effort, we smash through the gates and the Argive wall,
we will never return by the way we came here, unharmed,   210
but will leave many comrades behind, cut down by the Argives
as in desperation they fight to defend their ships.
This is how a seer would interpret the omen,
someone whose understanding the men can trust."

Hector answered him then, with an angry scowl:
"I do not care for your speech, Polydamas; you
could have come up with better advice than this.

But if indeed you mean what you say, then it simply
proves that the gods themselves have addled your brains,
since in your opinion I should ignore the will   220
of almighty Zeus and the solemn promise he gave me.
You tell me to put my trust in the flight of birds;
but why should I care which direction birds fly in—whether
to the right and the rising sun or the left and darkness?
The only thing we should trust is the will of Zeus,
who is king over all, immortals as well as mortals.
There is just one omen: that we should fight for our country.
And what do you have to fear from this battle? Even
if the rest of us are cut down at the Argive ships,
you needn't have any fear that *you* will be killed,   230
since you don't have the courage to fight. But this I swear:
If you ever hold back from battle, or if you persuade
anyone not to fight, you are a dead man;
I will come and cut you to pieces with my own spear."

With these words he led the way, and the others followed
with a deafening roar. And Zeus from the mountains of Ida
sent down a violent wind storm that hurled the dust
straight at the ships, bewildering the Achaeans,
and he granted the Trojans glory. Trusting the omen
and their own strength, they began to break through the wall.   240
They tore at the beams that supported the battlements
and tried to pry up the posts that the Argives had driven
into the ground to buttress the wall's foundations.
They struggled to pull these out in the hope that the whole
wall would collapse. But the Argives did not give way.
They patched the defenses with oxhides and from the top
kept hurling their missiles down as the Trojans came near it.

The Ajaxes ranged back and forth on top of the wall,
encouraging the Achaeans and cheering them on,
some men gently, some with harsh words of reproach   250
whenever they saw them hanging back from the battle:
"Dear friends, you may be among the best of our fighters
or you may not fight well or you may be somewhere in the middle,

since all are not equally gifted. But in this war
everyone has his job; you already know that.
No man must go to the ships when he hears his commander
urging him on; he must stand firm and keep moving forward,
and almighty Zeus will let us repel the attack
and send our enemies scurrying back to their city."
With words like these they roused the Achaeans' spirits.   260
And like snowflakes that thickly fall on a winter's day
when Zeus lulls the winds and pours down snow without ceasing
until it has covered the mountain peaks and the headlands
and the grassy plains and the rich farmlands of men,
and it pours down over the harbors and shores of the sea,
and only the waves keep it back as they beat against it,
but everything else is enfolded in its embrace:
so thick and fast did the stones fly from either side,
falling on both the Trojans and the Achaeans,
and the sound of pounding was heard the whole length of the wall.   270

Yet not even then would the Trojans and glorious Hector
have smashed through the gates of the wall and its massive crossbar
if Zeus had not sent Sarpedon, his own dear son,
to the Danäans, like a lion to grazing cattle.
Holding his shield before him—a lovely thing
that a smith had hammered of bronze, its layers of oxhide
stitched on with golden wire around the rim—
and a spear in each hand, he strode ahead like a lion
who has wandered for a long time in the mountains, hungry,
and his proud heart bids him break into a well-fenced homestead   280
and try for the sheep, and although the shepherds are there
guarding their flocks with dogs and spears, he refuses
to be chased from the farmhouse, and he leaps over the fence
and brings down a sheep and makes away with his kill,
or else he is hit by a spear from someone's quick hand:
just so was the heart of godlike Sarpedon inspired
to charge at the wall and break through the battlements.

But first he went over to Glaucus and spoke these words:
"Glaucus, why is it that we two are held in the greatest

esteem in Lycia and honored with pride of place,   290
the choicest meat, and our wine cups always refilled,
and all men look up to us both, as if we were gods,
and we each have a large estate on the banks of the Xanthus,
beautiful tracts of orchards and wheat-bearing farmland?
It is so that we may now take our stand in the front ranks
and lead our army into the thick of battle
and fight with courage, so that the soldiers will say,
'These men who rule us in Lycia are not unworthy.
They may dine on fat sheep and drink the best of the wines,
but they are strong, too, and brave, and they fight in the front ranks.'   300
Dear friend, if the two of us were to survive this war
and could live forever, without old age, without dying,
I wouldn't press on to fight in the front lines myself
or urge you into the battle. But as it is,
since death stands facing us all in ten thousand forms
and no mortal can ever escape it, let us go forward
and either win glory ourselves or yield it to others."
At these words, Glaucus nodded his head in agreement,
and the two men advanced with the Lycian army behind them.

When he saw them coming, the Argive commander Menéstheus   310
shuddered, since they were charging directly at him,
and he looked all along the wall's length, trying to find
some warrior who could save his men from destruction.
He saw the two Ajaxes, who were nearby, and Teucer,
who had just come from his hut; but although he was shouting
directly at them, he could not make himself heard,
so loud was the uproar—a din that reached to the heavens—
of battered shields and helmets and gates. (The gates
had been closed, and the Trojans were gathered in front of them, pounding
and battering them and trying to force their way through.)   320
And he sent the herald Thöótes to the two men:
"Run, Thöótes; find Ajax and tell him to come here—
or find both Ajaxes; that would be even better—
since a great disaster threatens to overwhelm us,
so ferocious is this assault from the Lycian commanders,
who have always fought valiantly in the thick of a battle.

But if heavy fighting has broken out there too, then
at least find Ajax the Tall and tell him come here,
and tell Teucer to come as well, with his deadly bow."

At once the herald did what his lord had commanded   330
and went running along the wall; and as soon as he saw
the two Ajaxes, he went up to them and said,
"Menéstheus needs your help now, right away. Go there,
fight alongside him, for even a little while—
the two of you go, if you can; that would be best—
since a great disaster threatens to overwhelm us,
so ferocious is this assault from the Lycian commanders,
who have always fought valiantly in the thick of a battle.
But if heavy fighting has broken out here too, then
he asked me come back at least with Ajax the Tall,   340
and Teucer should come as well, with his deadly bow."

At these words, Ajax the Tall, Télamon's son,
quickly turned to the son of Öíleus and said,
"Ajax, stay here, together with Lycomédes.
Stand firm, and stir up the Argives to fight their best.
I will follow the herald to where Menéstheus is standing
and will come back soon, once I fight off the attackers."
When he had spoken, Ajax the Tall moved onward,
and his half-brother Teucer went along, with his bow.

They hurried on, and as soon as they came to the place   350
where Menéstheus stood—the soldiers were being attacked
ferociously, as the Lycian troops and commanders
climbed up onto the battlements like a black whirlwind—
they flung themselves into the fight, and a great shout arose.
Ajax was first to kill a man: Épicles, one
of Sarpedon's comrades, hitting him on the head
with a jagged boulder that lay on top of a pile
of huge rocks inside the wall by the battlement's edge.
No man of today could easily lift such a boulder,
not even the strongest of men; but Ajax held it   360
above his head, and he hurled it down, and it hit

Épicles, and it crushed his four-plated helmet
and shattered his skull, and he let go and plunged from the height
like a diver, and the life spirit left his bones.
And Teucer hit Glaucus as he was climbing the wall;
seeing his arm unprotected, he drew back the bowstring,
and the arrow hit home and put a stop to his fighting.
But Glaucus jumped down quietly, so that no Argive,
noticing he had been wounded, would jeer in triumph.

Sarpedon was filled with grief as soon as he realized   370
that Glaucus was gone, but he did not retreat from the fighting.
He stabbed Alcmáon, Thestor's son, with his spear
and yanked the spear out; and Alcmáon followed its movement
and fell head first, and his armor clattered upon him.
And Sarpedon grabbed hold of the battlement, and he pulled,
and the whole section came off, and the top of the wall
was laid bare, and he had opened a passage for many.

Then Ajax and Teucer attacked him at the same moment.
Teucer let fly an arrow, which hit the thick strap
of his shield, on his chest, but Zeus saved his son, for now.   380
Then Ajax lunged forward, piercing his shield, and the spear
drove right through it and stunned him and pounded him back.
He retreated a little way, but he would not withdraw
from the battlement, because he still hoped to win glory.
And he turned around and shouted out to his troops:
"Lycian soldiers, where is your fighting spirit?
As strong as I am, it is hard for me by myself
to break through this wall and open a path to the ships.
So follow me now, and the more men who come, the better."
The Lycians were stung with shame at Sarpedon's rebuke,   390
and they all rushed in to rally around their commander.
Inside the wall, the Argives sent reinforcements,
and between the two armies a deadly struggle arose.
The mighty Lycians could not break through the defenses
and force their way to the ships, nor could the Argives
push them back from the wall once they had reached it.
But as two farmers, with measuring rods in hand,

quarrel about the boundaries of a small field
that they own in common, and each one demands his fair share:
just so did the two sides contend for the battlements,   400
and across the top they hacked at each other's defenses.

Many men's bodies were slashed by the pitiless bronze
when they turned and exposed their backs, and many were wounded
by spears that went through their shields, and in every place
the wall was drenched with the blood of men from both armies.
The Trojans kept trying to drive the Achaeans back,
but both sides held on. As an honest, hardworking woman
who spins for a living will hold the scales by the beam
and keep adding wool to a pan till the weight is balanced,
and thus she can earn a wretched wage for her children: 410
so evenly matched were the Trojans and the Achaeans
till Zeus gave Hector the glory of being the first
to leap inside the Achaeans' wall. With a shout
that moved all who heard him, he called out to his companions,
"Trojans, follow me! Now is the time to smash through
the Argive wall and light torches and burn their ships!"
With these words he cheered them on, and every ear heard him,
and they charged at the wall in one mass and began swarming
over the buttresses, thrusting their spears, and Hector
grabbed a huge rock that was lying in front of the gate.   420
Its bottom was thick and its top was pointed, and not
easily could the two strongest men in a town
have levered it up from the ground and onto a wagon,
but he lifted it by himself, since Zeus made it light.
And as when a shepherd carries the fleece of a ram
with one hand, easily, hardly aware of its weight:
just so did Hector carry the rock to the doors
that held together the close-fitted, high double gates.
(On the inside two massive bars kept them closed, crossing
over each other, and one bolt held them secure.)   430
And when he was right in front, he took his position
with feet wide apart to give more force to his throw,
and he hurled the rock at the center, and it smashed off
both the hinges. The rock was carried inside

by its own sheer weight, and the gates groaned loudly, the bars
shuddered and cracked, and the doors were shattered to pieces
from the force of the blow. And Hector charged on inside,
his face like the onrush of night, his terrible bronze
armor gleaming, and each hand holding a spear.
When he flung himself into the gateway, none but a god   440
could have held him back, and his eyes were blazing like fire.
He turned around and shouted out to the Trojans
to storm the great wall, and they all obeyed his command.
Some of them climbed the wall, and the others poured
in through the gate, and the Argives fled panic-stricken
toward their ships, and an ungodly uproar arose.

Book 13

When Zeus had brought Hector near the Achaean ships,
he left the two armies there to endure the anguish
of nonstop fighting, and turned his bright eyes away,
looking far north toward the land of the horse-breeding Thracians,
the Mysians, those hand-to-hand fighters, the Hippemólgi,
who live on mares' milk, and the Ábïi, justest of men.
He no longer turned his bright eyes toward Priam's city,
since he did not expect that any among the gods
would dare to bring help to the Trojans or the Achaeans.

But Poseidon noticed. High on the topmost peak   10
of forested Sámothrace, he too looked down at the battle,
marveling; from there he could clearly see
all of Mount Ida and Troy and the Argive warships.
He had come up out of the depths, and as he witnessed
the Argives being cut down, he was filled with pity,
and he felt a violent indignation at Zeus.
Immediately he strode down the side of the mountain,
and as he walked, the wooded hills all around
trembled beneath his feet. He took three long steps,
and with the fourth step he arrived at his goal, Ægæ,   20
in the depths of the sea, where his glorious palace is,
golden and gleaming, imperishable forever.
And when he arrived, he harnessed a pair of horses,
bronze-hoofed and swift as the wind, with long golden manes,
and he strapped on his golden armor and picked up his fine
golden whip and mounted his golden car,
and he drove out over the waves, and on every side
the dolphins swam up and leaped all around him with joy,
knowing their lord, and the sea in her gladness opened
a path for him, and so lightly the chariot flew   30
that the wheels' bronze axles were not even wet beneath it,
and the horses kept bounding on toward the Argive ships.

*

There is a cavern deep in the waters, halfway
between the isles of Imbros and Ténedos;
there he reined in the horses, unyoked them, and spread
a mound of celestial fodder before their feet,
and to each of them he fastened a golden hobble
that could not be broken or slipped, so that they would stay
until his return; and he went to the Danäan army.

The Trojans, like wind-driven fire, were following Hector   40
in one mass, raging, their voices a single roar,
and they all thought they would take the black ships that day
and slaughter the enemy. But the Earthshaker, Poseidon,
the Earth-encircler, cheered on the Argive commanders
in the likeness of Calchas the seer, with his tireless voice.
He spoke first to the two Ajaxes, who were already
eager for battle: "You two can save the Achaeans;
fight boldly on, and don't even think of fleeing.
Everywhere else I am sure that we will drive back
the Trojans, although they are swarming over the wall—   50
I know that our men are strong and can hold them off.
But here, where we stand on the battlements, I am afraid
disaster may overtake us, since that mad dog
is leading them on like a pillar of flame—that man Hector,
who boasts that he is a son of almighty Zeus.
May some god give you the strength to stand firm against him
and rally the others; and then, in spite of his fury,
you can drive him back from the ships and rout his whole army,
even if he is inspired by Zeus himself."

After he finished, the Earthshaker tapped them both   60
with his staff; he filled them with courage, gave them fresh strength,
and quickened their arms and legs. And as a hawk
will fly straight up from a sheer cliff, hover in air,
then swoop down to chase some smaller bird over the plain:
just so did Poseidon instantly leave. And the swift
son of Öíleus, Ajax the Smaller, knew
that it was a god, and he said to Télamon's son,
"Ajax, that must have been an immortal who left us,

an Olympian, who was taking the form of Calchas,
not the real man. I could tell from the way his feet moved   70
as I watched from behind; it is easy to know a god.
My heart has been struck by a jolt of courage, I feel
my body tingling all over, my arms and legs
surge with strength, and I long to go into battle."

Then Ajax the Tall, the son of Télamon, answered,
"I feel that too. A current runs through my hands,
they long for a spear, my legs want to sprint, my body
feels stronger than it has ever been, and I can't
wait to meet Hector and fight him in all his fury."
These were their words to each other as they exulted   80
in the joy of war that the god had put in their breasts.

Meanwhile Poseidon stirred up the other Achaeans
who were resting beside the ships in the rear of the battle,
trying to catch their breath. Their bodies were weak
with exhaustion, and deep despair had caught hold of their hearts
at the sight of the Trojans storming over the wall.
As they saw them come closer, tears welled up in their eyes;
they did not think they would ever escape destruction.
But Poseidon the Earthshaker, lightly moving among them,
aroused the courage of each man and gave him strength.   90
And he spoke to Penéleos, Teucer, Deípyrus,
Meriones, Léïtus, Thoas, Antilochus:
"Shame on you, Argives! You are the men I was trusting
to safeguard our ships; if *you* hold back from this battle,
the Trojans will certainly win and cut us to pieces.
I am amazed that we have come to this dreadful
turning point, which I never thought that my eyes
would look on: the Trojans fighting their way to our ships,
men who, before, were like timid deer in the forest,
food for jackals, panthers, and wolves, as they wander   100
terrified and defenseless, with no will to fight.
They have never been able to stand and face us—not even
a little, yet now they are cutting a path to our ships
because of our leader's weakness and the reluctance

of our troops, who are so disgusted with him that they
would rather die alongside our ships than defend them.
But even though King Agamemnon is absolutely
at fault in this, because he dishonored Achilles,
it is wrong for you to stand apart from the fighting,
since you are the army's finest. I wouldn't blame   110
some coward for hanging back; but you, of all men . . .
I am furious; I expect more from men like you.
Isn't it clear that you will cause even more damage
by hanging back? Have you all lost your sense of honor
and dignity? This is not just a minor skirmish:
Hector is here, he has smashed our gates, and the Trojans
are pouring through and have carried the war to our ships."

That is how Lord Poseidon stirred up the Achaeans.
And the troops took their stand around the two Ajaxes,
massing together. Not even Athena or Ares   120
would have found fault with them. As they awaited Hector
and the Trojan attack, the bravest men formed a wall,
spear upon spear and shield overlapping shield,
and the horsehair crests in the shining plates of their helmets
touched when they moved their heads, so closely packed
were the ranks, and their long-shadowed spears crisscrossed in the air.
And their minds did not waver; each of them longed to fight.

The Trojans charged in a mass, with Hector in front.
He drove with the force of a boulder that thunders down
the side of some mountain, torn out by winter floods   130
which have washed away the small rocks that held it in place,
and headlong it crashes down through the forest, smashing
everything in its path and gathering speed
till it reaches the level ground; it slows then; it stops;
it can move no farther, however strongly it wants to:
just so, for a while, did Hector threaten to crash
right to the sea through the Danäan huts and ships,
killing as he charged onward; but when he came
to the close-packed battalions, he stopped. And as the Achaeans
faced him, thrusting their swords and double-curved spear points,   140

they drove him back and, staggering, he gave way.
Then, with a piercing shout, he called to his comrades:
"Trojan, Lycian, Dardánian soldiers and friends,
stand by me. The Argives will not resist me for long,
even though they have formed a great wall against me.
They must soon give way if Zeus, the greatest of gods,
is, as he said, the one who inspired my onslaught."

With these words he stirred up the courage of every man.
Then, among them, his brother Deíphobus
strode from the ranks; he stepped forward nimbly, behind   150
the shelter of his round shield. Meriones aimed
and hit the shield, but before the spear could go through it,
the shaft broke off at the socket, behind the point;
he had held the shield well away from himself, frightened
that the spear would punch through it. And as Deíphobus stood there,
Meriones moved back into the ranks, disappointed
at the loss of his triumph, incensed that his spear had been shattered;
and he ran alongside the ships toward his hut, intending
to bring back one of the spears he had left behind.

The others fought on, and a ceaseless uproar arose.   160
Teucer was first to kill a man: Ímbrius,
son of Mentor, a wealthy man who raised horses.
He had lived in Pedǽon before the Danäans came
and was married to Médesicástē, a bastard daughter
of King Priam's, born to one of his concubines;
but after the Danäan fleet arrived, he had gone back
to Ilion and was prominent there, and he lived
in one of the rooms in the house of Priam, who loved him
and honored him as much as he did his own children.
Teucer thrust into his jawbone below the ear,   170
then yanked the spear out; and he fell to earth like an ash tree
chopped down on a mountaintop visible far and wide,
and its delicate leaves come toppling to the ground:
just so did he fall, and his armor clattered upon him.
Teucer rushed out from the ranks to strip off the armor,
and as he was running, Hector hurled his bright spear,

but Teucer saw the spear coming; he dodged to one side
and it missed him by inches and hit the man standing beside him,
Amphímachus, son of Ctéatus, grandson of Actor,
driving straight through his chest as he strode into battle;   180
he fell with a crash, and his armor clattered upon him.
As Hector rushed out from the ranks to pull off the helmet
from the head of Amphímachus, Ajax thrust with his spear,
but he could not get through to the flesh, since Hector was covered
in bronze, though he hit the knob of his shield with such
force that it pushed him back, and Hector gave ground,
and the Argives moved forward and dragged away the two bodies.
The Athenian leaders Stíchius and Menéstheus
carried Amphímachus back to the Argive ranks,
while the two Ajaxes, filled with the spirit of war,   190
carried the body of Ímbrius. As two lions
snatch a goat from a herd that is guarded by dogs—
they kill it and carry it off, through the thick brushwood,
holding it in their jaws high up from the ground:
just so did the two men hold the dead Ímbrius high,
stripped of his armor. And Ajax the Smaller, angry
at the death of Amphímachus, hacked off the head from the soft
neck and, swinging his arm back, sent the head whirling
over the crowd like a ball, and it fell and rolled
in the dirt and came to a stop at the feet of Hector.   200

When Lord Poseidon learned that Amphímachus,
his grandson, had fallen in battle, he was enraged,
and he went to the huts and ships of the Achaeans
to stir up the troops and inspire them to attack.
And Idómeneus met him, on his way back from helping
one of his men who had just come out of the battle
with a wound on the back of his knee; his comrades had brought him
off the field, and Idómeneus had instructed
the healers and now was going to his own hut,
since with all his heart he wished to return to the fighting.   210
Poseidon the Earthshaker spoke to him in the likeness
of Thoas, son of Andrǽmon, the ruler of all
the Ætólians who lived in the Cálydon hills

and in Pleuron, and whom the people revered as a god.
"Idómeneus, what has become of the victory threats
that the Argives used to level against the Trojans?"

And Idómeneus, counselor of the Cretans, answered,
"Thoas, no human is now to blame, as I see it.
We are all skilled in warfare; not one of us has been seized
by heart-stunning fear, nor is cowardice making us back off   220
from the evils of fighting. But such is the will, it seems,
of almighty Zeus—that the Argives should die here, far
from their homes, ingloriously. You have always been brave
and have urged the men on as well, whenever you saw them
shrink from the fighting. Don't stop now: keep urging
your troops to fight bravely, with all the strength they can find."

Poseidon the Earthshaker answered him with these words:
"Idómeneus, may the man who shrinks from this battle
stay here in Troy forever, and may the wild dogs
delight in his flesh. Come on; we need to act quickly   230
and combine our strength if we are to be of help.
Together, the worst of fighters can triumph; how much
more so can we, who have conquered even the bravest!"

And he moved, a god, on into the frenzy of mortals.
When Idómeneus reached his hut, he put on his armor
and seized two spears and strode like the lightning that Zeus
takes in his hands and hurls from the heights of Olympus
to reveal an omen to men in a blinding flash:
just so, as he ran, did the bronze of his breastplate glitter.

His brave lieutenant, Meriones, happened to meet him   240
not far from his hut. He was on his way from the battle
to get a spear when Idómeneus stopped him and said,
"Meriones, why have you left the fighting and come here?
Are you hurt? Are you in pain from a Trojan spear point?
Or have you been sent with a message? I need no prompting;
I am just about to leave and return to the battle."

*

Meriones, that clear-minded man, responded,
"I am coming to get a spear. Is there one in your hut?
Mine just broke on the shield of Deíphobus."

Idómeneus said, "You will certainly find a spear,   250
or twenty spears—as many as you could wish for—
leaning against the white inner wall of my hut:
Trojan spears, which I took from the men I killed.
It isn't my way to stand at a great distance
from my enemy when I fight. I have many spears there,
and helmets and shields and brilliantly gleaming breastplates."

Meriones answered, "I too have many trophies,
Trojan weapons and armor, inside my hut.
But my hut is too far away; I need a spear *now*.
I haven't forgotten my courage, I can assure you;   260
I fight up front whenever a battle breaks out.
There may be *some* men among the Achaeans who don't
know how I fight, but you know perfectly well."

And Idómeneus said, "I know what a brave man you are;
there is no need to tell me. I know that if all the best
of our captains were chosen now to go on an ambush,
even then no one would find any fault with your courage.
Nothing can show so convincingly what a man
is made of: who is a coward and who is brave.
The coward's face changes colors and goes dead white,   270
he can't sit still, but he fidgets, and as he squats,
he keeps shifting his weight from one foot to the other,
and his heart pounds loudly against his ribs, and his teeth
chatter as he imagines how death will seize him;
but the brave man's body is calm, and he doesn't feel
any great fear as he settles into the ambush,
but he longs to go into action as soon as he can.
And if you were hit by an arrow or stabbed in battle,
it would never be from behind, in your nape or back;
the weapon would seek you out in your chest or belly   280
as you sought the Trojans' embrace ahead of your soldiers.

But let us not stand here idly, talking like fools,
or the soldiers who see us may be resentful. So hurry,
go to my hut; choose any spear that you want."

He turned and ran toward the fighting. Meriones quickly
went to the hut and picked out one of the spears,
then followed Idómeneus, eager to fight again.
And just as man-killing Ares strides out to war,
and following him goes Panic, his son, who strikes terror
into the hearts of even the bravest men,   290
and they go out from Thrace to fight on behalf of either
the Éphyri or the Phlegians and give glory
to one of the sides but are deaf to the prayers of the other:
so terribly did Idómeneus stride into battle
with Meriones, both men armored in fiery bronze.

Meriones said to him, "Son of Deucálion, tell me:
Where do you think that we should rejoin the fighting—
on the army's right, in the center, or on the left?
The left is where the Argives, I think, are the weakest."

And Idómeneus answered, "Other great fighters among us   300
are defending the center. The Ajaxes both are there
and Teucer, who is the finest of all the Achaeans
with the bow, and a good man too in hand-to-hand fighting.
These men will saturate Hector with war, however
eager he is to fight now. It will be hard
for him to get past them, indomitable as they are,
to burn down the Argive ships, unless Zeus himself
tosses his blazing firebrands onto the decks.
But there is no man whom Ajax the Tall will yield to,
no mortal who eats the fruit of the earth, whose flesh   310
can be torn by spears and whose bones can be crushed by boulders.
Not even Achilles, breaker of men, could defeat him,
in close combat at least; for of course no mortal can win
in the open field over such an astounding runner.
So let us set out for the left of the battlefield; then
we can quickly know if the victory will be ours."

*

Meriones led, until they arrived on the left
of the battlefield. And as soon as the Trojans saw
Idómeneus coming, as powerful as a flame,
with his lieutenant, wearing their massive armor,   320
they gave a tremendous battle cry and moved toward them,
and furious hand-to-hand fighting took place by the ships.
As when gusts keep swirling under the whistling winds
on a day when the dust lies thick on the roads, and it rises
and hangs in the air for hours in a dense cloud:
just so did the armies collide, and the men were eager
to kill one another amid the thick press of battle.
The fighting bristled with long-shadowed, flesh-tearing spears,
and eyes went blind in the endless dazzle of bronze
helmets and new-polished breastplates and glittering shields   330
as the armies clashed there. Only a bold-hearted man
could rejoice at that sight and not be stricken with terror.

The two mighty sons of Cronus, opposing each other,
caused huge grief for the men who were in the battle.
Zeus wished the Trojans and Hector to have the triumph
in order to keep his promise. (He did not want
all the Achaean troops to be killed, but only
enough to give honor to Thetis and her great son.)
But Poseidon had risen out of the depths in secret
and was walking among the Argives and giving them courage;   340
it pained him to see them being cut down, and he felt
a violent indignation at Zeus. Both gods
came from the same stock, both of them had the same father,
but Zeus was the elder, the one with the greater knowledge.
So Poseidon avoided openly helping the Argives,
but he went through their ranks in secret, in human form,
always stirring them up and urging them onward.
So these two pulled on the rope of violent conflict
from opposite sides, and the battle went back and forth
continually, and brought death to many good men.   350

And Idómeneus, though his hair was already half-gray,

called to the Argives to follow him, and he charged
straight at the Trojans and made them flee in a panic.
He killed Othryóneus, a guest in Troy from Cabésus
who had recently come there, drawn by news of the war,
and had asked for Priam's most beautiful daughter, Cassándra,
without a bride-price. Instead, he had promised a triumph:
to drive the Achaeans out of the land of Troy.
King Priam had accepted his terms, and now
Othryóneus fought for him, trusting their solemn agreement.   360
Idómeneus hurled his spear and hit him full on
as he swaggered forward; the breastplate that he was wearing
did not protect him; the spear went right through his belly,
and he fell with a crash. And Idómeneus gloated above him:
"Friend, there is no one on earth whom I will admire
as much as you if you really fulfill your promise
to drive us out in return for King Priam's girl.
We too will make you a promise: We will agree
to give you King Agamemnon's most beautiful daughter;
we will sail her out here from Argos for you to marry   370
if only you help us tear down the walls of Troy.
So come along to the ships, and let us agree
on the terms of the marriage. We will not drive a hard bargain."

After he finished, Idómeneus took his leg
and dragged him off through the fighting. But Ásius
came to defend the body. He was on foot,
in front of his horses; his charioteer was holding
them so close that he could feel their breath on his shoulders.
He fought his best, but Idómeneus was too quick;
he punched the spear through his throat, just under the chin,   380
and Ásius fell like an oak tree or a white poplar
or a pine that carpenters, with new-whetted axes,
cut down in the mountains and hew into planks for a ship:
just so did he lie stretched out in front of his horses,
choking to death and clawing the blood-soaked dust.
And his charioteer panicked and lost his wits;
paralyzed, he stood there not daring to turn
the horses around to escape, and Antilochus hit him.

The spear passed right through his breastplate and into his belly,
and he fell to the ground from the chariot, with a gasp,   390
and Antilochus drove the horses to the black ships.

And Deíphobus, grieving for Ásius, came up close
to Idómeneus, and he aimed and hurled his bright spear.
But Idómeneus saw it coming and dodged aside
and took cover behind the shield that he always carried,
made out of oxhide circles and glittering bronze
and fitted in back with two crossbars. He crouched behind it,
and the spear flew over and clanged as it grazed the rim.
But the shot of Deíphobus was not wasted; it hit
Hypsénor, son of Híppasus, in the belly   400
and pierced his liver; at once he crumpled to earth.
And Deíphobus gloated terribly over his corpse:
"Now Ásius lies there avenged. Although he is going
down to the realm of Hades, I think he will be
pleased that I sent an escort to go along with him."
When they heard his boast, the Argives were filled with sorrow.

And Idómeneus still kept up his furious onslaught
and charged on, eager to wrap some Trojan in darkness
or go down fighting to save the Argives from ruin.
And he met Alcáthoüs, son of King Æsÿétes,   410
a great warrior and the son-in-law of Anchíses;
he had married the eldest daughter, Híppodamía,
adored by her father and mother, brought up in their palace
with the best of care; she excelled all girls of her own age
in beauty, wisdom, and all the womanly skills,
and her parents had picked Troy's noblest suitor for her.
Poseidon killed him, using Idómeneus;
he put him into a trance now, stunning his body,
and he could not move a muscle, but stood there bewildered,
fixed to the spot, like a gravestone or a tall tree,   420
while Idómeneus thrust and stabbed him right through the chest,
ripping a hole in the breastplate that until then
had protected him, and it clanged as the spear plunged through it,
and he fell with a crash; the spear point lodged in his heart,

and the heart still throbbed and made the whole length of the shaft
quiver, until at last its fury was spent.
And Idómeneus gloated terribly over him, shouting:
"Deíphobus, what do you think? I have killed three men
for the one that you boasted about. Shall we call it even?
If you feel lucky now, stand and face me yourself   430
so you can see what an offspring of Zeus is made of.
Zeus fathered Minos, the guardian over Crete,
and Minos in turn was Deucálion's father, and then
Deucálion fathered me, the king over many
in the land of Crete; and my black ships have brought me here
as a curse to you and your father and all the Trojans."

Deíphobus was of two minds: should he give ground
and join with some comrade, or take the man on by himself?
And in the end, he decided that it would be best
to look for Aeneas. He found him standing alone   440
behind the battle lines, brooding, angry at Priam
for not honoring him, though he was one of their bravest.
Deíphobus ran up and stood beside him and said,
"Aeneas, counselor of the Trojans, hurry, come
fight for Alcáthoüs, if you have any feeling
for your family. He was your brother-in-law, who raised you
in the palace when you were a child. Idómeneus
just killed him. We need to rescue his body, right now."

These were his words, and they made Aeneas's heart
beat faster; he ran out to look for Idómeneus, raging.   450
But Idómeneus did not flee like an untested boy;
he stood firm, confident as a wild boar in the mountains
who faces a rabble of hunters coming straight at him
in some desolate place; the bristles stand up on his back,
his eyes blaze, and he gnashes his knife-sharp tusks
in his fury, eager to fight off the dogs and men:
just so did Idómeneus stand without giving way
as Aeneas attacked. But he shouted out to his comrades
Ascálaphus and Deípyrus, who were nearby,
and Meriones, Antilochus, and Apháreus: 460

"Over here, friends; come help me. I am alone
and much afraid of Aeneas as he heads toward me,
a killer of men, and young, at the height of his powers.
If we were the same age, I wouldn't be calling for help;
I would fight him alone, and one of us would soon triumph."

When they heard his cry, they ran to him with one purpose
and closed in around him, leaning their shields on their shoulders.
And at the same time, Aeneas called out to *his* comrades,
Prince Paris and Deíphobus and Agénor,
and they hurried at once to help, and behind each captain   470
the soldiers followed, as when a flock follows the ram
when they leave the pasture and move off to drink at a pond,
and the heart of the shepherd is glad: just so Aeneas
was glad when he saw the number of troops that had come.
Then they all clashed in close fighting around the body
of Alcáthoüs, and the bronze on their chests rang out
terribly as the sharp-pointed spears hit their mark.
Idómeneus and Aeneas, above all, were straining
to tear through each other's flesh with the pitiless bronze.

Aeneas threw first, but Idómeneus saw the spear coming;   480
he dodged to one side, and the spear flew past him and stuck,
quivering, in the ground. And Idómeneus threw
his spear, and it hit Œnomáüs right in the belly
and tore through the front of his breastplate; his innards gushed out,
and he fell in the dust, clawing the earth with his nails.
Idómeneus pulled his spear from the body, but as
the missiles rained down, he could not strip off the armor.
His legs were no longer fast enough to charge in
after his spear or dodge the spear of another;
he could keep death at bay in close combat, but now his legs   490
were too weak to carry him quickly out of the battle.
And as he moved backward, Deíphobus, with fierce hatred,
aimed and threw his bright spear. But again he missed,
and instead he hit Ascálaphus, son of Ares;
the spear drove into his shoulder and out his back,
and he dropped to the ground and lay there, clawing the dirt.

And Ares was unaware that his son had fallen;
he sat on one of the peaks of Olympus, under
the golden clouds, restrained by the will of Zeus,
with the other gods, who were also barred from the fighting.   500

Then they all clashed in close fighting around the body
of Ascálaphus. Deíphobus stripped off his helmet,
but Meriones leaped in and thrust his spear, and it pierced
the Trojan's arm, and the helmet fell to the ground
with a clang. Meriones leaped in again like a hawk
and pulled the spear from his upper arm, then retreated
into the dense crowd of Argives. Quickly Polítes
ran to his brother Deíphobus, put his arm
around his waist, and led him out of the fighting
to the horses waiting for him at the rear of the battle,   510
with their charioteer and the handsome, bronze-inlaid car.
They carried him to the city, and he kept groaning
in his agony, and the dark blood poured from the wound.

The others fought on, and a ceaseless uproar arose.
Aeneas charged at Apháreus, son of Calétor,
and pierced his throat with his spear as he turned to face him;
and his head jerked back, and he fell, and his shield and helmet
clattered, and death engulfed him on every side.
Antilochus waited for Thoön to turn his back,
then rushed in and stabbed him and severed the vein that runs   520
along the spinal cord, all the way up to the neck;
he cut right through it, and Thoön fell on his back
and lay in the dirt, stretching his arms to his comrades.
As Antilochus warily started to strip off the armor,
the Trojans surrounded him, and they moved in and kept
thrusting at his bright shield, but they were unable
to pierce it and wound his flesh with the pitiless bronze,
since Poseidon stood guard and watched over Nestor's son
even as spears and arrows fell thickly around him.
Unable to shake off the enemy, he wheeled round   530
in every direction to face them, and his long spear
was never still for a moment, but it kept shaking

as he threatened to hurl it or suddenly lunge at a man.
Ádamas, son of Ásius, noticed him aiming
into the crowd, and at once he ran up and stabbed him.
But Poseidon weakened the spear point's thrust and denied it
the life of the Achaean. Half of it stuck
in the shield of Antilochus, like a fire-hardened spike,
while the other half fell to the ground, and Ádamas
shrank back into the crowd to avoid destruction.   540
But Meriones followed him as he left, and he stabbed him
midway between the genitals and the navel,
the most agonizing way for a man to die.
There the spear plunged, and Ádamas gripped the shaft,
writhing and bucking like some wild bull in the mountains
that herdsmen have caught with ropes and are dragging away:
just so did he writhe—a little while, not for long.
And Meriones came up and stood beside him and pulled
the spear from his flesh, and darkness covered his eyes.

Then Hélenus hit Deípyrus, stabbing him through   550
the temple with his huge Thracian sword, and the helmet
shattered and crashed to the ground, and one of the Argive
officers picked it up as it rolled at his feet;
and Deípyrus dropped, and black night covered his eyes.

On seeing this, Menelaus was wrenched by grief
and charged at Lord Hélenus, menacing him with his spear,
while Hélenus drew back his bowstring; the two attacked
at the very same moment. Hélenus hit Menelaus
on the front of his breastplate, but the keen arrow bounced off.
As when on a threshing floor the black beans or the chickpeas   560
leap from the shovel, under the whistling wind:
just so from the breastplate of Menelaus the arrow
bounced off and flew a great distance before it fell.
And Menelaus hit Hélenus on the hand
that was holding the polished bow, and the spear drove deep
into the hand, and it stuck in the bow itself,
and he shrank back into the crowd to avoid destruction
as his pierced arm dangled beside him, dragging the spear.

Agénor pulled out the spear point and bound up the hand
with a length of twisted wool as a makeshift sling.   570
(His attendant gave it to him as he stood beside him.)

And then Pisánder went charging toward Menelaus,
but an evil fate was leading him to his death,
to be cut down by you, Menelaus, in hand-to-hand combat.
When the two of them had advanced to within close range,
Menelaus hurled his spear, and it flew just past him,
and Pisánder stabbed and hit Menelaus's shield,
but he was not able to drive the spear through its layers;
the shield was too strong, and the spear snapped off at the socket.
And Menelaus rejoiced and hoped for a triumph,   580
and drawing his silver-bossed sword, he attacked Pisánder;
while he, from behind his shield, grabbed a bronze axe
set on a long polished handle of olive wood,
and both men struck at the very same moment. Pisánder's
axe hit the plate of the helmet, a little below
the horsehair crest; but just as Pisánder was charging,
Menelaus slashed at his forehead, above the bridge
of his nose. The bones cracked; his eyeballs, dripping with blood,
fell at his feet on the ground, and he doubled over
and fell down himself in the dirt. Menelaus set   590
his foot on his chest and gloated over the body:
"This is the way you Trojans will leave our ships,
you arrogant fools, who are always yearning for bloodshed.
You will bring down death on yourselves and will bring as well
the disgrace that you brought on me, you cowardly dogs,
since you had no fear in your hearts of the punishing rage
of Zeus, who holds sacred the bond between host and guest
and will therefore destroy your city. You carried away
my wife and much of my treasure, with no regard
for decency, even though she received you with kindness   600
and you were her honored guests. And now you are trying
to fling fire onto our ships and slaughter our men.
But you will be stopped, however determined you are.
Zeus our father, they say that you surpass all
others in wisdom, both men and gods, and from you

these things have come to us. How can you favor the Trojans,
those lawless men, whose violence knows no bounds?
Men reach their limit with everything, even with sleep
and lovemaking and sweet music and beautiful dance,
and most men try to fill their desire for such pleasures   610
rather than war; but these Trojans just long for more fighting."
And Menelaus stripped off the blood-stained armor
from the dead body and gave it to his companions;
then he went out to rejoin the front ranks of the fighters.

And the son of King Pylǽmenes charged straight at him,
Harpálion, who had come with his father to Troy
but never was to return to his own dear country.
He rushed out to Menelaus and stabbed at his shield,
but he was not able to drive the spear through its layers,
and he shrank back into the crowd to avoid destruction,   620
warily, so that no Achaean would wound him.
But as he retreated, Meriones aimed and shot
and pierced him in the right buttock, and the keen arrow
pushed up under the bone, straight into his bladder.
And sinking down on the spot, in the arms of his comrades
he breathed out his life and lay there stretched on the earth
like a dead worm; and the ground was soaked with his blood.
And the Páphlagónians gathered around and put him
onto a car and carried him sadly to Troy,
and his father, weeping bitterly, walked by their side;   630
but no blood-price would ever be paid to avenge the killing.

Paris was greatly enraged at Harpálion's death,
since they were guest-friends; he shot an arrow that hit
a man named Euchénor, son of the seer Polÿídus,
a wealthy man and well-born, whose home was in Corinth.
He had set sail for Troy in full knowledge that he was going
to his death, since his father had often told him that he
would either die in his bed of a painful disease
or else he would fall at Troy beside the beached ships.
So he came, to avoid the large penalty that the Achaeans   640
levied on those not willing to serve, and also

to save himself from the gnawing pain of the illness.
He was hit just under the ear, and quickly the life
fled from his limbs, and hideous darkness seized him.

And so they continued to fight, like a blazing fire.
Hector was in the middle; he did not know
that his men were being cut down to the left of the ships;
and soon the Achaeans might have triumphed, so strongly
was Poseidon the Earthshaker urging them forward to battle
and putting his own great power behind their efforts.   650
But Hector kept driving on where he first stormed through
the gates and the wall and shattered the close-packed ranks
of shield-bearing Danäans, near the place where the ships
of Ajax and Protesiláüs were drawn up beside
the shore of the gray sea. There the wall was built low,
and the Argives were putting up a ferocious defense.
But the Bœótians, Iónians, Lócrians, Phthians,
and Epéans could barely hold out against Hector's onslaught
as he rushed toward the ships like a fire, and they were unable
to drive him back. And there as well were the bravest   660
Athenians, led by Menéstheus, who was supported
by the commanders Stíchius, Phidas, and Bias;
the Epéans were led by Dracius, Meges, Amphíon;
and Podárces and Medon commanded the Phthian troops.

Ajax the Smaller, the swift-footed son of Öíleus,
stood by the other Ajax, not for a moment
leaving his side. As two oxen with equal strength
pull the plow over farmland that for a long time
has lain fallow, and sweat wells up at the base of their horns,
and only the yoke divides them as they keep straining   670
to cut the furrow and reach the far edge of the field:
just so did these two move forward, shoulder to shoulder.
Ajax the Tall was followed by many brave men
who had come to relieve him and carried his massive shield
whenever fatigue came over his sweat-drenched body.
But the Lócrians did not follow the son of Öíleus,
since they felt that they could not engage in hand-to-hand combat;

they did not have helmets or shields or spears, but had come
to Troy armed only with bows and arrows and slings
of twisted wool, and when they shot them, the missiles   680
fell thick and fast and could break the Trojan battalions.
So the other troops fought in front with their heavy armor,
while the Lócrians shot their arrows and stones from the rear.
And the Trojans, forced back by the missiles, began to lose heart.

And now they would have retreated miserably,
away from the ships and huts to the windswept city,
if Polydamas had not gone up to Hector and said,
"Hector, you are a very hard man to advise.
Because the gods have made you supreme in warfare,
you think that you always know best in tactics as well.   690
But you should not claim preeminence in all things.
The gods make one man an excellent warrior, while
in another man's breast Zeus puts a wise understanding,
which benefits many men and brings safety to many.
So I will speak out and tell you what I think best.
You can see that all around you the battle is blazing;
our troops have succeeded in storming the wall, but some
are standing idle, aside from the fighting, while others
fight in small groups, outnumbered, beside the ships.
Pull them back now, and summon our bravest commanders;   700
then we can make a sensible choice and decide
whether we should attack the ships, in the hope
that the gods will grant us the victory, or instead
draw back our troops for now, without any losses.
I am much afraid that the Argives will take their revenge
for yesterday, since a warrior hungry for battle
still lingers beside the ships, and I cannot believe
that he will hold back from the fighting for very much longer."

Hector was pleased at the good advice of his comrade;
he agreed with him, and he answered him with these words: 710
"Polydamas, stay here and hold back our bravest commanders
while *I* go into the thick of the battle. Soon
I will come back, after I give the men their commands."

*

With these words, he strode away like a snow-capped mountain
and, shouting instructions, swept through the Trojan ranks;
and they, when they heard him, rushed toward Polydamas.
Hector kept ranging among the front ranks, in search
of his comrades Deíphobus, Hélenus, Ádamas,
and Ásius, but none had escaped unharmed;
the last two were lying under the ships' sterns, cut down   720
by the Argives; the others were inside the city wall,
gored by a thrust of the spear or by a keen spear throw.
Soon, on the left of the battlefield, he found Paris,
who was cheering his men and urging them on to fight.
Hector came close and addressed him with shaming words:
"You miserable disgrace, most handsome of men
but woman-crazed, a seducer, a selfish fool,
where are Deíphobus, Hélenus, Ádamas,
and Ásius? Othrÿóneus—where is he?
If these great heroes have disappeared, Troy is doomed,   730
and we face the destruction of everything we hold dear."

Paris answered him, "Hector, why do you blame
someone who is quite blameless, for all you know?
At other times I may have held back from the fighting,
but not today; I was *not* born an utter coward.
From the very moment you stirred up your men to attack,
we have dug in here, engaging the Argives, without
a moment's respite. Three of these comrades are dead,
though Deíphobus and Hélenus have survived;
they are back in the city, both with deep wounds in the arm.   740
But now lead on, wherever your spirit moves you.
We will follow you gladly, and all of us will keep fighting
as long as our strength holds out. A man cannot fight
beyond his strength, no matter how willing he is."

With these words Paris softened his brother's heart,
and they set out and headed for where the battle was fiercest
as it raged near Cebríones and Polydamas,
Phalces, Orthǽus, Pólyphétes, and Palmys,

and Hippótion's sons, Ascánius and Morys,
who had come from Ascánia on the previous day,   750
as reinforcements, and fought in the thick of battle.

The Trojans attacked like the blast of a sudden squall
that swoops down to earth with lightning and thunder, churning
the dark sea into a fury, and countless waves
surge and toss on its surface, high-arched and white-capped,
and crash down onto the seashore in endless ranks:
just so did the Trojans charge in their ranks, each battalion
packed close together and glittering in the sunlight.
And leading the army, just like man-killing Ares,
was Hector. Before him he held out his round shield, thick   760
with oxhides and with a top layer of hammered bronze,
and upon his head shook the crest of his gleaming helmet.
He kept stepping forward to test the enemy ranks
at every point, to see if they would give way
as he pressed on behind the folds of his massive shield;
but he could not break the resolve in the Argives' hearts.

Then Ajax strode forward and challenged him: "If you feel lucky,
come a bit closer. Why are you trying to scare us?
We Danäans aren't newcomers to war; but the fatal
lash of Lord Zeus has struck and beaten us down.   770
Now, I suppose, you hope to destroy our ships;
but we too have hands to defend them. And long before
you can ever capture our ships, your city will fall
to our brave army, and we will plunder its riches.
I tell you truly: the time is approaching when you
will pray to almighty Zeus and the other immortals
to make your horses fly faster than hawks as they kick up
the dust on the plain and carry you back to your city."

As he was speaking, a bird flew by on the right,
a high-soaring eagle, and all the Achaeans shouted   780
for joy, and took heart at the omen. But Hector answered,
"Ajax, you sputtering ox, what nonsense you utter!
If only it were as certain that all my days

I was the son of Zeus, and Queen Hera my mother,
and was honored like Lady Athena and Lord Apollo,
as it is that this day brings evil to the Achaeans.
You too will die with the rest, if you dare to stand
against my spear, which will rip through your tender flesh,
and you will be food for Troy's dogs and carrion birds."
With these words he led the way, and his men followed   790
with a deafening roar, and behind them the whole army shouted.
And the Argives shouted in answer and did not lose courage,
but stood their ground as the Trojan army advanced.
And the uproar from both sides rose to the dazzling heavens.

Book 14

As Nestor was drinking wine in his hut, he noticed
the din of the battle outside, and he said to Macháon,
"Son of Asclépius, listen. The shouts keep getting
louder and louder. I wonder what we should do.
Stay here and drink your wine until Hecamédē
heats you a bath and washes the clotted blood off.
I will take a look and try to find out what has happened."

With these words he picked up the shield of his son Thrasymédes,
who had taken *his* shield, and he picked up a heavy spear.
As soon as he was outside, he saw, to his horror,   10
that the wall had been breached and the Argives were fleeing in panic
and the Trojans relentlessly driving them toward the ships.
As when the sea surges and heaves with a silent groundswell
and watches out for the rush of the whistling winds
and does not break or roll its waves this way or that
until some deciding blast sweeps down from the heavens:
just so did the old king ponder, divided between
two courses of action—should he move forward into
the mass of fighters, or look for King Agamemnon?
And in the end, he decided that it would be best   20
to search for the son of Atreus. Meanwhile the armies
kept slaughtering ceaselessly, and the harsh bronze clanged
as they thrust at each other with swords and double-curved spear points.

And Nestor was met by the wounded kings: Diomedes,
Odysseus, and Agamemnon, as they were coming
up from their ships, which were stationed upon the seashore
far from the fighting. The first of the ships to arrive
had been hauled a good distance inland onto the plain,
and in front of their sterns the Achaeans had built their wall.
For as wide as the beach was, it could by no means contain   30
all the ships, and the men did not have enough room,
and so they had drawn the ships up in rows and had filled

the entire shore of the deep bay between the two headlands.
So these three were late in hearing the uproar of battle,
and they all came together, each leaning upon his spear,
and their hearts were in anguish. When the old warrior met them,
Lord Agamemnon went up to him, and he said,
"Son of Neleus, glory of the Achaeans,
why have you left the fighting and come back here?
I am much afraid that Hector will make good the threat   40
that he once announced in the Trojan assembly, saying
he would never go back to Ilion from the black ships
until he had set them on fire and slaughtered our men.
These were his words, and now they are coming true."

Nestor said, "Yes. Indeed this has come upon us,
and not even Zeus the Thunderer can prevent it.
We thought that the wall would be an unyielding defense
for us and our fleet, but now it has been knocked over,
and the Trojans are fighting relentlessly by the ships,
and wherever you look, you cannot see which direction   50
the attack is coming from, so confused is the slaughter,
so great the chaos, an uproar rising to heaven.
We must think about what we should do now, if thought can do
anything. But you three shouldn't enter the battle,
since no man can fight when he is wounded as you are."

Then Agamemnon answered him with these words:
"You are right. They are fighting now at the sterns of the ships;
the wall and trench that we labored so hard over haven't
protected us, though we relied on them and we hoped
they would be an unyielding defense for us and our fleet.   60
Such is the will, it seems, of almighty Zeus.
I knew it when he was eager to come to our aid,
and I know that now he has shackled our hands and is giving
these Trojans the glory he gives to the blessed gods.
So listen now, and let us all do as I say.
We should drag the ships in front, the ones that are nearest
the sea, and pull them into the water and moor them
a little way out, with anchor stones, until night comes.

In the darkness we can drag down the rest of the fleet,
unless the Trojans keep fighting. There is no shame   70
in running away from disaster, even by night.
It is better to run and escape death than to be killed here."

Odysseus answered him then, with an angry scowl,
"Son of Atreus, what words have spilled from your mouth!
If you are so spineless, you should have been in command
of some other army, an army of cowards—not us,
to whom Zeus has given the task of carrying out
horrendous wars, from youth to old age, fighting on
till our very last breath. Is this how you want us to leave
Troy, the great city, for which we have suffered such hardships?   80
Don't say another word now or some of the men
will hear your idea, which no one in his right mind
would allow through his lips, especially such a king
as you are, in command of so vast an army.
Have you lost your mind? What has made you spout out
such contemptible nonsense? You tell us to launch our ships
in the midst of a battle, to hand the Trojans a sweet
victory at a time when they are attacking
and want nothing more than for us to go running home.
Besides, it would be a disaster for us. Our soldiers   90
will never fight on as their ships are hauled to the sea;
they will panic and run, and their disorder will cause
nothing but harm. Your advice will destroy them, Commander."

Then Agamemnon answered him with these words:
"You have stung my heart, Odysseus, with your rebuke.
But you are right. I will not order the Argives
to pull the ships into the sea if they do not want to.
Is there anyone who can put forth a better idea?
I would welcome it, whoever the man might be."

When he heard this, Diomedes spoke out: "That man   100
is standing right here, and you need not look any farther,
if you are willing to listen to what I say
and not be biased against it because I am young.

I too am proud to descend from a noble father,
Tydeus, whom the piled earth now covers in Thebes.
Three sons were born to Portheus; they lived in Pleuron
and the steep hills of Cálydon: Ágrius and Melas
and the third of the sons was Œneus, my father's father,
the bravest of them. He stayed there in Cálydon,
but my father had to leave home, and he settled in Argos;   110
such was the will of Zeus and the other gods.
There he married one of Adrástus's daughters
and lived on a large estate, with wheat-bearing plowlands,
abundant orchards, and fields filled with herds and flocks,
and of all the Achaean warriors he was the greatest.
You all know that this is true, so you won't dismiss
the words that I say—provided that they make sense—
on the grounds that my lineage is that of a coward.
Here is my thought: We should go at once to the battle,
we *must* go, though we are wounded. As long as we keep   120
beyond the range of the missiles, there is no chance
that we will add wounds to the ones we have; but from there
we three can encourage the others and send them out
with their spirits renewed, and even send those who until now
have been well disposed but have stood apart from the fighting."
They listened to him and agreed with what he had said,
then set out, with King Agamemnon leading the way.

Poseidon, who had been watching, went down to meet them
in the likeness of an old man, and he approached
Lord Agamemnon and took his right hand and said,   130
"Son of Atreus, now the hard heart of Achilles
must be filled with glee as he looks on this slaughter and rout.
There is no human feeling in him, not even a little.
May some god punish him for it. But I am sure
that the blessed gods are not wholly displeased with *you*.
A time will come when the Trojan lords and commanders
will kick up the dust on the plain, and you will see them
fleeing as fast as they can toward the walls of their city."
With these words he left, and he hurried across the plain
bellowing, and his roar was as loud as the shout   140

of ten thousand men as they join in the tumult of battle:
so mighty a voice did Poseidon the Earthshaker hurl
from his chest. And within the heart of each Argive soldier
he stirred up the strength to fight without any respite.

Meanwhile Hera looked down from the top of Olympus
and saw her brother and brother-in-law as he bustled
about and urged on the troops, and she was happy.
Then she saw Zeus as he sat on the highest peak
of Mount Ida, and suddenly hatred surged through her heart,
and she pondered how she could trick him and help the Achaeans.   150
And in the end, she decided that the best way
was to seduce him by making herself so alluring
that he would be overwhelmed by desire for her
and want to make love; and afterward she could pour
a warm, gentle sleep on his eyelids and cunning mind.
She went to her room, which her son Hephaestus with great skill
had fashioned, fitting its massive doors to the doorposts
with a secret lock, which no other god could open,
and she entered the room and closed the great doors behind her.
First she cleansed all the stains from her lovely body   160
with ambrosia, then she rubbed herself with perfumed
olive oil. (Its fragrance filled earth and heaven
as she moved about in the bronze-paved palace of Zeus.)
After she rubbed this all over her beautiful skin,
she combed her long hair and braided the glistening locks,
then put on a dress that Athena had made for her, richly
embroidered with many images, and she pinned it
at her breast with a golden brooch, and around her waist
she fastened a belt that was hung with a hundred tassels,
and in the pierced lobes of her ears she put earrings with brilliant   170
jewels that hung down in triple drops, gleaming with beauty.
She covered her head with a shawl of the finest linen
that had never been worn and was pure white as the sun,
and onto her feet she tied her elegant sandals.

After she finished adorning herself, she walked
out of her room, and she beckoned to Aphrodite

to come aside from the other gods, and she said,
"Will you do me a favor now, dear child, if I ask you?
Or will you refuse because you are still annoyed
that I am helping the Argives, though *you* love the Trojans?"   180

And Aphrodite, daughter of Zeus, replied,
"Queen of goddesses, daughter of mighty Cronus,
say what is on your mind. I will certainly do it
if I can and if it is something that may be done."

Then, with cunning deceitfulness, Hera said,
"Give me love and desire, with which you conquer
the hearts of all the immortals and of all men.
I am going now to the ends of the earth to see
Lord Ocean, the sire of the gods, and Mother Tethys,
who received me from Rhea and brought me up in their house   190
at the time when Zeus imprisoned Cronus, our father,
in the darkness beneath the earth and the restless sea.
I am going to visit them now and resolve their endless
quarrel; they are so furious at each other
that it has been a long time since they have made love.
If I can manage to reconcile them and bring them
back into bed to unite in love, they will always
be grateful to me and will honor me ever after."

And laughter-loving Aphrodite responded,
"Hera, I can't and shouldn't refuse what you ask,   200
since you are the one who sleeps in the arms of the greatest
of gods, Lord Zeus." And unfastening from her breasts
an embroidered sash that was inset with magic charms
of love and desire, flirtation, whispered endearments
that seduce the good judgment even of sensible men,
she handed it over to Lady Hera and said,
"Take this sash and put it between your breasts.
All my magic is in it, and I am sure
that you will be able to get whatever you wish for."
When she heard Aphrodite's instructions, Hera smiled,   210
and smiling she tucked the charmed sash into her bosom.

*

Aphrodite turned and walked into the palace,
and Hera flew down from Mount Olympus; she soared
over Piéria, over Emáthia, past
the snowy mountaintops of the horse-rearing Thracians,
and her feet never touched the ground. From Mount Athos she crossed
the waves of the sea till she came to the isle of Lemnos.
There she found Sleep, Death's brother. She took his hand
in hers, and she said, "Sleep, lord of all gods and all men,
you have listened to me before; listen again now,   220
and I will be grateful to you for the rest of my days.
Seal Zeus's eyes in slumber beneath his eyelids
as soon as we have made love. Do this for me
and I will give you a beautiful golden throne,
imperishable forever. My son Hephaestus,
the crippled god, will make it for you, with a footstool
to rest your glistening feet as you drink your nectar."

Then Sleep, the god of refreshment, said in response,
"Queen of goddesses, daughter of mighty Cronus,
I would readily grant your request if it were a matter   230
of anyone else among the immortal gods—
even Lord Ocean, the origin of us all.
But I dare not come close to Zeus or lull him to slumber
unless it is he himself who commands me to do it.
I was once before taught a lesson when I agreed
to something you asked for, when Zeus's arrogant son
Héracles sailed from Troy after laying it waste.
I made Zeus slumber, pouring my sweetness around him
while you plotted against his son and stirred up a gale
that swept him far from his friends, to the isle of Cos.   240
Zeus was enraged when he woke up; he began hurling
gods all over the palace and then he went looking
for me, and he would have flung me through empty space
to vanish into the sea, if Night, the subduer
of gods and men, had not saved me. I ran to her side
for protection, and Zeus drew back, in spite of his rage,
since he didn't dare to do anything she would dislike.

And now you are asking for one more impossible favor."

Then Hera smiled and answered him with these words:
"Why should you trouble your mind with such silly ideas?   250
Do you think that Zeus is as bent on helping the Trojans
as on helping his son, that time he was so enraged?
But all right, my dear; I will give you one of the Graces
for you to marry and call your beloved wife."

When he heard this, Sleep was overjoyed, and he answered,
"Well then, by the inviolate waters of Styx
swear to me, with one hand on the bountiful earth
and the other hand on the glistening sea—and let all
the gods who dwell in the lower depths with old Cronus
witness—that you will give me one of the Graces: 260
Pasíthea. I have longed for her all my days."

Hera nodded her head and did what he asked for.
She swore, invoking the names of those lower gods.
And after she had completed her oath, the two
shrouded themselves in mist and quickly set out,
leaving the cities of Lemnos and Imbros behind them.
Soon they came to Mount Ida, abundant in springs
and mother of many wild beasts, where they left the sea
at Lectos. From there they went on over dry land,
and the highest treetops trembled beneath their feet.   270
And then Sleep stopped, before Zeus's eyes could see him,
and he flew up into a pine tree, the tallest on Ida,
which reached through the mist and into the clear air above.
He perched at the top of it, hidden by the thick branches,
in the form of a shrill-voiced bird that lives in the mountains
(the gods call it Bronze-throat, but men's name for it is Hawk-owl).

Hera sped on to Gárgarus, Ida's summit.
And when Zeus saw her, desire overwhelmed his mind
as strongly as in the days when they first were lovers,
sneaking off to escape the eyes of their parents.   280
He stood there in a fever of lust and said,

"Hera, what brings you down from the heights of Olympus?
And where are your horses and chariot? I don't see them."

Then, with cunning deceitfulness, Hera said,
"Oh, I am off to the ends of the earth, to visit
Lord Ocean, the sire of the gods, and Mother Tethys,
who received me from Rhea and brought me up in their house.
I am going to visit them now and resolve their endless
quarrel; they are so furious at each other
that it has been a long time since they have made love.   290
My horses wait at the foot of the mountain, to take me
over dry land and sea. But to tell the truth,
you are the reason I came down here from Olympus.
I wanted to see you so that you wouldn't be angry
that I went to Lord Ocean's house without letting you know."

Then Zeus said, "My dear, you can visit them later on;
for now, let us go to bed and be joined in pleasure.
Never before has desire for goddess or woman
so inundated my heart and so overpowered it—
not even when I was in love with Ixíon's wife,   300
who bore me Piríthoüs, or with Acrísius's daughter
Dánaë, that girl with the lovely ankles,
who bore me Perseus, or with the daughter of Phoenix,
Európa, who bore me Minos and Rhadamánthys,
or with Sémelē, or with Alcména in Thebes,
who was the mother of Héracles, whereas the other
gave birth to Dionýsus, the joy of mankind,
or with Deméter, or Leto, or you yourself—
than now, when this sweet desire has overwhelmed me."

Then, with cunning deceitfulness, Hera said,   310
"Dread Lord, what do you mean? If you want to make love
on the summit of Ida, everybody will see.
What if one of the gods were to pass by and spot us
sleeping together and go and tell all the others?
It would be such a scandal that I could never go back
to Olympus. But if you really want to make love,

there is a very private room in your palace
that your son Hephaestus fashioned for you with great skill.
We can go there now, since lovemaking is your pleasure."

And Zeus answered, "Hera, I promise that no god or man   320
will see. I will cover you up in a golden cloud
so thick that not even Hélios could see through it,
though his eyesight is the most penetrating of all."
After these words, Zeus took his wife in his arms,
and beneath them the shining earth burst forth with spring flowers,
dewy clover and crocus and hyacinth,
thick and soft, which lifted them off the ground.
They lay there, concealed in a beautiful golden cloud,
and from it dewdrops fell glistening all around them.

As the Father lay there in peace on the top of Mount Ida,   330
subdued by slumber and holding his wife in his arms,
Sleep ran down to the black ships of the Achaeans
to bring the news to the god who encircles the earth.
And when he found him, he quickly came up and said,
"Go now, Poseidon; bring as much help to the Argives
as you have wanted to; give them the victory,
if only for a short time, while Zeus lies sleeping.
I sent him into deep slumber when Hera seduced him."

After these words, he flew off to visit mankind,
and he left the Earthshaker more determined than ever   340
to help the Argives. Poseidon ran up and shouted,
"Men, are we going to yield the triumph to Hector
and let him capture our ships and win all the glory?
He is boasting that this is what he will do, since Achilles
lingers behind, his heart still blazing with anger.
But we will not feel his absence too much if we all
fight our best and always stand by each other.
So listen now, and let us all do as I say.
Take the strongest shields that you can lay hold of,
put on your helmets, and come with your longest spears.   350
I will lead you myself, and Hector will never hold out

against our forces, for all his determination.
If any good fighter has a small shield, he should give it
to a weaker man and take a large shield himself."

When they heard his words, they did what Poseidon commanded.
And Diomedes, Odysseus, and Agamemnon,
although they were badly wounded, directed the others
and oversaw the exchange of armor—the best
fighters put on the best armor; the worst, the worst.
And when they had clothed their bodies in gleaming bronze,   360
they marched out, and Poseidon the Earthshaker led them,
holding his sword in his hand like a bolt of lightning
that flashed with terror, and no one dared to come near it.
Opposite them, the Trojans were led by Hector,
and Poseidon and he pulled tight the rope of the battle.
And the sea surged up to the huts and ships of the Argives
as the armies of both sides clashed with a deafening uproar.
Less loud is the boom of waves as they crash on the seashore,
thrust from the deep by the brutal blast of the north wind;
less loud is the roar that comes from a blazing fire   370
in a mountain gorge as it rages up through the forest;
less loud is the shriek of the wind among the high branches
of the oak trees when it is howling in all its fury
than this uproar was, with the din of the terrible war cries
that the Trojans and Argives were shouting as they attacked.

First Hector threw his bright spear at Ajax the Tall,
who had turned straight toward him. The spear hit Ajax directly
on the chest, at the point where two thick straps intersected,
one for his shield and one for his silver-bossed sword.
This saved him; the spear bounced off, and Hector was angry   380
that the shot, though it had been perfectly aimed, was wasted,
and he moved back into the ranks to escape destruction.
But as he was going, Ajax picked up a huge rock—
one of the many that lay there to wedge the ships
and, dislodged, were rolling amid their feet—and he hit him
above his shield's rim, on the chest, just below his neck,
and the blow made him stagger, spinning him like a top.

As when from a blast of lightning an oak tree falls
uprooted, and from it a horrible stench of sulfur
fills the air, and a man who comes close feels sheer   390
terror at seeing what Zeus's fire has wrought:
so Hector fell to the ground; and the long spear dropped
out of his hand, and the heavy shield crashed upon him.
And the Argives rushed forward with a thick volley of spears,
shouting their battle cries, hoping to drag him away.
But no one could hit him with a spear's thrust or a spear throw;
immediately he was joined by the best of the Trojans,
Aeneas and Polydamas and Agénor,
and Sarpedon and Glaucus. And none of the other men
failed to protect him; they all held their shields out in front   400
and lifted him up and carried him out of the fighting
to the horses waiting for him at the rear of the battle
with their charioteer and the handsome, bronze-inlaid car;
and they brought him, groaning with pain, back toward the city.
But when they came to the ford of the swirling Xanthus,
they lifted him out, laid him upon the ground,
splashed water over his face, and he came to
and opened his eyes and got up onto his knees
and coughed up dark blood, then sank back to earth, and night
covered his eyes, for the mighty blow still overwhelmed him.   410

And when the Argives saw Hector leaving the battle,
they rushed at the Trojans more fiercely, with freshened spirits.
In front was Ajax the Smaller, who lunged with his spear
and stabbed Sátnius, son of Enops; a water nymph
had conceived him as his father was tending his herds
beside the river Satníoïs. Ajax came close
and stabbed him below the ribs, and he fell to the earth
face upward, and all around him Trojans and Argives
clashed with one another in furious combat.
And quickly Polydamas came to defend him; he aimed   420
and threw his spear, and it hit Prothöénor, the son
of Arëílyeus, and it drove through his shoulder,
and he fell in the dust, clawing the earth with his nails.
And Polydamas gloated terribly over him, shouting:

"Another spear from the hand of the great-hearted son
of Pánthoüs, and it didn't leap out for nothing,
since one of the Argives has caught it. Now it can serve
as his staff, while he walks down the road to the realm of Hades."

The Argives were stung by his boasting, none of them more
than Ajax, since he was the closest to Prothöénor.   430
As Polydamas drew back, Ajax threw his bright spear;
Polydamas jumped to one side and escaped destruction,
but the spear hit Archélochus, one of Anténor's sons,
since the gods had ordained his death on this day; it hit him
at the place where the head and the neck join, at the topmost
vertebra, and it severed both of the tendons,
and the head flew off, and it fell face down in the dirt,
and after a moment the rest of his body crumpled.
And Ajax shouted these words to Polydamas: "Now,
Polydamas, think it over and tell me truly—   440
isn't the death of this man a fitting exchange
for Prothöénor? He doesn't appear to be
a common man or to come from a common family;
he could even be a brother of Lord Anténor
or perhaps a son—he bears such a striking resemblance."
(He knew quite well who it was.) And the Trojans were grieved.

But Ácamas straddled Archélochus, who was his brother,
and when a Bœótian named Prómachus tried to drag
the body off by the feet, he lunged and stabbed him.
And Ácamas gloated terribly over him, shouting: 450
"You Argive weaklings, mouths filled with pitiful threats,
our troops are not the only ones that will suffer.
You too will someday be killed like this man. Can you see
how your Prómachus sleeps, cut down by my mighty spear?
It seems that the blood-price that I was owed for my brother
has been promptly paid. This is the reason a man
prays that a brother remains to avenge his death."
The Argives were stung by his boasting, none of them more
than Penéleos; angered, he charged. And Ácamas did not
stand his ground before the Achaean's attack;   460

and Penéleos thrust and stabbed Ílioneus, the son
of Phorbas, a favorite of Hermes, who made him wealthy,
but this son was the only child his mother had borne.
Penéleos stabbed him under the eyebrow; the spear
knocked out the eyeball and then drove on through the socket
and out the neck; as he sank down backward, he reached
both arms to his friends. But Penéleos unsheathed his sword
and sliced off his head, and it fell to the ground in its helmet,
with the spear still stuck in the eye bone. He lifted it up
like a poppy upon its stalk, and he displayed it   470
before the eyes of the Trojans, shouting in triumph:
"Do me a favor, Trojans; go back to the city
and tell the father and mother of Ílioneus
that they should begin their mourning, just as the wife
of Prómachus will not rejoice to see *him* again
when the Achaeans sail back from the land of Troy."
At these words, each Trojan was seized by trembling and looked
around to see how he could escape destruction.

Tell me now, Muses, who have your homes on Olympus,
who was the first of all the Achaeans to win   480
the blood-stained spoils of an enemy killed in the fighting
after the Earthshaker turned the battle around?
It was Ajax the Tall; he was the first one. He stabbed
Hýrtius, the commander of the brave Mysians.
Antilochus then killed Mérmerus and Phalces,
Meriones cut down Hippótion and Morys,
and Teucer dispatched Prothóön and Periphétes.
Then Menelaus stabbed Hyperénor below
the ribs, in the side; the bronze point's thrust made his innards
gush out as it ripped them, then the life force came rushing   490
out through the deep wound, and darkness covered his eyes.
But the one who killed the most men was Ajax the Smaller.
There was no one as fast as he was in running down
the men who fled when Lord Zeus sent panic among them.

Book 15

But once the Trojans had fled past the stakes and the trench
and many of them had died at the hands of the Argives,
they reached their chariots and came to a halt there, pale
with terror. Now Zeus woke up on the heights of Mount Ida
where he was lying, and Hera was lying beside him.
He stood up and saw the Trojans fleeing in panic
and the Argives relentlessly driving them back from the ships,
with Lord Poseidon among them, leading the way.
And Hector was there on the plain—his comrades were kneeling
around him, and he lay stretched out, gasping for breath,   10
stunned with pain and coughing up blood, since the rock
had been hurled by the most powerful of the Achaeans.
When he saw him, the father of men and gods felt pity,
and he gave a ferocious scowl and said to Hera:
"You treacherous bitch, it must be your damned scheming
that knocked Hector out of the war and routed his army.
I am tempted to teach you a lesson and get my whip
and beat you senseless, since you are to blame for this mischief.
Don't you remember that time when I strung you up
with two anvils hung from your feet, and around your hands   20
an unbreakable golden cord? You dangled in midair
among the white clouds, and all the gods of Olympus
were furious, but no one could come to your rescue—
whomever I caught I hurled from the threshold of heaven,
and he fell to Earth and landed there, barely alive.
And still my heart wasn't eased of its aching sorrow
for Héracles, whom you and the north wind drove
spitefully, with violent hailstorms, over
the restless sea until he was swept away
to the isle of Cos. I rescued him there and brought him   30
back to the land of Argos after much grief.
I have brought this up in the hope of driving some sense
into that devious mind of yours. Don't imagine
that lovemaking will protect you in any way

from my rage, if I catch you trying to trick me again."

When she heard these words, Queen Hera shuddered and said,
"Let earth be my witness now and heaven above
and the downward-flowing waters of Styx—the greatest
and most terrible oath that we immortals can take—
and your sacred brow and the sacred bed of our marriage,   40
which I never would swear upon falsely, that it is not
through anything I have done that Poseidon has caused
grief to the Trojans and Hector, and helped the Argives.
It must be his own heart that prompts him; he must have seen
the Achaeans as they were overwhelmed near their ships
and must have felt pity for them. But I assure you,
Lord of the Dark Clouds, that I would advise him always
to follow your lead, wherever you wish to go."

At this, the father of men and gods smiled and said,
"From now on, Hera, if you agree to support me   50
when I make my will known in the council of the immortals,
then Poseidon, like it or not, will soon come around
and join us, changing his mind to suit our opinion.
But if you are really telling the truth, then return
to the gods on Olympus. Tell Iris I want to see her.
I will send her down to the army of the Achaeans
to command Lord Poseidon to leave the war and go home.
And tell Apollo to come here as well. I want him
to restore Hector's health so that he can rejoin the battle—
to breathe fresh power into his body and make him   60
forget the pains that are wracking his lungs, and then
to stir up terror and panic among the Achaeans
and drive back their army all the way to the ships.
I will not cease from opposing them. I forbid
any of the immortals to help the Argives
until the desire of Achilles has been fulfilled,
as I promised him at the beginning and bowed my head
on the day that Thetis came to Olympus and clasped
my knees and wept and implored me to honor her son."

*

At these words, Hera did what her husband had asked for   70
and flew from the mountains of Ida up to Olympus.
And as instantaneously as a thought in the mind
of a man who has traveled through many lands and calls up
many memories—"Let me be here, or there!"—
and, in a moment, he is: so quickly did Hera
fly through the air until she came to Olympus
and found the immortals gathered in Zeus's palace.
And when they saw her, they stood up and drank her health.
She passed by the rest of them, but she accepted a cup
from Themis, who ran out in front to meet her and said,   80
"Hera, why have you come here? You look upset.
What is the matter? Has Zeus abused you again?"

Then Hera said, "Please don't ask me about it, Themis.
You know how overbearing and stubborn he is.
But go ahead, lead the gods to the dinner table;
you will hear what a vile turn of events he is planning.
Even though some of you still may enjoy the feast,
I very much doubt that everyone will be happy."

With this Queen Hera sat down, and throughout the room
the heavenly gods were chilled. She laughed with her mouth,   90
but above her dark brows her forehead knit in a scowl.
Finally, she burst out with indignation:
"What fools we are when we try to quarrel with Zeus!
Do we think we can stop him or turn him aside by force
or by argument? He sits by himself, apart,
and he doesn't care about us or about our opinions,
since he knows that he is much stronger than all the immortals.
So make the best of whatever evil he sends you.
Already a sorrow has come to Ares. His son
Ascálaphus has been killed, the man he loved most."   100

When he heard this, Ares stood up, and he slapped his thighs
with the flats of his hands, and he howled out in his sorrow:
"Don't blame me now, you gods who live on Olympus,
if I go to the Argives' ships to avenge my son,

even if I am struck down by Zeus's lightning
and I lie there in pain amid the piles of the dead."

When he finished speaking, he ordered Terror and Panic
to yoke his horses, while he himself put on his armor.
Then Zeus would have been aroused to an even greater
and more calamitous rage against the immortals   110
if Athena, alarmed for their safety, had not at once
leaped from the golden chair where she had been sitting
and hurried outside. She caught up with Ares and snatched off
his glittering helmet and took the shield from his shoulders
and the spear from his massive hand, and she rebuked him:
"Are you crazed? Have you lost your mind? Don't you have ears
or a brain in that thick skull of yours? Didn't you hear
what Hera announced to us, coming straight from Mount Ida?
Do you want to be overwhelmed with evil, then forced
whimpering back to Olympus once you have sown   120
the seeds of disaster for all the other immortals?
Right away Zeus will leave the Trojans and Argives
and will come back here in a fury that you can imagine,
and batter each one of us, guilty and guiltless alike.
So I beg you now: let go of your dangerous anger.
Better men have already been killed before this,
and many good men will be killed in the future. It isn't
possible that we can safeguard everyone's children."

With these words Athena made Ares sit down again,
while Hera summoned Apollo outside the great hall   130
and Iris, the messenger of the gods, and she said,
"Lord Zeus commands you both to go to Mount Ida
immediately. And when you come into his presence,
you must listen closely and do whatever he says."

After she finished, Hera went back inside
and sat on her throne, and the two of them hurried away.
Quickly they came to Mount Ida, abundant in springs
and mother of many wild beasts. There they found Zeus
on the peak of Gárgarus, wreathed with a fragrant cloud.

They stood before him, and seeing them he was pleased   140
that they had been quick in obeying his wife's instructions.
He spoke first to Iris, the messenger of the gods:
"Hurry now, Iris; go to the lord Poseidon
and deliver this message, exactly the way I tell you.
Command him to leave the fighting at once and to go
straight to Olympus or into the shining sea.
And if he is tempted to disobey my command,
ask him whether he thinks he is strong enough
to withstand my attack. For I am much stronger than he is
and his elder by birth. Yet he has the gall to claim   150
that he is my equal, though all the other gods fear me."

When she heard this, Iris obeyed, and as swift as the wind
she flew from the heights of Mount Ida to sacred Troy.
And like the snow and the freezing hail that are driven
down from the clouds beneath the blast of the north wind:
so quickly did Iris fly to the plain of Troy.
And she found the Earthshaker, and she went up and said,
"Great Lord, I have come with a message from mighty Zeus.
He commands you to leave the fighting at once and to go
straight to Olympus or into the shining sea   160
And if you are tempted to disobey his command,
he threatens to come here himself and to make you leave
by force, and he solemnly warns you to keep far away
from his reach. He says that he is much stronger than you are
and your elder by birth. Yet you have the gall to claim
that you are his equal, though all the other gods fear him."

Greatly troubled by this, Lord Poseidon answered,
"What arrogance—to order me out of the battle
with a threat of force. Outrageous! The gall of *him!*
He may be the stronger, but I am most surely his equal.   170
We are three brothers, borne to Cronus by Rhea:
Zeus and I and Hades, the lord of the dead.
The world was divided in three, and each of us brothers
was given an equal share when the lots were cast.
I drew the restless sea as my realm forever,

and Hades the murky gloom of the underworld,
and Zeus the broad sky and the clouds and the upper air;
but the earth and the heights of Olympus were left to us all.
I refuse to live according to Zeus's whims.
He must stay in his third share, however strong he may be.   180
And let him not try to frighten me as he might
frighten a coward. It would be better for him
to threaten his sons and daughters. They are obliged,
being his children, to do whatever he tells them."

Then Iris said, "Great Lord, am I really to take
this harsh and defiant message to Zeus, or will you
perhaps reconsider? A noble mind can be changed.
And you know how the Furies always side with the elder."

Poseidon the Earthshaker answered, "What you just said,
Iris, is rightly spoken, and it is good   190
when a messenger has such sense and shows such discretion.
Nevertheless, it offends me that he has rebuked
someone who is his equal and has the same portion.
But all right—I will give in to him, though I am angry.
But I tell you this, and it is no idle threat:
If without my consent, and without the consent of Athena,
he spares this city and lets the Trojans survive
and doesn't grant triumph and plunder to the Achaeans,
between him and me there will be an unhealable rupture."
With these words the Earthshaker left the battle and plunged   200
into the sea. And the Danäans sorely missed him.

Now Zeus told Apollo, "Go, dear Phoebus, to Hector.
Poseidon has just plunged into the shining sea
to ease my dangerous rage and avoid a battle
whose uproar would have been heard by even the gods
imprisoned with Cronus, down in the deepest abyss.
It is better for me by far, and for him as well,
that he did what I asked, however offended he is,
because this wouldn't have ended without much grief.
Take the terrible storm shield and shake it above   210

the Achaean army and set their hearts wild with panic.
Then care for Hector and bring him back to full strength
so that he can make the Achaeans flee to their ships.
At that point, I will decide what needs to be done
to give the Achaeans breathing space from the battle."

When he heard these words, Apollo obeyed his father
and swooped from the heights of Ida as fast as a hawk,
the dove-killer, the swiftest of winged creatures.
And when he arrived, Hector was no longer lying
stretched on the ground, but sitting up. He had just   220
begun to collect his wits and was recognizing
his comrades around him, and all the gasping and sweating
had stopped, as the mind of Zeus sent strength to his body.
Apollo approached and stood beside him and said,
"Son of Priam, why are you sitting apart,
looking so feeble? Have you been badly hurt?"

Then Hector answered, in an unsteady voice:
"Which of the gods are you who ask me this question?
Haven't you heard? I was fighting beside the black ships
of the Argives, killing his comrades, when Ajax hit me   230
in the chest with a boulder and put a stop to my triumph.
Truly, I thought that today I would breathe my last
and go down among the dead in the realm of Hades."

And Apollo said to him, "Courage; Lord Zeus has sent
a mighty helper to stand by your side and protect you—
Phoebus Apollo, the god of the golden sword.
I have kept you from harm in the past, both you and your city.
Now you must rally your charioteers and command them
to drive toward the black ships. I will go first and smooth
the way for the horses and drive the Achaeans back."   240

With this he breathed a tremendous strength into Hector.
Just as a stabled horse who has fully eaten
breaks his tether and gallops across the plain,
eager to have a swim in the fast-flowing river:

so quickly did Hector run up and down as he urged on
the charioteers, in obedience to the god.
As when farmers have set their hunting dogs on a stag
or a wild goat, but it flees and escapes to some cliff
or shadowy wood, since they were not destined to catch it,
then, stirred by their shouting, a great bearded lion appears   250
and sends them all running away in spite of their courage:
just so had the Argives kept charging in mass formation
until then, thrusting their swords and double-curved spear points;
but when they saw Hector striding again through the ranks,
they were terrified, and their hearts sank down to their feet.

Then Thoas, the son of Andræmon, spoke to the army;
he was the bravest of all the Ætólians,
skilled in throwing the spear, but a good man too
in hand-to-hand fighting, and few were more eloquent
whenever the young men competed in a debate.   260
With confidence in his judgment, he spoke to the men:
"Look! Can this be? But I see it with my own eyes.
Hector is on his feet; he has come back to life!
We thought he had died at the hands of Ajax, but now
one of the gods, it appears, has saved him again.
So listen now, and let us all do as I say.
We must first make sure that most of the troops fall back
as far as the ships, while those of us in the front line,
who claim to be the best fighters, stand with our spears out,
ready to hold him off. However he rages,   270
his heart will shrink from plunging straight into our ranks."

When they heard his words, they did what Thoas had told them.
The men with Idómeneus, Ajax, Meriones, Teucer,
and Meges called for the best of their men to come,
and they formed a strong line to face the Trojans and Hector,
and behind them most of the troops fell back toward the ships.

The Trojans charged in a mass then, and Hector led them,
striding ahead. In front was Apollo, his shoulders
covered with mist, and he held the furious storm shield,

shaggy, blindingly bright, which the smith Hephaestus   280
had fashioned for Zeus, to curdle the blood of men;
with this in his hands, the god led the Trojan army.
The Argives stood firm, in dense ranks, and a shrill war cry
arose from both sides, and the arrows leaped from the bowstrings.
Many spears lodged in the bodies of quick young men,
and many spears, hungry to glut themselves on white flesh,
stuck in the ground before they could ever reach it.
As long as Apollo held the grim storm shield steady,
the weapons of both sides pierced, and the men kept dying.
But as soon as he shook it into the Danäans' faces   290
and uttered his deafening battle cry, he bewildered
their minds, and they abandoned their fighting spirit.
And like a great herd of cows or a flock of sheep
that two lions stampede when they come in the dead of night
suddenly, and the herdsman is nowhere near:
just so the Achaeans fled like cowards. Apollo
had terrified them and given the glory to Hector.

Then man cut down man as the Danäan front was scattered.
Hector killed Stíchius and Árcesiläüs;
the one was a prominent leader of the Bœótians,   300
the other was one of Menéstheus's trusted comrades.
Aeneas slaughtered Medon and Íasus—
Medon a bastard son of Öíleus, and brother
of Ajax the Smaller (he lived in Phýlacē, far
from his own dear country; he left it because he had killed
the brother of Eriópis, Ajax's mother);
Íasus was an Athenian captain, whose father
was Sphelus. Polydamas killed Mecísteus, Polítes
killed Échius in the front lines, and Agénor killed
Clónius; Paris's spear hit Dëíochus   310
from behind as he fled; the spear point drove hard into
the base of the shoulder and came straight out through his chest.

And while the Trojans were stripping the bodies, the Argives,
terror-stricken, were falling into the trench
and hitting the stakes, and were forced back behind their wall.

Then Hector ordered the Trojans in a loud voice
to charge the black ships and leave the armor behind:
"If any one of you shrinks back and doesn't follow,
I will have him killed on the spot, and his father and mother
won't be allowed to give him his due rites of burning,   320
but the wild dogs will tear him apart in front of our city."
With these words, bringing his whip down with all his force,
he lashed his horses ahead and rallied the Trojans.
Shouting out, they all drove their chariots onward
with a deafening roar; and in front of them Phoebus Apollo
kicked down the banks of the deep trench effortlessly
and pushed them into the middle to make a long causeway,
as wide as the distance a javelin flies when a sportsman
tests his strength by throwing as far as he can.
Across this they all poured, rank after rank, as Apollo   330
led the army, holding the terrible storm shield.
And with utter ease he knocked down the Argives' wall,
like a young child sitting and playing beside the sea
who amuses himself by building a sand castle, then
gleefully knocks it down with his hands and feet:
so you, Lord Apollo, demolished what the Achaeans
had toiled so hard to build, and drove panic among them.

They came to a halt alongside the ships, and they called out
to one another and cried to the gods with raised arms.
Nestor cried out the most fervently of them all,   340
stretching his hands to the sky, where the stars are hidden:
"Father Zeus, if ever in wheat-bearing Argos
any of us has burned in your honor the fat-wrapped
thighbones of oxen or sheep and begged you to send him
safely home, and you promised and nodded your head,
remember that now. Save us from doom; don't let us
all be wretchedly slaughtered like this by the Trojans."
That was his prayer, and Lord Zeus thundered in answer.
But the Trojans, when they heard Zeus's terrible omen,
rushed at the Argives more fiercely, with freshened spirits.   350

Like a monstrous wave that crashes down on a ship

when the sea runs highest, swollen by raging winds:
just so did the Trojans sweep over the wall with loud war cries,
driving their chariots inside. They fought at the ships' sterns
with double-curved spears; the Achaeans had climbed high up
on their ships, and from there they fought with the long bronze-tipped
pikes that lay on the decks for battles at sea.

And while the Achaean and Trojan armies were fighting
for control of the wall, Patroclus still sat in the hut
of Eurýpylus, cheering him up with his conversation   360
and applying herbs to his wound to relieve the dark pain.
But as soon as the Trojans broke through the wall, while the Argives
with panicked shouts were turning and running away,
he heard them and stood up, groaning, and slapped his thighs
with the flats of his hands and cried out to him in sorrow:
"I know that you need me, Eurýpylus, but I can't
stay here with you anymore—a great battle has started.
Your attendant will have to take care of you. I must hurry
to Achilles and urge him to enter the fighting. Who knows?—
if all goes well, I might move his heart with my words,   370
since a dear friend's advice can be a powerful thing."

With this he hurried away. Meanwhile the Argives
stood firm against the Trojan attack, but they could not
push them away from the ships, though the Trojans were fewer,
nor were the Trojan battalions, however they tried,
able to force their way through the Danäan lines.
But just as a cord keeps the cut of a ship's plank straight
in the hands of a skillful shipwright, knowledgeable
in all the ways of his craft, through Athena's guidance:
so evenly matched were the Trojans and the Achaeans.   380

The two armies battled all down the line of the ships.
Hector went straight for Ajax. The two of them fought
over one ship, and neither prevailed, since Hector
could not force Ajax away and set it on fire,
nor could Ajax push Hector back, once the god had brought him.
Then Ajax cut down Calétor as he was trying

to set the black ship on fire; the spear hit his chest,
he fell with a crash, and the lit torch dropped from his hand.
When Hector saw his dear cousin fall in the dirt,
he called to the Trojans and allies in a loud voice: 390
"Hear me, Trojans, Dardánians, and Lycians.
Don't give ground in this narrow space; come and rescue
Calétor's body in front of the ship where he fell,
and don't allow the Achaeans to strip off his armor."

With these words he aimed at Ajax with his bright spear.
He missed his mark but hit Lýcophron, son of Mastor,
an attendant of his, who had left his home in Cythéra
after killing a man and lived in Ajax's house.
Hector hit him above the ear as he stood
close to Ajax; he plunged to the ground, backward,   400
from the stern of the ship, and his body crumpled to earth.
Ajax shuddered and turned to his brother and said,
"Teucer, look: we have lost our trusted companion
Lýcophron, who came to our house from Cythéra
and whom we honored as much as our own dear parents.
Hector just killed him. Where are your deadly arrows?
Where is the bow that Phoebus Apollo gave you?"

When Teucer heard this, he ran up and stood beside him,
holding his bow and quiver, and quickly began
stringing the arrows and shooting them at the Trojans.   410
He hit Clitus, the son of Pisénor and close companion
of Polydamas, as he held the reins. His attention
was on his team; he was driving them where the battle
was fiercest, doing his best for the Trojans and Hector,
but evil came swiftly upon him; no one could stop it,
however greatly they wished to. The fatal arrow
pierced the back of his neck, and he fell to the ground,
and the horses swerved and rattled the empty car.
Polydamas saw it and rushed out to intercept them,
and handed them to Astýnoüs, Protiáon's   420
son, with instructions to watch him and keep them close by,
and then he himself returned to the front line of battle.

*

Then Teucer took out another arrow, for Hector,
and he would have put an end to his fighting if Zeus
had not noticed him as he stood there, and broken his bowstring
just as he aimed at Hector; the bronze-tipped arrow
flew to one side, and the curved bow fell from his hand.
Teucer shuddered and said to his brother, Ajax,
"Look, some god has ruined our plan of battle;
he has knocked the bow from my hand and broken the new   430
oxhide cord that I twisted and strung this morning
to last after hundreds of arrows had leaped forth from it."

Ajax answered him, "Well then, put down your bow
and your cluster of arrows, and let them be, since a god
with a grudge against the Achaeans has made them useless.
Pick up a spear, and a shield to cover your shoulders,
and fight like that, and urge on the rest of the men.
The Trojans may be successful for now, but let us
fight with our utmost strength and make sure that they don't
take our ships without a ferocious struggle."   440

At this, Teucer went and put the bow in his hut,
and over his shoulders he slung a shield four hides thick,
and upon his head he placed a glittering helmet,
and he picked up a heavy spear, pointed with bronze,
and set out at a run and was soon back at Ajax's side.

When Hector perceived that Teucer's weapons were useless,
he called to the troops around him in a loud voice:
"Trojan, Lycian, Dardánian soldiers and friends,
be men now. Onward; remember your fighting spirit;
attack the ships. I have seen with my own eyes   450
how Zeus has disabled the weapons of one of their best men.
It is easy to know when Zeus is helping an army,
when he grants some the glory of triumph and takes the heart out
of others, sapping their strength and refusing to help them.
He is fighting on our side now and crippling the Argives.
Keep moving forward. Fight in one solid mass.

And if any man should be hit by a missile, then let him
die; it is no dishonor for him to be killed
defending his land. He will leave his wife and his children
safe and his house undamaged once the Achaeans   460
have launched their ships and sailed back to where they came from."
With these words he stirred up the courage of every man.

On the other side, Ajax called out to his companions:
"Shame on you all! We must choose now—either we die
or we rescue ourselves by driving the enemy off.
Or do you suppose that if Hector captures our ships
we will all be able to walk back home at our leisure?
Can't you hear Hector cheering on his whole army?
He is desperate to burn our ships. He isn't inviting
his men to a dance, believe me, but to a battle.   470
Our only hope is to fight them with all our strength
in hand-to-hand combat. It is better to settle the matter
once and for all—whether we live or die—
than to have the life of us squeezed out like this near the ships
in the grind of battle, by men who are less brave than we are."
With these words he stirred up the courage of every man.

Then Hector killed Schédius, Perimédes' son,
a Phocian leader; and Ajax, Laódamas,
an infantry captain, one of the sons of Anténor.
Polydamas cut down Otus, who came from Cyllénē,   480
a comrade of Meges, a leader of the Epéans.
When Meges saw this, he charged at Polydamas,
but he ducked and swerved from beneath him, and Meges missed,
since the god would not let Polydamas be cut down;
but he did hit Crœsmus, right on the chest, with his spear,
and he fell with a crash. And as Meges was stripping his armor,
Dolops charged at him; he was an excellent spearman,
Laómedon's grandson, the bravest of Lampus's sons.
He ran up close and stabbed with his spear at the center
of Meges' shield, but the massive bronze of his breastplate   490
defended him well. (Phyleus, his father, had brought it
from Éphyra, from beside the river Selléïs.

His guest-friend Euphétes, king of men, had bestowed it
upon him, to wear into battle as a protection;
and now it protected his dear son from death.) Then Meges
thrust with his spear at Dolops and hit the ridge
of his shining helmet and sheared off the horsehair crest,
and it fell in the dirt, bright with its new scarlet dye.
But while Dolops, still hoping for victory, stood his ground,
Menelaus came up as well, from the other side,   500
unnoticed by him. He threw his spear, and it hit him
from behind, on the shoulder; the point sped eagerly on,
right through his chest, and he sank to the ground, face forward.
And as the two of them moved in to strip off his armor,
Hector called out to the many kinsmen around him,
and first he rebuked Hicetáon's son, Melaníppus,
who in earlier times had grazed his lumbering cattle
in Percóte, while the Achaeans were far away,
but after the fleet arrived, he had gone back home
to Ilion, where he was one of the prominent men.   510
Hector angrily shouted at him, "Are we going
to slack off like this, Melaníppus? Don't you have any
feeling about your cousin who was just killed?
Can't you see them stripping off Dolops's armor?
Follow me now. We can no longer fight from a distance;
we must fight with them hand to hand, until either we kill them
or they capture the high walls of Troy and slaughter our people."
With these words he led the way, and the other man followed.

Meanwhile Ajax the Tall urged on the Achaeans:
"Dear friends, be men now. Put courage into your hearts.   520
When men act with honor, more are saved than are killed,
but when they take flight, there is neither glory nor refuge."
The men were already resolved to defend themselves,
but they took his orders to heart, and they circled the ships
with a wall of bronze, as Zeus drove the Trojans against them.

Then Menelaus urged Antilochus on:
"Antilochus, none of the younger Achaean fighters
is faster than you or more courageous in battle;

so why don't you charge and cut down one of the Trojans?"
With this he drew back, but Antilochus was excited,   530
and he hurried out from the front line and, glaring around him,
he aimed his bright spear. The Trojans pulled back as he threw it,
and the spear point hit Melaníppus, full in the chest,
beside the nipple, as he moved into the fighting.
Antilochus charged at him like a dog that leaps
on a wounded fawn which a hunter has shot as she bounded
out of her lair, and she stops short and crumples to earth:
just so did Antilochus leap on you, Melaníppus,
to strip off your armor. But Hector was quick to notice,
and at once he attacked him through the thick of the battle.   540
Antilochus could not stand firm, as brave as he was;
he fled like a wild beast that has done something wrong,
has killed a dog or a herdsman beside his cattle,
and it runs off before a crowd can be gathered to chase it:
just so did Antilochus flee, and the Trojans and Hector
with a deafening roar rained hundreds of spears upon him,
and he did not stop and turn till he reached his comrades.

The Trojans charged at the ships like ravenous lions,
doing the will of Zeus, who constantly spurred
them on and increased their strength, but bewildered the hearts   550
of the Argives, denying them glory and helping the Trojans.
He still intended to give all the glory to Hector
and to let him throw deadly fire onto the ships
and so fulfill the unrighteous request of Thetis.
He was waiting to see the blaze of a burning ship;
from that moment on, he intended to turn the battle
around and to drive the Trojans away from the camp
and give the Danäans victory. With this purpose
he urged Hector on, though Hector needed no urging.
He was raging like Ares or like an unstoppable fire   560
that rages through a dense forest among the mountains.
He foamed at the mouth, his eyes blazed under his savage
brows, and his helmet shook terribly as he fought.
And now he tried to break through the ranks, attacking
wherever he saw the most men and the finest armor;

but however fiercely he fought, he could not break through;
they closed ranks in tight formation and stood their ground.
They were like a steep cliff at the edge of the restless sea,
which stands firm against the swift paths of the whistling winds
and the swollen waves that keep pounding against the shore: 570
just so did the Argives withstand the fierce Trojan onslaught.
But Hector charged in among them, blazing with fury,
and fell on the mass of men like a towering wave
whipped up by a storm, which crashes over a ship
and hides it in spray, and the violent blast of the wind
howls against the mast, and the hearts of the sailors
tremble with fear as they try to move out of death's reach:
just so stirred up was the heart of every Achaean.

He fell on them like a murderous lion attacking
a herd of cows as they graze, too many to count,   580
at the bottom of some low-lying marsh, and among them
is a herdsman who does not know how to fight off a wild beast
from an animal's carcass; he walks alongside the cattle
in front or alongside the ones in back, but the lion
charges the middle and leaps on a cow and devours it
as the others stampede: just so did the Danäans flee
from Hector and Father Zeus in unearthly dread.
But Hector killed only Periphétes, the son
of Copreus, who had often been sent with a message
from Eurýstheus to Héracles, to assign him his labors.   590
The son grew up a much better man than his father
in all respects; he could run fast and was a great fighter,
and in understanding, no man in Mycénæ surpassed him.
He now gave Hector a triumph; as he turned back,
he tripped on the rim of the body-length shield he carried
to protect him from spears; entangled in it, he fell
on his back, and around his temples his helmet clanged
terribly as he hit the hard ground. And Hector
was quick to notice; he ran up and stood beside him,
then lifted his spear and plunged it into his chest   600
before the eyes of his comrades, and they could do nothing
to help him, however much they grieved for their friend,

since they themselves were deathly afraid of Hector.

Now they were in among the black ships, encircled
by the outermost row of the first ones drawn up on shore.
But the Trojans kept pouring in after them, and the Achaeans
were forced to pull back from the outermost row. They stopped
when they reached the huts, and they stood their ground in a mass
and did not scatter; honor and fear held them
as they stood there shouting encouragement to their comrades.   610

And Nestor called out the most fervently of them all,
begging each man to stand firm for the sake of his parents:
"Dear friends, be men now. Put courage into your hearts
and act honorably in the sight of your comrades in battle.
Think of your children and wives, your houses and farmlands,
and your dear parents, whether alive or dead.
I beg you, for their sakes, to stand firm and never flee."
With these words he stirred up the courage of every man.

And now Athena lifted the veil of darkness
that had covered their eyes, and light streamed from both directions,   620
from back toward the ships and from out where the battle was raging.
And all the Achaeans could see the enemy clearly,
those who had fallen back to defend the huts
and those who were fighting so fiercely beside the black ships.

But Ajax refused to retreat with the other Achaeans.
He went to and fro on the ships' decks, with long strides,
waving a pike that sailors use for sea battles,
fitted together with bolts and thirty feet long.
As when an expert trainer has harnessed four horses
together, choosing them out of many, and comes   630
tearing ahead at full speed along the main highway
to some large city, and many look on in wonder,
both women and men, as he constantly, with sure footing,
leaps from one horse to another while they dash forward:
just so did Ajax keep striding from one ship's deck
to another. With mighty, blood-chilling shouts he kept urging

the Danäans to defend their ships and their huts.
Nor did Hector remain among the mass of the Trojans;
as a flame-colored eagle swoops on a flock of birds
feeding beside a river—wild geese or cranes   640
or long-throated swans: so Hector charged straight ahead
at one of the ships, and Zeus was driving him onward
with his great power and urging the troops to follow.

And now there was bitter fighting beside the ships.
You would have thought that the armies were fresh and rested,
so furiously did they battle. And as they fought on,
this is what the men on each side were thinking:
The Achaeans could not imagine that they would escape;
they expected to die; while every one of the Trojans
could feel the heart in his chest beat fast in the hope   650
of burning the ships and slaughtering the Achaeans.
These were their thoughts as they battled. And Hector took hold
of the stern of the ship that had brought Protesiláüs
to Troy but never carried him back to his country.
Around this ship now the Trojans and the Achaeans
were killing each other in hand-to-hand combat, no longer
awaiting the rush of arrows and spears from a distance
but fighting at close range, both sides with equal fury,
as they hacked at each other with battle-axes and hatchets
and thrust their long swords and their spears with double-curved points.   660
Many fine blades that were bound with dark thongs at the hilt
fell to the ground in the fighting, out of their hands,
or were cut from their arms, and the dark earth ran with their blood.

Hector never let go of the stern he had seized,
but gripped the stern-post and shouted out to the Trojans,
"Bring fire here, all of you. Fight as hard as you can,
for this day has been given to us by Zeus; it is worth
all the others. Today we will capture the ships
that came to our city against the will of the gods
and have caused so much misery, only because our elders   670
were cowards who held me back when I wished to push on
to the Argive camp and fight at the sterns of the ships.

But even though Zeus was confusing our minds then, today
he is on our side and is urging us onward to glory."
When they heard this, they charged at the Argives even more fiercely.

Ajax, under the onslaught of hurtling spears,
thinking that he would die if he stayed where he was,
left the raised deck at the stern and retreated a bit
to the cross-bench, seven feet wide, across the ship's middle,
and he took his stand there. Whenever a Trojan came   680
to set fire to the ships, he would drive him back with his pike,
and always with blood-chilling shouts he urged on the Argives:
"My dear friends, Danäan soldiers, companions in battle,
be men now; have courage; remember your fighting spirit.
Or do you think we have allies waiting to help us,
or some stronger wall that might rescue us from disaster?
We don't have a city nearby that we can retreat to
or people who will supply us with reinforcements.
We are here by ourselves upon the wide plain of the Trojans,
with our backs to the sea and far from our own dear country.   690
So our only salvation is fighting with all our strength."
As he spoke, he kept stabbing furiously with his pike,
and whenever a Trojan climbed up with a flaming torch,
Ajax was waiting for him with a deadly pike thrust.
And he wounded twelve men as they fought in front of the ships.

Book 16

As the armies kept fighting by Protesiláüs's ship,
Patroclus came to Achilles shedding hot tears
like a spring of water that pours its dark stream down over
some goat-steep cliff. And Achilles felt pity and said,
"Why are you crying, Patroclus, like some little girl
who runs to her mother and tugs at her skirts and begs
to be comforted and gets in her way and keeps
crying until the mother at last picks her up?
Are you crying because you have some bad news to report
to the Myrmidons and to me, some message from Phthia?   10
But as far as I know, Menœtius is still alive,
your father, and Peleus, my father, lives on too,
for whom we would both mourn bitterly if they died.
Or is it because you are grieving for the Achaeans
as they die by the black ships, through their own arrogant folly?
Tell me. Don't keep it hidden; let me know too."

Then, with a deep groan, you gave him this answer, Patroclus:
"Achilles, great champion of the Achaeans, don't
be angry. I weep for the pain that has overwhelmed us.
All the men who until now have been our best fighters   20
are back in their huts in agony: Diomedes
has been pierced by an arrow, Odysseus and Agamemnon
have been stabbed, and Eurýpylus has been shot in the thigh.
The healers attend to them now with their soothing herbs,
trying to cure them. But you are impossible
to deal with, Achilles. I hope I am never seized
with such anger as yours. What good is your excellence? How
will it benefit others, now or in times to come,
if you hold it back and refuse to save the Achaeans?
Your father cannot have been Lord Peleus, nor   30
can Thetis have been your mother. The rough sea bore you,
the harsh cliffs fathered you, since your heart has no pity.
But if some heavenly sign has been holding you back,

some prophecy from Zeus that your mother has brought you,
at least you can send *me* out now, and let the rest
of the Myrmidons follow, and I can be a great light
to all the Argives. And you can give me your armor
to wear into battle; the Trojans will take me for you,
and they will pull back, and the Argives can catch their breath,
worn down as they are. I and our men are fresh   40
and the Trojans exhausted. I could soon push them all
the way to the walls of their city, back from our ships."

Thus he begged his companion—great fool that he was,
since what he begged for turned out to be his own death.
Disturbed by the proposal, Achilles answered,
"Patroclus, what are you talking about? There is no
sign from heaven that has been holding me back,
no prophecy from Zeus that my mother has brought me,
only this one bitter thought that keeps troubling my heart:
that a man of my own rank dared to dishonor and rob me   50
of my beautiful prize, because he had greater power.
This causes me endless grief, after all I have suffered.
The girl whom the Argives chose for me as my prize,
whom I won with my own strong spear when I plundered her city—
Agamemnon took her from me, treating me like
some filthy tramp or some outcast who has no rights.
But all this is over and done with, so let it be;
I can't be angry forever. Although I said
that I wouldn't relent or put an end to my rage
until the fighting advanced as far as my ships,   60
you can go ahead now and fight. Put on my armor
and lead the war-loving Myrmidons into battle,
since the Trojans surround the ships in a dark stormcloud
and the Argives are being driven back to the seashore
and hold just a narrow strip of ground. The whole city
has taken heart and descended upon them because
they no longer see my helmet blazing among them.
They would soon have been running in panic, and every gully
would have been stacked with their dead, if Lord Agamemnon
had treated me kindly; but now they swarm through the camp.   70

So go, Patroclus; attack them with all your strength;
don't allow them to get to our ships and burn them
and take away any chance of our longed-for return.
Now listen closely; remember all my instructions
and carry them out, so that you can win me great honor
from all the Argives, and they will decide to give back
that beautiful girl, with many fine gifts in addition.
And when you have driven the enemy from our ships,
come back. Even if Zeus puts a glorious triumph
within your grasp, you mustn't push on without me;   80
if you do, you will take the honor that should be mine.
And in the delight of war, as you slaughter Trojans,
don't press forward to Troy, or one of the gods
might come from Olympus and enter the battle against you—
you know how dearly Apollo loves Troy. But once
you have saved the ships, come back to me without fail,
and let the others keep fighting across the plain.
By Father Zeus and Athena and Lord Apollo,
I wish that not one of the Trojans remained alive,
and not one of the Argives, but that you and I were the only   90
ones to survive and smash Troy's towers to rubble."

While they were speaking, Ajax, under the constant
onslaught of hurtling spears, was forced to give ground,
subdued by the will of Zeus and the Trojan weapons.
His glittering helmet rang out with dreadful clangs
as the arrows and spear points kept hitting against its cheek plates,
and his left shoulder ached from the weight of his shield; yet with all
the missiles they hurled, they could not knock it away.
But his heart was pounding inside his chest, and the sweat poured
down all over his body, he could not catch   100
his breath, and on every side of him there was danger.

Tell me now, Muses, who have your homes on Olympus,
how fire was first hurled onto the Argive ships.
Hector came up and slashed at Ajax's spear
with his heavy sword, hitting it at the socket
behind the spear head and shearing it off, and Ajax

kept wielding the shaft, still unaware that the spear head
was gone; it flew off and fell to the ground with a clatter.
Then Ajax saw it and knew that the gods had done this,
and he shuddered that Zeus had ruined his plans and had given   110
victory to the Trojans, so he drew back
out of range of the spears, and the Trojans threw torches
onto the ship, and unquenchable fire blazed through it.

The flames spread raging around the ship's stern, and Achilles
slapped his thighs in alarm and said to Patroclus,
"Up now, Patroclus; now is the time to fight.
I see flames nearby. We mustn't allow the Trojans
to destroy our ships and with them our chance of returning.
Put on the armor. I will assemble our men."

And Patroclus began to put on the glorious armor.   120
First, he strapped the bronze greaves to his lower legs
and fastened them onto his ankles with silver clasps.
Next, on his chest he put the finely wrought breastplate,
glittering like a star, that Achilles had worn.
He slung the bronze, silver-bossed sword over his shoulder,
and above it his massive shield. And last he put on
his bronze helmet with its blood-chilling horsehair crest,
then took two powerful spears that fitted his hand.
But he did not pick up the famous spear of Achilles,
huge and heavy, which none of the other Achaeans   130
was able to hold; Achilles alone could use it.
It was made of ash, and the centaur Chiron had brought it
from Pélion as a gift to Achilles' father.

Patroclus next had Automedon harness the horses.
He was the man whom Patroclus honored the most
after Achilles; he trusted that in a battle
he would keep the chariot close and answer his call.
So Automedon brought the horses under the yoke,
the immortal Xanthus and Bálius, who could fly
with the breezes; they were sired by Zéphyrus,   140
the west wind, out of the storm-mare Podárgē as she

was grazing beside the Ocean. In the side traces
he put a fine horse named Pédasus, which Achilles
had brought back after taking Ëétion's city;
it was mortal but could keep up with the deathless pair.

Meanwhile Achilles went everywhere in the camp
and commanded his men to arm. And they rushed out
like ravenous wolves, their hearts filled with boundless fury.
And Achilles urged on the soldiers and charioteers.

There were fifty ships that Achilles had brought to Troy,   150
and in each there were fifty men who had manned the oarlocks.
He had appointed five leaders, men whom he trusted,
and he himself was commander over them all.
The first line of ships was led by Menésthius,
son of Sperchéüs, the river fed by the heavens;
he was borne by a daughter of Peleus named Polydóra,
a woman who slept with a god; in name, however,
he was the son of Borus, who made her his wife
openly and gave a very large bride-price.
The second line of ships was led by Eudórus,   160
Polyméla's son. She was an unmarried mother;
Hermes had fallen in love with her when he saw her
among the chorus of girls who were dancing in honor
of Ártemis; he went up to her room and in secret
made love to her. She conceived a glorious son,
who turned out to be a preeminent runner and fighter;
and when the pain-dealing goddess of childbirth brought
Eudórus into the world and he saw the sunlight,
Echécles, the son of Actor, gave an enormous
bride-price for her and took her home as his wife,   170
and her father, Phylas, took charge of the boy and raised him
and loved him as dearly as if he were his own son.
Pisánder, the son of Mæmelus, led the third;
he was the best in spear-fighting, except for Patroclus.
The fourth line of ships was led by the old commander
Phoenix; the fifth by Álcimus, son of Laérces.

*

And when Achilles had stationed them with their leaders
in the right order, he gave them these stern instructions:
"Myrmidons, do you remember the victory threats
that you used to level against the Trojans, throughout   180
the time of my rage? You would all accuse me and say,
'You are hard, Achilles; your mother nursed you on bile
not milk, so unfeeling you are. You keep us, your comrades,
here by the ships, not letting us go into battle.
It would be much better to sail home at once, since this wretched
anger has utterly taken over your heart.'
That is what you were saying about me; but now
you are faced with the great battle you all have longed for.
So each of you, fight the Trojans with all your strength."

With these words he stirred up the spirit of every man,   190
and the ranks drew closer together once he had spoken.
As when a man builds the walls of a high-roofed house
with close-fitting stones to keep out the force of the winds:
so tightly did helmets and shields fit together; shield pressed
on shield, and helmet on helmet, and man on man,
and the horsehair crests in the shining plates of their helmets
touched whenever they moved their heads, so close-packed
were their ranks. And two men stood armed in front of them all,
Automedon and Patroclus, both with one purpose,
to lead the Myrmidons out to war. But Achilles   200
went to his hut and opened the finely carved lid
of the beautiful chest that Thetis had put on his ship
and had packed with tunics and warm cloaks and woolen rugs.
Inside it he kept a golden cup that no man
but himself might drink from, nor would he pour a libation
from it to any god except Father Zeus.
He took this cup from the chest, and he purified it
with sulfur and rinsed it in clear water; then he washed
his hands, and he filled the cup with glistening wine.
And he stood in the courtyard, looking up to the heavens,   210
and poured a libation and prayed, and Lord Zeus saw him.
"Almighty Father, lord of Pelásgia, who dwell
far from us and rule over wintry Dodóna

where your prophets live, the Selli with unwashed feet,
who sleep on the ground—hear me now, just as you did
when I prayed before, and you honored me and attacked
the Achaean army and caused them great casualties.
Grant me my prayer now. I myself will remain here
where the ships are gathered, but I am sending my comrade
out to fight at the head of the Myrmidons. Grant him   220
victory, Zeus. And when he has driven the Trojans
away from the ships, grant that he come back unharmed,
with all his armor intact, and the comrades he fought with."
This was his prayer, and Zeus heard him; and in his wisdom
he granted him half, but the other half he refused.
He granted the part where Patroclus would push back the Trojans
from the black ships, but he did not let him return.

After Achilles had prayed and poured the libation,
he entered his hut and put the cup back in the chest.
Then he came out and stood there; he was still eager   230
to watch the fierce battle between the Trojans and Argives.

Meanwhile the Myrmidons, greatly exhilarated,
advanced with Patroclus leading and charged at the Trojans,
swarming out all at once like wasps on a roadside
that boys, in their childish sport, have stirred up to anger,
poking them over and over again in their nest,
the little fools, creating a public nuisance
for many people; and if a man passing by
jostles the nest and disturbs them, they all fly out
in a seething rage to attack him and fight for their young: 240
with a spirit like this, the Myrmidons all swarmed out
from the ships, and their furious battle cries filled the heavens.

When the Trojans caught sight of Patroclus and his attendant,
Automedon, both of them glittering in their armor,
their hearts were stricken with panic. They thought that Achilles
had abandoned his rage, for his friends' sakes, and each man looked
wildly around him to see how he could escape.

*

Patroclus was first to let fly his shining spear
into the midst of the fighting where men pressed thickest,
by the stern of the ship that Protesiláüs had brought.   250
And he hit Pyræchmes, who led the Pæónian horsemen
from Ámydon and the wide-flowing Áxius river;
he hit him on the right shoulder, and with a scream
Pyræchmes fell onto his back. And his comrades fled
in panic—Patroclus had terrified all the troops
when he killed their leader, the bravest of them in battle.
He drove them away from the ships and put out the fire,
and the ship was left there half-burned, and the Trojans scattered
with screams of terror; the Argives poured after them, charging
among the ships, and a deafening uproar arose.   260
As when Zeus moves a thick cloud away from the crest of a mountain,
and the outlines of peaks and headlands and valleys appear,
and unspeakably brilliant air spills down from the heavens:
just so when the Danäans drove the fire from the sterns
they were able to catch their breath. But the fight was not over.
The Trojans were not yet pushed back in a headlong rout;
they were forced to withdraw from the ships, but still they stood firm.

Then man killed man, as the Trojan front lines were scattered.
Patroclus hit Areílycus in the thigh
at the moment when he was turning to flee; the spear point   270
shattered the bone, and he fell face down in the dirt.
And Menelaus stabbed Thoas above the rim
of his shield, where his chest was bare, and he crumpled to earth.
And Meges, when Ámphiclus charged at him, was too quick
and ran him through at the top of the leg, where the muscle
is thickest; and as the spear point drove in, the tendons
were completely severed, and darkness covered his eyes.
And Antilochus stabbed Atýmnius in his side
with a thrust of his spear, and he toppled forward. And Maris,
enraged that his brother Atýmnius had been killed,   280
stood in front of the body and, close up, lunged
at the son of Nestor, thrusting at him with his spear;
but Thrasymédes, another of Nestor's sons,
was too quick for him and before he could do any damage

he stabbed his shoulder; the keen point tore off the arm,
shearing it from the muscles and smashing the bone;
and he fell with a crash, and darkness covered his eyes.
So both of them were slaughtered by the two brothers,
and they went down to Hades, these brave men, friends of Sarpedon
and sons of Amisódarus, who had brought up   290
the Chimǽra, that raging monster who killed so many.
Then Ajax the Smaller charged straight at Cleobúlus
and took him alive as he stumbled amid the rout;
but immediately he killed him, slashing his neck
with his sword, and the blade grew warm with his blood, and death
took hold of him, veiling his eyes in a purple mist.
And Penéleos and Lycon rushed at each other;
they had missed with their spears, so each drew his sword and charged,
and Lycon's sword struck the ridge of the Argive's helmet
and shattered. And quickly Penéleos sliced through his neck   300
under the ear, and the whole blade sank in, and only
a flap of skin kept the head attached, and it dangled
to one side for a moment, and then he crumpled to earth.
And Meriones ran down Ácamas with long strides
and stabbed him in the right shoulder as he was fleeing;
as he fell from his chariot, mist poured over his eyes.
And Idómeneus then stabbed Érymas in the mouth
with his pitiless spear, and the point passed all the way through,
up under the brain, and smashed the white bones; his teeth
were knocked out, and a stream of blood gushed from both eyes,   310
and he spurted blood through his nostrils and gaping mouth
as he gasped for breath, and death in a black cloud took him.

So each of these Danäan leaders dispatched his man.
And like ravening wolves that fall upon lambs or kids
when they are alone on the hillside, apart from their mothers
through the carelessness of the shepherd, and seeing them
defenseless, the wolves pounce quickly and tear them to pieces:
just so the Danäans fell on the Trojans, who panicked
and lost their nerve and scattered with a shrill uproar.

Ajax the Tall kept looking out for a chance   320

to take Hector down with a spear throw. But he, skilled in battle,
kept his broad shoulders behind his shield, well protected,
and watched for the whistle of arrows and thud of spears.
He realized now that the battle had turned against him,
but he stood his ground and was trying to save his companions.

As a huge thundercloud, after clear weather, spreads out
over the sky from Olympus when Zeus sends a storm:
just so did the Trojans, panicked, spread out from the ships,
and they crossed back in great disorder. Hector's swift horses
carried him off, and he left the army behind,   330
disastrously penned in by the Argive trench.
Team after team of horses plunged into it, snapped
their yoke-poles off, and ran free, leaving their masters
trapped. And Patroclus kept pressing on, with loud war cries,
and violence in his heart. The Trojans were screaming,
running away in every direction, and dust
went swirling up to the clouds as their horses galloped
back toward the city, away from the ships and huts.
Cheering his men, Patroclus drove on, wherever
he saw the most Trojans fleeing, and many fell   340
under his wheels as their chariots crashed and tipped over.
And his horses galloped ahead and leaped over the trench;
he tried to catch up with Hector, longing to kill him,
but Hector's swift team had carried him off to safety.
And just as beneath a storm the dark earth is heavy
on an autumn day when Lord Zeus sends violent rain,
because he is angry at men who give crooked verdicts
in the assembly and drive out justice, with no
fear about being punished for it by the gods,
and then all their rivers fill, overflowing their banks,   350
and many hillsides are cut off and look like islands
in the torrents that headlong rush from the mountains, roaring
down to the turbulent sea, and the tilled fields are ruined:
so loud were the Trojan chariots as they fled.

When Patroclus had cut through the front battalions, he forced them
back toward the ships and blocked their retreat to the city;

in the space between ships and river and the high wall
he kept charging into their midst and slaughtering them,
making them pay for the many deaths of his comrades.
First he speared Prónoüs, where his chest was exposed   360
above his shield, and he fell to earth with a crash.
Next, he rushed straight at Thestor, the son of Enops,
who was huddled up in his chariot, out of his mind
with terror; the reins had slipped from his hands, and Patroclus
came up and stabbed him on the right side of his jaw
and drove the spear through his teeth. Then, gripping the spear shaft,
he pivoted back and lifted him over the rail
like a fisherman who sits on a jutting boulder
and hauls a tremendous fish up out of the sea
at the end of his line, caught on the bright bronze hook: 370
just so did Patroclus haul him up out of his car,
mouth gaping around the spear point, and tossed him down
on his face, and he lay there flopping until life left him.
Then Eryláüs charged at him, and Patroclus
smashed his head with a rock, and inside the helmet
the skull cracked in two, he fell, and death poured around him.
And then he killed Érymas and Amphóterus
and Tlepólemus, son of Damástor, and Pyris and Ipheus
and Échius and Euíppus and Polymélus,
and they lay down, one by one, on the bountiful earth.   380

When Sarpedon saw his companions being cut down
by Patroclus, he angrily shouted out, "Shame on you, Lycians!
Where are you running off to? Now is the time
to stand and fight the Achaeans. I will go face
this man, whoever he is, who has done us so much
damage and killed so many of our brave men."

He leaped to the ground from his chariot, in full armor,
and Patroclus too, when he saw him, leaped to the ground.
And as two eagles, with curved beaks and crooked talons,
clash high above some towering rock face, screaming: 390
just so with loud screams did the two men rush at each other.

*

Seeing them, Zeus felt pity and said to Hera,
"I am sad at heart because the appointed time
has come that Sarpedon, dearest of men to me,
must meet his fate and be killed. My mind is divided:
should I go to Troy and snatch him out of the fighting
and put him back down amid the rich fields of Lycia,
or should I destroy him now at Patroclus's hands?"

Then Hera responded, "Dread Lord, what are you saying?
Do you want to take a mere mortal and set him free   400
from a death that has been ordained for him? Do as you wish,
but be aware that not all the gods will approve.
And one thing more: If you rescue Sarpedon now,
it will set a precedent; someday, because of this,
some other god will feel entitled to rescue
his own dear son from another dangerous battle.
Many men fighting around the great city of Priam
are sons of gods, and you will cause bitter resentment.
But if this man is so dear to you, and your heart
is so grieved, you can let him be cut down now in this combat   410
at Patroclus's hands, and when the spirit has left him
send Death and sweet Sleep to carry him off the field
and tenderly bring him home to the land of Lycia,
where his family and kinsmen will bury him in all honor,
with mound and gravestone, the privilege of the dead."

Zeus bowed his head and did as his wife had told him,
but he sent a shower of bloody raindrops to Earth
to honor his son, whom Patroclus was now to kill
on the plain of Ilion, far from his own dear country.

When the two of them had advanced to within close range,   420
Patroclus killed Thrasydémus, the charioteer
of Lord Sarpedon; the spear plunged into his belly,
and he crumpled to earth. Sarpedon then threw his spear
and missed, but hit the horse Pédasus in the right shoulder;
it shrieked as it gasped out its life, then fell in the dirt,
whinnying, and its spirit fluttered away.

The other two horses shied, the yoke creaked, the reins
tangled around the third one, who now lay dead.
But Automedon saw what to do. Drawing the sword
at his thigh, with a single blow he cut loose the trace horse,   430
and the team straightened out and pulled the reins tight in their harness.

The two great warriors charged at each other again
in heart-crushing combat. Sarpedon again hurled his spear;
it missed Patroclus, sailing above his left shoulder.
But Patroclus charged forward and hurled *his* spear, and it hit
in the place where the lungs envelop the beating heart,
and Sarpedon fell like an oak tree or a white poplar
or a pine that carpenters, with new-whetted axes,
cut down in the mountains and hew into planks for a ship:
just so did he lie there stretched out in front of his horses,   440
choking to death and clawing the blood-soaked dust.
Like a bull that a lion attacks and kills as it stands
sleek and tall and proud in a herd of cattle,
and it bellows its life out under the lion's jaws:
just so, brought down by Patroclus, the Lycian commander
bellowed and struggled to speak a few words to his comrade:
"Glaucus, my dear friend, now is the time to show
your courage and fight over me with your whole heart; now
you must long for nothing but victory. Hurry and call
all the Lycian commanders to come and defend   450
my body, and you too defend it with all your strength.
It will be a great shame and disgrace to you, all the days
of your life, if you let the Achaeans strip off my armor
and do not protect my body where I have fallen.
Stand your ground now, and call our brave men to help you."

As he said these words, death covered his eyes and nostrils.
And Patroclus, bracing his foot on his chest, drew out
the spear from his flesh, and the lungs too came wrapped around it
as he pulled the point out, and with it Sarpedon's life.
The Myrmidons held his horses in place, as they snorted   460
and strained to run off, since they knew that they had no driver.

*

Glaucus felt bitter grief as he heard his friend,
and his heart was distraught that he was unable to help him.
And he took his own arm in his hand and squeezed it, tormented
by the wound that Teucer, fighting to keep devastation
from his comrades, had made with an arrow as Glaucus stormed
the Achaean wall. And he called to Apollo in prayer:
"Hear me now, Lord Apollo. You may be in Lycia
or you may be in Troy, but wherever you are, you can hear
a man in great trouble, for trouble has come upon me.   470
I have a dangerous wound, and the pain is piercing
my arm, and my blood won't dry, and my shoulder is
a dead weight; I can't even hold a spear, and I can't
go out to fight. And the best of our men has been killed,
Sarpedon, the son of Zeus, who didn't protect
his own dear child. But hear me now, Lord. At least
ease my great pain, and heal this terrible wound,
and give me the strength to call my companions and urge them
to come here and help me fight for my dead friend's body."

He ended his prayer, and Apollo was swift to answer.   480
He stopped the pain instantly, dried the dark blood that was flowing
from the wound, and he put fresh courage into his heart.
And right away Glaucus realized what had happened
and was overjoyed that the great god had heard his prayer.
At once he hurried to all the Lycian commanders
and urged them to rally around the corpse of Sarpedon;
then, with long strides, he hurried off to the Trojans,
to Polydamas and Agénor and farther on
to Aeneas and Hector. And when he found him, he said,
"Hector, you are neglecting your allies. These men   490
are fighting and losing their lives for *your* sake, far
away from their families and friends; but you will not help them.
Sarpedon is dead, our commander and king, who ruled
Lycia with his great strength and his just decrees;
Ares has cut him down by Patroclus's spear.
So come with me, friends, stand by his side and ward off
the disgrace of having the Myrmidons strip his armor
and disfigure his corpse in their anger for all the Achaeans

we slaughtered as we were fighting beside the black ships."

At these words, the Trojans were utterly overwhelmed   500
by unbearable, inconsolable grief, since Sarpedon
had always been the support of their city, although
he came from another land; and of the many
men who came with him he was the bravest of all.
And they charged at the Argives fiercely, as Hector led them,
angry about Sarpedon. Meanwhile the Argives
were being urged on by Patroclus, who called out first
to the two Ajaxes, both of them eager for battle:
"Ajaxes, make it your job now to push back the Trojans,
the way you have fought before, or even more bravely.   510
The man who was first to break through our wall—Sarpedon—
is dead. We must try to seize and disfigure his corpse
and strip off his armor and, with our pitiless bronze,
cut down whoever comes to defend his body."
And now they were even more eager to stand their ground.

When the leaders of both the armies had strengthened their ranks,
Trojans and Lycians, Myrmidons and Achaeans,
they clashed with fierce battle cries over the dead man's body,
and their armor clanged. And Zeus sent down a thick darkness
to make the fight for his dear son even more brutal.   520

At first the Trojans pushed back the Achaeans, killing
one of the best of the Myrmidons, Lord Epígeus,
the son of Ágacles; he had once ruled in Budíon
but had murdered one of his kinsman and taken refuge
with Peleus and Thetis, and they had sent him to Troy
under Achilles' command, to attack the Trojans.
Now, as he moved in, Hector brought down a heavy
rock on his head; the skull cracked apart in the helmet,
and he fell face down on the corpse, and death poured around him.

Patroclus was filled with grief for his fallen comrade,   530
and he raced through the warriors in the front line, like a hawk
when it swoops down on jackdaws and starlings: so fast did you charge,

Patroclus, straight at the Lycians and Trojans, angry
at heart, with a fierce desire to avenge your comrade.
And you hit Stheneláüs, the son of Ithæmenes,
on the neck with a massive boulder, snapping the tendons.
Then Hector and the front ranks of the Trojans retreated
as far as a javelin flies when an athlete throws it
with all his might as he tests himself at the games:
so far did the Trojans give ground, pushed back by the Argives.   540

The first one to turn was Glaucus; he killed a man
named Báthycles, son of Chalcon, who lived in Hellas
and was famous among the Myrmidons for his wealth.
He stabbed him, suddenly turning as Báthycles chased him
and was getting closer; the spear drove right through his chest,
and he fell with a crash. And grief took hold of the Argives,
that such a brave man had been killed. The Trojans rejoiced,
and they rallied and stood around Glaucus, but the Achaeans
lost none of their fighting spirit and kept moving forward.

And Meriones killed Laógonus, son of Onéstor,   550
a priest of Zeus, and revered as a god by his people;
the spear hit his jawbone, under his ear, and the life
fled from his limbs, and hideous darkness seized him.
And Aeneas threw his spear at Meriones, hoping
to kill him as he moved forward under his shield,
but Meriones saw it coming and ducked to avoid it,
and behind him the spear point stuck in the ground, and the butt end
quivered until at last its fury was spent.
Aeneas was angry that he had missed, and he said,
"Meriones, what a fine dancer you are! But my spear   560
would have stopped your dancing forever if it had hit you."

Meriones answered, "Aeneas, for all your courage,
you may find it hard to defeat every man who comes near you.
You too are a mortal, just like the rest of us here.
If I were to throw my spear and my aim were true,
in spite of your strength you would quickly grant me the triumph
and would have to give up your soul to Death, the pale horseman."

*

But after he finished his speech, Patroclus rebuked him:
"If you are so brave, Meriones, why keep talking?
Believe me, dear friend, no insult will make the Trojans   570
pull back one inch from Sarpedon's body. Before
they do that, many of them will be covered in dirt.
You can save your words for the council; battles are won
by deeds. What we need now isn't more talk, but more fighting."
As he said this he led the way, and Meriones followed.

And as a crashing arises when men cut timber
in a mountain glade, and from far off the noise can be heard:
just so from the earth arose the thud and the clang
of bronze striking bronze and tearing through oxhide shields
as the men kept thrusting with swords and double-curved spear points. 580
Even sharp eyes would never have known Sarpedon
as he lay dead on the ground there, completely covered
with weapons and blood and dirt, from his head to his feet;
and men swarmed around the body like buzzing flies
in a sheepfold in spring, when milk overflows the buckets.
Lord Zeus did not turn his eyes from the brutal combat
but kept looking down at it, pondering in his heart
when he should kill Patroclus. Should it be now,
in the battle over Sarpedon, that Hector's sword
would cut him down and his armor would be stripped off,   590
or should he increase the sorrow of even more men?
And in the end, he decided that it would be best
for Patroclus to drive the Trojans and Hector far
back toward the city and take more lives. So he put
cowardice into the heart of Hector, who jumped
into his chariot and turned it around to flee
and called to the Trojans to follow him, for he knew
that the scales in the hands of Zeus were tipping against him.
Not even the Lycians could stand firm now; the whole army
ran when they saw that Hector's courage had failed.   600
And at once the Achaeans stripped the glittering armor
from Sarpedon's corpse, and Patroclus told his companions
to take it and carry it back to the Argive ships.

*

At this Zeus said to Apollo, "Dear Phoebus, go
and lift Sarpedon out of range of the missiles,
wipe off the blood, take him away and wash him
with ambrosia, dress him in robes that will never decay,
and give him into the care of the swift escorts
Sleep and Death, those twin brothers, who quickly will bring him
back to his home amid the rich fields of Lycia,   610
where his family and kinsmen will bury him in all honor."

When he heard this, Apollo did as his father had asked.
He flew from the heights of Mount Ida into the battle,
and immediately he lifted Sarpedon out of
range of the missiles, took him away and washed him
with ambrosia, dressed him in robes that would never decay,
and gave him into the care of the swift escorts
Sleep and Death, those twin brothers, who quickly brought him
back to his home amid the rich fields of Lycia.

Patroclus commanded Automedon now to follow   620
close behind with the chariot, and he pressed on
recklessly in pursuit of the Trojans and Lycians,
fool that he was; if only he had obeyed
Achilles' instructions, he would have escaped his death.
But the mind of Zeus is always stronger than man's is,
and Zeus is the one who put the urge in his breast.

Who was the first and who the last that you killed,
Patroclus, now that the gods were calling you deathward?
Adréstus first and Autónoüs and Echéclus
and Périmus and Epístor and Melaníppus   630
and Élasus and Múlius and Pylártes—
these were the men that Patroclus cut down; and their comrades,
seeing his fury, were filled with panic and fled.
And then Patroclus would surely have seized the high gates
of Troy as he raged unstoppably through the ranks
if Apollo had not come down and taken a stand
on top of the battlements, with his mind determined

on ending Patroclus's life and helping the Trojans.
Three times Patroclus started to climb the wall;
three times Apollo flung him back down, barely   640
touching the bright shield with his immortal hands.
But when for the fourth time Patroclus attacked in a frenzy,
Apollo shouted to him in a voice like thunder:
"Go back at once, Patroclus! It is not fated
for the Trojans' city to fall by means of your spear
or the spear of Achilles, a man far greater than you are."
At this, Patroclus gave ground, but only a little,
avoiding the wrath of the god who strikes from afar.

Hector had reined in his team at the Scaean Gates,
uncertain if he should drive back into the turmoil   650
or call the army to gather inside the wall.
And while he was thinking about this, Apollo drew near
in the likeness of Ásius, a powerful man
who was Hector's uncle and Hécuba's brother, and lived
in the land of Phrygia, beside the Sangárius river.
Taking his form, Apollo came up and said,
"What are you doing here, Hector? Why have you stopped
fighting? It is unworthy of you. How I wish
that I were as much your better as you are mine!
Then I would make you regret withdrawing from battle.   660
But go back and drive your chariot straight toward Patroclus.
You might kill him now; Apollo might grant you that triumph."
And he moved, a god, on into the frenzy of mortals.

Hector commanded his driver, Cebríones,
to whip the horses and head for the thick of the fighting,
and Apollo charged in and spread a terrible panic
among the Argives and gave the Trojans fresh courage.
But Hector ignored all the Argives and did not try
to kill them; he drove his chariot straight toward Patroclus.
Patroclus, for his part, jumped from his chariot, holding   670
a spear in his left hand, and with his right hand he seized
a glittering, jagged stone, which his hand could just cover,
and he took his position and threw it. He did not hit him,

but his throw was not wasted; the huge stone flew on and hit
Cebríones, a bastard son of King Priam,
who was holding the horses' reins. It hit him between
the eyes and smashed through his brows and shattered his skull,
and his eyeballs fell on the ground in front of his feet;
backward he pitched from the blow, and he fell like a diver
over the chariot's rail, and the life left his bones.   680
Then, Lord Patroclus, you uttered these mocking words:
"My, what a nimble acrobat this man is!
I am sure that he would be skillful fishing for oysters;
he could feed many people with all the oysters he found
when he dived from his fishing boat, even in stormy weather,
to judge by this easy somersault onto the plain.
I never knew that the Trojans were such good divers."
And he charged at Cebríones with the attack of a lion
who is hit in the chest as he lays waste to the sheepfolds
and his own courage destroys him: just so, Patroclus,   690
did you charge ahead at Cebríones in your fury.

Hector also jumped to the ground from his car,
and they battled over Cebríones like two lions
on top of a mountain, both desperate in their hunger,
who find a deer's carcass and grapple for it to the death:
just so did these two great warriors clash, each eager
to tear through the other's flesh with his pitiless bronze.
Hector caught hold of the head and would not let go,
and Patroclus seized on a foot; meanwhile, around them,
Trojans and Argives clashed in ferocious combat.   700
As the east wind and the south wind strive with each other
in a mountain glade to toss the deep stands of oak
and ash and slender dogwood, and in the uproar
their tapering branches lash against one another
with a furious noise and the cracking of broken timber:
just so did the Trojan and Argive battalions clash,
cutting down men, and neither side would give way.
Around Cebríones many sharp spears stuck fast
and feathered arrows that leaped from the bowstring, and many
huge rocks struck against the bronze shields with a clang   710

as men fought around him. He lay in the swirling dust,
magnificent still, with his horsemanship gone forever.

As long as the sun stood bestriding the top of the sky,
the weapons of both sides pierced, and the men kept dying.
But when it sank to the hour for unyoking the oxen,
the Achaeans proved to be stronger, beyond what was fated.
They dragged Cebríones out of range of the missiles
and away from the battle's din, and stripped off his armor,
and Patroclus charged at the Trojans, his heart filled with murder.

Three times he charged them, as furiously as Ares,   720
with a blood-chilling war cry, and three times he killed nine men.
But when for the fourth time he rushed at them in a frenzy,
for you, Patroclus, the moment of death appeared:
Apollo met you and greeted you with his terror.
And Patroclus never saw the god moving through
the turmoil; Apollo had covered himself in mist
and stood behind him and hit him between the shoulders
with the flat of his hand, and Patroclus's eyes whirled round.
Apollo knocked off the glittering, visored helmet,
and, clanging, it rolled on under the horses' hooves,   730
and the hair of its crest was defiled in blood and dust.
Before this moment, the gods had never allowed
the helmet to be defiled, since it had protected
the mighty head and the handsome face of Achilles,
that godlike man. But now Zeus gave it to Hector
to wear for a while, as destruction swiftly approached him.
In Patroclus's hand the heavy, long-shadowed, huge
bronze-pointed spear was shattered, and from his shoulders
the tasseled shield with its thick strap fell to the ground,
and Apollo, the son of Zeus, unfastened his breastplate.   740
Bewilderment seized Patroclus's mind, and his legs
went limp, and he stood in a daze. And then, from behind,
a Dardánian fighter stabbed him between the shoulders
with his spear—Euphórbus, the son of Lord Pánthoüs,
who excelled all men of his own age in throwing a spear,
in running and horsemanship also; and in this battle,

the first he had fought as a novice charioteer,
he had knocked twenty men from their chariots to the ground.
He was the one, Patroclus, who wounded you first,
but he did not kill you. He pulled his spear from your back   750
and retreated into the crowd, since he was reluctant
to challenge you face to face, unarmed though you were.

Patroclus, overcome by the spear and the god's blow,
tried to retreat as well, to avoid destruction.
But when Hector saw him wounded and moving back
into the ranks, he charged through the crowd and stabbed him
in the lower belly and drove the spear all the way through,
and he fell with a crash, and the Argives were filled with anguish.
As a lion defeats a wild boar in a fierce combat
when they fight on top of a mountain, both in high fury,   760
over a little spring that they both want to drink from,
and the boar, breathing hard, succumbs to the lion's power:
just so did Hector end the life of Patroclus,
the killer of many, stabbing him with his spear.
And he spoke these exultant words as he stood above him:
"Patroclus, you must have thought you would plunder our city
and take the freedom away from the women of Troy
and carry them off in your ships to your own dear country,
fool that you were. But defending them, Hector's swift horses
race into battle, and with my long spear I am foremost   770
among all the war-loving Trojans, and I have saved them
from slavery. And as for you, I will leave you
here on the plain for the vultures to feast on. Poor fellow,
not even Achilles, great as he is, could protect you.
He must have given you strict commands as you left:
'Don't come back to the ships, Patroclus, until
you have wounded Hector and ripped through his tunic and soaked it
with his heart's blood.' Something like this is what I imagine
he said, and you were insane enough to believe him."

Then, with your strength quickly fading, Patroclus, you answered,   780
"Boast while you still can, Hector. Your triumph was given
by Zeus and Apollo. They were the ones who really

brought me down; they disarmed me and gave me to you.
For if even twenty such men as you are had faced me
here on their own, my spear would have killed all twenty.
No, it was fate and Apollo who cut me down,
and of humans Euphórbus; you were the third in the killing.
And one thing more: You too will die before long,
for at this moment your irresistible fate
is approaching, and you will be killed by Achilles' hands."   790
As he said these words, death covered him, and his soul
fluttered out of his body and went down to Hades,
bewailing its lot and the manhood it left behind.

And Hector answered him, though Patroclus was dead,
"Patroclus, why do you prophesy my destruction?
Who knows? It could happen that Thetis's son, Achilles,
will be cut down first by *my* spear and will die before me."
With these words he braced his foot against him and pulled
the spear from the wound, then kicked him onto his back.

And immediately he charged straight ahead at Achilles'   800
charioteer, Automedon, eager to kill him.
But the Argive was carried away by the deathless horses
that the gods had once brought to Peleus as their gift.

Book 17

When Menelaus saw that Patroclus had fallen
and was lying there dead, he moved through the foremost ranks,
armored in fiery bronze, and straddled the body,
as a cow stands, threatening, over her first-born calf:
just so did Menelaus stand over Patroclus,
holding his shield and his spear out in front of him,
determined to kill whoever came near the dead man.

Euphórbus as well had seen Patroclus cut down,
and he moved toward the body and called to Lord Menelaus:
"Son of Atreus, commander of men, go back;   10
do not defend the corpse and the blood-stained armor.
I was the first of the Trojans and their brave allies
to stab Patroclus. Let me gather the spoils
and win great honor and glory among the Trojans,
or else with my spear I will take your honey-sweet life."

Greatly troubled by this, Menelaus answered,
"Father Zeus, how foolish this boasting is!
The pride of the leopard, the lion, the vicious wild boar
is nothing compared to the pride of you and your brother.
Yet Hyperénor's life didn't last for long   20
after he met me with insults, saying that I
was the most contemptible fighter among the Achaeans.
If my memory is correct, he didn't go home
on his feet, to gladden the hearts of his wife and parents.
And if you continue to challenge me, I will take
your life as I took your brother's. So go on back
and do not oppose me now, or you may get hurt.
Only a fool will wait for disaster to teach him."

But his words had no effect on Euphórbus, who answered,
"Lord Menelaus, boast all you want about killing   30
my brother, but now you will pay the price for his death.

273

You widowed his wife inside her new bridal chamber
and caused our dear parents, Pánthoüs and Phrontis,
unbearable grief and sorrow, which I would relieve
if I brought them your severed head along with your armor.
But why should we wait? Let us begin right now,
and we will soon know which one of us is the stronger."

With these words he lunged at Menelaus's shield,
but the spear head did not break through; its point was bent back
by the shield's great mass. Then Menelaus got ready   40
to strike with his spear, first praying to Father Zeus;
and, charging forward, he stabbed at his white throat, leaning
into the spear thrust with all his weight, and the point
tore its way through the tender flesh of the neck,
and he fell with a crash, and his armor clattered upon him,
and blood soaked his hair, which was like the hair of the Graces,
the long locks plaited with spirals of silver and gold.
As when a man tends an olive shoot, and it grows
in a place of its own where water wells up in abundance,
and it flourishes and trembles under the breath   50
of every breeze, and it bursts forth into white blossoms;
then suddenly a fierce windstorm arises, rips it
out of its trench, and flings it onto the ground:
just so did Euphórbus fall and lie there face down,
and Menelaus began to strip off his armor.
As when some lion confidently approaches
a grazing herd and picks a fat heifer and leaps
onto her back and cracks her neck in his jaws,
then laps up her blood and gorges himself on her entrails
while around him the dogs and hunters cry out but keep   60
their distance, unwilling to come close, since pale fear has seized them:
just so not a single Trojan dared to approach.

And then Menelaus would easily have been able
to take Euphórbus's armor away if Apollo
had not begrudged him the victory and alerted
Hector against him, appearing in human form
as Mentes, the leader of the Cicónes, and said,

"All this time, Hector, you have been running around
in pursuit of the unattainable: the swift horses
of Peleus's son, impossible for a mortal   70
to master or ride—for any mortal, that is,
except for Achilles, whose mother, they say, is a goddess.
Meanwhile Lord Menelaus has taken a stand
over Patroclus and killed Euphórbus, the best
of our men, and put a stop to his fighting forever."
And he moved, a god, on into the frenzy of mortals.

The mind of Hector was darkened by terrible grief,
and he looked through the ranks and saw the two men, one taking
the glorious armor, the other face down in the dirt
as blood poured out from the savage gash in his throat.   80
With a shrill war cry, he ran through the foremost ranks,
armored in fiery bronze. And when Menelaus
saw him, he thought, "What should I do? If I leave
this armor here, with the corpse of Patroclus, who died
avenging the wrong that was done to me, any Achaean
who sees me withdraw will blame me. But if, from a sense
of honor, I fight single-handed against the Trojans,
they will cut me off and surround me, and I will be trapped,
since Hector is on his way with a large contingent.
But why do I need to debate these things with myself?   90
When a man defies the gods' will and fights against someone
helped by a god, disaster rolls down upon him.
Surely no Argive will blame me if I give way
to Hector now, since a god is certainly with him.
If only I could find Ajax, together we two
would call up our fighting spirit and go into battle
even against the gods' will, to rescue the body
for Achilles, and that would be the least bad of our choices."

But while he thought these things over, the Trojan ranks
bore down upon him, with Hector leading the way.   100
Then Menelaus began to move back from the corpse,
still turning to face them, like some great bearded lion
who is chased away from a sheepfold by dogs and men

with spears and shouting, and the brave heart in his breast
is chilled, and against his will he abandons the farmyard:
just so did Menelaus move back from Patroclus.
But he took his stand as soon as he reached his comrades,
and he looked around for Ajax the Tall, and he quickly
caught sight of him on the left of the battlefield, cheering
his men on and encouraging them to fight.   120
(Apollo had filled them with an unearthly panic.)
And he ran toward him, and as he approached, he shouted,
"Ajax, dear friend, Patroclus is dead. Come quickly!
We might at least save his body, to bring to Achilles.
It is lying there naked. Hector has stripped off the armor."
These words went right to Ajax's heart. In a fury
he strode through the front ranks, and Menelaus went with him.

When Hector had stripped Patroclus and taken his armor,
he began to pull him away; he wanted to cut
his head off and fling the trunk to the wild dogs of Troy.   130
But Ajax arrived, with his body-shield like a tower,
and Hector retreated into the crowd and jumped
onto his chariot, telling the men to bring
the armor to Ilion, where it would add to his glory.

Then Ajax covered Patroclus with his huge shield
and stood over him like a lioness over her cubs
when she leads them out of her den and is met by hunters,
and confidently she faces them, drawing the skin
of her forehead down in a scowl that covers her eyes:
just so did Ajax stand in defense of Patroclus,   140
and Menelaus stood too, grief swelling his heart.

Then Glaucus, the Lycian leader, came up to Hector
and rebuked him, glaring at him with an angry frown:
"Hector, most handsome of men, but pathetic in battle,
what good is your fame, since you are as cowardly as
a woman? From now on, your city will have to be saved
by men who were born here. None of us Lycians will fight
for Ilion, since a man has no thanks for his tireless

struggle against the enemy, day in, day out.
How will you ever rescue a lesser man   150
when you callously left Sarpedon, your guest-friend and comrade,
to the Argives, and he became their spoil and their prize—
a man who was such a help to you and your city
while he was alive—and you haven't taken the trouble
to keep the wild dogs from his flesh. So if any Lycian
will listen to me, we will all go home and leave Troy
to its devastation. If only the Trojans possessed
the unshakable strength that enters men who are fighting
with all their hearts in defense of their own dear country,
we would soon drag Patroclus's body out of the battle   160
and into Troy; and the Argives would soon return
Sarpedon's armor, and we would be able to bring
his body also inside the walls of the city—
so great is the man whose comrade you killed, the bravest
of all the Argives, and served by the bravest troops.
But you didn't have the courage amid the fighting
to stand against Ajax and look him straight in the eye
or do battle with him, since he is the better man."

Hector answered him then, with an angry scowl:
"This insolence doesn't become you, Glaucus. I thought   170
that you were a man of good sense, beyond all others
in Lycia; but now I see that I was mistaken.
Your judgment is worthless. You say that I was afraid
to face the gigantic Ajax; but trust me, war
and the noise of thundering cars are nothing to me.
Yet Zeus's mind is always stronger than man's is;
he can easily make a brave man panic and run
in battle, or he can inspire him to fight his best.
But come and stand by my side, friend, and see what I do—
see whether I am a coward now, as you think,   180
or whether I put an end to more than one life
while the Danäans fight in defense of Patroclus's body."

Then Hector, in a loud voice, addressed the army:
"Trojan, Lycian, Dardánian soldiers and friends,

be men now. Onward; remember your fighting spirit.
Now I will put on Achilles' glorious armor,
which I took when I killed Patroclus and stripped his body."

And Hector withdrew from the battle and ran at full speed
in pursuit of the men who were taking the armor to Troy.
Soon he caught up; they had not gone very far.   190
And standing there at some distance from all the fighting,
he took off his armor and handed it to the men
to carry to Priam's city; then he put on
the indestructible armor that the immortals
had brought as a wedding gift to Achilles' father
and that Peleus in his old age had given his son.
But Achilles was not to grow old in his father's armor.

When Zeus looked down and saw Hector as he put on
the armor of Peleus's son, that godlike man,
he shook his head and said to himself, "Poor fool,   200
death doesn't loom in your thoughts, and yet before long
it will hurry toward you, even while you are wearing
the indestructible armor of that great man
who makes all others tremble. Now you have killed
his friend, who was gentle and brave, and you took the armor
from his head and shoulders—something you shouldn't have done.
But I will grant you great power for the time being,
in recompense for the fact that never again
will you see your home, and Andromache will not ever
greet you as you arrive in Achilles' armor."   210

Thus Zeus decreed, and he bowed his dark brow to confirm it.
He looked down and made the armor fit Hector's body
perfectly. And a terrible lust for killing
entered his bloodstream, and a fresh surge of power
rushed through his limbs. And with a thunderous war cry
he strode to rejoin the allies, and he appeared
in front of them all, resplendent there in the dazzling
armor of the great-hearted son of Peleus.
And he went to each captain and said a few words to inspire him—

to Mesthles and Glaucus, Thersílochus and Medon,   220
Asteropǽus, Hippóthoüs, and Disénor,
Chrómius, Phorcys, and Énomus the bird-prophet:
"Listen to me, you uncountable tribes of our allies.
When I called you here from your towns, it was not mere numbers
I needed, but men who would fight here with all their hearts
to defend the Trojans' wives and their little children
from the bloodthirsty Argives. That is why I have been
impoverishing my own people as they supply you
with gifts and food, to sustain you and strengthen your spirits.
So charge at the enemy, every one of you; choose   230
to live or die in the brutal caress of war.
And whichever man drags Patroclus's corpse to our side
and makes Ajax yield—I will give him half of the spoils,
and he will share with me equally in the glory."

At these words, they raised their spears and charged at the Argives,
and each man hoped in his heart that he would be able
to pull the corpse out from under the feet of Ajax—
fools that they were, for many men lost their lives there.

Then Ajax shouted, "Lord Menelaus, dear friend,
I don't expect that we will survive this battle.   240
Not only am I afraid that Patroclus's body
will become a meal for the wild dogs and vultures of Troy,
but also that you and I will soon be cut down,
since a dark cloud of war has surrounded us on all sides.
Hurry now, shout to our captains. Someone may hear you."

Then Menelaus did what Ajax had said;
he called with a mighty shout that moved all who heard him:
"My friends, commanders and captains of the Achaeans,
you who keep drinking your wine at the public expense
by the side of Agamemnon and Menelaus   250
and share their command, by the will of almighty Zeus—
it is hard for me to recognize each of you here,
so huge is the blaze of war that flares up around us;
I cannot call you by name, but come here and help

defend Patroclus's body. Ward off the disgrace
of having Troy's dogs devour him and gnaw his bones."

These were his words, and Ajax the Smaller heard them
and came running through the confusion to join Menelaus,
and Idómeneus followed, along with Meriones.
But what man's mind could remember the names of all those   260
who answered the call to fight in defense of Patroclus?

The Trojans charged in a mass, with Hector in front.
As at the mouth of a river the huge waves roar
against the current, and on both sides the wide beach
booms with the thunder of salt water pounding in:
such was the roar of the Trojans as they moved forward.
But the Argives stood firm around Patroclus, united
in purpose, behind a solid wall of bronze shields.
And Zeus spread thick darkness over the shining helmets;
he had not disliked Patroclus while he still lived   270
as Achilles' attendant, and now he hated the thought
that he would become a meal for the enemy's dogs.

At first the Trojans drove back the Argives and forced them
to abandon the body and give ground; yet even so,
they did not succeed in killing a single man
among the defenders, though they all tried their utmost,
but they did start dragging the corpse away. The Achaeans
fell back, but just for a short time, since they were quickly
rallied by Ajax, who was, in stature and prowess,
the greatest of all the Danäans after Achilles.   280
He charged through the front ranks fiercely, like a wild boar
that easily scatters a pack of dogs and young hunters
in a mountain glade when it suddenly wheels and charges:
just so did Ajax scatter the Trojan battalions
that were standing around Patroclus, intending to haul him
off to Troy and cover themselves with glory.
Hippóthoüs, the son of Pelásgian Lethus,
had tied his shield strap to one of Patroclus's ankles
and was dragging him by the foot through the thick of the fierce

battle, doing his best for the Trojans and Hector.   290
But evil descended upon him; no one could stop it,
however greatly they wished to, since Ajax came charging
into the crowd and quickly caught up with him
and stabbed him, driving his spear through the bronze-cheeked helmet,
and the helmet was split apart, and brains and blood spurted
out from the wound, drenching the spear point's socket;
and he dropped Patroclus's foot, and he pitched face forward
and died on top of the body, far from his home
in the fertile land of Laríssa, unable to pay
the debt that he owed his dear parents for bringing him up,   300
since his life was cut short by the point of Ajax's spear.

Hector then aimed and hurled his own spear at Ajax.
But Ajax saw the spear coming; he dodged to one side,
and it missed him by inches. Instead, it cut Schédius down,
the son of Íphitus; he was by far the bravest
of the men who had come to Troy from Phocis; he lived
in Pánopeus, where he ruled over many people.
The spear drove into him, hitting him just below
the collarbone, in the middle, and went right through,
and the point came out at the base of his shoulder blade,   310
and he fell with a crash, and his armor clattered upon him.

Then Ajax's spear hit Phorcys, the son of Phænops,
in mid-belly as he stood near Hippóthoüs,
and it broke through the front of his breastplate; his innards gushed out,
and he fell in the dust, clawing the earth with his nails.
Hector and the front ranks of the Trojans fell back,
and the Argives gave a loud shout and dragged off the bodies
of Hippóthoüs and Phorcys and stripped off their armor.

And soon the Trojans would have been driven back
inside the walls of Ilion, overcome   320
by their own lack of fighting spirit, and the Achaeans
would have won glory beyond what Zeus had decreed
if Apollo had not urged on Aeneas, taking
the form of the herald Périphas, who had grown old

as herald to old Anchíses, Aeneas's father—
a family friend and devoted to Lord Aeneas:
"Aeneas, if it were true that the gods were against you,
how could you and our army ever save Troy?
I have known great leaders who saved their country by trusting
their own strength and courage, though most of their troops were afraid.   330
Zeus is on *our* side; he wants *us* to win, not the Argives;
yet you are all fleeing in panic and will not fight."

Aeneas knew that it was a god when he saw
Apollo's face, and he called out with a loud cry:
"Hector, and all you Trojan and allied commanders,
it will be a disgrace if we are now driven back
inside the walls of Ilion, overcome
by our own lack of fighting spirit. Besides, a god
just came to me and looked in my eyes and said
that Zeus is on *our* side and favors *us* in this battle.   340
So let us make sure that the Danäans have to work hard
before they can bring Patroclus to the black ships."

He charged out and took a stand far ahead of the front ranks,
and they rallied and turned to fight against the Achaeans.
Aeneas first stabbed Leócritus with his spear,
the son of Arísbas and comrade of Lycomédes.
And as he fell, Lycomédes was filled with pity,
and he moved in close; he hurled his spear, and it hit
Apisáon, son of Híppasus, in the belly
and pierced his liver; at once he crumpled to earth.   350
(He had come with the Pæónians and was the best
fighter among them, after Asteropǽus.)
When he fell there, Asteropǽus was filled with pity,
and he too rushed forward, eager to fight the Achaeans,
but he could do nothing; they had surrounded Patroclus
with a wall of shields and with spears pointed straight ahead.
Ajax had gone among them with firm instructions:
Not one of them was to move back behind the body
or move out in front of the others, but they were all
to stand their ground and defend it in hand-to-hand fighting.   360

This had been his command; and the earth was soaked
with blood, and the men died on top of each other in heaps,
Trojans and their brave allies, and Argives as well,
who did not fight without losses, though many fewer
of them were cut down in the slaughter, because they stood there
in a solid mass and warded off death from each other.

And so they continued to fight, like a blazing fire.
You would not have thought that the sun and moon still existed,
so thick was the darkness that covered all the brave men
who had taken their stand around Patroclus's body.   370
The rest of the Trojans and Argives fought unimpeded
under a clear blue sky, with the piercing sunlight
spread upon them and not a cloud to be seen
above the plain and the mountains. The armies fought,
then pulled back and stood out of range of each other's missiles.
But there in the center, the bravest warriors suffered
as they fought in the dark, ground down by the pitiless bronze.
Two men, however, Nestor's sons Thrasymédes
and Antilochus, had not heard that Patroclus was dead.
They were trying to ward off panic and death from their troops   380
some distance away from the center, as Nestor had told them
when he sent them off to the battle from the black ships.

So all day long the ferocious struggle continued,
and the sweat poured ceaselessly down the men's arms and legs
and into their eyes as they fought for Achilles' comrade.
As when a man gives an enormous bull's hide to his people
for stretching, once it is soaked in fat, and they take it
and pull at it as they stand around in a circle,
and quickly its moisture leaves and the fat sinks in
as the hide is stretched to its utmost with many hands pulling: 390
just so did both sides pull back and forth at the body,
their hearts filled with hope that they would drag it away,
the ones to the city, the others back to their ships,
and the struggle around it was fierce. Not even Ares
or Athena, at their most savage, would have found fault.
Such was the slaughter that Zeus sent down on that day

to horses and men in the struggle over Patroclus.

But Achilles did not yet know that Patroclus was dead.
They were fighting under the wall of Ilion, far
away from the ships, and he never dreamed that his comrade   400
could have been killed there. He thought that he would press on
right to the gates, then return; he never expected
that Patroclus would try to storm the city without him,
or with him either, since many times he had heard
his mother say that according to Zeus's plan
Patroclus would never take part in Ilion's fall.
But this time she did not tell him about the disaster:
that Patroclus, his most beloved companion, had died.

Meanwhile the two sides kept fighting over the body,
and many of them were cut down by thrusts of the spear.   410
And sometimes an Achaean captain would shout,
"My friends, it would be a disgrace to retreat and surrender
Patroclus's corpse to the Trojans, for them to drag it
back to Troy and cover themselves with glory.
It would be far better for us to let the dark earth
gape open and swallow us all where we are standing."
And sometimes a Trojan captain would shout, "My friends,
even if we are destined to be cut down
beside this body, let no one pull back from the fighting."
With such words, they stirred up the spirit of every man.   420

Thus the fierce fight went on, and the iron outcry
rose through the air up into the sky of bronze.
But apart from the battle, Achilles' horses were weeping;
they had not stopped since the moment they learned that Patroclus
had just been cut down at the hands of man-killing Hector.
Automedon did whatever he could; he hit them
again and again with his whistling whip, and he tried
persuading them with soft words, then angry threats.
But the horses refused to budge; they would not go back
to the ships, nor would they go forward into the fighting.   430
Motionless as a gravestone that has been set

upon the funeral mound of some lord or lady,
they stood there in front of the chariot, hanging their heads.
Hot tears flowed from their eyes and fell to the ground
as they mourned for their charioteer, who was gone forever,
and their long, luxuriant manes became filthy and trailed
in the dirt, from the collar on either side of the yoke.

When he saw them weeping, Lord Zeus was filled with pity,
and he shook his head and said to himself, "Poor fools,
why did we give you to Peleus, a mortal man,   440
when you are unaging and deathless? Was it to let you
share in the wretched sorrow of humankind?
For there is nothing so miserable as humans
among all the creatures that live and breathe on the earth.
But at least you will not see Hector drive you away
along with your chariot. That I will not allow;
it is quite enough that he gloats in Achilles' armor.
I will send fresh strength to your legs and your hearts, so that you
can bring Automedon safely out of the battle.
But I will give strength to the Trojans and let them keep on   450
killing, until they come to the Danäan ships."

With these words he breathed great power into the horses,
and they shook the dust from their manes and galloped ahead
into the thick of the battle. Automedon fought
standing behind them, however he grieved for his comrade;
he swooped on the Trojan ranks as an eagle swoops down
on a flock of geese. He could easily gallop clear
of the turmoil, and he could easily rush back in
to pursue a man, but although he drove on with fury
he could not kill them, since he was alone in the car,   460
unable to lunge with his spear or even to hold it;
he needed both hands to control the galloping horses.

At last, his companion Álcimus, son of Laérces,
noticing him, ran up to the chariot and said,
"My friend, what god has put this senseless idea
into your head and taken away your reason?

How can you fight the Trojans alone as you are
in your chariot? Your comrade-in-arms has been killed,
and Hector is strutting around in Achilles' armor."

Automedon answered, "Álcimus, there is no man   470
who can equal you in mastering these immortal
horses, except for Patroclus, while he was alive;
but now he has met his fate, and pale death has claimed him.
So come up beside me; take the whip and the reins,
and I will dismount from the car and fight on the ground."

At these words, Álcimus leaped up behind the horses
and took the whip and the reins, and Automedon
jumped down with his spear. And Hector caught sight of them
and said to Aeneas, who was standing nearby:
"Aeneas, dear friend, great counselor of the Trojans,   480
I can see Achilles' horses come into the battle
with inferior men in charge. If you will help me,
I am sure that I can capture them, since the two Argives
will never dare to withstand us when we attack."

Aeneas agreed and did what Hector had asked for;
and the two of them charged ahead, with their shoulders covered
by shields that had many layers of dried and toughened
oxhide, with a top layer of hammered bronze;
and Chrómius and Arétus followed close after.
The spirits of all these men were fired up; they hoped   490
to cut down the two Achaeans and capture the horses,
fools that they were, since they would not get away
from Automedon without bloodshed. He prayed to Zeus,
and the dark heart within him was filled with courage and strength.
And quickly he said to Álcimus, his companion:
"Dear friend, follow me now with the horses; hold them
so close that I can feel their warm breath on my back.
For if Hector is not cut down in the front lines himself,
he won't be stopped until he has killed us and taken
the horses and put the whole Danäan army to flight."   500

*

After he gave these instructions, he shouted out
to the Ajaxes and also to Menelaus:
"Ajaxes, Menelaus, each of you—hurry,
leave the corpse with the best of our men. They will stand
stalwartly here and hold off the enemy troops
while you come to defend the living as well. We need you;
Aeneas and Hector are bearing down hard upon us.
But I know that everything rests in the hands of the gods.
I will throw my spear, and Zeus will decide the outcome."

He aimed, then threw his long-shadowed spear, and it hit   510
Arétus's shield with such force that it passed through it
and drove right through his belt and into his belly.
As when a strong man takes a sharpened axe in his hands
and brings it down on a bull's neck, behind the horns,
and severs the tendons; the bull jerks forward, then drops:
so Arétus jerked forward, then fell on his back, and the spear
lodged in his bowels, trembling, and cut off his life.
Then Hector threw his bright spear at Automedon,
but Automedon saw it coming and ducked to avoid it,
and behind him the spear point stuck in the ground, and the butt end   520
quivered, until at last its fury was spent.

And now they both would have charged in, drawing their swords,
if the Ajaxes had not rushed over and forced their way through
the mass of men when they heard Automedon calling.
When they saw them, Hector, Aeneas, and Chrómius,
terrified, retreated and left Arétus
lying there, with the life torn out of his body.
Automedon stripped off his armor and said in triumph,
"Now I have given my grieving heart a small comfort
for the death of Patroclus, although the man that I killed   530
was hardly his equal." After he said this, he picked up
the blood-stained armor and put it into the chariot
and climbed on; his legs and arms were covered with blood,
like a lion that has been gorging upon a bull.

And now the ferocious, grief-laden fighting began

once again over Patroclus, urged on by Athena,
who had come down from heaven at the command of Zeus
to encourage the Danäans, since he had changed his purpose.
As Zeus sends a shimmering rainbow across the sky
to warn mankind of a war or a chilling rainstorm   540
that halts men's work on the land and troubles the flocks:
just so Athena, wrapped in a shimmering mist,
strode into the battle and stirred up the Danäans' courage.

The first warrior that she spoke to was Menelaus.
Taking the form and voice of Phoenix, she said,
"You, Menelaus, will bear the brunt of the shame
if Achilles' beloved comrade is torn to pieces
by the wild dogs roaming under the wall of Troy.
So stand your ground now, and call our brave men to help you."

And Menelaus answered her, "Phoenix, old friend,
dear father, if only Athena would grant me strength   550
and keep me safe from the onslaught of hurtling spears,
then I would gladly stand by Patroclus's body
and fight for him, since his death has so touched my heart.
But Hector is on the rampage, cutting men down
everywhere, ceaselessly, like a devouring fire.
Zeus today has decided to give him the glory."

When she heard him say this, Athena's heart was delighted
that she was the god he prayed to before all others.
She put strength into his shoulders and legs and gave him   560
a horsefly's boldness; no matter how often a man
brushes it from his skin, it keeps trying to bite him,
so sweet for it is the savor of human blood:
such was the boldness she poured into his dark spirit,
and he stood over Patroclus and threw his spear.
There was a Trojan named Podēs, Ëétion's son,
a wealthy man and well-born, much honored by Hector,
a dear friend of his and often his dinner companion;
the spear hit the back of his belt as he turned to flee,
and it went straight through, and he fell to the ground with a crash.   570

And Lord Menelaus dragged Patroclus's body
away from the Trojans and into the Argive ranks.

Apollo came up to Hector and urged him on
in the likeness of Phænops, Ásius's son, the dearest
of all his guest-friends, who had his home in Abýdus:
"Hector, which of the Argives will fear you again
if you cringe before Menelaus, who has in the past
been such a weak fighter? Yet single-handedly
he has snatched a dead body out of the Trojan lines
and gotten away with it; it was your loyal comrade,   580
that excellent warrior Podēs, Ëétion's son."
As he spoke, a black cloud of sorrow enfolded Hector,
and he strode through the front ranks, armored in fiery bronze.
Then Zeus picked up the glittering, tasseled storm shield
and covered Mount Ida in clouds and sent down his lightning
and thunder and shook the storm shield, giving the glory
to the Trojans and scattering the Achaeans in panic.

The first man to run was Penéleos the Bœótian;
he had been steadily facing the Trojan army
when a spear from Polydamas, who had run out through the ranks   590
and hurled it at close range, hit him on top of the shoulder;
it did not go deep, but it pierced him and grazed the bone.
Then Hector thrust and stabbed Léïtus in the wrist,
the son of Aléctryon, putting him out of action;
he looked around in dismay, and he pulled back, knowing
that he could no longer grip a spear in his hand.
And Idómeneus threw his spear as Hector was charging
at Léïtus, and it hit him beside the nipple
on his massive breastplate; but the long spear broke off
at the socket. The Trojans cheered loudly, and Hector threw   600
at Idómeneus, who by now had mounted a car;
he narrowly missed him, but hit Meriones' friend
Cœranus, who had sailed with the troops from Lyctus.
When Idómeneus had come from the ships that day,
he had come on foot, and he would have given the Trojans
a triumph if Cœranus had not driven up close,

saving his life and warding off certain destruction,
but it cost him his own life. Hector's spear hit him just under
the ear, and it knocked out his teeth and sliced his tongue
down the middle; he fell from the chariot, dropping 610
the reins. Meriones bent down and picked them up
and called to Idómeneus, "Whip on the horses—hurry!
Go back to the ships, and drive as fast as you can;
you can see for yourself that the Argives have lost this battle."
When he heard these words, Idómeneus lashed the horses
back to the ships. A great fear had entered his heart.

Ajax and Menelaus were just as aware
that Zeus was turning the course of the battle and giving
the Trojans victory. Ajax was first to speak:
"What a disaster! Even a fool can see 620
that Father Zeus himself is now helping the Trojans.
All their missiles are hitting home, whether they fly
from the hands of brave men or cowards; Zeus makes them all
fly straight, while all our missiles stick in the dirt.
So we need to help ourselves now and come up with a plan
for dragging the body away and at the same time
escaping and going back to bring joy to our friends,
who must be distraught as they look on and think that nothing
can stop the Trojans from hurling themselves on the ships.
If only someone could take a word to Achilles 630
without delay; I am sure that he hasn't heard
the bad news that his beloved friend has been killed.
But I cannot see an Achaean able to do this;
they are all covered in thick mist, both men and horses.
Father Zeus, save us. Lift this terrible darkness;
make the sky clear, bring light, so that at least
we can see what we are doing. Go ahead, kill us
if that is your will, as long as you do it in sunlight."
His tears fell as he prayed, and the Father took pity,
and at once he scattered the mist and dispelled the darkness, 640
and the sun broke through, and the battle came into sight.

Then Ajax said, "Look around you now, Menelaus.

If you can find Antilochus still alive,
tell him to run to Achilles to bring him the news
that Patroclus, his most beloved friend, has been killed."

And Menelaus did what Ajax had said
and called to Meriones and the Ajaxes:
"Ajaxes and Meriones, each of you, think
of poor Patroclus, his gentleness, the kind way
he had with everyone while he was still alive;   650
but now he has met his fate, and pale death has claimed him."

With this Menelaus left them, looking around
like an eagle, which of all winged creatures (men say)
has the keenest sight, and though he is far above,
he can spot the quick-footed hare as it lies crouching
under a bush, and he swoops down and seizes it
in his deadly claws and tears the life out of its body:
just so did your eyes, Menelaus, scan up and down
the ranks of all your comrades-in-arms to see
if Nestor's son was still alive somewhere. And quickly   670
you caught sight of him on the left of the battlefield, cheering
his men on and encouraging them to fight.
And Menelaus ran over to him and said,
"Antilochus, come here quickly. I have to tell you
the awful news—I wish it had never happened.
I think that you can already see, with your own eyes,
that a god is rolling disaster upon the Argives
and the battle belongs to the Trojans. But now the best
fighter among the Danäans has been killed:
Patroclus. It is a wretched loss for us all.   680
Quickly, run to the ships, take word to Achilles,
and tell him to bring the corpse to his ship, right away.
It is lying there naked. Hector has stripped off the armor."

When he heard these words, Antilochus shuddered with horror.
For a long time he was speechless; his eyes filled with tears,
and his strong voice failed. But he nodded to Menelaus
and ran off, leaving his armor with his companion

Laódocus, who had been keeping his horses close by.

And his swift feet carried him out of the battle, weeping,
to bring the unbearable news to Achilles. And you   690
decided not to remain, Menelaus, and help
the embattled troops of the Pýlians who were left there
by Antilochus—a loss that they all felt sharply—
but you put Thrasymédes in charge, while you yourself ran
to Patroclus and to the Ajaxes, and you said,
"I have done as you asked and sent that man back to the ships,
but I don't expect Achilles to come out soon.
However intense his fury at Hector may be,
he cannot enter the battle without his armor.
So we need to help ourselves now and come up with a plan   700
for dragging the body away and at the same time
ourselves escape death at the hands of the Trojan battalions."

Then Ajax the Tall, the son of Télamon, answered,
"What you say, Lord Menelaus, is right and proper.
Quickly now, you and Meriones lift the body
up on your shoulders and carry it out of the fighting,
while the two of us keep close behind you and drive back the Trojans.
We are one in heart, as in name; often before this
we have fought side by side and stood firm in the thick of battle."

When they heard this, they took the body up in their arms   710
and lifted it high off the ground, with a huge effort.
Behind them the Trojans gave a loud shout when they saw
the two men lifting the corpse and beginning to move it,
and they charged in like dogs pursuing a wounded boar
ahead of the hunters; for a short time they rush forward,
determined to leap upon him and tear him to pieces,
but when he suddenly turns on them, they recoil,
terrified, and they scatter in all directions:
just so did the Trojans keep charging at them in one mass
for a short time, thrusting their swords and double-curved spear points; 720
but whenever the Ajaxes wheeled around to confront them,
their flesh went pale; not one of them had the courage

to charge straight ahead and fight for Patroclus's body.

Thus they worked hard to take the corpse out of the fighting
to the black ships; and around them the battle raged
as violently as a sudden fire that breaks out
and sets a whole city ablaze, and the houses collapse
in the flames as the wind's force whips them into a roaring
devastation: just so, as they moved back, the tumult
of chariots and soldiers continued on every side.   730
Like mules that exert their great strength to haul a ship's beam
or an enormous timber down from the mountains
along a path strewn with rocks, and the pair keep straining,
worn out from the work, their bodies covered with sweat:
just so did the two of them strain to carry the corpse,
and behind them the Ajaxes kept back the Trojan battalions.
And as a wooded ridge that crosses a plain
keeps back a flood and holds off even the most
destructive torrents, diverting them over the plain,
and no river current is strong enough to break through it: 740
just so did the Ajaxes hold off the Trojan attack.
But the Trojans kept coming, led by Aeneas and Hector;
and as a cloud of starlings or jackdaws flies out
screeching in fear when they see a hawk approach, bringing
death to small birds: just so the young Argives fled,
screaming, as soon as Aeneas and Hector charged forward,
forgetting their will to fight and their joy in combat.
On both sides of the trench, many fine pieces of armor
fell as they ran. And there was no pause in the fighting.

Book 18

And so they continued to fight, like a blazing fire,
while Antilochus ran to Achilles. He found him sitting
in front of his black ships, feeling an intuition
of what had already happened; his thoughts were uneasy,
and he said to himself in dismay, "Why are the Argives
once again being driven across the plain
in panic, back toward the ships? I pray that the gods
haven't brought down on me the unbearable sorrow
that my mother told me about: that while I still lived
the best man among us would fall, cut down by the Trojans.   10
Patroclus must have been killed. He has done something reckless.
I *told* him not to fight Hector and to return
as soon as he saved our ships from the enemy's fire."

While he was brooding on all this, Antilochus
arrived at his hut with tears pouring down his cheeks
and said, "Son of Peleus, I am sorry to bring you
dreadful news—I wish it had never happened.
Patroclus is dead. They are fighting over his body.
It is lying there naked. Hector stripped off the armor."

A black cloud of sorrow enfolded Achilles. He stooped   20
and with both his hands he picked up some soot and dust
and poured it over his head, and his handsome face
was filthy with it, and black ashes fell all over
his sweet-smelling tunic. And out of the huts came running
the women slaves that he and Patroclus had won.
They were sobbing aloud in their hearts' grief, and they surrounded
Achilles, beating their breasts, and their knees went weak,
and they sank to the ground. And Antilochus cried out and wept,
holding Achilles' hands as the great man groaned softly.

Achilles then let out a terrible scream, and his mother   30
heard him at once, although she was far away,

sitting beside the Old Man of the Sea, her father.
She cried out loud, and the goddesses gathered around her,
the daughters of Néreüs, there in the depths of the sea.
The shimmering cave soon filled with them, and they all
beat their breasts, and Thetis began her lament:
"Néreïds, sisters, listen to me and hear
the grief that is in my heart. How wretched I am!
I bore a son who became the greatest of heroes,
strong and handsome; he shot up like a young sapling,   40
and I tended him like a tree on an orchard hill,
and when he grew up, I sent him to Ilion
to fight the Trojans. But never again will I see him
return to his home, the house of Peleus. And yet
every day of his life he will have to suffer,
and there is no way I can help him. But I will go
to my dear child and find out what dreadful sorrow
is crushing him while he sits apart from the fighting."

With these words she left the cave, and the others went with her
in tears, and the waves of the gray sea parted before them.   50
As they came to the land of Troy, one after another
they stepped out onto the shore, where the Myrmidon ships
were drawn up in close formation around Achilles.
Thetis came up and took his head in her hands
as he groaned, and with tears of pity she said to him, "Child,
why are you weeping? What has caused you this sorrow?
Tell me. Don't keep it hidden; let me know too.
All that you wished for has been accomplished by Zeus,
when you held out your hands and prayed that the Achaeans—
because you were no longer fighting for them—would be penned in   60
beside the ships and undergo great misfortunes."

Then, with a deep groan, Achilles said to his mother,
"True, the Olympian has indeed answered my prayers;
but what good can that do me, when my beloved friend
has been killed?—Patroclus, a man whom I held in such honor
and loved as much as my own life. Now I have lost him;
and Hector, who cut him down, has stripped off his massive

glorious armor, a marvel of grace and beauty,
which the gods gave my father, Peleus, on the day
when they put you into the bed of a human being.   70
If only you could have stayed at home with the sea nymphs
and Peleus had taken a mortal woman as bride!
But as it is, your heart will be filled with endless
grief for the death of your child. For you will never
welcome me back to my home, since my spirit commands me
not to live on among men unless Hector first
is cut to pieces by my own weapon and pays
in full the blood-price for killing my friend Patroclus."

Thetis, weeping, answered him, "Then, my child,
from what you are saying, you must die very soon,   80
since right after Hector dies, your own death stands waiting."

Achilles said, "May I die soon then, since I allowed
my beloved friend to be killed when I could have saved him.
Far from his home he died, and it was my fault.
And because I will never return to my own dear country
and haven't been able to save Patroclus or help
the many other companions who have been cut down
by Hector, while I—a man who is without equal
among the Achaean warriors—I have sat here
idly, a useless burden upon the earth . . .   90
If only strife could vanish from gods and mortals,
and anger, which makes even sensible men flare up
and get caught in violent quarrels and which, far sweeter
than trickling honey, expands in the breast like smoke:
such is the anger that Agamemnon has caused me.
But all this is over and done with, so let it be;
however it hurts, I must force down my bitter heart's passion.
Now I will go out to find the man who destroyed
the life of my dearest friend. As for my own death,
whenever Zeus and the other immortal gods   100
wish it to come, I will welcome it. For not even
Héracles, the strongest of men, could escape
his death, though he was the favorite child of Zeus,

but fate overtook him, and the fierce anger of Hera.
So I too will die, whenever my time has come.
But for now, while I am alive, let me win glory
and make many Trojan and many Dardánian women
wipe the tears from their tender cheeks with both hands
as they wail in their endless grief, so that they know
how long it has been that I have held back from the fighting.   110
And Mother, although you love me, do not attempt
to hold me back any further. I will not listen."

Then Thetis answered him, "Child, what you said is true;
it is right to save your companions from certain death
when they are so overwhelmed. But your fine armor
lies in the hands of the Trojans; Hector himself
is wearing it on his shoulders. I do not think
that he will enjoy it for long, since his own death
is fast approaching. But please don't enter the battle
until I return. I will come in the morning, at sunrise,   120
with glorious, newly made armor from Lord Hephaestus."

She turned away from her son and addressed her sisters:
"Go back into the sea; dive down to the house
of our father, and tell him everything that has happened.
As for myself, I will go to Olympus and ask
Hephaestus, the master craftsman, if he is willing
to make some glorious armor for my dear son."
As soon as they heard this, they all plunged into the sea,
while Thetis went off to make her request to Hephaestus.

As she hurried away to Olympus, the Argives were fleeing   130
Hector's onslaught, with cries of despair and terror,
until they came to their ships and the Hellespont.
They could not pull Patroclus's corpse from the hurtling
missiles, because the Trojans had launched an attack—
men and chariots and Hector blazing like fire.
Three times he seized the corpse from behind, by the feet,
determined to drag it back, and yelled to the Trojans;
three times the Ajaxes, filled with the spirit of war,

turned him away. But confident of his strength,
he kept charging into the thick of the fight, or he stood there   140
and rallied his men with loud war cries, not yielding an inch.
Like shepherds who find a huge, hungry lion standing
over a carcass and cannot chase him away:
just so the two Ajaxes could not chase away Hector.
And now he would surely have dragged off Patroclus's corpse
and won for himself imperishable glory
if Iris had not come hurrying down from Olympus
to tell Achilles that he must prepare to fight;
Hera had sent her, without the knowledge of Zeus
or the other immortal gods. She came up and said,   150
"Arise, son of Peleus, most negligent of all men.
Go and defend Patroclus; a deadly struggle
is raging over his body in front of the ships.
They are butchering one another, some trying to save him,
while the others keep trying to seize him and drag him to Troy.
The most determined is Hector; he wants to cut off
Patroclus's head from his tender neck and impale it
on one of the stakes in the palisade. So get up now.
Don't hang back from the fighting; ward off the disgrace
of having Troy's dogs devour him and gnaw his bones.   160
It will be your fault and your shame if the corpse is disfigured."

Achilles answered her, "Iris, which of the gods
was it who sent you down with this message for me?"

Iris said, "Hera. Zeus knows nothing about it,
nor does any other immortal on snow-capped Olympus."

Achilles answered, "But how can I enter the fighting?
Those men have my armor, and my dear mother told me
not to get ready until I see her again;
she promised to bring me new armor, made by Hephaestus.
And what other man has armor that I could put on,   170
except for the shield of Ajax? But he himself
is using it, I am sure, as he fights in the front ranks,
slaughtering Trojans over Patroclus's body."

*

Iris said, "We, too, know that your glorious armor
lies in their hands; but go to the trench as you are
and show yourself to the Trojans. Fill them with terror
at the sight of you, and they may pull back from the fighting."

With these words Iris left, and Achilles got up,
and around his powerful shoulders Athena flung
the tasseled storm shield and circled his handsome head   180
with a golden mist and made fire shoot from his brow.
As when plumes of smoke rise into the sky from a city
on some distant island that enemies have attacked,
and all day long men fight from the city walls,
and when the sun sets, a line of beacon fires blazes
to alert the neighboring islanders in the hope
that they will set sail and rescue them from disaster:
just so did the light blaze up from the head of Achilles.
He went out beyond the wall and stood at the trench,
but respecting his mother's command, kept back from the fighting.   190
He stood there and shouted his war cry—from far off Athena
shouted as well—and he stirred up unspeakable panic
among the Trojans. As when the sound of a trumpet
cries out in a town that has been attacked and besieged:
so piercingly clear was the sound of Achilles' voice.

When the Trojans heard his bronze call, they were shaken with terror;
even the horses sensed danger and started to pull
their chariots around. The charioteers were appalled
at the terrible flames from his head, which Athena had kindled.
Three times Achilles shouted across the trench;   200
three times the Trojans and allies were thrown into panic.
And then and there twelve of their bravest men were cut down,
trampled by their own chariots or stabbed by their spears.
Then, gratefully, the Danäans dragged Patroclus
out of the reach of the hurtling missiles and placed him
on a litter; he lay there, and all his dear comrades gathered
around him, weeping. Achilles also went with them,
shedding hot tears when he saw his faithful companion

lying there dead and mangled by the sharp bronze—
the friend he had sent out to fight, with his horses and chariot,   210
and never again would welcome on his return.

Then Hera ordered the tireless sun to go down
into the stream of Ocean. And the sun set
unwillingly, and the Argives could stop their fighting.
The Trojans also pulled back from the brutal conflict
and unyoked their horses; and before they took thought of supper,
they gathered in an assembly, all of them standing.
No one dared to sit down; they were all seized
by terror, because Achilles had reappeared
after the many days when he had been absent.   220

The first to speak was that clear man Polydamas,
the only one in the whole assembly who saw
what lay ahead of them all and what lay behind them.
He was a comrade of Hector—they were both born
on the same night—but Polydamas was a better
orator, as Hector was better in fighting.
With confidence in his judgment, he spoke to the men:
"It is time to act. Consider both sides of the issue
carefully, friends. But I, for my own part, urge you
to go back now and not wait for dawn to arise   230
here by the ships, so far from the city walls.
As long as this man was enraged at Lord Agamemnon,
it was easier for our troops to fight the Achaeans,
and I too was overjoyed that we spent the night
close to their fleet, in the hope of taking the ships.
But Achilles has now returned, and I am afraid.
He is a violent man, and he won't be happy
to stay on the plain, where we and the Danäan army
have been fighting on equal terms; he will soon attempt
to storm our city and carry off our dear wives.   240
We should go back now. Trust me, I know what will happen.
For the moment, night has disabled him; but tomorrow
he will move into action and catch us, and we will all
once again find out what he is made of. Whoever

escapes his spear will be thankful to get back to Troy,
and many of us will be eaten by wild dogs and vultures.
Take my advice, whatever misgivings you have:
We should pull back our forces and keep them safe in the city,
in the marketplace, protected by the strong walls
of Ilion, by the gates and thick wooden doors   250
yoked together and shut tight and bolted fast.
Then early tomorrow, at daybreak, let us all arm
and go out along the walls to defend the city.
And if Achilles should come from the ships and try
to attack our position, so much the worse for him;
he will have to return to his camp when he has exhausted
his horses, driving them back and forth under the walls.
But however he fights, however intense his fury,
he will not break through our lines, and he will never
conquer our city. Before that, the dogs will devour him."   260

Hector answered him then, with an angry scowl:
"I do not care for your speech, Polydamas; you
say we should go back and shut ourselves in the city—
but haven't you all had enough of being cooped up
inside our walls? Before the war Troy was famous
throughout the world for its riches of gold and bronze,
but all this treasure has disappeared from our houses,
and many of our possessions have had to be sold
to the Phrygians or the Mæónians, since the anger
of Zeus almighty began to descend upon us.   270
But now, when at last he has granted me all the glory
and allowed me to pin the Achaeans against the sea,
don't be such a great fool as to speak this nonsense.
So listen to me, and let us all do as I say.
Have supper throughout the army, in your divisions;
post your guards, and each of you stay awake.
And any man who is worried about his possessions
can share them among us all, for the common good;
better that *we* should have them than the Achaeans.
Then early tomorrow, at daybreak, let us all arm   280
and attack them with all our strength beside the black ships.

And if it is true that Achilles has moved into action,
then so much the worse for him. I will never run
but will stand face to face against him, and we will see
whether he wins or I do. The god of war
is impartial; he kills the man who has been the killer."

Thus Hector spoke to them all, and they roared their approval,
fools that they were, for Athena had robbed them of judgment.
They applauded Hector, though *his* plan led to destruction,
and not Polydamas, who had advised them well.   290

Then the whole army sat down to eat their supper.
Meanwhile the Argives grieved all night for Patroclus;
Achilles led them, putting his man-killing hands
on the breast of his comrade and uttering ceaseless moans,
like a great bearded lioness whose cubs have been stolen
by a man out hunting in the dense woods; she comes back
too late and, sick at heart, she moves through the valleys
tracking his footsteps, drawn on by boundless grief:
just so did Achilles groan. And at last he said,
"What empty words I spoke to that great man Menœtius   300
on the day that I tried to encourage him in our house!
I told him that once Troy fell, I would bring his son back
to Ópoïs, covered in glory and with great plunder.
But Zeus doesn't favor everything men propose.
Both of us have been fated to stain the ground red
in the land of Troy, because I will never return
to be welcomed at home by Lord Peleus in his halls
or by my mother; the earth will bury me here.
But now, Patroclus, since I will follow you soon
under the ground, I will hold off your funeral rites   310
until I have brought before you the armor and head
of the man who killed you: Hector; and at your pyre
I will cut the throats of a dozen splendid young Trojans
to appease my anger. But until that time, you will lie
beside my ships, just as you are, and around you
the Trojan and Dardánian women slaves
that we two worked hard to win by our strength and prowess

when we plundered the rich towns of Ilion, will lament
and keen for you, and their tears will fall night and day."

And Achilles ordered his men to put a large tripod   320
over the fire, in order to wash the clotted
blood from Patroclus's body without delay.
They put a three-legged cauldron for heating baths
onto the glowing fire and filled it with water
and brought wood to burn underneath it. And the flames licked
at the cauldron's belly, the water grew hot, and when
it came to a boil inside the glittering bronze,
they washed him clean and rubbed him with olive oil
and filled his wounds with long-seasoned ointment and placed him
on a funeral bed and covered him head to toe   330
with a sheet of fine linen and over that a white cloak.

Then for the rest of the night the Myrmidons stood
around Achilles and grieved and moaned for Patroclus.
And Zeus said to Hera, "So: you have had your way
once again; you have stirred Achilles to action.
One might almost think that the Argives were your own children."

Hera answered him, "Dread Lord, what are you saying?
Surely even a human can have his way
and do what he wants to another man, though he is mortal
and knows less than we do. And I, who am the greatest   340
of goddesses, both because of my noble birth
and because I am married to you, who rule over all
the immortal gods—why shouldn't I bring great trouble
upon the Trojans because they have made me angry?"

While Zeus and Hera were having this conversation,
Thetis arrived at the starry house of Hephaestus,
which the clubfooted god had fashioned with his own hands
from imperishable bronze and which stood out, shining,
among the gods' houses. She found him sweating with toil
as he bustled about his forge and worked at the bellows,   350
making a set of twenty tripods to stand

along the wall of his house. He had fitted golden
wheels under each of their legs, so that they could move
by their own power and enter the gods' assembly
any time he commanded them to and then
return to his house—a marvelous sight to behold.
They were not quite finished; he still had to put on the fine
ear-shaped handles, and he was forging their rivets.

While he was working at this, his beautiful wife,
Charis, came out and saw her. And taking her hand,   360
she said, "What brings you, Thetis, to honor our house?
You are always most welcome—and what a long time it has been!
But come with me now, and let me offer you something."

With these words the gracious goddess led her inside.
She had her sit down on a splendid chair that was richly
inlaid with silver (a footstool lay underneath it),
and she went in and found the master craftsman and said,
"Hephaestus, come out here. Thetis would like to see you."

The master craftsman, the clubfooted god, responded,
"I am glad she has come. I honor her and respect her   370
for saving me when my mother, that bitch, had thrown me
from heaven into the sea; she wanted to make me
disappear from her sight because of my lameness.
And I would have suffered even more agonies then
if Thetis, along with the sea nymph Eurýnomē,
daughter of Ocean, had not taken me in.
I lived in their house for nine years, making all kinds
of jewelry—brooches and spiral bracelets and earrings
and necklaces—down in their cavern, and endlessly
the Ocean roared all around us. Nobody else   380
knew I was there but the two who had rescued me, Thetis
and Eurýnomē. Now that Thetis has come to visit,
I must pay her all that I owe her for saving my life.
Please make her comfortable, serve her our finest nectar,
while I store my bellows and put away all my tools."

*

He stood up from the anvil, panting, a monstrous form,
with his massive torso and arms, and the stunted legs
bustling nimbly beneath him. He moved the bellows
away from the fire and gathered his tools and stowed them
in a silver box. And then, with a sponge, he wiped off   390
his face and both arms and his neck and his shaggy chest,
and he put on a tunic and picked up a thick staff to lean on
and limped toward the door, and his handmaids ran up to help him;
they were fashioned of gold, but they looked like real, breathing girls;
he had given them all intelligent minds; they could speak
and act on their own and had learned their skills from the gods.
While they scurried around to support their master, he came
hobbling up to where Thetis was, and he sat down
on a glittering chair, and, putting his hand in hers,
he said, "What brings you, Thetis, to honor our house?   400
You are always most welcome—and what a long time it has been!
Say what is on your mind. I will certainly do it."

Then, shedding hot tears, Thetis answered, "Hephaestus,
is there any goddess who ever endured such grief
as the sorrows that Zeus has sent me beyond all others?
I was the only one, out of all the sea nymphs,
who was forced to marry a human—Peleus, son
of Æacus—and I had to submit and endure
his embraces in bed, though it was against my will.
And now he lies in his house, worn out with wretched   410
old age; but there is still more now that I must suffer.
Zeus gave me a son who became the greatest of heroes,
strong and handsome; he shot up like a young sapling,
and I tended him like a tree on an orchard hill,
and when he grew up, I sent him to Ilion
to fight the Trojans. But never again will he come home,
and every day of his life he will have to suffer,
and whatever I do, there is no way that I can help him.
The girl whom the Argives picked out for him as his prize—
Lord Agamemnon took her back, and Achilles   420
has been eating his heart out in grief for her. Then the Trojans
penned the Achaeans in by the sterns of the ships

and wouldn't let them break out; and the senior commanders
came to his hut and pleaded with him and named
the many glorious gifts they would give him. But he
refused to ward off disaster from them; instead
he let Patroclus put on his armor and sent him
into the fighting, with a large force of men.
All day long he fought by the Scaean Gates
and did much damage and would have taken the city   430
if Lord Apollo had not interfered and killed him
in the front ranks and given Hector the glory.
That is why I have come here today, to implore you
to make for my son—who is fated to die so early—
a shield and a helmet, and also a pair of greaves
fitted with ankle clasps, and a strong breastplate,
since the armor he had was lost when his comrade died."

The master craftsman, the clubfooted god, responded,
"Take courage, and don't be troubled by all these things.
I only wish that I had the power to save him   440
from death, when it comes, as I have the power to fashion
a set of armor for him, so magnificent
that any mortal who sees it will be astonished."

With these words he left her there and moved back to the bellows.
He turned them to face the fire and commanded them
to get to work, and all twenty bellows started
to blow on the crucibles, blasting the flames up high
when he needed them to; and when he was not so busy
they blew with a gentler force, in whatever direction
he wanted, so that the work could proceed. And he threw   450
bronze on the fire, and tin and silver and gold,
and he placed the great anvil upon its block, and with one hand
he picked up a pair of tongs to hold the hot metal
and with the other one picked up the mighty hammer.

He began by making a huge and powerful shield,
embellishing it all over. Around its edge
he put a glittering rim, of a triple thickness,

and from it he hung a shield strap inlaid with silver.
The shield itself had five layers, and on the top one
he created marvels with his unmatchable skill.   460

Upon it he fashioned the earth and the sky and the sea
and the tireless sun and the moon as she grows into fullness
and all the constellations that crown the sky,
the Pleiades, Hyades, and the hunter Oríon,
and the Great Bear (men also call it the Wagon),
who turns in the same place and keeps a close eye on the hunter
and never goes down to bathe in the stream of Ocean.

Upon it he made two cities, alive with people.
In one there were weddings and feasts; they were leading the brides
from the women's chambers, under the blaze of torches   470
and through the wide streets, and the wedding song rang out among them.
Young men were leaping and twirling around in the dance,
and the flutes and lyres played joyfully, and the women
stood in their doorways, looking on with delight.
At the place of assembly, meanwhile, a crowd had gathered.
A quarrel had broken out, and two men were disputing
about the blood-price for someone who had been killed.
One man was claiming the right to pay for the death,
while the other refused to accept any compensation,
and each was eager to plead his case to the judges.   480
The people were cheering them on, some taking the side
of one, some taking the other's side, while the heralds
tried to control the crowd, and the city elders
were seated on polished stone chairs in the sacred circle,
holding the heralds' staffs. The men stood before them,
and each made his case, and the elders rose and gave judgments.
Two bars of solid gold, one from each side,
were displayed in the center; they were to be awarded
to the judge who was thought to give the clearest opinion.

Around the other city two forces were camped   490
in their shining armor. They were debating two plans:
One side wished to attack and plunder the city,

while the other side wished to spare it and, in return
for withdrawing, to claim one half of the city's possessions.
But the city would not consent; they were secretly arming
for an ambush, hoping to break the siege, and their wives
and children were standing upon the wall to defend it
along with the men who were too old to fight now. The others,
the warriors, were marching out from the city
led by Athena and Ares, fashioned in gold,   500
both of them huge and beautiful in their gold armor,
and they stood out above the rest, as is fitting for gods;
he had made the humans who marched at their feet much smaller.
And when they arrived at a likely place for the ambush,
in a riverbed where the cattle would come to drink,
they took their position, covered in shining bronze.
At some distance, two scouts were stationed to watch for the sheep
and cattle of the besieging army. These soon
appeared, and two herdsmen came with them, happily playing
on shepherds' pipes, with no premonition of danger.   510
And when the ambushers saw them, they charged out and quickly
cut off the herds of cattle and flocks of sheep
and killed the herdsmen. But when the besiegers, still
debating the issue, heard the loud noise from the cattle,
they leaped up onto their chariots and rode off
in pursuit, and they soon caught up with them. Then, by the banks
of the river, they took their position and fought a battle,
and both sides were hurling their bronze-tipped spears at each other,
all of them struggling in combat like living men
and dragging away the enemies they had killed.   520

Upon it he set rich farmland that had been lying
fallow the year before. It had just been plowed
three times, and plowmen were wheeling their teams across it,
back and forth and up and down the deep furrows.
When they reached the edge of the field and before they turned,
a man would hand them a cup of honey-sweet wine;
then they would turn back, eager to plow through the soil
and reach the other edge of the field for the next turn.
And the land darkened behind them and looked as if

it had just that moment been plowed, although it was fashioned   530
of pure gold: so marvelous was the craft of its forging.

Upon it he set the estate of a nobleman,
where the hired farmhands were reaping the grain with their sickles.
Some handfuls fell to the ground as they moved through the swath,
and the binders were tying other handfuls in sheaves
with rope made of twisted straw. Three binders stood by,
while behind the reapers children were gathering
the bound sheaves in armfuls and taking them off to be stored,
and the nobleman stood beside them, holding his staff
and silently watching the work with a joyful heart.   540
Apart from the reaping, under an oak tree, heralds
were preparing a feast; they had sacrificed a large ox
and were busy cutting it up, and the women took barley
and sprinkled the flesh with it for the workers' dinner.

Upon it he set a large vineyard heavy with grapes;
it was golden and beautiful; and the rich hanging fruit
was dark, and the vines were trained around poles of silver.
He set a ditch of dark-blue enamel around it,
and around that, a fence of tin. One single path
led to the vineyard; the grape-pickers came and went   550
along this path whenever they gathered the vintage.
Girls and young men, carefree, with innocent laughter,
carried the honey-sweet fruit in their wicker baskets.
In their midst a boy who was plucking his clear-toned lyre
played heart-pleasing music and sang the ancient lament
for Linus. His voice was clear and lovely, and they
moved to the powerful rhythm; their nimble feet pounded
the earth as they followed him, singing and shouting with joy.

Upon it he fashioned a large herd of straight-horned cattle,
of gold and tin; they were moving from farmyard to pasture   560
by a murmuring stream and a swaying thicket of reeds.
Along with the cattle four golden herdsmen were walking,
and nine dogs were running beside them. But at the front
of the herd, two ferocious lions had caught a bull,

and he, with loud bellows, was being dragged off, while the dogs
and young men pursued them. The lions had ripped through the bull's hide
and were lapping his blood and gorging themselves on his entrails
while the herdsmen were vainly setting the dogs on them, trying
to frighten them off, but the dogs were afraid, and they stood there
at a distance, barking, and would not move any closer.   570

Upon it the master craftsman, the crippled god,
made a large meadow, filled with a flock of sheep
grazing, and shepherds' stalls and roofed huts and sheepfolds.

Upon it he inlaid a dancing-floor, like the one
that Dædalus built in Knossos for Ariádnē.
Young men and rich-dowried girls were dancing upon it,
moving gracefully, holding each other's wrists.
The girls wore long linen robes, and the young men wore tunics
of fine-spun cloth, which glistened with olive oil;
and the girls were crowned with garlands of flowers, and the men   580
wore golden daggers that hung from sword belts of silver.
Sometimes they circled around on their knowing feet,
as when a potter sits at his wheel and holds it
between his palms, to make sure it is turning smoothly;
sometimes their rows came close and merged with each other.
And around the beautiful dancers stood a large crowd,
watching with utter delight as two solo performers
went spinning and whirling among them, leading the dance.

And he set the powerful river of Ocean flowing
on the marvelous shield, along its outermost rim.   590

Once he had fashioned the shield, he made him a breastplate
brighter than fire, and a beautiful inlaid helmet
with a golden crest, and two greaves of hammered tin.

Then, when the master craftsman had finished his work,
he took it and put it in front of Achilles' mother.
And she, like a hawk, came swooping down from Olympus
carrying the bright armor, the gift of Hephaestus.

Book 19

When dawn with its saffron glow came up from the Ocean
to bring light to the immortal gods and to men,
Thetis arrived at Achilles' hut with the armor.
She found her son lying face down, holding Patroclus
in his arms, bitterly weeping, and many comrades
stood around him in tears. The goddess came close
and said to Achilles, taking his hand in hers,
"My child, we must let him lie here, for all our sorrow,
since it is the will of the gods that he was cut down.
But take this armor, fashioned for you by Hephaestus,   10
more splendid than anything mortals have ever worn."

With these words Thetis set down the glorious armor
in front of Achilles, and each of the pieces clanged.
All the Myrmidons trembled with awe; not one
dared to look at it; all of them backed away.
But the more Achilles kept looking, the more his rage
at Hector grew, and his eyes burned as if they were flames,
and his heart rejoiced to hold the gifts of Hephaestus.

And when he had taken his pleasure and finished gazing
at the marvelous craftsmanship, he said to his mother,   20
"Mother, this dazzling gift of the god is truly
fit for immortals; no human being could have made it.
I can now get ready for battle. But I am afraid
that flies will crawl into the wounds that the bronze has cut
in Patroclus's body, and maggots will breed to defile him
now that the life has gone, and his flesh will rot."

Thetis answered him, "Child, please don't be troubled
by any of this. I promise that I will protect him
from the savage flies that feed on men killed in battle.
Patroclus could lie here for a whole year, and still   30
his flesh would remain as it is—perhaps even fresher.

So call an assembly; have all the Achaeans come,
and declare an end to your rage against Agamemnon.
Then quickly put on your armor and go out to fight."
As she said these words, she filled him with strength and courage,
and through Patroclus's nostrils she dripped ambrosia
and red nectar, to preserve him from all decay.

At once Achilles strode out along the seashore
with terrible war cries and stirred the Achaeans to action.
Even those who would normally stay at the ships,   40
the helmsmen who were in charge of the steering oars
and the stewards on board who dealt out all the provisions—
even these men rushed out to hear Lord Achilles,
who had reappeared now after such a long absence.
And Diomedes came limping along, with Odysseus,
each leaning upon a spear, since their wounds were still painful;
they came and sat down in the front row of the assembly.
And last of all was that king of men, Agamemnon,
and he too was suffering; Coön, the son of Anténor,
had wounded him with his spear in the thick of the fighting.   50
Then, when all the Achaeans had gathered, Achilles
stood up and turned to Lord Agamemnon and said,
"Son of Atreus, could anyone say that this quarrel
has been good for us, you and me, when the two of us flared up
in grief-filled, heart-crushing conflict over a girl?
I wish that Ártemis had taken an arrow
and shot her down on my ship the day that I won her
after destroying Lyrnéssus; then all those many
comrades would still be with us, the ones who were slaughtered
in battle while I was furious. Only Hector   60
and the Trojans have profited from it; as for the Argives,
they, I am sure, will remember it for a long time.
But all this is over and done with, so let it be;
however it hurts, we must force down our bitter hearts' passion.
Now, as for me, I declare an end to my anger;
I will not rage on, relentlessly and forever.
So stir up the heart of every man in the army,
and I will go out to face the Trojans again

and see if they still want to spend the night by our ships.
Many of them, I think, will be glad enough   70
to rest their legs if they can escape from my spear."

He sat down, and all the Achaeans shouted, rejoicing
that the great-hearted son of Peleus had put an end
to his deadly rage. Then Agamemnon addressed them
without standing up from the chair in which he was seated.
"My dear friends, Danäan soldiers, companions in battle,
it is good when a speaker can stand and be listened to
without interruption, which makes it hard to proceed;
but when the crowd keeps on shouting, how can a man
talk or hear himself? Even the clearest of speakers   80
would be drowned out by all this deafening noise. I am now
going to open my mind to the son of Peleus;
the rest of you men should listen and pay attention.
Many of you have criticized me for this matter.
But it really isn't *my* fault; the blame belongs
to Zeus and fate and the Fury who walks in darkness.
They put the savage madness into my mind
on that day when I seized Achilles' prize for myself.
What else could I do? At such moments, a god takes possession.
It was Madness, the eldest daughter of Zeus, who deceived me.   90
She deludes all mortals. Her step is soft, and she doesn't
walk on the ground but hovers above men's heads,
damaging them and ensnaring one after another.
Even Lord Zeus, who they say is the greatest of gods,
was deluded by her when Hera, though a mere female,
tricked him with cunning wiles on the day Alcména
was about to give birth to Héracles in the strong-walled
city of Thebes, and he boasted to all the gods:
'Listen to me, you gods and you goddesses,
while I speak to you what the heart in my breast commands.   100
Today the goddess of childbirth will bring to the light
a baby boy who has come from my very own loins;
he will grow up to rule over all those who live around him.'
Then, with cunning deceitfulness, Hera said,
'Is that so? Well, often you don't do what you have promised.

Swear to me now, with a binding oath, that the child
who drops out on this day between the feet of a woman,
this baby boy descended from your own loins,
will indeed rule over all those who live around him.'
These were her words, and Zeus didn't see through the trick,   110
but swore a great oath, blinded by his delusion.
Then Hera flew down from the summit of Mount Olympus
and quickly arrived in Argos, where, as she knew,
the wife of Sthénelus, son of Perseus, was pregnant
with a son, although she was just in her seventh month.
But Hera brought him into the light prematurely
and kept the spirits of childbirth away from Alcména
and went back to Zeus to bring him the news herself:
'Father Zeus, I have wonderful news to report.
A great man has been born, who will rule over all the Argives: 120
Eurýstheus, son of Sthénelus, son of Perseus—
your great-grandson—so it is right that he should be king.'
When he heard this, a sharp pain pierced him deep in his heart,
and, furious, he grabbed hold of the shining hair
of the goddess Madness and swore a powerful oath
that never again would Madness, who brings delusion
to all of us, be allowed to return to Olympus.
And he swung her around and hurled her down from the starry
heavens, and soon she landed on earth, among men.
Afterward Zeus couldn't think of her without groaning,   130
whenever he saw his dear son as he performed
some shameful labor Eurýstheus had piled upon him.
That is exactly how I have felt. When Hector
was slaughtering Argives penned near the sterns of the ships,
I couldn't forget that goddess and the delusion
she had blinded me with. But since I was out of my mind
when I did that thing, and Zeus took away my senses,
I am willing to make amends and give you abundant
compensation. So go ahead, lead out your men.
I am ready to hand over all the gifts that Odysseus   140
promised you in your hut before yesterday's fighting.
Or, if you like, though I know you are eager for battle,
you can wait here while my attendants run to my camp

and bring you the gifts, which will certainly please your heart."

And Achilles stood up and answered Lord Agamemnon,
"Most glorious son of Atreus, king of men,
do what you want with them. Whether you give me the gifts,
as is proper, or keep them—that decision is yours.
But now we must call up our fighting spirit. We shouldn't
hang around wasting our time here in idle chatter;   150
there is hard work to be done on the field of war.
When each of you sees Achilles again in the front lines
destroying the Trojan troops with his mighty spear,
remember that image as you are attacking your man."

And Odysseus stood up before the army and said,
"You are great as a fighter, Achilles, but please don't tell
our troops to advance toward the city and fight the Trojans
without having something to eat first, since the battle
is going to last a long time once the two armies
have clashed and the god breathes fury into both sides.   160
Command the Achaeans beside the black ships to take
food and wine, which give a man strength and courage.
For there is no man who is able to keep on fighting
all day long until sunset without any food.
At first his heart may be eager for battle, but then,
before he knows it, his body weakens, and thirst
and hunger set in, and his legs start stumbling beneath him.
But when a man has his fill of roast meat and wine,
he can fight the enemy all day long, and his heart
beats high in his breast with confidence, and his body   170
doesn't grow tired until the battle is over.
So dismiss the men and command them to take a meal.
As for the gifts, let Agamemnon present them
here where we are, in the middle of the assembly,
so all the Achaeans can see them with their own eyes
and your heart can be satisfied. Furthermore, he should stand up
in front of the whole assembly and swear an oath
that he never made love with the girl or entered her bed,
and, in return, your heart should learn to be gracious.

Then, as amends, he should feast you inside his hut   180
so that you can be given everything that is your due.
And son of Atreus, you will be all the more ready
to give others their due. It is no disgrace for a king
to make amends when he was the first to get angry."

Then Agamemnon answered, "I am delighted,
son of Laértes, with everything that you said;
you have dealt completely and properly with each point.
I am not only willing but eager to swear this oath
and will not swear falsely before the gods. But Achilles
should stay here, however impatient he is to fight,   190
and the others as well should stay here until the gifts
arrive from my hut and we offer a sacrifice
to seal my great oath. And I will entrust you, Odysseus,
with this task: to choose the finest young men in the army,
and bring from my camp the treasures that yesterday
I promised to give Achilles, and bring the women.
And let Talthýbius quickly prepare a boar
for me to kill in the presence of the whole army
for Zeus and for Hélios, who beholds all things."

Achilles stood up and answered Lord Agamemnon,   200
"Most glorious son of Atreus, king of men,
you ought to attend to these things at some other time,
when there is a lull in the fighting and when my heart
isn't so swollen with fury. But they are still
lying out there on the wide plain, mangled—the men
whom Hector cut down when Lord Zeus gave him the glory.
And you two want us to eat now? I would command
the Achaeans to go out and fight, unfed and hungry,
until we avenge our shame; and after the sun sets,
they can have a big meal. But as for me, not one bite   210
of food or one sip of drink will pass down my throat
as long as my dead companion lies in my hut,
mangled by the sharp bronze, with his feet still pointed
out toward the door and his comrades mourning around him.
I cannot think about eating. All I can think of

is slaughter and bloodshed and the loud groans of the dying."

Odysseus answered, "Son of Peleus, Achilles,
you are by far the bravest of the Achaeans,
far greater than I am, far mightier with the spear.
But my judgment might be a good deal sounder than yours.   220
I am older than you are, and my experience is wider;
so listen now to what I am going to tell you.
Men soon grow tired of fighting, where the sharp blades
reap bodies like stalks of grain and scatter them thickly
upon the ground, though the gain is small when Lord Zeus
has tipped his scales and decided which army will win.
But an empty belly is no way to mourn the dead.
Too many Achaeans, day after day, are falling—
when would we ever come to an end of the fast?
No, we must bury our comrades, bracing our hearts,   230
and mourn on that one day. Those who are left alive
must take thought of food and drink, so that we can be strong
and fight the enemy nonstop, hour after hour,
as tough as the bronze that covers our bodies. But once
the meal is done, you should all return to your ranks,
and no man should hold back and wait for a summons to action.
This is the summons to action, and there will be big
trouble for anyone skulking behind near the ships.
All our troops must assemble and move ahead
together, and loose the fury of war on the Trojans."   240

With these words he left the assembly, and he took with him
seven warriors: Nestor's sons Thrasymédes
and Antilochus, Meges, Thoas, Meriones,
Creon's son Lycomédes, and Melaníppus,
and they went to Lord Agamemnon's hut. Once they were there,
as soon as the order was given the task was done.
They brought out the seven tripods that had been promised
and twenty glittering cauldrons and twelve racehorses,
and then they brought out the seven women, all skilled
in their craft; the eighth was that lovely woman Briséïs.   250
And Odysseus weighed out ten bars made of solid gold

and led back the young men, who carried the gifts behind him.

They set them down in the middle of the assembly,
and Agamemnon stood up, and Talthýbius,
whose voice was like the immortals', stood up beside him,
holding the boar with his hands and pulling its head back.
The son of Atreus quickly drew out the knife
that always hung beside the great sheath of his sword,
and he cut some hairs from the boar as an offering,
then lifted his arms in prayer to almighty Zeus,   260
while all the Achaeans sat where they were, in silence,
as is right and proper, listening to the king.
And looking into the boundless heavens, he prayed:
"May Zeus almighty, the greatest of gods, be my witness,
and Earth and Sun and the Furies that under the ground
punish the dead who have broken their solemn vows,
that I never laid hands on the girl Briséïs, either
for the purpose of sex or for any purpose whatever,
and as long as she lived in my hut she remained intact.
If any word of this oath is false, may the gods   270
curse me with all the misery of an oath-breaker."
With these words, he slit the boar's throat with the pitiless bronze,
and Talthýbius swung the carcass around and hurled it
into the vast gray sea for the fish to devour.

Then Achilles stood up and addressed the Achaean army:
"Lord Zeus, how great is the madness you send to men!
The son of Atreus would never have roused my heart
to such a fierce anger or arrogantly insisted
on taking the girl away from me if somehow
Zeus had not willed that many Achaeans should die.   280
Now go eat your meal, and gather strength for the battle."
And after he said these words, he dismissed the assembly.

The army scattered, and each man went to his camp.
The Myrmidons took the splendid gifts for Achilles
to his black ship and stored them inside the huts
and settled the women there, while his attendants

took the horses and drove them off to his herd.

But when Briséïs, as lovely as Aphrodite,
saw Lord Patroclus lying there dead, mangled
by the sharp bronze, she threw herself onto his body   290
with a loud scream and dug her nails into her skin
and tore her breasts and her neck and her beautiful face
that was like a goddess's, crying out in her anguish:
"Patroclus, dearest of men to my wretched heart,
you were still alive when I was sent from this place,
and now, when I have come back here, I find you dead.
In my life, always, one grief follows another.
I saw the husband my father and mother gave me
mangled by the sharp bronze in front of our city
and saw my three brothers, whom my own mother bore   300
and whom I loved, cut down on the very same day.
But when Lord Achilles killed my husband and plundered
the city of Mynēs, you told me I shouldn't weep;
you promised that you would make me the lawful wife
of Achilles and that you would take me back in your ships
to the land of Phthia and give me a wedding feast
among the Myrmidons. So, my dearest Patroclus,
I will never stop mourning your death. You were always kind."
Thus she grieved, and the women joined in her wailing
for Patroclus, and each one wept for her own private sorrows.   310

Around Achilles the senior commanders assembled
and begged him to eat, but he refused with a groan:
"Friends, if you really care about me, don't ask me
to eat or drink when this terrible grief has come.
I will wait and fast and endure like this until sunset."
With these words, he sent away the other commanders,
but the two sons of Atreus stayed, along with Odysseus,
Nestor, Idómeneus, and the old warrior Phoenix;
they stood there and did what they could to comfort Achilles
in his great anguish; but he would never find comfort   320
until he entered the blood-dripping mouth of war.

*

And as he remembered, he heaved a deep sigh and said,
"How often have you, poor friend, my beloved comrade,
quickly and deftly set out a meal in my hut
when all the Achaeans were arming and getting ready
to bring the war and its misery to the Trojans.
But now I have no desire, as you lie here mangled,
for food or drink, so deep is my longing for you.
Nothing worse could have happened, no greater sorrow,
not even if I had heard of the death of my father,   330
who must now be shedding hot tears in far-away Phthia,
missing his son, while I am here fighting the Trojans
for the sake of that woman Helen, who makes my flesh creep."
Thus he mourned, and all the commanders joined him,
each one remembering what he had left at home.

When he saw them weeping, Lord Zeus was filled with pity,
and immediately he turned to Athena and said,
"My child, you have deserted your favorite human.
Have you lost all interest in Lord Achilles? He sits there,
mourning his friend beside the black ships. The others   340
have gone to their meal, but he will not eat. So drip
nectar into his breast, and ambrosia, so that
no hunger will overcome him and weaken his body."

This made Athena glad; she was eager to act.
And like a long-winged sea hawk, with a loud shriek,
she swooped down from heaven. Then, while the Achaeans
were arming for battle throughout the wide camp, she dripped
nectar into his breast, and ambrosia, so that
no hunger would overcome him and weaken his body.
Then she went back to the palace of Zeus, her father,   350
and all the Achaeans swarmed from their huts and ships.
As when snowflakes fly thick and fast as they fall from the heavens,
driven on by the chilling blast of the north wind:
so thickly did the bright helmets and shields and spears
and massive breastplates emerge from among the ships.
Their gleam rose up to the sky, and the earth around them
shone with the flash of bronze and shook with the thunder

of marching feet. And Achilles began to arm.
First, he strapped the bronze greaves to his lower legs
and fastened them onto his ankles with silver clasps.   360
Next, on his chest he put the finely wrought breastplate,
and over his shoulder he slung his bronze sword, embellished
with silver studs, and above it his dazzling shield.
Like a fire that sailors see blazing while they are far out
at sea, as it burns in a lonely farmstead high up
in the mountains, while the fierce storm winds carry them out
over the fish-teeming waters, away from their loved ones:
just so did the light from the marvelous shield of Achilles
blaze out, up through the air and into the heavens.
He lifted the massive helmet crested with horsehair,   370
and put it over his head, and it shone like a star;
and above it the gold plumes waved, which the master craftsman
Hephaestus had set in thickly along its ridge.
Achilles tried out the new armor to see if it fit him
and if his magnificent limbs moved freely inside it;
and he felt elated, buoyant, as if he had wings.
Then from its case he took out his father's spear,
huge and heavy, which none of the other Achaeans
was able to hold; Achilles alone could use it.
It was made of ash, and the centaur Chiron had brought it   380
from Pélion as a gift to Achilles' father.
Automedon and Álcimus yoked the horses
and fastened the handsome yoke straps around their chests,
and they set the bits in their mouths, and they drew the reins back
into the car. Automedon took the bright
bronze-handled whip and jumped up behind the horses,
and Achilles mounted beside him, blazing like sunlight,
and he called to his father's horses with a loud voice:
"Bálius, Xanthus, Podárgē's illustrious offspring,
this time be careful to bring your charioteer   390
back to his comrades after we finish fighting.
Don't leave him out there dead, as you left Patroclus."

Then Xanthus spoke to him, bowing his graceful head,
and his long, luxuriant mane trailed down from the yoke pad

and touched the earth. (Hera had given him human speech.)
"Certainly, Master, we will bring you back safe
once again this time. But death is hurrying toward you,
caused not by us, but by a powerful god
and inexorable fate. It was not through our slowness
or carelessness that the Trojans stripped off the armor   400
from Patroclus. It was Apollo, the best of gods,
who cut him down, and he gave the glory to Hector.
We two can run with the speed of our father, the west wind—
men say that nothing is faster. But it is your fate
to be overcome at the hands of a god and a mortal."

As he said this, the Furies cut off his power to speak.
Greatly troubled by these words, Achilles answered,
"Xanthus, there is no need to foretell my death.
I know well enough that it is my fate to die here,
far from my father and mother. But even so,   410
I will not stop killing until I have crammed the Trojans
full with sorrow and sickened them of this war."
And with a loud shout he drove the horses straight onward.

Book 20

Then, son of Peleus, around you, beside the ships,
the battle-ravenous Argives put on their armor,
and so did the Trojans, upon the rise of the plain.
And high on Olympus, Zeus told Themis to summon
all the gods, and she rushed out to do his bidding.
None of the rivers stayed away except Ocean,
and none of the nymphs who dwell in the lovely groves,
the springs, the limpid pools, and the grassy meadows.
They all came to Zeus's palace and took their seats
along the tall colonnades of bright-polished marble   10
expertly built by Hephaestus for Father Zeus.

As they assembled inside the palace, Poseidon
also heard the goddess's summons and came
out of the sea. He sat down among them and said,
"Why have you summoned the gods, great lord of the lightning?
Are you thinking about the Trojans and the Achaeans,
since the fighting down there is about to burst into flames?"

Zeus answered, "Shaker of Earth, you already know
what I am thinking and why I called you together.
I *am* concerned: so many of them will die.   20
But now I will sit here at ease on a ridge of Olympus
where I can watch, to my heart's delight, as you others
go down to join the Trojan or Argive forces
and help the side that you favor, whichever it is.
If Achilles goes on to attack the Trojans like this,
they won't be able to hold out against him, not even
a little. They used to tremble whenever they saw him,
and now that his fury is stirred up because of his comrade,
I greatly fear that he will break through the wall
and lay waste to the city before its appointed time."   30

And the gods went down to the fighting, on different sides:

Hera went to the Argive ships with Athena
and Poseidon and Hermes, who is the first of the gods
in cunning of mind. Hephaestus went along too;
he limped, but his thin legs bustled nimbly beneath him.
And Ares went to the Trojans, as did Apollo,
Leto, Ártemis, Xanthus, and Aphrodite.
As long as the gods kept away from the human fighters,
the Achaeans won, since Achilles had reappeared
at the head of their forces after such a long absence.   40
Terror seized all the Trojans; they were appalled
at the sight of Achilles marching to battle, blazing
in his glorious armor, the peer of man-killing Ares.
But when the Olympians mingled among the humans
and Strife, the inciter of armies, rose in her strength,
Athena cried out, now standing beside the trench,
now shouting loudly along the thunderous seashore.
And from the opposite side, like a black whirlwind,
Ares cried out, urging the Trojans onward,
now from the heights of the city, now as he ran   50
toward Cállicollóne hill, by the Símoïs river.

Thus did the blessed gods urge on both armies
as the bitter conflict burst out among themselves.
The father of men and gods sent blood-chilling thunder
down from on high; and beneath them Poseidon shook
the boundless earth and the lofty crests of the mountains,
and all the foothills and peaks of Mount Ida trembled,
and the Trojans' city, and the Achaeans' black ships;
and in the underworld, Hades, lord of the dead,
was terrified, and he leaped from his dark throne, screaming,   60
afraid that Poseidon would split the earth open above him
and the house of the dead be revealed to the sight of all,
that ghastly place that even gods shudder to think of:
so loud was the sound of immortals clashing in battle.
Opposite Lord Poseidon Apollo stood
with his winged arrows; Ares was faced by Athena
and Hera by Ártemis, sister of Lord Apollo,
goddess of the loud hunt; against Leto stood Hermes,

and against Hephaestus stood the great, deep-swirling river
that the gods call Xanthus and human beings Scamander.   70

Thus gods clashed against gods. In the meantime Achilles
burned in his heart to face Hector and feed his blood
to the fierce god of war. But Apollo instead sent Aeneas.
He spoke with the voice of Lycáon, a son of Priam:
"Aeneas, counselor of the Trojans, what
has become of the brave words you uttered as you drank wine
with the princes of Troy, when you boasted that you would soon
go out to face Lord Achilles in single combat?"

Aeneas answered, "Lycáon, why do you urge me
to fight Achilles, when I have no heart to do it?   80
This would not be the first time that I have faced him.
Once before now he drove me away with his spear
from Mount Ida—that time when he came to attack our cattle
and plundered Lynéssus and Pédasus; but Zeus saved me,
sending me strength and charging my legs with great speed.
Otherwise I would surely have been cut down
by Achilles and by Athena, who went before him
and protected him and urged him to slaughter us all,
Lelégēs and Trojans alike, with his mighty spear.
Fighting Achilles means certain death for a mortal;   90
there is always some god at his side to ward off destruction.
And even without that, his straight-flying spear doesn't stop
until it has passed through human flesh. But if ever
a god were to make the fight equal, he wouldn't win
so easily, though he thinks he is made of bronze."

Apollo answered, "If that is true, you should pray
to the deathless gods. Men say that you are the son
of Aphrodite, he of a lesser goddess;
your mother's father is Zeus, while Thetis's father
is the Old Man of the Sea. So go, attack him,   100
and don't allow his taunts or his threats to stop you."
With this he breathed a great power into Aeneas,
who then strode forward, armored in fiery bronze.

*

And right away Hera noticed Anchises' son
moving fast through the crowd as he hunted Achilles,
and immediately she said to the other immortals,
"Poseidon, Athena, both of you, help me decide
how this affair should proceed and what we should do.
Aeneas is moving fast to attack Achilles
at Apollo's urging; so we must now turn him back,   110
or one of us three must stand at Achilles' side
and give him strength and not let his courage fail him.
He should know that he is loved by the greatest of gods,
while those who have saved the Trojans from total disaster
are weaklings, nobodies. We have come down from Olympus
to protect Achilles from all harm, at least for today.
Later on he must endure what Destiny spun
for him with her thread on the day that his mother bore him.
But if he is never told about our protection,
he will be frightened when some god meets him. The true form   120
of a god can terrify even the bravest mortal."

Poseidon answered, "Hera, there is no need
to let your anxiety cloud your good sense. For myself,
I would not want gods to clash against gods in combat.
Instead, we should all move off to one side and sit down
where we can watch, and leave this war to the humans.
Of course, if Apollo or Ares should join the fighting
and hinder Achilles in any way, then we too
would rush in immediately and fight to defend him;
soon, I think, they would flee from the field of battle   130
and return to Olympus, overwhelmed by our might."

With these words the god with the dark-blue hair proceeded
to the mound of heaped-up earth that the Trojans had built
for Héracles, with Athena's help, as a way
to shelter him and protect him when the sea monster
came out of the waves and drove him up toward the plain.
There, Poseidon sat down with Athena and Hera,
and they covered themselves with impenetrable mist,

while the gods on the other side sat on Cállicollónē
around you, Apollo, and Ares, destroyer of cities.   140

And so the gods sat, on opposite sides, each planning
what to do next, each hesitant to step into
the battle, though Zeus had urged them to go and fight.
Meanwhile the plain was alive with men in bright armor
and horses and cars of glittering bronze, and the ground
trembled beneath their feet. And before the battalions
clashed with each other, two of the greatest heroes
entered the open space between the two armies:
the son of Anchíses, Aeneas, and godlike Achilles.
Aeneas came forward first, with menacing strides,   150
the crest of his helmet fiercely nodding; he held
his shield in front of his chest, and he shook his long spear.
Toward him Achilles rushed out like a ravening lion
that a whole village has gathered to hunt and kill,
and he pays no attention to them and goes on his way;
but when some young hunter wounds him with his long spear,
he crouches and snarls and foams at the mouth, and from deep
in his powerful chest he roars, and he lashes his tail
from side to side, over his ribs and his flanks,
to work himself up, and with a ferocious glare   160
he charges straight at them, determined to kill a man
or himself be killed as he enters the front line of battle:
just so Achilles, aroused by his boundless fury
and his courageous heart, strode out toward Aeneas.

When they had come within range and were facing each other,
Achilles called out, "Aeneas, why have you walked
so far ahead of the ranks to stand here and face me?
Do you feel an overwhelming desire to fight
in the hope that you will succeed to the throne of Priam
and rule the Trojans? But even if you do kill me,   170
that is no reason for Priam to hand you his kingdom.
He has sons of his own; he is strong and not feeble-minded.
Or have the Trojans marked out their best land for you,
a beautiful tract of vineyards and fertile fields,

to possess if you win? But winning is not so easy.
The last time we met, I drove you away with my spear—
or have you forgotten that day? I caught you alone,
and I made you flee from your cattle, all the way down
the slope of Mount Ida, as fast as your legs could take you;
you didn't even have time to look over your shoulder.   180
You ran all the way to Lyrnéssus, but I pursued you
and destroyed that town with the help of Athena and Zeus,
and I captured the women and took their freedom away,
though Zeus and the other gods saved your skin. But this time
I don't think that he will rescue you; so go back
and do not oppose me now, or you may get hurt.
Only a fool will wait for disaster to teach him."

Aeneas answered, "Achilles, you shouldn't attempt
to scare me with words, as if I were a mere child.
I too am quite adept at bandying insults.   190
We both know each other's lineage, for although
you never set eyes on my parents, nor I on yours,
we have long heard the famous tales that are told about them.
Men say that you are the son of Lord Peleus and Thetis,
the lovely goddess born of the sea; for my part,
I am proud to claim that I am the son of Anchíses
and my mother is Aphrodite, daughter of Zeus.
One of these couples today will mourn for the death
of their son, since I think that we won't settle this matter
on the field of battle with just a few childish words.   200
So let us not stand here idly, talking like fools.
I am eager to fight, and no words you can say will stop me.
Let us begin now and fight it out, man to man."

He threw his spear at the great and terrible shield,
and loudly the shield rang out when the spear point hit it.
Achilles, alarmed now, thrust the shield from his body;
he thought that Aeneas's spear would easily drive
through it, fool that he was, since he did not realize
that the gifts of the gods are invulnerable and cannot
be damaged by mortal men. And indeed the spear   210

did not break through; the first, golden layer stopped it.

Achilles in turn threw *his* sharp, long-shadowed spear,
and he hit Aeneas's shield on the edge of the rim
where the layer of bronze and the oxhide backing were thinnest.
The ashen spear ripped right through it, and the shield clanged,
and, frightened, Aeneas crouched, and he held the shield out
in front of him; and the eager spear tore through both layers
and flew on past and stuck quivering in the ground.
And he stood there in shock, appalled that the spear had just barely
missed. And Achilles, drawing his sword, charged at him   220
with a blood-chilling war shout. Meanwhile Aeneas recovered
and picked up a boulder that no two men of today
would be able to lift, and he held it above his head.

Aeneas would surely have thrown the huge rock and hit
his helmet or shield, but Achilles would have kept coming,
wielding his great sword, and would have cut down Aeneas
if Lord Poseidon had not been so quick to notice.
Immediately he said to the other immortals,
"Hurry! We need to rescue Aeneas, right now—
in a moment he will be killed by the son of Peleus   230
and descend to the realm of Hades. He is a fool
for listening to Apollo, who will not save him.
But why should this innocent man be required to suffer
for affairs that are not his own? He has always given
due sacrifices to the immortal gods.
So let us snatch him from death, since Zeus will be angry
if he is cut down by Achilles. It is his fate
to survive and save the Dardánian race from extinction,
for Zeus loved his ancestor Dárdanus more than all
the other children he fathered by mortal women,   240
and, as it is, he has turned against Priam's family.
When Ilion falls, Aeneas will rule the Trojans,
and so will his children's children in ages to come."

Then Hera answered, "It is for you to decide,
Earthshaker, whether to rescue Aeneas or leave him.

Athena and I have often sworn, in the presence
of all the immortals, never to save a Trojan."

When Poseidon heard this, he went out into the fighting.
He strode through the rain of spears and arrived at the place
where Aeneas stood and Achilles was fast approaching,   250
and he poured a dense mist down over Achilles' eyes
and pulled the great ashen spear from the shield of Aeneas
and set it down at Achilles' feet. And he lifted
Aeneas high off the ground, and he sent him flying
over the ranks of soldiers and chariots
and put him down at the edge of the battlefield
where the Caucónēs were armed and ready to fight.
Poseidon approached and stood beside him and said,
"Aeneas, what god has put you up to this madness
and told you to fight Achilles? He is far stronger   260
than you are, and more beloved by the immortals.
Whenever you come up against him, you must retreat
immediately, or else you will surely go down
to the realm of Hades before your appointed time.
But after Achilles is dead, you can take courage
and return to the front line, since no other Argive will kill you."

With these words he left him standing there, and he quickly
took away the dense mist from Achilles' eyes.
Achilles stared for a while, then said to himself,
"Astonishing! My spear lies here on the ground,   270
but the man I was trying to kill has completely vanished.
It is clear that Aeneas too is loved by the gods,
though I thought his claims were nothing but idle chatter.
Well, let him go. He won't be too eager to meet me
again, since he knows that he barely escaped this time.
Now I will urge on the Danäans, then I will see
what harm I can do when I face the rest of the Trojans."

And he ran back into the ranks and urged on the men:
"Forward, Achaeans! Don't stand here waiting; charge
at the Trojans now and fight them with all your fury.   280

As strong as I am, it is hard for me by myself
to take on so many men and defeat them all;
not even immortal gods like Athena or Ares
could single-handedly win a great battle like this.
But I will do all I can with my speed and courage
and prowess and won't hold back for even a moment;
I will charge straight ahead through their front lines, and any Trojan
who comes within range of my spear will be sorry he did."

As he was speaking, Hector urged on his troops:
"Take heart, you Trojans, and have no fear of Achilles.   290
I too could face the immortal gods if the fight were
of words alone; but spears are a different matter.
Believe me, Achilles will never accomplish all
that he says he will, for even the greatest man
accomplishes some things, while others he leaves unfinished.
Now I will take him on, though his hands are like fire,
though his hands are like fire and his courage like gleaming iron."

At these words the Trojans lifted their spears to attack;
and a thunder of war cries arose as the two sides clashed.
As Hector moved forward, Apollo came up and said,   300
"Hector, you mustn't challenge Achilles to combat;
stay back and wait for him here in the surging crowd,
or else he will spear you or run you through with his sword."
And quickly Hector retreated into the ranks,
seized with fear as he heard what the god was saying.

But Achilles, exalted, charged ahead with a fierce
war cry. The first man he killed was Iphítion,
son of Otrýnteus, a leader of many men;
his mother, a water nymph, bore him under the peak
of snow-covered Tmolus in the rich land of Hydē.   310
As he came on against him, Achilles let fly his spear,
and it hit the man's head, cracking his skull in two,
and he fell with a crash, and Achilles triumphed above him:
"Lie here, son of Otrýnteus, most reckless of men.
You will breathe your last here, far from your birthplace beside

the Gygǽan Lake, where your forefathers had their land
by the fish-teeming Hyllus and swirling waters of Hermus."

As he triumphed, darkness covered Iphítion's eyes,
and the Danäan chariots' wheel rims cut him to pieces.
Next, Achilles charged at Demóleon,   320
Anténor's son, a courageous defensive fighter.
The spear hit his temple and drove through his bronze-cheeked helmet,
which could not withstand the force of it, and the spear point
tore right through it and right through the bone, and his brains
splattered inside the bronze, and he fell in the dirt.
Then, as his driver Hippódamas jumped away
from the chariot and started to run off in terror,
Achilles caught up and punched a spear through his back,
and he gasped out his life, roaring, the way a bull roars
when the young men drag it up to Poseidon's altar   330
at Hélicē, to the Earthshaker's deep delight:
just so did he roar as the proud spirit left his bones.

Next, Achilles went after a son of Priam,
Polydórus. His father had never allowed him to fight,
since he was the youngest son and the one he loved best.
Now he was foolishly showing off his great speed
by dashing through the front ranks, which cost him his life.
As he passed, Achilles threw his long spear and hit him
in the mid-back, at the place where the golden belt clasps
were fastened and where the breastplate was doubled over,   340
and the spear point drove into his flesh and out through his navel,
and he fell to his knees, screaming, and darkness embraced him,
and he sank down, trying to hold in his guts with his hands.

When Hector saw Polydórus, his young brother,
sink to the ground, clutching his own intestines,
a mist spread over his eyes, and he could no longer
bear to keep at a distance; he charged at Achilles
like a bright flame, shaking his spear. And the very moment
Achilles saw him, he rushed out and said to himself,
"Here is the man who wounded my heart most deeply   350

when he killed my beloved friend. There will be no more
cowering from each other among the crowd."
And, with an angry scowl, he said to Hector,
"Come closer to me, the sooner to meet your death."

Then, with no hint of fear, Hector responded,
"Son of Peleus, Achilles, you shouldn't attempt
to scare me with words, as if I were a mere child.
I too am quite adept at bandying insults.
I know how mighty you are and that I am much weaker,
yet these things lie in the hands of the gods. Although   360
I am the lesser man, I might still take your life
with a throw of my spear. It is as sharp as yours is."

And drawing his spear back, he hurled it. But with the lightest
puff of her breath, Athena turned it away,
and it came back and landed at Hector's feet. And Achilles
charged, with a blood-chilling shout, in a frenzy to kill.
But Apollo swept Hector away from the battle with ease,
as a god can do, shrouding him in dense mist.
Three times Achilles charged at him in his fury;
three times he lunged and hit nothing but empty air.   370
Then, with a terrible war cry, he shouted at Hector:
"Once again you have escaped, you cowardly dog,
though death came close; but your precious Apollo saved you.
Do you pray to him very sweetly before you dare
to walk out amid the hum of our hurtling missiles?
I will make sure to finish you off the next time I meet you,
if I too have a god helping me. But for now
I will see what other Trojans I can bring down."

With these words he charged and stabbed Dryops right through the neck
with a thrust of his spear, and Dryops crashed at his feet.   380
And he left him there and hurled his spear at Demúchus,
the son of Philétor, a huge and powerful man;
the spear hit his knee and brought him down, and Achilles
ran over and stabbed him with his great sword. Then he charged
at Laógonus and Dárdanus, sons of Bias,

and he knocked them both from their chariot onto the ground,
one with his spear and one with a powerful sword slash.
Then Tros, the son of Alástor, ran up to clasp
his knees and beg him to spare his life and to take him
prisoner and ransom him and not kill him   390
and have pity on him because they were both the same age—
fool that he was. He did not know that Achilles
would never listen, because he was not sweet-tempered
or soft-hearted, but a man of the fiercest passions.
As Tros was trying to clasp his knees and to beg him
for mercy, Achilles plunged his sword into his liver,
and the liver slid out through the gaping wound, and the blood
poured out all over his belly and soaked his lap,
and darkness covered his eyes as the spirit left him.
And Achilles ran up to Múlius, and his bronze spear point   400
punctured one ear and came straight out through the other.
And he stabbed Echéclus, Agénor's son, in the head
with his sword, and the whole blade grew warm with his blood, and death
took hold of him, veiling his eyes in a purple mist.
Achilles then stabbed Deucálion's arm with his mighty
spear, in the place where the tendons join at the elbow.
Deucálion stood there, his heavy arm useless beside him,
seeing his death approach, and Achilles sliced through
the neck with his sword, and the head flew off in its helmet
and landed a distance away, and the marrow spurted   410
out through his spinal cord as he lay in the dust.
Achilles next went after Rhigmas, Piras's son,
a Thracian. He threw, and the spear drove into his belly,
and he crashed down from his chariot onto the ground.
And as his charioteer, Arëíthoüs,
was turning the horses around, Achilles rushed in
and stabbed him, piercing his back with his spear, and knocked him
over the rail, and the horses panicked and bolted.

As a ravaging fire rages through the parched valleys
in the mountains, and the dense-wooded forest burns   420
as the wind whips the flames and everywhere whirls them around:
just so Achilles ran everywhere, in a frenzy,

and he killed as he went, and the black earth flowed with the blood.
As when a man yokes two oxen to tread the white barley
on a threshing floor, and quickly the grains are husked
under the feet of the bellowing oxen: just so,
driven straight on by Achilles, the horses trampled
over the bodies and shields of those who had fallen,
and the axle below and the chariot rails were splattered
with the blood flung up by the horses' hooves and the wheel rims.   430
And Achilles pressed on, eager to win great glory,
and his huge invincible hands were dripping with gore.

Book 21

When the Trojans came to the ford of the swirling Xanthus,
Achilles proceeded to cut their army in two.
One part he forced toward the city, across the plain,
where the Argives themselves had been pushed back the day before
when Hector was raging; there they stampeded, and Hera
spread a dense mist before them to hold them back.
The rest were forced to the edge of the fast-flowing river,
and they flung themselves in with loud splashes, and the high banks
echoed on every side with the sound of men screaming
as they thrashed around and struggled to stay afloat.   10
As when locusts rise in a swarm and fly to a river
to escape a fire that has suddenly broken out
and keeps roaring on and chasing them till they plunge
into the water: just so, in front of Achilles,
a huge mass of horses and men filled up the swift currents
of the deep-swirling Xanthus, struggling in utter confusion.

Achilles left his spear on the riverbank, leaning
against a tamarisk. Then, in a frenzy, he jumped in
with his naked sword, and with butchery in his heart
he laid about him, slashing in all directions,   20
and hideous screams arose from the men being hacked
and maimed and killed, and the water was red with blood.
Like shoals of fish that dart away, fleeing the huge
jaws of a dolphin, and crowd into every nook
of some sheltered harbor, terrified for their lives:
just so did the Trojans cower beneath the steep banks
of that terrible river. And when his arms had grown weary
from all the slashing, Achilles chose twelve young men
and took them out of the river alive, as the blood-price
for Patroclus's death. He drove them onto dry land,   30
dazed with terror like fawns, and he tied their hands
behind their backs with the leather belts they were wearing
around their tunics and gave them to his companions

to take to the Myrmidon ships. Then he charged down
to the banks of the Xanthus, still in a frenzy to slaughter.

There he met one of the sons of Priam, Lycáon,
who had just escaped from the river. Achilles had caught him
once before, in a night raid, and taken him captive
from his father's orchard, where he was cutting the green
shoots of a fig tree to bend back for chariot rails,   40
when suddenly, out of nowhere, Achilles appeared.
He put him aboard his ship and took him to Lemnos
and sold him there to Eunéüs, the son of Jason;
from there he was bought by Ëétion of Imbros,
a friend of his family, who ransomed him for a huge price
and sent him on to Arísbē, which he soon left,
and he made his way back to his father's palace in Troy.
For eleven days he had lived with his friends and family,
celebrating; but on the twelfth day some god
once again threw him into the hands of Achilles,   50
who this time was going to send him down to the realm
of Hades—a trip he did not look forward to taking.
Achilles saw him, unarmed, without shield or helmet
or spear; he had thrown them away as he was escaping,
and he stood there exhausted, sweaty, his legs limp beneath him.
Taken aback, the great man said to himself,
"Astonishing, but I see it with my own eyes:
Even the Trojans I killed are arising again
from the darkness below the earth, just as this fellow
has escaped and returned here after I sold him on Lemnos;   60
and the deep sea, which hinders so many people, could not
keep him away. But now he will taste my spear point,
and we will see if the man will come back from Hades
this time, after I kill him, or if the earth,
which holds down even the strongest, will hold him too."

These were his thoughts as he waited. Lycáon came close,
dazed with terror, desperate to beg for mercy,
with only one thing in mind: to escape his doom.
Achilles lifted his long spear, ready to stab him,

but Lycáon ducked and ran in to hug his knees,   70
and the spear passed over his back and stuck in the ground,
quivering, still hungry for human flesh.
Lycáon cried out, grasping his knees with one hand
and with the other one clutching his spear: "I implore you,
spare me, Achilles. Have mercy on me; I am here
at your feet, a holy suppliant, and I beg you
to honor my claim, since you were the first man whose bread
I shared on the day that you captured me in our orchard
and carried me far from my father and friends and sold me
on Lemnos. I earned you the price of a hundred oxen,   80
and then I was bought for a ransom of three times as much,
and this is just the twelfth day since I came back to Troy
after my many hardships, and once again fate
has put me into your hands. Father Zeus hates me—
he must, since he made me your captive a second time.
And the life that my mother gave me will be cut short:
Leóthoē, daughter of Altes, the old, honored king
of the warlike Lelégēs, who live upon the steep hills
of Pédasus, beside the Satníoïs river.
My father, King Priam, married this girl—he had many   90
other wives—and Leóthoē had two sons,
and you will have butchered us both. You cut down my brother
Polydórus in the front line with your deadly spear,
and now I also must die. And I do not think
that I will escape you again, now that some power
has delivered me into your hands. But one thing more:
Remember, I wasn't born from the same womb as Hector,
who killed Patroclus, your gentle and brave companion."

In this way the son of Priam implored Achilles
with pitiful words. But the answer he got had no pity.   100
"Fool, don't say a word to me about ransom.
Before Patroclus had met his appointed fate
I was better disposed to spare the life of a Trojan;
many of them I captured alive and sold.
But now no Trojan, not one, shall ever escape
death when a god delivers him into my hands,

and least of all Priam's sons. So courage, my friend;
you too must die. Why all this moaning about it?
Even Patroclus died, and he was a better
man than you are. And don't you see *me*—how huge   110
and handsome I am? My father is a great king
and my mother a goddess. Yet death stands waiting for me
as well. There will come a dawn or an evening or noon
when someone will take my life too amid the fighting
with a throw of his spear or an arrow well aimed from his bowstring."

When he heard this, Lycáon's knees went limp and his spirit
sank. He let go of the spear and sat back, with both hands
spread wide. And Achilles drew his double-edged sword
and hit him just under his collarbone, and the sword plunged
in, to its hilt, and he fell and lay there face down,   120
stretched out at full length, and his blood soaked into the earth.
Achilles grabbed one of his feet, and he flung his body
into the river and called out to him in triumph:
"Lie with the fish now; they will lick the blood clean
from your wound, without rituals. Though your dear mother won't
lay you out and mourn for you, the Scamander
will carry you with it, into the lap of the sea."

At these words, the god of the river became incensed
and began to consider how he might stop Achilles
in his rampage, and save the Trojan troops from disaster.   130
Meanwhile Achilles, in a great frenzy to kill,
charged at Asteropǽus, Pélagon's son.
(Pélagon had been born to the Áxius river
and a daughter of Ácessámenus, Peribœa,
when the deep-swirling river had lapped her around with his love.)
Achilles attacked when Asteropǽus had just
climbed out of the water; he faced him holding two spears,
and Xanthus put courage into him, since he was angry
that Achilles had savagely butchered so many men
along his stream. And when the two had advanced   140
to within close range, Achilles was first to speak:
"Who dares to approach? Who are you? Where do you come from?

Unhappy are those whose sons have stepped out to face me."

Without any fear, Asteropǽus answered,
"Son of Peleus, why do you ask who I am?
I come from distant Pæónia and have led
my troops here; it is eleven days since we arrived.
I descend from the god of the Áxius river, who fathered
the famous warrior Pélagon, who, men say,
is my own father. But now let us fight, Achilles."   150

At this, Achilles lifted his mighty spear,
but Asteropǽus, just as skilled with his left hand
as he was with his right hand, hurled his two spears at once.
One of them hit Achilles' shield, but the spear
did not break through; the first, golden layer stopped it.
The other one grazed Achilles' right arm at the elbow,
and the blood spurted out, but the spear kept flying on past him
and stuck in the ground, still hungering for his flesh.
Achilles in turn threw his spear at Asteropǽus,
but he missed his man and hit the high riverbank   160
so hard that the spear drove half its length into the dirt.
Then, drawing his sword from his hip, he charged with a war cry
as Asteropǽus was trying in vain to pull out
Achilles' great ashen spear that was stuck in the bank.
Three times he pulled at it, struggling with all his might;
three times he had to give up the effort. The fourth time
he was trying again to bend and snap the huge spear,
but before he could do that, Achilles ran up and killed him
with a sword thrust that sliced his belly down from the navel,
and his innards gushed out, and darkness covered his eyes   170
as he gasped for life. And Achilles leaped on his chest
and stripped off his armor and gloated over the body:
"So much for you. You see how hard it is, even
for a river's grandson, to fight with the children of Zeus.
You said that you were descended from a wide river,
but I can claim my descent from the greatest of gods.
My father is Peleus, son of Æacus, king
of the Myrmidons, whose father was Zeus himself;

and just as Lord Zeus is greater than any river,
his descendants are greater than any river's descendants.   180
You may think that the mighty river beside us will help you,
but no one can fight against Zeus; not even the god
of the mightiest river of all, Achelóüs, can match him,
or the powerful deep-flowing river of Ocean, from which
all rivers flow and all seas, brooks, springs, and deep wells—
even he fears the lightning of Zeus almighty
and his terrible thunder that crashes down from the heavens."
With these words he pulled his spear from the bank, and he left
Asteropǽus dead there. Then he went after
the Pæónian warriors who were still crouching in terror   190
beside the fast-swirling river where they had seen
their greatest fighter cut down by Achilles' sword.
And he killed Thersílochus, Mydon, Astýpylus,
Thrásius, Ǽnius, Mnesus, and Opheléstes.

And now he would have killed even more men if Scamander
had not grown angry. Taking on human form,
he called to him from the depths of one of his pools:
"Achilles, you are supreme among men, both in strength
and in violence, since the gods themselves always protect you.
But if Zeus really wants you to cut down every last Trojan,   200
at least go elsewhere; do your grim work on the plain.
My beautiful streams are clogged now with dead men's bodies,
and I cannot pour myself into the shining sea,
choked as I am with the dead. Enough of this brutal
slaughter, Achilles. Stop now. I am appalled."

Achilles answered, "So be it: I will move out
onto the plain and do as you wish, Lord Scamander.
But I will not stop killing Trojans until I have penned them
inside their walls—until I meet Hector and fight him
man to man, and he kills me or I kill him."   210
With these words he charged the Pæónians in a frenzy.

Scamander said to Apollo, "Shame on you, lord
of the silver bow—you aren't obeying the orders

of Zeus, your father. He told you to stand by the Trojans
and see that they are protected until dusk comes
to cast its wide shadows over the land around us."

When he heard this, Achilles leaped from the bank and plunged
into the stream. But Scamander rose up against him
in a towering wave and whipped himself into a turmoil
and swept away all the Pæónians whom Achilles   220
had slaughtered and who were clogging his stream. He flung them
onto the dry land, bellowing like an ox,
and he saved the survivors by hiding them in the deep
pools where the water was calm. And enormous waves
surged up around Achilles, battered his shield,
and crashed on his head. He lost his footing and grabbed
an elm tree, but it came out by its thick roots, tearing
the whole bank away, and it fell straight across the river
and dammed it up with its tangle of roots and branches.
In terror Achilles scrambled out of the current   230
and ran toward the plain as fast as his legs could take him,
but the god was not done with him yet; in a darkening swell
he rose up and followed him out in order to stop him.
Achilles ran for the length of a spear throw, moving
as fast as an eagle swoops, the dark one, the hunter,
the swiftest of winged creatures; he sprinted away,
and his armor clanged on his chest as he tried to run out
from under the huge wave, desperate to escape,
but the river surged on in pursuit with a thunderous roar.
As a gardener cuts a channel from a deep spring   240
to water the plants in his garden—mattock in hand,
he clears away all the obstacles from the trench—
and as the water starts flowing, it sweeps the pebbles
out of the way, and soon it pours down the slope,
singing, and it outpaces the man who made it:
just so did the huge wave keep overtaking Achilles
as fast as he ran, since gods are much stronger than mortals.
Whenever Achilles would try to stand and fight back
to see whether all the gods had united against him,
a wave from the river came after him, crashing down   250

over his shoulders. Panicked, he tried to jump clear,
but the river kept grabbing his legs with its fierce current
and eating away the ground from beneath his feet.

And Achilles cried out, gazing up at the heavens:
"Zeus our father, isn't there even one god
who will pity me and rescue me from Scamander?
I would rather be killed in any way except this one.
Of all gods, none is to blame so much as my mother,
who deceived me with her predictions; she said I would die
under Troy's wall, brought down by one of Apollo's   260
deadly arrows. If only Hector had stabbed me,
and the bravest of Trojans had killed the bravest Achaean.
But now I am fated to die an ignoble death,
trapped in this river like some small boy herding pigs
swept up by a torrent while trying to cross in a rainstorm."

When he heard this, Poseidon came quickly, along with Athena,
in the form of humans; they took his hands, and they tried
to reassure him. Poseidon was first to speak:
"Son of Peleus, don't be afraid. We are here,
Athena and I; we have come from Olympus to help you,   270
with Zeus's approval. We know that it isn't your fate
to be killed by a river. This one will settle down,
as you will soon see. And here is some good advice;
we hope you will listen: Do not pull back from the fighting
until you have penned the whole Trojan army inside
the walls of Troy—whoever escapes from your fury.
And do not go back to the ships until you have taken
Hector's life. We guarantee you that triumph."

At this, the two of them left to rejoin the immortals,
and Achilles, greatly encouraged by the god's words,   280
walked on across the plain, which was now flooded,
and much fine armor of young men slaughtered in battle
floated upon the water along with their corpses.
With high steps he hurried on; the river could not
hold him back, since Athena had filled him with power.

But Scamander did not give up; he redoubled his fury
and piling his waters high in a monstrous wave,
he rolled toward Achilles and called out to Símoïs,
"Dear brother, let us join forces to kill this man
or soon he will storm the walls of Priam's great city   290
and the Trojans will not be able to hold him back.
Quick, come help me. Open your springs and fill
your channels with water; stir up your mountain torrents,
then lift a huge wave and hurl down a thundering tumult
of tree trunks and boulders, and let us finish this wild man
who is wreaking such havoc and thinks he is like the gods.
I say that neither his strength nor his speed will save him,
nor his magnificent armor, which somewhere far down
in the depths of me will lie buried in slime, and his body
will be wrapped in sand, and tons of silt will pour down   300
over him, and I will pile him so high with mud
that the Argives will never be able to find his bones.
This will serve as his grave mound; he will not need
his comrades to build him a mound for the funeral rites."

With these words he raged and surged and charged at Achilles,
his water seething with foam and blood and dead bodies,
and a dark wave hung over Achilles, about to destroy him.
But Hera, afraid for him, screamed out, thinking that he
would be swept away by the furious deep-swirling river,
and she called to Hephaestus: "Hurry, Clubfoot, my child.   310
We are counting on you, since you are the one who opposed
Xanthus in battle. Quick now, come to the rescue;
start a great fire, and I will go to stir up
the west wind and south wind to send a fierce gale from the sea
that will spread the flames and consume all the bodies and armor.
Go burn up the trees along the banks of the Xanthus
and set the river himself on fire, and don't
let him stop you, however he wheedles or threatens.
Keep pressing him hard, and don't hold back till you hear me
shout to you. Only then should you put out the flames."   320

When he heard this, Hephaestus set a prodigious fire.

It began on the plain and burned up the many scattered
bodies of men, whom Achilles had cut down; the whole
plain was dried up, and the shimmering water vanished.
As when the north wind in autumn quickly dries up
a field that was soaked by rain, and the farmer rejoices:
just so the whole plain dried up and the bodies burned.
Then he directed his roaring flames to the river.
The elm trees burned, the willows and tamarisks burned,
the clover burned, and the reeds and rushes and all   330
the plants that grew lush on the lovely banks of the river.
And the eels and fish in the deep pools were writhing in pain,
and in every direction they tried to leap out of the water
to escape the fiery blast that Hephaestus had set.
The mighty river himself was on fire, and he shouted,
"Hephaestus, none of the gods can withstand your fury.
It is useless for me to fight these devouring flames.
Stop now, and let Achilles drive all the Trojans
from Priam's city. What business is it of mine?"

By now the beautiful stream had begun to boil.   340
As a cauldron is brought to a boil over a fire
and melts down the lard of some fatted hog, and it bubbles
all around as the dry logs burn underneath it:
just so did his waters heat until they were boiling,
and he could not flow, but came to a halt, so afflicted
he was by the blasts of fire that Hephaestus had kindled.
He called out to Hera and begged her to help him: "Hera,
why has your son attacked me and caused me such pain?
I haven't done much to deserve it, compared with the other
immortal gods who have given aid to the Trojans.   350
But I will stop right away if that is your wish,
as long as Hephaestus stops too. And I will swear
that never again will I try to rescue the Trojans,
not even when their whole city goes up in flames
on the day that the ferocious Achaeans burn it."

When Hera heard this, she called to Hephaestus: "Enough.
You can stop now, my glorious child. It isn't right

to harm an immortal god for the sake of these mortals."
At this Hephaestus put out his prodigious fire,
and once more the river could flow along in his channel.   360

With the fury of Xanthus quelled, the two gods stopped fighting,
since Hera had held them back in spite of her anger.
But among the rest of the gods a fierce conflict broke out,
since their sympathies drove them apart in different directions.
And they charged at each other and clashed with a deafening uproar,
and the wide earth groaned, and the heavens blared like a trumpet.
Zeus heard the noise as he sat on his throne, and he laughed
to see the immortals rushing together in battle,
no longer restraining their fury. Ares began
by attacking Athena, shaking his huge bronze spear   370
as he bellowed insults: "Why are you once again
inciting the gods to combat, you nasty bitch?
What has your impudence pushed us into this time?
Don't you remember that day when you made Diomedes
stab me, and you yourself took hold of the spear
and drove it straight on and mangled my handsome flesh?
Now you will pay for what you did to me then."

With these words he lunged at the terrible tasseled storm shield,
so impenetrable that even the lightning of Zeus
is unable to pierce it, and stabbed at it with his spear.   380
But Athena stepped back, and with one hand she picked up a huge
jagged black rock that men of an earlier era
had put there to mark the boundary of one of their fields.
She hurled it and hit Ares' neck, and he crumpled to earth,
and his armor clattered, his long hair was fouled in the dust,
and he lay there prostrate, stretched out on seven acres.
And Athena laughed as she stood above him in triumph:
"What a fool you are! Haven't you learned by now
that you cannot beat me, since I am much stronger than you are?
This is the price you pay for your mother's curses.   390
She is angry and wishes you harm because you deserted
the Argives and gave your help to the insolent Trojans."

*

With these words she turned her eyes from him in contempt.
Then Aphrodite took Ares and led him away
groaning and barely conscious. When Hera saw it,
immediately she called to Athena and said,
"Can you believe it? Look at them, daughter of Zeus.
There goes that stupid twit through the thick of the battle,
leading him off the field. Go after her—now!"

When she heard these words, Athena rushed off, delighted,   400
and as she caught up, she punched Aphrodite hard
in the breast; she reeled and fell to the ground and took
Ares down with her. The two of them lay stretched out
on the bountiful earth, and Athena shouted in triumph:
"All those who help the Trojans—may they end up
like this, and may they be as heroic as she was
when she came out to rescue Ares and faced my fury.
If that had been so, we would long since have put an end
to this war, and stormed the strong walls of the city of Troy."

Meanwhile Poseidon, the Earthshaker, said to Apollo,   410
"Phoebus, why keep our distance? It isn't right,
when other gods have been fighting; it would be shameful
to return to the bronze-paved palace of Zeus on Olympus
without a tussle. Begin now, since you are the younger.
It isn't my place to start, and it wouldn't be fair
if I did. And I tell you, you are a fool; you lost
your mind when you decided to help the Trojans.
Don't you remember the misery that we suffered,
we two, cut off from the gods, that time when Zeus sent us
to work for Laómedon, that most arrogant king?   420
For a whole year we had to work for him as his servants,
and he kept us busy; we both had to do what he wanted.
I built a wall for the Trojans around their city,
a wide and beautiful wall that couldn't be breached;
and you, Phoebus, had to herd the sleek, lumbering cattle
along the valleys and wooded slopes of Mount Ida.
But when the glad seasons brought the end of our labor,
Laómedon robbed us of all our wages and sent us

away and threatened to bind our hands and our feet
and sell us and ship us out to some distant island,   430
and he even said he would cut off our ears. So we left
in a fury about the wages that he had promised
and never paid. And that is the man whose people
you are favoring now, when you should be working instead
with the rest of us to destroy these insolent Trojans
utterly, along with their wives and children."

Apollo said, "Earthshaker, I would be out of my mind
if I fought with you for the sake of these wretched mortals,
who are like the leaves: for a short time they blaze with life,
then wither and fall to the ground. So let us withdraw   440
from the battlefield now, and let them do their own fighting."
With these words he turned and left, since he thought it wrong
to enter a combat against his own father's brother.

But his sister, Lady Ártemis, came and rebuked him.
"So, you are running away. You have yielded the whole
victory to Poseidon without an effort.
Why do you even bother to carry a bow
if you can't use it? Some hero you are, with your boasting
to all the immortal gods in our father's palace
that someday you would challenge Poseidon and beat him."   450

Apollo did not reply, but Hera was angry.
"How dare you oppose me, you sniveling little bitch?
I am dangerous to confront, though you carry a bow
and Zeus has made you a lioness to all women
and allowed you to kill any mother you wish in childbirth.
But stick to *them* and to killing deer in the mountains.
When you challenge me, I will teach you a lesson or two
about fighting, and show you which of us is the stronger."
She grabbed both her wrists with her left hand, and with her right hand
she took her quiver and bow, and with her own weapons   460
she smacked her around her pretty ears, all the while smiling
as Ártemis wriggled and squirmed, and the arrows tumbled
out of the quiver. The goddess burst into tears

and fled from her like a pigeon that flies from a hawk
into the cleft of some rock, where it cannot be taken:
just so she ran off, leaving her bow behind her.

Hermes the messenger turned to Leto and said,
"I will not fight with you, Leto; it isn't safe
to stand up and take on any of Zeus's wives.
So go ahead now and boast to all the immortals   470
that you overwhelmed me in combat and won a great triumph."
Then Leto picked up the bow and quiver and arrows
that had fallen out all around in the swirling dust,
and she followed her daughter back to the heights of Olympus.

When Ártemis came to the bronze-paved palace of Zeus,
she went to her father and, weeping, sat down on his lap,
and her long robe shook as she sobbed. And her father held her
and spoke to her with a gentle laugh: "My dear child,
which of the gods did this terrible thing to hurt you?"

Ártemis answered, "Father, it was your wife.   480
It was all her fault. She is always causing us trouble."

As they spoke, Apollo entered the sacred city,
concerned that the Argives would break through the walls that day
and lay waste to Troy before its appointed time.
But the other immortal gods went up to Olympus,
some of them angry, others greatly exulting,
and they sat down beside the lord of the dark clouds, their father.

Meanwhile Achilles was slaughtering men and horses.
As when plumes of smoke fly up from a burning city
into the sky when the gods' rage sets it on fire   490
and brings hardship to all its people and grief to many:
just so did Achilles bring hardship and grief to the Trojans.

Priam, the old king, stood on the tower and saw
gigantic Achilles and how he was driving the Trojans
in panic before him, and no one was there to help them.

He groaned in dismay and at once climbed down from the tower
and gave orders to all the gatekeepers by the wall:
"Hold the gates open until you see all our men
return to the city. Achilles is close behind them,
pushing them back; we are facing a great disaster.   500
As soon as they are inside the walls, catching their breath,
shut the gate tight and keep this butcher outside it."

When they heard this, they pushed back the bars and opened the gate,
and this brought the Trojans safety. And then Apollo
rushed out to meet them and rescue them from destruction.
They were running straight toward the city and its high wall
in a cloud of dust, their throats all ragged with thirst,
while Achilles chased them. A violent mad-dog rage
gripped his heart, and he was intent on glory.

And now the Achaeans would surely have taken Troy   510
if Apollo had not stepped in and stirred up Agénor,
a brave and powerful fighter, Anténor's son.
He put boldness into his heart, to save him from death's
heavy hands, as he leaned back against the oak tree,
wrapped in dense mist. When Agénor saw that Achilles
was approaching, he stood his ground, but his heart was in turmoil.
He waited there and, troubled, said to himself,
"What should I do? If I run away from Achilles
with the rest of the men who are fleeing, he will still catch me
and slit my throat like a coward. But if I run   520
in the other direction, away from the wall, to the plain,
and reach the foothills of Ida and hide in the thickets,
then, when the sun goes down, I could wash off my sweat
in the cool of the river and make my way back to Troy.
But why do I need to debate these things with myself?
He is bound to see me moving away from the city
and will chase me and hunt me down, and I will have no
chance against him, since he is such a fast runner
and stronger than all men, and I will certainly die.
But suppose I stand and face him in front of the city.   530
He isn't a god; his flesh can be pierced by bronze

like anyone else's; he doesn't have more than one life,
and only through Zeus's will has he won such glory."

With these words he braced himself to await Achilles,
and his heart was firm and eager to stand there and fight.
And as a leopard charges from a dense thicket
to attack a hunter and is not afraid when she hears
the baying of hounds, and even if the man hits her
she rushes on with a spear in her side, undaunted,
until she can bring him down or is brought down herself: 540
just so did Agénor stand firm. He held up his shield,
aimed his spear, and called out in a loud voice:
"You probably thought, Achilles, that you would conquer
the city of the proud Trojans this very day.
What a fool you are! There is much grief that you and your comrades
will suffer before we are finished. Many brave men
will fight before Ilion, holding you off and defending
our parents and wives and children. And you will die here,
however ferocious a warrior you may be."

With these words he hurled his spear, and he hit Achilles   550
below the knee, on the shin, and the new tin greave
clanged loudly, but the bronze point bounced off it; it could not
pierce the magnificent armor the god had made.
Then in his turn Achilles charged at Agénor,
but Apollo did not allow him the triumph; he snatched
Agénor away and covered him in dense mist
and quietly sent him to Troy. And he tricked Achilles
to keep him away from the Trojan troops who were fleeing;
he stood there taking Agénor's form. And Achilles
rushed off in hot pursuit, and Apollo kept running.   560
Achilles pursued him across the wheat-bearing plain,
driving him toward the deep-swirling river Scamander,
and Apollo stayed just a little ahead and lured him
on, and Achilles kept thinking that he would catch him.

Meanwhile the rest of the Trojans, stampeding in panic,
reached the city and crowded in with relief.

Not one of them even dared to wait for the others
outside the walls and find out who had escaped
and who had died in the fighting, but they all poured
into the city—all those whose legs could save them.   570

Book 22

When the Trojans had entered the city, panicked like fawns,
they dried the sweat from their bodies and quenched their thirst,
leaning against the battlements. Meanwhile the Argives
advanced on the wall, bracing their shields on their shoulders.
But destiny shackled Hector and kept him standing
in front of the wall of Troy and the Scaean Gates.

Apollo then turned around and called to Achilles,
"Son of Peleus, why keep chasing me? Never
will you catch me, since you are a mortal and I am a god.
Haven't you noticed? Haven't you understood   10
that as you pursued me, you have lost sight of the Trojans?
You routed them, but now they have entered their city
while you were being lured in the other direction.
You will never kill me. I have no appointment with death."

Greatly troubled by these words, Achilles answered,
"That was a nasty trick, Lord Apollo, cruelest
of gods. If you hadn't lured me away from the wall,
many more Trojans by now would have chewed the dirt
before they could ever reach Ilion. You have robbed me
of a great triumph, and at no risk to yourself,   20
since there is no retribution you have to fear.
I would certainly pay you back if I had the power."
With this he raced off toward Troy like a prize-winning horse
that gallops ahead of its chariot effortlessly
over the plain: so fast were the legs of Achilles.

King Priam was first to see him as he ran back
across the plain toward Ilion, like the star
that comes in late summer in all its brilliance, outshining
the countless stars in the depths of the night sky (men
call it Oríon's Dog), a bright portent of evil,   30
bringing high fevers down on unfortunate humans:

just so, as he ran, did the bronze of his breastplate glitter.
The old king moaned and lifted his hands above him
and pounded his head and with a loud groan called out,
pleading with his dear son, who had taken a stand
in front of the gate, determined to fight Achilles.
He stretched out his arms and begged his son to have pity:
"Hector, my dear child, please do not face that man
alone, with no one to help you, or you will surely
meet your death, since he is so strong and ruthless.   40
I wish the immortals loved him as little as I do;
then dogs and vultures would eat his body, and this
bitter grief would be lifted out of my heart.
He has bereaved me of so many sons; he has killed them
or shipped them off as slaves to some distant island.
Even now there are two of them whom I can't
see among those who have crowded into the city:
Lycáon and Polydórus, Laóthoë's children.
If these two are still alive in the enemy camp,
we will ransom them with the treasures of bronze and gold   50
that Laóthoë's father, King Altes, gave as her dowry.
But if they are dead and gone to the realm of Hades,
then that will be one more grief for their mother and me;
to the rest of our people the grief will be shorter-lived,
if only Achilles doesn't cut *you* down. So come
inside the walls, my child; come into the city,
and save the men and the women of Troy. Don't give
a great victory to that man and lose your own life.
Have pity on me, while I am still living, before
Father Zeus kills me after I see many horrors: 60
my sons destroyed, my daughters raped and dragged off,
the palace ransacked, infants tossed from the walls
and smashed on the ground, my sons' wives grabbed by the deadly
hands of the Argives. And I myself, last of all,
my own dogs will tear me and eat me in front of my own
door, when some soldier enters the gate and spears me—
the watchdogs I raised in my house and fed at my table
will greedily lap up my blood, then lie in the gateway.
When a young man is killed and mutilated in battle,

there is no disgrace: though he falls and his flesh is torn,   70
he is beautiful, and the wounds are his marks of honor.
But when an old man is killed and the dogs defile
his gray head and beard and chew his genitals, nothing
more shameful can ever occur to a wretched human."
With these words Priam took hold of his hair and started
pulling it out. But he could not change Hector's mind.

Now Hector's mother lamented and wept and opened
the folds of her robe and held out one of her breasts:
"Hector, my child, take pity on me, if ever
I gave you this breast to suckle. Remember those times   80
and fight off this brutal man from inside the wall.
Don't be stubborn and stand your ground there; come in.
If he kills you now, I won't be able to mourn you
or lay you out and weep for you on your deathbed,
my own dear boy, nor will your beloved wife.
Far off, by the Argive ships, the dogs will devour you."

Thus the two of them cried out, begging their son
over and over, but Hector would not be swayed;
he stood his ground while Achilles, hugely, came closer.
As a snake in the mountains waits for a man at the entrance   90
to its hole, when it has eaten poisonous herbs
and is gripped by a savage anger and glares with malice:
just so Hector stood there, immovable in his resolve,
with his shield propped up against the projecting tower.
And as he awaited Achilles, he said to himself,
"What should I do? I could back off and enter the gate,
but Polydamas would be quick to accuse me of rashness.
He begged me to lead the troops back inside the city
during this last disastrous night, when Achilles
arose again and returned to the fighting; but I   100
didn't take his advice. It would have been far
better for me if I had. And now that my own
reckless conduct has ruined us, I feel shame
at facing the men and the long-robed women of Troy.
What if some lesser man were to say of me, 'Hector

thought he could trust his own strength and destroyed his people'?
Men will say this, and that is why it is better
to face Achilles; either I cut him down
or I die a glorious death in front of the city.
But what if I laid down my shield and helmet and leaned   110
my spear up against the wall and went out to meet him
and promised to give back Helen to Menelaus
along with all the possessions that Paris took
in his ships to Ilion—which was how this war started—
and promised as well to divide all our riches and give
half of them to the Argives and take an oath,
the elders and I, on behalf of the Trojan people,
not to hold anything back, to divide it completely . . . ?
But why do I need to debate these things with myself?
If I went up to him and begged, he would show me no mercy   120
but would cut me down on the spot, unarmed like a woman.
There is no way that he and I can talk about these
irrelevant things or waste time chatting together
like a girl and boy in their love talk, a girl and a boy
loving each other's sweet names and whispered endearments.
It is better to go and fight him immediately
and see which one of us Zeus will allow to triumph."

These were his thoughts as he waited. Achilles came close,
looking as fierce as Ares in his huge helmet
and shaking his terrible spear above his right shoulder.   130
All around him, his armor blazed like the flames
from a raging fire or the light of the sun as it rises.
When he saw him this close, Hector was seized by trembling.
He lost his nerve; he no longer dared to stand
his ground but, leaving the gate, he ran off in terror,
and Achilles ran after him, confident in his great speed.
As a mountain hawk, the fastest of winged creatures,
swoops down on a fluttering dove and she flies off in panic
and he, with shrill cries, keeps striking at her, determined
to have her: just so did Achilles rush after his prey.   140
And Hector kept running beneath the wall of the Trojans,
desperately, as fast as his legs could take him.

*

They ran past the lookout post and the windswept fig tree
along the thin wagon path that skirted the city
a little away from the wall, and they came to the two
lovely springs that feed the river Scamander.
One spring flows with hot water, and from it steam rises
as if a fire were burning beneath the current;
but the other one, even in summer, flows cold as hail
or freezing snow or water that turns to ice.   150
Beside these springs were the wide troughs, hollowed in rock,
where the Trojan wives and daughters would wash their clothing
in the time of peace, before the Achaeans arrived.
The two men ran past this, one fleeing, the other pursuing,
a brave man in front, but a greater one at his heels,
both running their hearts out, and what they were trying to win
was not the usual prize for a footrace, a bull
to sacrifice or an oxhide shield; they were running
now for the life of Hector, tamer of horses.

As when champion chariot horses gallop around   160
the turning-post at full stretch, and some splendid prize
has been set out, a beautiful tripod or female slave,
at the funeral games for some warrior who has been killed:
just so did they race around and around the city.
Three times they circled it, and the immortals were watching.
The father of men and gods was the first to speak:
"How dreadful! A man I love is being pursued
around the wall of the city. My heart grieves for Hector,
who has burned the thighbones of so many bulls for me
on Mount Ida's peaks and the heights of Ilion also.   170
But now Achilles, whom no one can match in running,
is chasing him down. All of you—we must decide
whether to save him from death or allow Achilles
to finish him off, brave fighter though Hector is."

Athena answered, "Dread Father, what are you saying?
Do you want to take a mere mortal and set him free
from a death that he has been destined for? Do as you wish,

but be aware that not all the gods will approve."

And Zeus said, "All right. Don't you worry, dear child;
I didn't mean what I said. You can have your own way.   180
Go down to Earth now, and do whatever you want to."
This made Athena glad; she was eager to act,
and down from the topmost peak of Olympus she flew.

Meanwhile Achilles drove Hector relentlessly on.
Like a fawn that is flushed by a dog from her mountain lair
and he chases her through the valleys, and though she escapes
for a while and cowers under a bush, the dog
keeps sniffing her out and hunting until he finds her:
just so did Hector fail to escape from Achilles.
Each time he headed toward the Dardánian Gates   190
to get close enough to the wall for the warriors on it
to protect him by showering down their arrows and spears,
Achilles would cut him off by dashing between
him and the wall, and forcing him back toward the plain.
And as in a dream a man is unable to catch
someone he is chasing—the harder he tries to run,
the less he can move: just so Achilles could not
narrow the distance, and Hector could not outrun him.
And how could Hector have kept clear of death until then
if Apollo had not supported him with fresh power   200
and fresh speed, though this was the last time that he would do it?
And now Achilles signaled his men, with a shake
of his head, that they were all to refrain from shooting
their arrows and spears, so that none of them would hit Hector
and win the glory and he himself come too late.
But when they had circled around to the springs for the fourth time,
the Father held out his golden scales, and upon them
he put two portions of death—one for Achilles,
and one for Hector—and lifted the scales by the middle,
and Hector's portion began to sink and kept sinking   210
down toward the realm of death. And Apollo left him.

Athena came up and stood by Achilles and said,

"Now it is time, Achilles, beloved of Zeus,
that the two of us bring great glory to the Achaeans
and return to the ships. Our chance has come to kill Hector.
However fiercely he struggles, it is no longer
possible that he can escape, though Apollo
may grovel as much as he wants before Father Zeus.
But stay here now and recover your breath, while I
go and persuade him to fight with you man to man."   220
When he heard these words, he obeyed, and his heart rejoiced,
and he stood there and rested, leaning on his great spear.
Athena left him and, taking the form and voice
of Deíphobus, she went up to Hector and said,
"Brother, Achilles is wearing you out. You will never
pull away from him; no one is faster than he is.
So stop. We will make a stand and see who is stronger."

Hector replied, "Deíphobus, you were always
my favorite brother of all the sons born to Priam
and Hecuba. Now I will honor you even more,   230
since you had the courage to leave the wall when you saw me,
and you came here while all the others remained inside."

Athena said, "Brother, with all respect, it is true
that our father and mother and all our comrades implored me
to stay where I was, so terrified are they all
of that man Achilles. I had to come, though; my heart
was aching for you when I saw you. Now let us charge
straight at Achilles. Soon we will know whether he
will kill us both and carry our bloodstained armor
back to the ships or himself be cut down by your spear."   240

When they had come within range of Achilles, they faced him,
and Hector spoke first: "Son of Peleus, no longer
will I run away from you. You have already chased me
three times around the city. I haven't dared
to stop and await your attack. It is time now. My heart
commands me to fight; I will kill you or else be killed.
But first let us swear an agreement and call on the gods

as our witnesses. I swear, if Zeus grants me the triumph,
not to defile your body; all I will do
is strip off your glorious armor, then give your corpse   250
back to the Argives. Swear you will do the same."

Achilles answered him then, with an angry scowl,
"Don't talk to me of agreements, you son of a bitch.
No solemn oaths are sworn between lions and men;
wolves and lambs don't bargain to make a truce
but hate one another for all time. There can never
be friendship for you and me, nor will there be oaths
sworn between us till one or the other has fallen,
gorging mad Ares with blood. Now is the moment
to summon up all your courage and all your skill   260
as a warrior—and I promise that you will need it.
But nothing will save you. Athena will cut you down
with my spear, and soon you will pay me back the full price
for all the grief that I felt when you killed my comrades."

With these words he aimed and hurled his long-shadowed spear.
But Hector saw it coming and crouched to avoid it,
and the spear flew over his head and stuck in the ground.
Athena, unseen by Hector, pulled out the spear shaft
and gave it back to Achilles. Then Hector shouted,
"You missed! So it seems that Zeus, after all, told you nothing   270
about my death, although you pretended to know.
It was empty talk; you were using your power with words
to frighten me and make me forget my courage.
But I will not flee and allow you to stick a spear
in my back; if a god lets you win this fight, you will have to
thrust your spear through my chest as I charge straight at you.
Now it is your turn; avoid my spear if you can.
May it find you and drive through your body with its whole length.
This war would be that much easier for the Trojans
if I killed you here, since you are our greatest affliction."   280

With these words he aimed and hurled his long-shadowed spear,
and he hit the great shield dead on, but the spear bounced off

and stuck in the ground at a distance. Hector was angry
that the shot, though it had been perfectly aimed, was wasted,
and he stood there dismayed, since that was his only spear.
He called out loud to Deíphobus to come bring him
another one. But Deíphobus was not there.
And suddenly Hector realized the truth. He said,
"Ah, so the gods did summon me to my death.
I thought that Deíphobus was standing beside me,   290
but he is behind the wall. Athena has tricked me.
Now death is on its way here. I can feel it coming;
there is no escape. This end must have been decided
a long time ago by Zeus and Apollo, however
often they came to protect me. It always seemed
that they were on *my* side; but fate is about to seize me.
Let me at least die gloriously, with a struggle,
and do some great deed that men will praise for all time."

With these words, he drew the long sword that hung at his side,
and gathering all his strength, he swooped like a high-flying   300
eagle that plunges to earth through the dark cloudbanks
to snatch up a tender lamb or a cowering hare:
just so did he charge, with his sword held out above him.
Achilles charged also, his heart filled with savage fury,
and his wondrous shield was in front of him, and the crest
of his glittering four-plated helmet shook fiercely above him.
Like the evening star as it shines among other stars
in the depths of the night, the loveliest star in the heavens:
such was the gleam from the point of Achilles' spear
as he held it in his right hand, determined to cut down   310
Hector, scanning his armor, looking for bare
skin. The rest of his body was covered in bronze;
in only one spot could the flesh be seen: on his throat,
where the collarbone separates neck from shoulders. At this spot,
as Hector attacked, Achilles thrust, and the spear drove
into the tender flesh of the neck and pushed
all the way through, though it did not sever his windpipe.
(He could still make sounds, and he was just able to speak.)
And he fell in the dirt, and Achilles triumphed above him:

"Hector, you must have thought, as you killed Patroclus,   320
that you would be safe from the consequences. You never
had me in mind; you thought I was far away.
Fool, I was there in the background, a much greater man,
to hunt you down and take my revenge. And now
I have killed you. And while the Achaeans treat him with honor
and give him full funeral rites, the wild dogs and birds
will be tearing at you and mauling you hideously."

Then Hector forced out these words, and his voice was feeble:
"I implore you, by your own life, your knees, and your parents—
don't let the dogs devour me by your ships,   330
but accept a ransom for me. My mother and father
will give you great treasures of bronze and gold, if only
you return my body and let them take it back home
so that the men and the women of Troy can give me,
once I am dead, the burning that is my due."

Achilles answered him then, with an angry scowl,
"You filthy dog—how dare you beg for your body!
I only wish that this fury inside my heart
would drive me to carve you in pieces and eat your flesh raw
myself, for what you have done to me. You can be sure, though,   340
that no man is going to keep the dogs from your head,
not even if he were to come and offer me ten
or twenty times what you are worth, as a ransom—not even
if Priam offered to pay me your weight in gold,
not even then would your mother be able to touch
your face on your deathbed and mourn for the son she gave birth to.
The dogs and birds will consume you, and they will leave nothing."

Then Hector said to Achilles with his last breath,
"I know you well; I was sure that I had no chance
of moving you. Your heart is as hard as iron.   350
But be careful now, or you may bring down the gods' anger
on the day that must come, when Paris and Lord Apollo
cut you down in your strength at the Scaean Gates."
As he said these words, death covered him, and his soul

fluttered out of his flesh and went down to Hades.

And Achilles answered him, even though Hector was dead,
"Die. And as for my own death, I will accept it
whenever Zeus and the other gods wish it to come."

With this he pulled out his spear and set it aside
from the corpse and began to strip off the bloodstained armor.   360
And the other Achaeans came running up, and they stood
gazing in wonder at the huge, beautiful body.
And a man would turn to his neighbor, laughing, and say,
"Well, Hector is certainly easier now to handle
than when he attacked us and almost burned down our ships."
Thus they would gloat, and each of them came and stabbed him.

Achilles stripped off his armor, then stood up and said,
"My friends, commanders and captains of the Achaeans,
the gods have allowed us to triumph over this man
who has done so much harm to us, more than all other Trojans   370
put together. So let us advance and find out
what they intend to do next, whether they mean
to abandon their citadel now that this man has fallen
or whether they are determined to fight on without him.
But why do I need to debate these things with myself?
There is a dead man lying inside my hut,
unmourned, unburied—Patroclus, whom I will never
forget, as long as I breathe and have life in my body.
And even if others forget their dead when they go down
to Hades, I will remember him there as well.   380
So let us return to the ships, carrying this one
and singing a song of praise to the gods for our triumph.
We have won high glory, since we have killed the great Hector,
whom the Trojans honored in Ilion like a god."

And Achilles began to mutilate Hector's body.
He sliced the tendons of both feet and cut large holes
in the space between the ankles and heels and threaded
oxhide straps through the holes he had made and tied

the straps to the rear of his chariot, so that the head
would be left to drag on the ground behind. And he lifted   390
his famous armor into the chariot and climbed up
and touched his whip to the backs of the horses, and gladly
they flew off, and Hector was dragged behind them, and dust
swirled around him, and his dark hair streamed out
in back, and his head, which had once been so handsome, bounced
along in the dirt, since Zeus had given him over
to his enemies, to defile him in his own country.

His head and body were dragged through the dirt, and his mother
tore her hair and flung off her glistening shawl
and began to scream when she saw it; his father groaned;   400
and throughout the city the people were overcome
by wailing and lamentation. It was as if
Troy itself on its towering rock were in flames.
The people could barely hold back the old man in his anguish
as he headed for the Dardánian Gates, and he groveled
there in the dung and begged them to let him go:
"Leave me alone, friends. I know how concerned you are
for my welfare, but let me go out to the Argive ships
and beseech that shameless, violent man; perhaps
he will look at me and take pity on my old age.   410
He too has a father—Peleus, as old as I am,
who reared him to be a deadly scourge to the Trojans.
On me above all he has brought much grief, so many
sons of mine has he killed in the flower of their youth.
And yet, though I mourn for all of them, there is one
I lament even more: Hector. My sorrow for him
will drag me down to Death's house. If only he could have
died in my arms! We would have been able to weep then
over his body and given him his due rites—
his mother who bore him to sorrow, and I myself."   420
Thus he mourned, and the people joined in his wailing.

And Hecuba led the women in lamentation:
"My child, how unhappy I am! How can I live
with this misery, now you are dead? You were my pride

every day of my life, and a blessing to all
the men and the women of Troy, who greeted you like
a god, because you were their great glory as well."

Thus she lamented. But Hector's wife had not heard
anything yet; no one had brought her the news
that her husband had stayed outside the wall of the city.   430
She was at work in her chambers, in front of the loom,
weaving a purple robe in which she was making
a pattern of colored flowers. She called to her handmaids
to put a large three-legged cauldron over the fire
so that hot water would be there for Hector's bath
when he returned. Poor innocent, how could she know
that far from all baths Athena had cut him down
at the hands of Achilles? But now she heard the loud noise
of wailing and lamentation that came from the tower,
and her body began to shake, and the shuttle dropped   440
from her hands. And she called again to her servants: "Come,
two of you, quickly. I need to find out what happened.
That was the voice of my husband's mother. My heart
is pounding all the way to my throat, and my legs
tremble beneath me. Something terrible must have
happened to one of Priam's sons. May I never
hear such news, but now I am deathly afraid
that Achilles has caught my brave Hector alone and cut him
off from the city and driven him out to the plain
and put an end to that fatal courage he had—   450
he would never stay back in the ranks, but he always rushed
ahead of everyone, second to none in his daring."

With these words she hurried out of the house, in a frenzy,
like a madwoman, and her handmaids ran out behind her.
When she came to the tower, where groups of soldiers had gathered,
she stood on the wall and looked down and saw him as
he was being dragged off in front of the city; horses
were brutally dragging him toward the Achaean ships.
Black night covered her eyes, and she fell backward
and breathed out her soul, and her lovely headdress fell off—   460

the diadem and the cap and the plaited clasp
and the shawl—that were given to her by Aphrodite
on the day that Hector had taken her as his wife
from Ëétion's house, having paid an enormous bride-price.
Her husband's sisters and brothers' wives all crowded
around, and they held her, stunned, almost, to death.

When she revived and the soul returned to her body,
she burst into sobs and wails, and she cried out and said,
"Oh Hector, how wretched I am! It seems that we two
were born to the same fate, you in the house of Priam,   470
and I in Ëétion's house in Thebē, where he,
an ill-starred father, brought up his small doomed child.
I wish I had never been born, now you are going
down to Hades, under the depths of the earth,
and have left me behind to mourn, in an anguish that has
no end, a widow, and our dear child just a baby—
Astýanax, who would sit on his father's lap
and be fed only marrow and the rich meat of lambs,
and when he was sleepy and done with playing, his nurse
would carry him off in her arms and would gently put him   480
into his soft bed, his heart full of happy dreams.
But now, with his father gone, he will suffer greatly.
And beside the black ships, far from your parents, naked,
the wriggling maggots will eat you, after the dogs
have had their fill. And with all the beautiful clothes,
woven by craftswomen, stored for you in our house . . .
I will burn them all, since you can no longer use them
or even be wrapped in them on your funeral pyre.
That is how I will honor you with the Trojans."
Thus she mourned, and the women joined in her wailing.   490

Book 23

As the Trojans were mourning throughout the city, the Argives
withdrew to their camp on the shore of the Hellespont.
There they scattered, and each man went to his ship.
But Achilles would not dismiss his comrades. He said,
"Myrmidons, friends, my faithful companions in battle,
it is not yet time to unyoke our horses; still mounted
as we all are, let us drive up close to Patroclus
and mourn for him—the privilege of the dead.
Once we have taken comfort from our lamenting,
we will come back, unyoke the horses, and have a meal."   10

As he spoke of Patroclus, they burst into lamentation.
Three times they drove around the body, in tears,
and Thetis intensified their desire for weeping.
The sands were wet, their armor was wet, with tears,
so formidable was the warrior they were mourning.
And Achilles led the Myrmidons in their lament,
putting his man-killing hands on the breast of his comrade:
"Go well, Patroclus, even in Hades' realm.
Already I am accomplishing what I promised.
I have dragged Hector here and will feed him raw to the dogs,   20
and in front of your pyre I am going to cut the throats
of a dozen splendid young Trojans to soothe my anger."

With these words, he treated Hector shamefully, flinging
his body face down into the dirt by the pyre.
All of them took off their armor, unyoked their horses,
and sat down beside Achilles' ship in their thousands,
and Achilles set out a magnificent funeral feast.
Many sleek bulls fell, bellowing, under the knife;
many plump sheep and goats were slaughtered, and many
white-tusked hogs were stretched out to singe on the flames,   30
and around Patroclus's body the blood flowed in streams.

*

And Achilles was led by the Argive commanders to feast
with Agamemnon, though it had been hard to persuade him,
since his heart was still full of anger about Patroclus.
And when the group had reached Agamemnon's hut,
immediately they commanded the heralds to place
a large, three-legged cauldron over the fire
in the hope of persuading Achilles to wash the clotted
gore from his face and body. But he refused:
"No, by Zeus almighty, the greatest of gods,   40
I will never wash or let any water come near me
until I have put Patroclus upon the flames
and heaped a grave mound above him and cut my hair,
since no second grief will touch me as deeply as this one
while I am among the living. We have to eat now,
though the thought of food repulses me; but tomorrow
you, my lord Agamemnon, king of men,
order the troops to collect enough wood and bring
everything that a dead man should have when he journeys
down to the gloomy darkness below the earth,   50
so that fire can burn him and he can quickly be taken
out of our sight and our men can return to the fighting."

Everyone listened carefully and agreed.
They quickly prepared the meal, and when it was ready
they feasted, and all of them had their fair share and were happy.
And when they had had enough of eating and drinking,
each man went back to his own hut to get some sleep.
But Achilles lay down on the shore of the loud-roaring sea,
groaning, amid the thousands of Myrmidon troops,
in an open space where the waves surged up on the seashore.   60
And when sleep took hold and poured out its sweetness around him,
dissolving the cares of his heart (his glorious limbs
were exhausted from chasing Hector around the city),
the spirit of poor Patroclus appeared and stood there,
in every way like the man, with his height and voice
and beautiful eyes, and dressed in the clothes he had worn.
It stood there above his head and spoke to him softly:
"You are sleeping, Achilles; you have forgotten me now.

You were always attentive to me when I was alive,
but now I am dead, you neglect me. Bury me quickly,   70
so I can pass through the gates of Hades. The spirits—
the phantoms of those who have died—are keeping me out;
they won't allow me to cross the river and join them.
Give me your hand, I beg you, for never again
will I come back from Hades after I have my burning.
Never again will we sit apart from our comrades
in intimate talk. The fate that was mine at birth
has opened its jaws around me and swallowed me up.
And you, Achilles—you too are fated to die
under the wall of Troy. But there is one more   80
thing that I have to ask, and I hope you will do it.
May my bones not be buried apart from your bones, Achilles.
May they lie together, just as we grew up together
when my father brought me from Ópoïs to your house
on the day that I killed the son of Amphídamus. I was
only a boy. I didn't do it on purpose;
we were having a childish quarrel about some dice.
It was then that Lord Peleus welcomed me in his home,
and he brought me up kindly and let me be your attendant.
So may one urn hold the bones of us both together."   90

Achilles answered, "Dear friend, why have you come here
and made these requests? But I will do everything
you asked me to do, exactly as you have stated.
Come closer now. Let us embrace, if just for a moment,
and take a small bit of comfort in grieving together."
He reached out but could not touch him. The spirit vanished
like smoke and flew underground, squeaking. At this Achilles
awoke from his sleep in astonishment and cried out,
"So something exists then, even after we die!
All night long the spirit of poor Patroclus   100
stood at my side, weeping and mourning, and told me
what I must do. It was wondrously like himself."
With these words he stirred in them all the desire for weeping.

When the flush of dawn appeared in the heavens, they still

were weeping around the body. Lord Agamemnon
sent mules and soldiers from every part of the camp
to gather wood, and a good man was placed in charge:
Meriones, Lord Idómeneus's attendant.
They set out with axes and heavy ropes in their hands,
with the mules ahead of the men; and without stopping,   110
uphill and downhill, sideways and zigzag they went,
and when they finally came to the spurs of Mount Ida,
they began to fell the tall oaks with their long-bladed axes,
and the trees kept crashing down loudly. Then the Achaeans
chopped up the trunks and tied them in back of the mules,
and the mules tore tracks in the ground as they strained through the dense
underbrush in their eagerness to return.
The woodcutters carried wood too, as they had been ordered,
and when they arrived at the seashore, they stacked the logs
in rows, where Achilles was planning to build a huge   120
burial mound for Patroclus and for himself.

After they finished stacking the logs, they sat down
in one large crowd and they waited. And soon Achilles
ordered the Myrmidon troops to put on their armor
and yoke the horses. They rushed off and armed and mounted
their chariots, both fighters and charioteers,
then pulled out in front, and a mass of foot soldiers followed,
thousands of them. And as the procession advanced
with Patroclus borne up in the middle by his companions,
the Myrmidons covered his body with locks of hair   130
that they cut off and dropped on it as it passed, and behind it
Achilles walked, and he cradled the head and grieved
bitterly for the friend he was sending to Hades.
When they reached the place that Achilles had pointed out,
they put down the body and started to heap up the wood.

And one further thought struck Achilles. He moved away
from the pyre and cut off a lock of his long blond hair,
which he had let grow luxuriantly since the time
he had dedicated it to the river Sperchéüs.
Looking out on the wine-dark sea toward his own land,   140

he called to Spérchéüs, "God of the river, in vain
did my father, Peleus, vow that when I returned
I would cut off this lock for you and offer you also
fifty ungelded rams alongside the river
by your sacred grove and your altar, fragrant with burning.
That was his vow, but you failed to do what he asked for.
So because I will never return, I will give this lock
to my dear Patroclus, to take to the underworld with him."
As he said this, he put the lock in his comrade's hands,
and all those who watched him were overpowered with weeping.   150

And now the sun would have set on their lamentation
if Achilles had not approached Agamemnon and said,
"Son of Atreus, you are the one the Achaeans
obey most willingly. Men can have enough mourning,
so send them away from the pyre for now and command them
to have their meal. Those of us who were closest
to our dead companion will take care of what must follow.
And let the commanders stay here with us as well."
When he heard this, Agamemnon dismissed the soldiers,
but the Myrmidons stayed there and built up huge piles of wood   160
and made a pyre of a hundred feet on each side,
and with grief in their hearts they placed the body upon it.
In front of the pyre they slaughtered, skinned, and dressed
many plump sheep and lumbering bulls. And Achilles
took the fat from them all and covered Patroclus
from head to toe and heaped the bodies around him,
then put some two-handled jars of honey and oil there
leaning against the funeral bed, and with groans
he slaughtered four horses and threw them onto the pyre.
Patroclus had nine pet dogs that he fed at his table,   170
and Achilles took two of them, killed them, and threw their bodies
onto the pyre, and with butchery in his heart
he ordered his men to bring the dozen young Trojans,
and he slit their throats with his knife, one after the other,
and threw them onto the pyre and lit the wood
so that the flames would spread and consume it all.
He uttered a groan and called out to his dear comrade,

"Go well, Patroclus, even in Hades' realm.
I have brought to completion everything that I promised.
The dozen young Trojan captives are on the pyre,   180
and the flames will consume them together with you. As for Hector,
not fire but dogs will lick the flesh from his bones."

This was his threat. But no dogs took care of Hector.
Aphrodite kept them away from him day and night,
and every dawn she rubbed him with an immortal
oil of roses, so that he would not be torn
to shreds when Achilles dragged him around the city.
And Apollo brought down a cloud from the sky and shaded
the ground where the corpse was, so that the sunlight would not
shrivel the flesh around his limbs and his sinews.   190

But the pyre of the dead Patroclus refused to burn.
And a further thought struck Achilles. He moved away
from the pyre and prayed to the north wind and to the west wind,
and promising them rich sacrifices, he poured
libations to them from a golden cup, and he begged them
to come and ignite the wood and spread the fire quickly
so that the bodies would be consumed in the flames.
And Iris heard him and rushed to the winds with his message.
They were all at a feast in the house of the stormy west wind
as Iris ran in and stood there on the stone threshold.   200
They all leaped up, and each one invited her
to sit beside him; but Iris refused their requests:
"There is no time; I have to get back to the Ocean,
to the land of the Ethiopians, where they are making
sacrifices to all the immortals—hundreds
of oxen and goats—and I want to share in the feasting.
But Achilles is sending prayers to you, North Wind and West Wind,
and promises you rich offerings if you come
to fan the fire where Patroclus's body is laid,
whom all the Argives with bitter tears are lamenting."   210
At this she left. And with a tremendous howl
the two winds arose now, sweeping the clouds before them.
They whipped out over the sea, and the sea's waves swelled

under their whistling blast, and at Troy they swooped
onto the pyre, and the flames shot up with a roar.

All night long, from different directions, they blasted
the fire with their howling currents, and all night long
Achilles, using a two-handled cup, drew wine
from a golden bowl and poured it onto the ground
till the earth was soaked, and called on Patroclus's spirit.   220
As a father laments his just-married son whose death
has filled his parents with inconsolable sorrow:
just so did Achilles weep as he burned his comrade,
moaning and moving with slow steps around the pyre.

At the time when the morning star announces the daylight
all over the earth and dawn spreads its saffron glow
upon the wide waters, the flames began to die down,
and the two winds flew back, and they crossed the Thracian sea,
stirring it into a frenzy. Achilles turned
away from the smoldering pyre and sank down, exhausted,   230
and in an instant sweet sleep descended upon him.

But soon Agamemnon and those who had remained
came crowding around, and their voices and their loud footsteps
awakened him. And Achilles sat up and said,
"Son of Atreus, and you Achaean commanders,
first of all, go to the funeral pyre and extinguish
whatever embers are still hot; then let us gather
the bones of Patroclus, singling them out from the others.
That will be easy, because he was lying alone
in the center, apart from the rest of them, men and horses,   240
who burned at the pyre's edges. After we wrap
the bones in a double layer of fat, we will place them
inside a golden urn, until I myself
descend to the realm of Hades. As for his grave mound,
I do not want you to build him a very large one,
but one that is moderate. Afterward, you Achaeans
can build it up further, making it broad and high—
whoever survives the fighting when I am gone."

                                    *

When they heard these words, they did as Achilles had told them.
First they extinguished with wine whatever embers   250
were still hot, as far as the flames had reached on the pyre,
where the wood had burned and left a thick layer of ash.
Then weeping, they gathered the bones of their gentle friend,
wrapped in two layers of fat, in a golden urn,
and they covered it with a sheet of fine linen and placed it
inside his hut. Around the base of the pyre
they put a circle of boundary stones, and they heaped
earth on top of it, forming a burial mound.
After they finished, they turned around to go back.
But Achilles made them sit down, thousands of them,   260
for funeral games, and he sent to his ships for prizes.
When the prizes arrived, he set them out in the middle:
cauldrons and tripods, horses, mules, and fine oxen,
along with some lovely women and precious iron.

The first of the prizes were for the chariot race:
a woman skilled in the arts of spinning and weaving
and a twenty-two-gallon tripod with ear-shaped handles
for the winner; for second place, a six-year-old mare
not broken in, with a baby mule in her womb;
for third place, a beautiful cauldron that held four gallons,   270
untarnished by fire and as bright as when it was new;
for fourth place, two solid gold bars; and for fifth, a shining
two-handled bowl. And he stood up and said to the Argives,
"Son of Atreus, and you Achaean commanders,
I have set out the prizes here for the chariot race.
Of course, if the games were in anyone else's honor,
I would certainly come in first, for you know how greatly
my horses excel all others. They are immortal,
a gift that Poseidon brought to Peleus, my father,
and my father gave them to me. But I will remain here   280
with my horses, and we will not compete in this race.
They have lost their splendid charioteer, the kind man
who often would wash them down with clear water, and comb
olive oil into their manes. So they stand there in mourning,

bowing their heads, and their manes trail down in the dirt,
and they will not move, so boundless is their hearts' sorrow.
But the rest of you should get ready—any Achaean
who is confident of his skill as a charioteer."

After he finished, five commanders came forward.
The first on his feet was Eumélus, that king of men,   290
Admétus's son, who was an outstanding horseman.
And the son of Tydeus, Diomedes, stood up
to yoke the marvelous horses that he had captured
from Aeneas, when Lord Apollo rescued their master.
And after him Menelaus, Atreus's son,
harnessed his team: Podárgus, who was his own horse,
and Æthē, the mare of his brother, King Agamemnon.
Antilochus was the fourth of them to come forward,
the son of King Nestor; the horses that pulled his car
were bred in Pylos. His father came up and gave him   310
some good advice, though the young man could think for himself:
"Antilochus, young as you are, Poseidon and Zeus
have loved you and made you into an excellent horseman,
so there is no need at all for me to instruct you;
you certainly know how to make the turn. But your horses
are awfully slow, and I think that you will have trouble.
Yet though the other horses are faster, their drivers
are no more skillful than you are. So use that skill
and do not allow the prizes to slip from your fingers.
It is skill, not brute force, that makes a woodsman effective;   320
and by skill a good pilot can keep a straight course on the sea
even when strong gales are pounding down on his ship;
and one driver beats another one only by skill.
The man who stupidly leaves too much to his horses
goes wheeling around the turning-post in a wide circle
and his chariot zigzags aimlessly down the track;
but a skillful man, though driving inferior horses,
always keeps watching the post and turns tightly around it,
and he knows when to pull on the reins and when to let go
and give his horses their head, and he firmly controls them   330
while keeping his eye on the charioteer in the lead.

As for the turn, it is very clear; you won't miss it.
There is a dried-out tree stump, an oak or a pine,
which rain has not rotted; it stands about six feet high,
and two white stones stand against it, one on each side;
this is the halfway mark where the homestretch begins,
and there is smooth turning for horses around it. Maybe
it marks the grave of some man who died long ago,
or maybe the men of a former age put it there
as a goal for a race. Anyway, it is the landmark   340
that Achilles has set as the turning-post. Stay as near it
as you can when you make the turn, and lean to the left
as you stand on the plaited straps of the chariot. Keep
whipping your right-hand horse and shouting him on,
and give him rein, while you pull on the inside horse
and drive him so close to the turning-post that the hub
of the wheel seems to graze the edge of it. But be careful
to avoid the stone, or else you will injure your horses
and wreck the chariot—which would delight your rivals
and bring great disgrace upon you. In short, my dear boy,   350
use your wits and always be on your guard.
Keep close behind them, then surge ahead at the post;
if you do, no man will be able to overtake you,
not even if he were driving Adrástus's stallion,
the great Aríon, sired by one of the gods,
or Laómedon's horses, the best ever bred in this country."
When he finished, Nestor went back and sat in his place,
having told his son the essential points to consider.
And Meriones was the fifth man to harness his horses.

Then they all mounted their chariots and threw in their lots,   360
and Achilles took hold of the helmet and shook it, and out
jumped the lot of Antilochus, who thus drew
the inside track. Eumélus's lot was next,
and after his lot came Menelaus's; fourth
came Meriones', and the last one was Diomedes',
the best of them all as a driver. They took their places
side by side, with Antilochus on the left,
and Achilles showed them the turning-post far in the distance

out on the plain. He had placed an umpire beside it,
Phoenix, his father's attendant, to keep a close watch   370
and bring them a clear and truthful account of what happened.

They lifted their whips above the backs of the horses,
and at the signal they lashed them and shouted them on,
and the horses broke out and galloped away from the ships
across the plain, and under their chests the dust
rose and hung in the air like a large thick cloud,
and their manes streamed back in the wind. Sometimes the wheels
ran smoothly along the plain, and sometimes they bounced
violently, and the drivers stood firm in their cars,
and each man's heart was pounding with the desire   380
for victory, and each shouted out to his horses,
and they all flew over the ground in a swirl of dust.

But when the horses had turned and were racing back
on the final stretch toward the seashore, each of the drivers
showed his true worth, and the horses strained to the utmost.
Quickly the mares of Eumélus surged out in front;
close behind came the stallions of Diomedes,
and at every moment it looked as if they would leap
into Eumélus's chariot, and his broad back
and shoulders were warm with their breath as they flew along   390
leaning upon him. And now Diomedes would have
passed Eumélus or made the race a dead heat
if Apollo, who was still angry at him, had not
knocked the whip from his hand. And tears of frustration
poured down his cheeks when he saw Eumélus's mares
pulling ahead, while his own horses were starting
to fall behind, since there was no whip to urge them.

But Athena saw how Apollo had fouled Diomedes
to slow him down, and she hurried to pick up the whip
and returned it to him and gave fresh strength to his horses.   400
Then in her anger she rushed ahead to Eumélus
and smashed his yoke. His mares ran apart, to the left
and right of the track, the yoke pole fell to the ground,

and Eumélus flew headlong over the wheel, and the skin
was torn from his nose, his mouth, and his elbows, his forehead
was bruised, and his eyes filled with tears, and his strong voice failed.
And Diomedes swerved to drive past the wreckage
and pulled far ahead of the other men, since Athena
had filled his horses with strength and given him glory.

Next after Diomedes came Menelaus.   410
But Antilochus shouted out to his father's horses,
"Faster now! Give it everything that you've got!
We don't have a chance of catching that pair ahead,
Diomedes' horses—Athena has filled them with speed
and given him glory. But run as fast as you can
and catch up with Menelaus's team; don't let them
leave you behind. Quick now, or Æthē will shame you,
although she is only a mare. Why are you lagging?
I swear to you, and I mean it: If you slack off
and I win anything less than the second prize,   420
Nestor will punish you; yes, he will slit your throats
at the end of the race. Hurry now, run your hearts out,
and I, for my part, will think of some way of slipping
past him where the track narrows. He won't escape me."

When they heard the words of their master, the horses were frightened,
and they picked up their pace for a while. And Antilochus
saw a spot where the track grew sunken and narrow;
the water from winter rains had collected there
and broken the edge and made a large rut all around.
As he came to this place, Menelaus did not leave room   430
for a second car to come up and move alongside him.
But Antilochus pulled his horses completely off
the track; he drove outside it and kept drawing closer
to Menelaus and sped on in full pursuit.
And Menelaus was terrified, and he shouted,
"Antilochus, don't be a maniac! Rein in your horses;
the track is too narrow; pass me when it gets wider.
Be careful or you will hit me and wreck us both!"
But Antilochus whipped his team and drove even faster,

as though he were deaf. They ran abreast for the length   440
that a discus flies when swung from the powerful shoulder
of a young man testing his strength, and then Menelaus
pulled on the reins so the galloping horses would not
collide and wreck the two cars and leave both drivers,
in their fierce desire to win, sprawled out in the dirt.

Then Menelaus shouted at him in anger,
"Antilochus, there is no mortal more reckless than you are.
I thought that you were a sensible man, but now
I know better. And do not think that the prize will be yours
unless you can take an oath that you won it fairly."   450

After he said this, he shouted out to his horses,
"Don't hold back now, however upset you are.
That pair ahead—their feet and knees will get tired
far sooner than yours will, since both are no longer young."
When they heard the words of their master, the horses were frightened,
and they picked up their pace and soon pulled close to the others.

Meanwhile everyone sitting in the assembly
was looking out at the chariots as they flew
toward them over the plain in a swirl of dust.
The Cretan commander, Idómeneus, was the first man   460
to see them. He was sitting apart from the crowd
on higher ground, and he heard a charioteer
far away from them shouting out to his horses,
and he knew the voice and recognized one of the pair,
who was chestnut all over except for a little patch
of white on his forehead, as round as the full moon.
He rose to his feet and called out to the assembly,
"My friends, commanders and captains of the Achaeans,
am I the only one here who can see the horses,
or can you all see them too? It appears to me   470
that another team is in front, with another driver.
Eumélus's mares were in first place on the way out,
but something must have happened to them; they must
have run into trouble. I saw them in front at the turn,

but now I no longer see them, though I have been looking
everywhere. Perhaps he lost hold of the reins
and couldn't control his horses around the post
and failed to complete the turn. He must have been thrown
and his chariot smashed, and his mares must have bolted in panic.
Look for yourselves. Though I can't be certain, the driver   480
in front appears to be an Ætólian . . .
a king of Argos . . . Tydeus's son: Diomedes."

Then Ajax the Smaller shouted out to him rudely,
"Idómeneus, you are always shooting your mouth off.
Those mares are still out on the plain, with a long way to go.
You must know that you aren't young anymore, and your eyes
aren't too sharp, but you are a goddamned loudmouth!
Why blabber about it like this, since so many men here
see better than you? I say that the horses in front
are the same ones that led before: Eumélus's horses,   490
and that he is still in his chariot, holding the reins."

The Cretan commander was furious, and he said,
"Ajax, you are a talented fellow at insults,
but at nothing else—the stupidest man among us
and the nastiest. Would you care to make a small wager?
I bet you a cauldron or tripod; let Agamemnon
referee. We will soon see who is the winner.
When you have to pay up, perhaps you will learn your lesson."

Then Ajax too was enraged and ready to utter
more abuse, and the quarrel would have gone further   500
if Achilles himself had not stood up then and said,
"Stop it now, Ajax. Idómeneus, you too: no more.
It is wrong of you both to attack each other like this.
You would each be the first to criticize anyone else
who acted this way. Now sit back down in your places
and look for the horses. Soon they will race across
the finish line, and each of you will be able
to see for yourself who wins and who comes in second."

*

Then Diomedes drove in; he was lashing his horses,
swinging the whip from his shoulder with all his might,   510
and the horses kicked high as they galloped on down the homestretch.
Sand and dirt kept swirling around the driver
and the gold- and tin-inlaid chariot seemed to fly
above the ground, and its wheels left hardly a trace
in the dust beneath. And when he arrived at the finish,
the sweat poured down from the necks and chests of the horses
and soaked the ground. And quickly he jumped from his car
and leaned his whip on the yoke, and his faithful attendant
Sthénelus lost no time in claiming the prizes.
He handed the woman over to his companions   520
and also gave them the tripod with ear-shaped handles
to take back with them, and then he unyoked the horses.

Antilochus drove in next to take second place,
having outstripped Menelaus by cunning, not speed.
But even so, Menelaus was close behind him;
the distance between a chariot wheel and a horse
when he gallops across the wide plain, pulling his driver,
the tip of his tail just brushing against the wheel rim
with hardly a space between them: that was how small
was the distance that Menelaus came in behind   530
Antilochus, after trailing him by as much as
a discus throw. But he closed the gap, and he almost
drew even, as Agamemnon's noble mare Æthē
showed her spirit; and if the race had been longer,
Menelaus would surely have passed him, beyond a doubt.
Next, Meriones came in, a spear throw behind;
his team was the slowest one in the race, and he
was the least skilled driver. And last of all was Eumélus,
who came in on foot, pulling his car behind him,
with his horses trotting in front. Achilles felt pity   540
when he saw him, and he stood up and said to the crowd,
"The man who is the best driver has come in last.
But I want to give him a prize, as is only fitting:
the second prize, since Diomedes was first."

*

When they heard this, they all assented to his idea;
and Achilles would have given the mare to Eumélus
with the army's consent if Antilochus had not stood up
and objected: "Achilles, I will be very angry
if you do what you have proposed. The prize should be mine.
You are going to rob me of it because Eumélus 550
got into trouble, although he is such a fine driver.
He should have prayed to the gods; if he had, he would never
have come in last. But since you are sorry for him
and like him so much, there is plenty of gold in your camp,
and bronze and sheep and serving-women and horses.
So choose something else. Give him an even better
prize later on, or right now; the troops will agree.
But I will not give up my mare. If anyone tries
to take her away, he will have to flatten me first."

When he heard these words, Achilles smiled in amusement 560
at the pluck of Antilochus, his companion, and said,
"Antilochus, if you want me to give Eumélus
some extra prize from my camp, I will certainly do that.
I will give him the breastplate I took from Asteropæus.
It is bronze, inlaid with a circle of shining tin,
and it is of very great value—a fitting prize."
And he told his comrade Automedon to go get it,
and he went to the hut and brought it back for Eumélus.

Then Menelaus stood up in the crowd, outraged
and furious at Antilochus, and a herald 570
placed the staff in his hand and shouted for silence,
and Menelaus addressed these words to the men:
"Antilochus, you were once a sensible fellow,
but look at what you have done. You have brought shame
on my valor and robbed me of victory, cutting in
across my path, though your horses are slower than mine.
I ask the commanders and captains of the Achaeans
to judge between us impartially, without favor,
so that no one will ever be able to say about this,
'Oh, Menelaus—the only way he could beat 580

Antilochus was by lying. That's how he walked
away with the mare. He lost; his horses were slower,
but later he took advantage of his high rank.'
Now I myself will propose a solution; I don't
think that any Achaean will find it unfair
or blame me for it. Antilochus, come here now
and in front of us take an oath, as custom decrees.
Stand here beside your team and your chariot, holding
the whip that you drove with, then put your hand on the horses
and swear by the god who encircles the earth and shakes it   590
that you didn't cut in on purpose and block my way."

Antilochus, that clear-minded man, responded,
"Bear with me now, sir; I am much younger than you,
and you, King Menelaus, my elder and better,
know very well how a young man can go too far;
sometimes his spirit will rush ahead of his judgment.
So be patient with me. I am perfectly willing to give up
the mare that I won and hand her over to you.
And if you demand some other, more costly token
of my esteem, I am more than ready to give it   600
immediately, rather than lose your favor
for all my days, and offend the immortal gods."

After he said this, he went and led the mare over
and gave her to Menelaus, whose heart was warmed
like drops of dew on the ears of the ripening grain
in spring, when the fields are bursting forth with new shoots:
just so, Menelaus, the heart in your breast was warmed.
And you looked at Antilochus, and you quickly responded,
"Antilochus, now it is my turn to give up my anger.
You have never been foolish or reckless before, but this time   610
your impulsiveness got the better of your discretion.
In the future, don't ever try to outsmart your elders.
Any other Achaean wouldn't have found me
so easy to placate, but you have worked hard and suffered
for my sake, and so have your noble father and brother.
So I will accept your apology and will give you

the mare, although she is mine, so that everyone here
can see that my heart isn't arrogant or vindictive."

With these words he handed over the mare to Noémon,
a friend of Antilochus. He himself took the cauldron,   620
and Meriones claimed the fourth prize, the two gold bars.
But nobody claimed the two-handled bowl, the fifth prize,
so Achilles gave it to Nestor. He walked through the crowd
with the bowl in his hands and gave it to him and said,
"Take this, sir, with my compliments. It is a treasure
to commemorate these funeral games for Patroclus,
whom you will not see again among the Achaeans.
I give you this prize as an honor, and not for winning
one of the contests, since you will not box or wrestle
or enter the spear-throwing contest or run in the foot race,   630
for the difficulties of old age lie heavy upon you."

And he placed the two-handled bowl in the hands of Nestor,
who accepted it with delight and said to Achilles,
"Your words about my old age, dear child, are true;
this body is not what it used to be. If only
I were still as strong as I was on that famous day
when King Amarýnceus was buried by the Epéans
at Buprásion, and his sons held games in his honor.
There was not a man who could match me among the Epéans
or the Ætólians or my comrades from Pylos.   640
In boxing I beat Clytomédes, the son of Enops,
and in wrestling, Ancǽus of Pleuron. Then in the foot race
I defeated Íphiclus, and in the spear-throwing contest
I threw even farther than Phyleus or Polydórus.
It was only at chariot racing that I was beaten—
by the sons of Actor, two against one; they were twins,
and they forged ahead of me, lashing their horses, trying
everything they could come up with, so desperately
did they want to win, since that race had the biggest prize;
one of them did the driving and lashed the horses   650
with the reins, while the other kept lashing them with his whip.
Well, that is the kind of fellow I used to be.

Nowadays I must leave these things to the young ones
and bow to old age—though in *my* time, as I have said,
I was the best among some very great men.
But go now, see to these games in your comrade's honor.
I accept your gift with much pleasure, and I am delighted
that you think of me as a friend and never forget
the respect that I should be paid among the Achaeans.
May the gods, in return for this, grant you your heart's desire."   660

When Achilles had listened to everything Nestor said,
he went back through the assembly, and he brought out
the prizes for the next contest, the boxing match.
For the winner he set out and tethered a female mule,
unbroken and six years old (which is an age
when it is hardest to break them), and for the loser
a two-handled cup. And he stood and said to the men,
"Son of Atreus, and you Achaean commanders,
these are the prizes for boxing. We need two men,
the best among you, to put up their fists and begin.   670
The one who is granted endurance by Lord Apollo,
whom all of you judge the winner, can take this mule
as his prize, and the loser will get the two-handled cup."

At these words Epéüs, son of Panópeus, stood up,
a tall, powerful man and an excellent boxer.
He put his hand on the back of the mule and said,
"If anyone wants the cup, let him step forward.
The mule is mine; no other Achaean will win her
by beating me in this match, since I am the greatest.
I may not be such a good warrior—no one is good   680
at everything—but I can assure you all
that whoever stands up against me will never win.
I will quickly pulverize him and crush his bones.
His friends had better be ready to cart him away
to his own funeral, once I have finished with him,
since certainly they will find him more dead than alive."

When he had spoken, no one could say a word.

Only Eurýalus dared to stand up against him;
he was the son of Mecísteus, who had once
come to the city of Thebes for the funeral games   690
when Œdipus fell, and he won all the prizes there.
And Diomedes went over (he was his cousin),
and volunteered as his second, and he was eager
for him to win, and he helped him prepare for the match.
First he set out a loincloth for him, then bound
oxhide thongs on his hands. And when the two men
were ready, they walked out into the center, put up
their fists, and began to punch, and the blows fell quickly.
There was a terrible cracking of jaws, and the sweat poured
down their bodies. And then, as Eurýalus looked   700
for an opening, Epéüs rushed in and hit him
full on the cheek. He was lifted up off the ground
like a fish that leaps from the shallow seaweed-strewn waters
and falls back into the dark waves: just so did he leap,
and his legs collapsed underneath him, and down he fell.
But generously Epéüs gave him a hand
and pulled him again to his feet; and his comrades gathered
and led him out through the crowd with his legs dragging,
spitting out blood, and his bruised head hung to one side.
They sat him down in their midst, and he was so groggy   710
that they themselves had to claim the two-handled cup.

And Achilles brought out the prizes for the third contest,
the wrestling match, and showed them to the Achaeans:
for the winner, a large tripod to stand on the fire—
its value was set at twelve oxen; and for the loser
he placed in their midst a woman skilled in the arts
of spinning and weaving, valued as worth four oxen.
And then he made this announcement to the assembly:
"Two of you, stand up now to compete for the prize."

When he heard this, Ajax the Tall, Télamon's son,   720
stood up, and so did Odysseus, master of cunning.
They put on their belts and walked out into the center,
and they took each other's arms in their powerful grips

and stood like steep-angled rafters joined by a builder
in the roof of a house to keep out the whistling winds.
Their backs creaked under the pressure of massive hands,
and the sweat poured down, and blood-red welts rose along
their shoulders and ribs, but they struggled on for the tripod.
Odysseus was as unable to throw his opponent
as Ajax was, and both men's bodies stood firm.   730
But when the assembly began to grow bored and restless,
Ajax said, "Son of Laértes, let us now try
a different way: I will lift you first, and then you
try to lift *me*—the rest will be up to Zeus."

With these words he lifted him off the ground. But Odysseus
did not forget his cunning; with a swift kick
in the back of the knee, he caught the huge man and knocked
the legs out from under him. Ajax collapsed and fell
backward onto the ground, and Odysseus landed
on top of his chest, and the crowd looked on in amazement.   740
Then in his turn Odysseus struggled to lift him.
He slightly shifted his weight off the ground but could not
lift him clear, so he hooked a leg quickly around
Ajax's knee, and the two of them toppled over
and lay side by side, and both were filthy with dust.
And they rose and would have wrestled for the third time
if Achilles had not stood up and told them to stop:
"End the match now, and don't exhaust yourselves further.
You have both won. You both deserve equal prizes.
Take them and go, so that other men can compete."   750
They listened to his decision, and both agreed,
and they wiped off the dirt from their bodies and put on their tunics.

Next was the foot race. Achilles set out the prizes:
the first was a silver mixing bowl, beautifully crafted,
which held six gallons—by far the loveliest bowl
in the world, a masterpiece made by Sidónian craftsmen.
It had been brought into port by Phoenician traders
over the misty sea; when they disembarked,
they had given it to King Thoas, whose grandson Eunéüs,

the son of Jason, had given it to Patroclus   760
as the ransom price for Lycáon, the son of Priam.
And now Achilles was putting it out as the first prize
for the fastest runner, in honor of his dead friend.
As the second prize, he brought out a well-fattened ox,
a large one, and as the last prize a half-bar of gold.
Then he stood up and announced the event to the Argives:
"All those who wish to compete for this prize, come forward."
When he heard this, Ajax the Smaller stood up, that quick man,
and Odysseus too, and Antilochus, Nestor's son,
who of all the younger men was the fastest runner.   770
They took their places along the starting line, side
by side, and Achilles showed them the turning-post.
Then, at the signal, they all flew off at full speed,
and right away Ajax surged out in front, but Odysseus
kept close behind him, as close as the weaving-rod
comes to the breast of a woman who carefully pulls it
toward her and draws the spool through the opening, past
the warp, and the rod comes almost to touch her: so close
did Odysseus follow. His feet stepped in Ajax's footprints
before the dust settled into them, and his warm breath   780
from inches behind streamed down onto Ajax's head.
All the Achaeans kept cheering him on and shouting
encouragement as they saw him straining his utmost.

But when they were in the homestretch, Odysseus made
a silent prayer to Athena: "Hear me now, goddess.
Be kind and come to my aid and lighten my feet."
These were the words of his prayer, and Athena heard him
and gave him fresh power and quickened his arms and legs.
And as they approached the finish line, Ajax slipped;
Athena had tripped him. The ground was strewn with the dung   790
of the bellowing cattle Achilles had slaughtered to make
Patroclus's funeral feast, and Ajax's mouth
and nostrils were stuffed with dung. Odysseus shot past
and finished first, and he went up to claim the bowl.
Ajax took second place, and as he stood there
with his hands on one of the horns of the fattened ox,

spitting out dung, he shouted to the Achaeans,
"It was *her* fault—she tripped me, that goddess who always stands
at Odysseus's side and cares for him like a mother."
These were his words, and the audience burst out laughing.   800

Antilochus claimed the last prize, smiling, and said,
"Friends, I will tell you all something you know already:
To this day the gods still favor the older men.
Ajax is only a little older than I am,
but Odysseus is of an earlier generation.
He is a tough old bird, as they say; it is hard
for any of us to beat him, except for Achilles."
With these words he honored Peleus's swift-footed son.

Achilles answered, "Your words won't go unrewarded;
I will add to your prize another half-bar of gold."   810
And he handed the gold to Antilochus, who was delighted.

And next Achilles set out before the assembly
a massive spear, and with it a shield and helmet,
the arms of Sarpedon—Patroclus had taken them from him.
He stood up now and announced the event to the Argives:
"We invite two men to come forward, the best ones among you,
to fight for these prizes: to put on their armor, take spears,
and test each other's prowess in front of the troops.
The first one to make a hit on the other's body
will receive from me this beautiful silver-bossed sword,   820
fashioned in Thrace, which I took from Asteropǽus.
Both combatants can share the armor between them,
and then I will offer them both a feast in my hut."

When they heard this, Ajax the Tall, Télamon's son,
and the son of Tydeus, Diomedes, stood up.
And when the two men had armed and taken their weapons,
they walked out into the center, eager to fight,
both glaring fiercely. Excitement seized all who watched.
When they had come within range and were facing each other,
three times they charged and lunged, and after three lunges   830

Ajax hit Diomedes' shield, but the spear did not touch him;
his breastplate stopped it. And Diomedes kept thrusting
over the huge shield of Ajax, right at his neck
with the point of his shining spear. And now the Achaeans
were frightened for Ajax and shouted for them to stop
and share the prizes. Achilles, though, gave the great sword
to Diomedes, along with its sheath and a sword strap
of figured leather, as a reward for his valor.

Then he set out a huge lump of rough-cast iron,
which had been King Ëétion's once, who was strong enough   840
to be able to use it himself in weight-throwing contests.
When Achilles plundered his town, he had taken this with him
on his ships, along with many other rich spoils.
He stood up now and announced the event to the Argives:
"All those who wish to compete for this prize, come forward.
The winner of this will have enough iron for five years,
however distant his fields are—no shepherd or plowman
of his will have to go into town to get iron,
since this will provide him with everything that he needs."

When he finished, four huge and powerful men stood up: 850
Polypœtes, Leónteus, Ajax the Tall, and Epéüs.
They stood in a row, and Epéüs picked up the weight,
swung it and threw, and the audience burst into laughter.
The second to throw was Leónteus. Ajax went third,
hurling it well beyond the marks of the others.
But when Polypœtes picked up the weight and threw it,
it sailed out over the whole space marked for the contest,
as far as a herdsman can send his throwing-stick when
he flings it and it goes spinning among the cattle.
The troops cried out in amazement; and Polypœtes'   860
comrades stood up and carried the prize to their ships.

Achilles then brought out the archery prizes: ten iron
double-edged axes and ten with a single edge.
He set up the mast of a blue-prowed ship, at a distance,
in the sand of the seashore, and had a dove tethered to it

by a thin cord around her foot, and he told the crowd
that she was the target: "Whichever contestant hits her
can take all the double-edged axes home as his prize.
And if someone misses the bird but still hits the cord,
he will win second prize and take home the single axes."   870

When he heard these words, Lord Teucer stood up, and so did
Meriones, Lord Idómeneus's attendant.
They took two lots and shook them in a bronze helmet,
and Teucer drew the first place, and he aimed and shot
an arrow that flew straight up to the dove; but he had
forgotten to promise a sacrifice to Apollo,
so he missed the bird—Apollo grudged him the prize.
But he did hit the cord that tied the bird by her foot.
His arrow cut through it; the dove flew away, up into
the sky, and the cord hung down, and the audience cheered.   880
But Meriones snatched the bow from Teucer's hands quickly
(he was already holding an arrow), took aim,
and vowed to the lord Apollo, who strikes from afar,
to sacrifice a hundred fat lambs in his honor.
Then high up under the clouds he spotted the dove.
As she circled around, he shot, and the arrow hit her
below the wing and passed through and fell back down
and stuck in the ground in front of Meriones' feet.
The bird's head drooped, and her wings went slack, and the life
fluttered out of her body, and down she fell,   890
far from the mast; and the crowd looked on in amazement.
And Meriones went and claimed the double-edged axes,
while Teucer took the single ones back to his ships.

And now Achilles set out before the assembly
a massive spear and a cauldron untouched by fire
(it was worth one ox), with a pattern of flowers on it.
Two men stood up to compete in the spear-throwing contest:
the son of Atreus, wide-ruling Agamemnon,
and Meriones, Lord Idómeneus's attendant.
And Achilles said, "Son of Atreus, we all know   900
that no one can match your strength in throwing the spear.

So take this prize and carry it back to your ships.
And let us award the spear to Meriones,
if that is acceptable. This is what I propose."

When he heard these words, Agamemnon did as he said.
He gave the bronze spear to Meriones, and he handed
his own splendid prize to Talthýbius, his herald.

Book 24

The assembly broke up, and the troops all scattered and went
back to their own ships. Everyone else was thinking
of supper and then the pleasure of sleep; but Achilles
wept as he remembered his dear companion,
and all-mastering sleep could not hold him: he tossed and turned;
now he would lie on his side, now on his back,
now on his face, then finally he would get up
and, desolate, pace the length of the seashore until
dawn arrived to light up the sea and the beaches.
Then he would yoke his chariot and tie Hector   10
to the back of it and drag him three times around
Patroclus's tomb, then go to his hut to rest,
leaving Hector stretched out face down in the dirt.
But Apollo pitied the man although he was dead,
and protected him, covering him with the golden storm shield
so his body would not be torn as the chariot dragged him.

And so Achilles kept trying to mutilate him
day after day; but the gods felt pity for Hector,
and they even asked Hermes to steal the corpse. But while this
found favor with all the others, it did not please Hera   20
or Poseidon or the gray-eyed daughter of Zeus;
they hated the Trojans as passionately as they did
on the day when Paris committed that act of madness.

But when the twelfth dawn after Hector's death had arrived,
Apollo spoke up and said to the other immortals,
"You are hard-hearted, all of you—and ungrateful as well.
Did Hector never make sacrifices to you,
burning the thighs of unblemished oxen and goats?
Yet now you won't even bother to save his body
for his wife to see and his mother and his small child   30
and his father, Priam, and all his people, who quickly
would burn him and give him the proper funeral rites.

Instead, you favor Achilles, that ruthless man
whose heart is devoid of all decency. He will never
bend; he rages as savagely as a lion
who, giving in to his arrogance and his power,
goes out to feast on the flocks of mortals: just so
Achilles has lost all pity, all sense of shame.
He is not, after all, the first man to have a friend die:
men have lost loved ones before, who were even closer   40
than this man was—a brother, perhaps, or a son,
and they wept and mourned for their dead, and then it was over,
since the Fates have put an enduring heart in mankind.
But this man has taken Hector's life and now ties him
to the back of his car and drags him around the tomb
of his dear companion, as if that will do him some good.
Great as he is, he ought to beware of our anger."

Then Hera, furious, answered, "Even in *your* words,
lord of the silver bow, there might be some truth
if the gods meant to honor Hector as much as Achilles.   50
But Hector is a mere mortal, who grew up suckling
a woman's breast, while Achilles was born of a goddess.
I myself brought her up and gave her in marriage
to Peleus, a man who was very dear to the gods,
and all of you came to their wedding. And so did you,
Apollo, friend of the wicked; you sat at the banquet
with the rest of us, in your treachery, strumming your lyre."

And Lord Zeus answered her, "Hera, don't be so angry.
These two mortals will never be shown the same honor.
And yet of all the people in Ilion, Hector   60
was dearest to the immortals. He certainly was
dearest to me, since he always offered me gifts
and never withheld the abundant feast from my altar,
the wine spilled for me, the savor of burning fat—
oblations that are the honors due to us gods.
But stealing Hector's body is out of the question.
In any case, it cannot be done, since Achilles
would know it; his mother is constantly at his side,

night and day. But one of the gods should tell her
to come here. I have a sensible plan: for Achilles   70
to accept a ransom from Priam and give back the body."

Swift as the storm wind, Iris left with his message.
And midway between the island of Sámothrace
and rocky Imbros, she leaped down into the waves,
and the sea crashed moaning around her, and down she plunged
into the depths, like the lead weight tied to the end
of an angler's line that brings death to the hungry fish.
Thetis was in her cave with the other sea nymphs
gathered around her, and in their midst she was weeping
for her handsome son, who soon was fated to die   80
on the plains of Ilion, far from his own dear country.
Iris quickly approached and said to her, "Thetis,
Zeus in his infinite wisdom summons you. Come."

Thetis answered her, "What does Zeus want with *me*?
I am ashamed to visit the gods on Olympus,
so measureless is the sorrow that grips my heart.
But of course I will go and do whatever he tells me."

With these words the goddess snatched up a shawl, the darkest
one that she had, and Iris, swift as the wind,
led the way, and the sea surge parted before them.   90
Quickly they came out on shore, and quickly they flew
into the sky, and there they found Zeus, with the other
blessed eternal gods assembled around him.
Athena gave up her place, and Thetis sat down
beside Father Zeus, then Hera placed in her hand
a beautiful golden cup and welcomed her gently,
and Thetis drank from the cup, then returned it to Hera.

The father of men and gods was the first to speak:
"Welcome, Thetis. You came in spite of your sorrow.
I know what incurable anguish you must be feeling.   100
Still, I will tell you why I have called you here.
For nine days the gods have been quarreling over Achilles

and the body of Hector; they even want Hermes to steal it.
Instead, I intend to honor Achilles greatly
in order to keep your respect and the friendship we have.
Quickly now, go to your son's camp and bring him this message:
Tell him that we are displeased with what he is doing
and that in particular I am exceedingly angry
that in his rage he still keeps the body of Hector
beside his ships and refuses to give it back.   110
Perhaps he will listen and, fearing me, will release it.
I will also send Iris down to King Priam, to tell him
he must go to the Argive ships with a fitting ransom
of splendid gifts that will soften Achilles' heart."

When she heard the command of her father, Thetis was quick
to do his bidding. Down from the peaks of Olympus
she flew, and she came to Achilles' hut, where she found him
heartsick with grief, while all around him his comrades
were bustling about, preparing their morning meal,
cooking the meat from a large ram they had just slaughtered.   120
She entered the hut and went and sat down beside him
and stroked his hair and spoke to him softly: "Child,
how long will you gnaw your own heart with sorrow and longing
and not think of food or rest? Yet it would do you
good to make love with a woman. You will not live
much longer; already your fated death is here, standing
close by. But listen; I bring you a message from Zeus.
He says that the gods are displeased with what you are doing
and that in particular he is exceedingly angry
that in your rage you still keep the body of Hector   130
beside your ships, refusing to give it back.
Let go of it now. Accept a ransom. Return it."

Achilles answered, "Let somebody bring the ransom
and take the body, if that is what Zeus commands."

As mother and son continued their conversation,
Lord Zeus sent Iris down to the city of Troy:
"Hurry, Iris, and leave Olympus right now.

Fly down to Troy with an urgent message for Priam.
Tell him to go to the ships with a fitting ransom
of splendid gifts that will soften Achilles' heart.   140
He must go alone; let no other man go with him
but one of the older heralds to drive the mules
and the four-wheeled cart that will carry back to the city
the dead man there, the one that Achilles cut down.
He shouldn't fear death or have any fear whatsoever.
We will give him a guide: Hermes, the finest of escorts,
who will lead him in safety, through the wide camp, to Achilles.
And when he has led him into Achilles' hut,
that man won't kill him, nor will he let anyone harm him;
he isn't a madman, a fool, or an evildoer,   150
but will treat a suppliant kindly and spare his life."

Swift as the storm-wind, Iris left with his message.
She came to the house of Priam, where she heard moaning
and lamentation. His sons were all sitting near him
within the courtyard, their clothing wet with their tears,
and the old king was hunched up, wrapped head-to-toe in his cloak,
his face and neck caked with the dung he had rolled around in
and smeared on himself. His daughters and his sons' wives
were wailing throughout the palace, thinking of all
their dear ones who had been slaughtered by the Achaeans.   160
Iris came up and addressed him now, and she spoke
softly; yet his whole body began to tremble.
"Take courage, Priam, and don't be afraid. I have come here
to bring you a message—not about anything harmful
but something good. I bring you a message from Zeus,
who pities and loves you, although he is far away.
He commands you to go to the ships with a fitting ransom
of splendid gifts that will soften Achilles' heart.
You must go alone, and nobody must go with you
but one of the older heralds to drive the mules   170
and the four-wheeled cart that will carry back to the city
the dead man there, the one that Achilles cut down.
You shouldn't fear death, or have any fear whatsoever;
he will give you a guide: Hermes, the finest of escorts,

who will lead you in safety, through the wide camp, to Achilles.
And when he has led you into Achilles' hut,
that man won't kill you, nor will he let anyone harm you;
he isn't a madman, a fool, or an evildoer,
but will treat a suppliant kindly and spare your life."

When Iris had delivered this message, she left him.   180
And Priam ordered his sons to bring out a mule cart
with a large wicker receptacle fastened on top,
and then he went down into the fragrant storeroom,
high-roofed and lined with cedar and bright with his treasures,
and he summoned his wife. When Hecuba came, he said,
"My dear, a goddess has brought me a message from Zeus.
I must go at once to the ships with a fitting ransom
of splendid gifts that will soften Achilles' heart.
But I want to know your opinion: what do *you* think?
As for myself, my heart fiercely commands me   190
to go down and enter the wide camp of the Achaeans."

At these words, Hecuba let out a shriek and answered,
"Good god! Are you out of your mind? Where is your wisdom,
which once was famous all over the earth? How can
you think of going alone to stand face to face
with the man who slaughtered so many of your brave sons?
Your heart must be made of iron. If that man gets you
within his grasp—but he is a savage beast
and not a man—he will kill you without even blinking.
Please don't go. We can mourn for our son right here   200
as we sit in our own house. This must be what Fate spun
when I gave him birth: to be food for the wild dogs,
far from his parents. That butcher! If I could get
my hands on him, I would tear out his liver and eat it
raw! That would give me some small revenge for my son,
who wasn't a coward when he was killed, but was holding
his ground in defense of the men and the women of Troy,
and did not think of running away or hiding."

Then, in response to her, Priam, the old king, said,

"I have made up my mind, so don't be an evil omen;   210
you can't convince me to stay, however you plead.
If any human had told me to go to Achilles—
some prophet or priest—I would have called him a liar.
But I heard the goddess's voice; I saw her myself
with my own eyes. So of course I must do what she told me.
And if I am fated to die near the Argive ships,
so be it. Achilles can slaughter me once I have taken
my son in my arms and wept to my heart's content."

With these words he lifted the lid of his storage chests
and took twelve beautiful robes and twelve long cloaks,   220
and an equal number of covers, white capes, and tunics,
and two gleaming tripods, four cauldrons, and one large cup
of exquisite beauty, given to him by the Thracians
when he went to that land on an embassy. It was a priceless
treasure, but Priam did not withhold even this,
so powerful was his desire to ransom his son.
Then he dismissed all the people waiting around
the colonnade, and rebuked them with shaming words:
"You disgraces! Failures! Get out! Don't you have loved ones
to mourn for in your own homes without coming here   230
and causing me grief? Do you think it isn't enough
that Zeus has brought me this sorrow and I have lost
the best of my sons? His death means ruin for Troy,
as you will soon learn for yourselves. Without his protection,
there is nothing that stands between us and the Argives' fury.
I only hope I am dead and in Hades before
my city is burned to the ground and my people slaughtered."

As he said this, he drove them out with his staff, and they fled
from the old king's anger. Then he called to his sons,
rebuking them too: Hélenus, Paris, Pammon,   240
Ágathon and Antíphonus and Polítes,
Deíphobus, Hippóthoüs, and Dius.
He shouted at these nine sons and gave them his orders:
"Move now, you sorry excuses for men. If only
the lot of you had been cut down instead of Hector!

How wretched I am! I fathered the bravest men
in the land of Troy, yet not one remains alive—
not Mestor or Troilus or Hector, that god among men,
who seemed like the son of a god, not of a mortal.
All of them fell in this war, and now I am left   250
with cowards, liars, pretty-boys, heroes at dancing,
parasites, loungers, robbers of lambs and kids,
who live off the people's sweat. Do I have to beg you?
Would your lordships be so kind as to bring me a mule cart
and load it with all these things, so that I can get started?"

Terrified by their father's rebuke, they brought out
a four-wheeled mule cart, a fine one, newly constructed,
and tied the wicker receptacle onto its back.
Then from a peg they took down the boxwood mule yoke
with a knob in the middle, fitted with rings for rein guides,   260
and with it they brought out a strap that was twelve feet long
for binding the yoke. They set the yoke carefully down
onto the polished shaft in the notch at the front end,
slipped the bronze yoke ring onto its pin, then bound
the strap three times around the knob on each side,
wound it over and over, all the way down
the shaft, then tucked the loose end beneath the tongue.
Then they went down to the storeroom and brought out the glorious
ransom for Hector's body and piled the treasures
onto the cart, then yoked the two powerful mules,   270
a splendid gift that the Mysians had given Priam.
And they wheeled out his chariot, and they yoked the two horses
that he kept for his own use and fed at his polished manger.

And so the herald and Priam, with many thoughts
in their minds, stood there as the teams were yoked in the courtyard.
And Hecuba, troubled at heart, came up to them, bringing
a golden cup that was filled with heart-cheering wine
in her right hand, for Priam to pour out before he left.
In front of the horses she gave it to him and said,
"Take this, and make a libation to Father Zeus.   280
Pray that you come back safe from the enemy, since

your heart commands you to go to the ships, although
I don't approve of it. Pray to the son of Cronus,
the lord of the dark clouds, who has his abode on Mount Ida
and looks on the whole land of Troy as it spreads beneath him.
Ask for his swift-flying messenger to appear—
the mightiest of all birds and the dearest to him.
If it flies to your right, you will know that you have his favor
and in confidence can go to the Argive ships.
But if Zeus doesn't send you his messenger, then I beg you   290
to stay here in Troy, however you long to go."

Then, in response to her, Priam, the old king, said,
"I will do what you say, my dear—of course. It is always
good to lift up one's hands and ask Zeus for mercy."

With these words he told his housekeeper to pour
clear water over his hands. She quickly came up
and stood beside him, bringing a jug and a basin.
He washed his hands, then took the cup from his wife
and stood in the courtyard and poured out wine to the gods.
And looking to heaven, he lifted his hands and prayed: 300
"Zeus, our father, you who rule from Mount Ida,
most glorious king, now grant that Achilles receive me
with kindness and mercy. Send me a bird of good omen;
let your swift-flying messenger now appear—
the mightiest of all birds and the dearest to you.
If it flies to my right, I will know that I have your favor
and in confidence I can go to the Argive ships."

That was his prayer, and in his wisdom Zeus heard him,
and quickly he sent an eagle, the surest omen
among all birds—his favorite, the dark one, the hunter.   310
As wide as the massive doors in the high-ceilinged room
of a rich man's house: so wide did its wings spread out
as it flew to the right. And everyone's heart was elated.

The old king quickly mounted his chariot and passed
out through the gates and the echoing colonnade.

In front was the mule team, pulling the four-wheeled cart,
which Idæus drove, that sensible man, and behind them
were the horses. The old king whipped them into a trot,
and they drove through the streets. His family all followed, weeping
and mourning, as though he were going off to his death.   320

But when they passed through the gates and arrived at the plain,
his sons and sons-in-law turned and went back to Troy.
Zeus was watching the two men as they began
crossing the plain; he saw the old king and felt pity,
and quickly he gave this command to his dear son Hermes:
"Hermes, you above all gods delight in befriending
mortals, and you are happy to answer their prayers.
So go down to Troy; guide Priam across the plain
to the Argive camp and make sure that nobody sees him
until he has safely arrived at Achilles' hut."   330

Right away Hermes did as Zeus had commanded.
He laced to his feet the beautiful golden sandals
that could fly him across the water and over the earth
as fast as the wind, and he picked up the rod that spellbinds
the eyes of men and puts them to sleep or wakes them;
and holding it lightly, he flew in an instant to Troy.
From there he proceeded on foot, and he took the form
of a handsome young prince, with the first slight traces of hair
on his lips and cheeks, in the loveliest prime of youth.

And when the two men were past the great tomb of Ilus,   340
they halted their mules and horses to let them drink
at the river, since darkness was fast coming on. And the herald
looked and saw Hermes approach, and he said to Priam,
"Be careful now, Sire. Danger is looming ahead.
I see an Argive who may be coming to kill us.
Let us escape in the chariot, leaving the cart—
or else let us clasp his knees and beg him for mercy."

At these words the old king's mind was filled with confusion.
The hairs stood on end all over his body, and he

waited there in a daze. But when Hermes came closer,   350
he stood beside Priam and took his hand and said gently,
"Where are you headed, Father, leading your mules
and horses like this in the dead of night, while all other
mortals are sleeping? Don't you feel frightened now
of your enemies, those violent men, the Achaeans?
You are coming into their camp, and if one of them saw you
bringing such treasures here through the swift black night,
what would you do then? You are no longer young,
and your driver is an old man and cannot defend you
if anyone picks a fight. You are lucky I came;   360
I will protect you and keep off any Achaean
who threatens you. You remind me of my own father."

Then, in response to him, Priam, the old king, said,
"Thank you, dear child. What you have spoken is true.
One of the gods must be holding his hand above me,
at least for the moment, to send you here. You have come
to me as a good omen, and I am encouraged
by your wondrous beauty, your well-spokenness, and your mind's
intelligence. How blessed your parents must be!"

Then Hermes, the cunning guide of travelers, said,   370
"That is quite true, sir; you don't know how right you are.
But speak to me in all frankness, and answer my question:
Are you sending these splendid treasures out of the country
for safekeeping? Are you all abandoning Troy
because your bravest fighter is dead, your dear son,
who stood as your greatest champion against the Achaeans?"

Then, in response to him, Priam, the old king, said,
"Who *are* you, my good young friend? Who are your parents?
You have spoken such noble things of my ill-fated son!"

Then Hermes, the cunning guide of travelers, said,   380
"You are testing me, sir; you want to know about Hector.
Well, I have seen him in battle with my own eyes,
many times. I have seen him forcing the Argives

back to the ships and killing them with his spear.
We all stood by, and we marveled at him; Achilles
was holding us back, in his anger at Lord Agamemnon.
I know Achilles—am one of his close attendants;
I came to Troy on the same ship that carried him here.
I am one of the Myrmidons, and my father is named
Polýctor. He is a rich man, as old as you are.   390
He has six other sons at home with him; I am the seventh,
and when we drew lots, I was chosen to sail here. Now
I have come to the plain to prepare for tomorrow's battle.
The Achaeans intend to attack the city at dawn.
They are tired of waiting, and they are so eager to fight
that their commanders can no longer hold them back."

Then, in response to him, Priam, the old king, said,
"If you really are Lord Achilles' attendant, tell me:
Is my son still there, or has Lord Achilles hacked him
limb from limb and given him to the dogs?"   400

Then Hermes, the cunning guide of travelers, said,
"Sir, he has not been eaten by dogs or birds.
He is inside Achilles' hut, still looking exactly
as he looked when he died. This is now the twelfth day
he has been there, and yet his body has not decayed,
nor have the worms that feed on men killed in battle
begun to chew it. Each day when dawn appears,
Achilles brutally drags him around the tomb
of his comrade, but so far he hasn't damaged the body.
In fact, you would be astonished to see how alive   410
it seems, as it lies there. It looks as fresh as the dew.
Every wound on the flesh has been healed completely,
though many Achaeans stabbed it. Such is the care
that the blessed gods have shown for your dear son, even
for his dead body—so close is he to their hearts."

When he heard these words, the old king rejoiced and said,
"My child, it is truly a good thing to give the immortals
the gifts that are due them. My son (if he ever existed)

didn't neglect to honor the gods in our home,
and so they have cared for him now, if only in death.   420
But here: accept this beautiful cup, with my thanks,
and please escort me—with the gods' help, of course—
safely, until I come to Achilles' hut."

Then Hermes, the cunning guide of travelers, said,
"You are testing me, sir, because I am younger than you are.
But I cannot accept a present from you behind
Achilles' back. I fear and respect him too much
to rob him of what is his; there would be trouble
for me if I did. But I am most willing to serve
as your escort—if need be, all the way back to Achaea—   430
and will take good care of you, whether on ship or on foot.
No one will dare to attack you if I am here."

He leaped on the car, took hold of the whip and reins,
and breathed great power into the mules and horses.
When they reached the fortifications around the ships,
between the wall and the trench, where the sentries were busy
preparing their supper, Hermes poured sleep on them all,
then quickly pulled back the bar and opened the gate
and drove Priam in, along with the cartload of treasures.

They soon reached Achilles' quarters—a high building   440
that the Myrmidons had constructed for him of pinewood
and roofed with the shaggy thatch they had reaped in the meadows.
They had made a large courtyard around it and fenced it in
with stakes set closely together. The gate was fastened
by a single huge beam of pinewood, which took three men,
straining with all their might, to push in or draw back;
but Achilles could move it easily by himself.
Now Hermes opened it and drove into the courtyard
with the cart that held the glorious gifts for Achilles.
And then he jumped to the ground, and he said to Priam,   450
"The truth is, sir, that I am a god—I am Hermes.
My father sent me to go with you as your guide.
Now I must hurry back. I mustn't appear

in Achilles' hut, since it would be most offensive
for one of the gods to be welcomed like that by a mortal.
But go in yourself now. Clasp his knees and entreat him."
With this he departed and flew back up to Olympus.

Priam got down from the car and went to Idæus,
and leaving him in charge of the mules and horses
he walked straight across the courtyard and reached the house   460
where Achilles most often was. He found him inside.
The rest of his men were sitting apart, but two—
Automedon and Álcimus—were nearby,
waiting on him. He had just finished his supper,
and the table was still there. Priam walked in, unseen,
and went to Achilles. He clasped his knees, then he kissed
his terrible hands, the deadly hands that had slaughtered
so many of Priam's sons. As when a man
who is gripped by madness murders someone in his homeland
and escapes to another country and then seeks refuge   470
in the house of some lord, and all who look on are astounded:
just so was Achilles astounded when he saw Priam,
that godlike man. And everyone in the hut
was astounded as well, and they looked around at each other.

Then Priam spoke to Achilles in supplication:
"Remember your father, Achilles. He is an old man
like me, approaching the end of his life. Perhaps
he too is being worn down by enemy troops,
with no one there to protect him from chaos and ruin.
Yet he at least, since he knows that you are alive,   480
feels joy in his heart and, every day, can look forward
to seeing his child, whom he loves so dearly, come home.
My fate is less happy. I fathered the bravest men
in the land of Troy, yet not one remains alive.
I had fifty sons before the Achaeans came here,
nineteen from a single woman, and all the rest
were borne to me by other wives in my palace.
Most of my sons have been killed in this wretched war.
The only one I could truly count on, the one

who guarded our city and all its people—you killed him   490
a few days ago as he fought to defend his country:
Hector. It is for his sake that I have come,
to beg you for his release. I have brought a large ransom.
Respect the gods now. Have pity on me; remember
your father. For I am more to be pitied than he is,
since I have endured what no mortal ever endured:
I have kissed the hands of the man who slaughtered my children."

With these words he stirred in Achilles a wild longing
to weep for his father. Taking the old man's hand,
he gently pushed him away. And each of them sat there   500
remembering. Priam, crouched at Achilles' feet,
sobbed for Hector; Achilles wept now for his father,
now for Patroclus. And every room in the house
rang with the sound of their mourning and lamentation.

But when Achilles had had enough, and the aching
sorrow had eased from his mind and body, he stood
and took Priam's hand and lifted him from the ground;
and with pity for his white hair and white beard, he said,
"Unfortunate man, what grief you have had to endure!
Sit down on this chair, and let us both rest from our tears.   510
Heart-chilling anguish can do us no good. The immortals
have spun out the thread of life for us human beings
so that, however we can, we must learn to bear
misfortune like this, but *they* live free of all sorrow.
There are two urns in the house of almighty Zeus,
one of them filled with evil, the other with blessings.
If Zeus pours gifts for a man from both of these urns,
he sometimes encounters evil, sometimes good fortune.
But when Zeus pours gifts from the urn of misery only,
he makes a man hate his life, and a ravenous hunger   520
drives him restlessly over the shining earth,
and he wanders alone, despised by both gods and mortals.
Consider Peleus. All his life, from the start,
the gods gave him splendid gifts; he surpassed all men
in power and wealth and was king of the Myrmidons,

and though he was mortal, they gave him a goddess as wife.
Yet even on him a god brought evil, because
no sons were born in his house to take over his kingdom:
only a single child, who was doomed to die early,
and I am not able to care for him in his old age.   530
I am idly sitting around in the land of Troy,
a long way from home, a curse to you and your children.
And you too, sir—we hear that you once were happy.
Men say that in all the lands of your realm, from Lesbos
in the south, where Macar ruled, and to Phrygia eastward,
and northward and westward as far as the Hellespont,
you reigned supreme, with vast wealth and many children.
But ever since the immortals brought you these troubles,
there is ceaseless fighting and slaughter around the walls
of your great city. It is something that you must bear.   540
Even if you should endlessly grieve for your son,
it would do no good; you will never restore him to life
before some other new misery comes upon you."

Then, in response to him, Priam, the old king, said,
"Don't ask me to sit, my lord, while Hector is still
lying uncared-for inside your hut. Release him
quickly and let me see him with my own eyes.
Accept the great ransom I bring here. May you enjoy it
and return home safely, because you have spared my life."

Achilles answered him then, with an angry scowl,   550
"Don't push me too far, sir. I have already decided
to release Hector's body to you, since Zeus commands it.
He sent me word; the messenger was my own mother,
the daughter of the Old Man of the Sea. And also
I am well aware, Priam—you haven't hidden it from me—
that some god escorted you here to the Argive ships.
No mortal would dare to come to our camp. However
young and strong he might be, he would never get past
the sentries or push back the beam that fastens our gate.
So do not provoke my grieving heart any further,   560
or else, disobeying Zeus's command, I may not

spare even you, sir—suppliant though you are."

The old man, recoiling in terror, at once sat down.
Then, like a lion, Achilles sprang out the door,
not alone: two attendants followed his steps,
Automedon and Álcimus, whom Achilles
loved more than any comrade except for Patroclus.
They unyoked the horses and mules, then brought in the herald
and seated him on a stool. Then from the cart
they unloaded the magnificent ransom for Hector,   570
leaving two robes and a tunic there, for Achilles
to put on the body and wrap around it, before
he presented it for the old king to carry home.
And then Achilles called for his handmaids and told them
to wash and anoint the dead man, but somewhere else,
in another part of the house, so that Priam would not
see his son—in case, in his anguish of heart,
he might not be able to keep from voicing his anger
and Achilles' own heart flare up into violent rage.
When the body was washed and anointed with olive oil   580
and dressed in the fine-spun tunic and handsome robe,
Achilles lifted it onto a pallet and then
with the help of his comrades he put it onto the cart.
And he groaned aloud and addressed his beloved companion,
"Don't hold it against me, Patroclus, if down in Hades
you hear a report that I have given back Hector
to his old father. The ransom he brought is worthy,
and of course I will give you your own fair share of the gifts."

After he said this, Achilles returned to the hut,
sat down on the inlaid chair that he had jumped up from,   590
against the opposite wall from Priam, and said,
"Your son has now been released, sir, as you requested.
He is lying upon a pallet. Tomorrow, when daybreak
appears in the camp, you will see him yourself, with your own eyes,
as you take him away. But for now, let us think of supper.
For even Níobē came to the point of eating,
and that was after all twelve of her children were killed,

six daughters and six sons, in the prime of their youth.
Apollo shot down the sons with his silver bow,
and Ártemis shot down the daughters. They were both angry   600
at Níobē for boasting that she was the equal
of Leto, because the goddess had borne just two,
while she herself was the mother of many children;
so the pair, though only two of them, slaughtered her many.
For nine days they lay in their blood, since there was no one
to bury them—Zeus had turned the people to stones.
But on the tenth day the gods came and buried the children,
and exhausted by weeping, Níobē finally ate.
Somewhere among the rocks in the lonely hills
of Sípylus, where men say that the wood nymphs sleep   610
when they dance on the banks of the Áchelésius river,
she still continues, although she is made of stone,
to brood on the desolation that the gods brought her.
So come, sir; it is time that you think of eating.
Afterward, when you have taken your dear son to Troy,
you can mourn for him; and many tears will be wept then."

With this Achilles stood up and slaughtered a sheep,
and his comrades skinned and prepared the carcass and cut it
expertly into small pieces and skewered them
and roasted them on the flames. And Automedon   620
took loaves of bread and passed them around the table
in fine wicker baskets. Achilles then served the meat,
and they helped themselves to the food that was set before them.
And when they had had enough of eating and drinking,
Priam gazed at Achilles in wonder—how tall
he was and how handsome, like one of the blessed gods.
And Achilles gazed at Priam in wonder, admiring
his noble face and the brave words that he had spoken.

But when they had gazed their fill, Priam said, "Give me
a bed, if you please, my lord. I am weary; I need   630
to lie down as soon as I can and sleep a little.
Never beneath my eyelids have my eyes closed
since the moment when my dear child died at your hands.

All that time I have stayed awake, moaning and brooding
over my countless sorrows. But now I have eaten
and drunk some wine. Before, I had eaten nothing."

When he heard this, Achilles ordered his men and handmaids
to put beds outside that were covered with fine purple rugs
and blankets on top and wool-lined cloaks to keep warm in.
The women went out of the room with torches and quickly   640
prepared the two beds. And Achilles said, with a hint,
"You must sleep outside, dear sir, in case some Achaean
commander arrives. They are constantly coming to me
to ask my advice about tactics; that is our custom.
If one of them saw you here in the dead of night,
he immediately would report it to Agamemnon,
and that would mean a delay in releasing the body.
But speak to me in all frankness, and answer my question:
How many days will you need for the funeral?
I will wait that long, and will hold back the army as well."   650

Then, in response to him, Priam, the old king, said,
"If you really are willing to let me give Hector full
funeral rites, you would do me a kindness, Achilles,
by calling a truce. You know how we are cooped up
behind our walls; we must travel to gather wood
a long way off in the mountains, and all our men
are afraid of leaving the city. So if you agree,
for nine days we will lament for him in our houses,
then bury him on the tenth day and have the feast,
and on the eleventh day we will build him a grave mound.   660
On the twelfth day the war can begin again, if it must."

And Achilles the godlike, the greatest of warriors, answered,
"Yes. I agree, sir. This too shall be as you say.
I will hold off the war for the time that you have requested."
As he spoke these words, he clasped the old king's right hand
at the wrist, so that he would have no fear in his heart.

And so the herald and Priam, with many thoughts

in their minds, lay down to sleep outside on the porch.
But Achilles slept in the innermost part of the hut,
and by his side lay that beautiful girl Briséïs.   670

Now all the other immortals and all the humans
slept through the night, subdued by sleep's gentle power.
But sleep did not overcome Hermes; he stayed up and pondered
how he could lead King Priam away from the ships
unseen by the sentries. At last he went over to Priam,
stood there above his head, and spoke to him softly:
"Sir, since Achilles spared you, you have no thought
of danger, but you are asleep in the enemy's camp.
You have ransomed your son for a large price; and now, to get you
back alive, your family would have to pay   680
three times that much as a ransom if Agamemnon
or the other commanders discovered that you were here."

At this the old king was frightened and woke up the herald.
Hermes then yoked the horses and mules, and himself
quickly drove through the camp, and nobody saw them.

And when they came to the ford of the swirling Xanthus,
Hermes left them and went to Olympus, as dawn
was spreading its saffron glow over all the earth.
With groaning and lamentation they drove the horses
on toward Troy, and the mule cart carried the body.   690
No one saw them at first, neither man nor woman.
But Cassándra, who was as lovely as Aphrodite,
from the top of Pergamus caught sight of her father
coming to Troy in the chariot . . . then the herald . . .
and then she saw *him,* on a pallet inside the mule cart.
She let out a scream and shouted to the whole city,
"Come and see Hector, you men and women of Troy,
if you ever were glad to see him return from the war,
so great a joy he was to our city and people."

When they heard her cry, they were seized by uncontrollable   700
wailing. And soon no one was left in the city,

not one man or woman. They all went outside the gates
to meet Priam. In front were Hector's wife and his mother,
tearing their hair in grief. They ran to the cart
and touched his head, while the crowd stood weeping around them.
And all of them would have stayed there in front of the gates
for the rest of the day until sunset, weeping and mourning
for Hector, if the old king had not said to the people,
"Let me pass through! Make way for the mule cart! Later,
once he comes home, you can mourn as much as you want."   710
When they heard this, they pulled back on either side and made way.

The family brought him into the palace and placed him
on a large bed and put ritual singers around him
to lead the dirge; and they chanted the song of sorrow,
and all the women responded with a shrill keening.
And cradling Hector's head, Andromache cried out,
"My husband, you died so young and left me behind,
a widow, with our beloved child just a baby,
and I doubt that he will ever become a man.
Before that, Troy will be plundered and burned, because   720
now you are dead, the one man who could have saved us,
Troy's loyal wives and our little children; and now
they will all be carried away in the Argive ships,
and I among them. And you, my child, will go also,
to work as a slave and perform the most shameful tasks,
toiling for a harsh master, or else some Achaean
will grab your arm and fling you down from the wall
to a horrible death—a warrior angry at Hector
for taking the life of his brother or father or son.
And indeed there were many Achaeans who sank their teeth   730
into the dirt at your father's hands; he was not
a gentle man in the thick of the fighting, and that
is why they mourn him so bitterly all through the city.
You have brought unbearable grief to your parents, Hector;
and I, more than all the rest, will be left with unending
misery, that you didn't die in your bed
reaching your arms out to me or in your last moments
speaking some word full of meaning, which I can remember

both day and night in my heart as I weep for you always."
Thus she mourned, and the women joined in her wailing.   740

Then Hecuba led the women in lamentation.
"Hector, by far the dearest of all my children,
you were also dear to the gods while I had you alive,
and even in death they have cared for you, I can see.
My other sons Achilles would sell if he caught them,
sending them over the restless sea to the islands
of Sámothrace, Imbros, or misty Lemnos. But you—
when he had taken your life with his sharp-edged spear,
he dragged you around the tomb of his comrade Patroclus
many times, yet this didn't bring him to life.   750
But you have come home to me now, and you lie here looking
as fresh as the dew, as if you had just now died,
like someone Apollo has killed with his gentle arrows."
Thus she lamented and stirred them to violent weeping.

And Helen was third to lead them in lamentation:
"Hector, you were by far the dearest of all
my brothers-in-law, and in all these years since I came here,
leaving my country behind, I have never heard you
speak to me with a harsh or an unkind word.
And if anyone in the palace spoke to me rudely—   760
one of your brothers or sisters or brothers' wives
or your mother (although your father was always kind,
as if he were my own father)—you intervened
and you stopped them from their abuse and you won them over
by the strength of your gentleness and your gentle words.
Now I am heartsick. I weep for both you and me,
because there is no one left here to treat me kindly
and be my friend; but everyone sees me and shudders."
Thus she lamented, and the crowd moaned along with her.

Then Priam, the old king, addressed the people and said,   770
"Trojans, go out and bring firewood back to the city.
Don't be afraid of an ambush; Achilles gave me
his solemn word when he let me depart from the ships

that he won't attack until the twelfth dawn arrives."
When they heard his command, they yoked their oxen and mules
to their carts and quickly assembled in front of the city.

For nine days they went and gathered great stores of firewood.
And on the tenth day, when dawn appeared in the heavens,
they carried out Hector's body, and they were all weeping,
and they put it on top of the funeral pyre and lit it.   780

As soon as the flush of dawn appeared in the heavens
on the next day, they assembled around the pyre.
First they extinguished with wine whatever embers
were still hot. And then his brothers and his companions
gathered up the white bones, lamenting, and tears
poured down their cheeks. They took the bones, and they put them
in a golden urn, wrapped in soft purple robes,
and laid the urn in a grave and covered it quickly
with large stones set close together, then piled the earth
over it as a grave mound, and posted guards   790
in case the Achaeans attacked before they were finished.
When they had piled up the mound, they returned to the city,
and they gathered again and held a magnificent feast
in the palace of Priam, their revered, god-ordained king.
Thus did they bury Hector, tamer of horses.

Notes on the Introductory Sections

Introduction

p. xv, *monuments of our own magnificence:* W. B. Yeats, "Sailing to Byzantium": "Nor is there singing school but studying / Monuments of its [the soul's] own magnificence." Yeats may not have been thinking of Homer when he wrote these lines, but it is partly thanks to the scholars of Byzantium that the texts of the *Iliad* were preserved and that we can read them today.

p. xv, *Every time I study this priceless work:* To C. E. Schubarth, January 12, 1821. Goethe also wrote, "We can consider this work the most admirable in its elements, and the most perfect in its execution, that we possess, and we should forever acknowledge it with gratitude" (to C. von Knebel, December 17, 1820).

p. xv, *more than twenty thousand people: Ion* 535d.

p. xv, *I was in Alice Springs:* Email from Pico Iyer, January 21, 2010.

p. xvi, *In 1990, the Colombian Ministry of Culture:* Alberto Manguel, *The Iliad and the Odyssey: A Biography* (New York 2007), p. 6.

p. xvi, *a brilliant and famous essay:* "L'Iliade ou le poème de la force." However brilliant the essay is, Simone Weil had a blind spot about the Hebrew Bible, though for understandable reasons. And at one point she says, astoundingly, that "the Gospel is the last and most marvelous expression of the Greek genius." The *Greek* genius? Is she talking here about Jesus of Nazareth, who drank in the Psalms and the Prophets with his mother's milk?

p. xvi, *a treasury of all military virtue:* Plutarch, "Life of Alexander."

p. xxi, *He was probably born:* This paragraph is based on the great classical scholar M. L. West's eye-opening *The Making of the Iliad*, which should be required reading for every serious student of the *Iliad* in Greek. (The title is hereafter abbreviated as *MI*.)

p. xxi, *around 700 BCE: MI*, p. 19.

p. xxi, *wasn't named Homer:* West, "The Invention of Homer," p. 364.

p. xxi, *a traditional language that had evolved: MI*, p. 4.

p. xxi, *As an epic singer: MI*, p. 21.

p. xxi, *four-stringed lyre:* West, "The Singing of Homer and the Modes of Early Greek Music," pp. 115–21.

p. xxi, *expanding his early draft:* "The key to understanding the making of the *Iliad* is, in my view, the recognition that its poet . . . did not proceed in a straight line from the beginning to the end but, working over many years, made insertions, some of them lengthy, in what he had already written. I say written, because I think it probable that he wrote out his poem himself, though the alternative possibility, that he used an amanuensis or a series of amanuenses, cannot be excluded. The essential point is that he made insertions in parts of the poem that were already fixed; and fixed means written, because if they were only fixed in his head they would naturally have moulded themselves round the insertions more pliably than they have done" (*MI*, p. 3). "The major expansions are thousands of lines long; there are also various self-contained episodes of several hundred lines that have been inserted, and many shorter passages, of a few dozen lines, or of only one or two, inserted within or between episodes" (*MI*, p. 58).

p. xxi, *to four or five times its original length:* "Comparing [the poet's] uncompleted *Ur-Ilias* with his finished epic, we see most obviously a huge increase in size, to four or five times the length of the original. The overall structure of the story remains, but its coherence has been compromised; the logical consecution of scenes has been disrupted by the ever more numerous expansions. This is a loss, but in several ways the poem has gained. Many of the new episodes are of the highest poetic quality, and constitute some of the most memorable parts of the *Iliad*. They introduce us to a wider variety of heroes and divinities" (*MI*, p. 67).

p. xxi, *amazingly intact:* According to West, 95 percent of the traditional text is the work of the original poet (*MI*, p. 7).

p. xxii, *the massive Trojan walls: MI*, p. 24.

p. xxii, *killed the men:* Aeneas is the exception among the major heroes.

p. xxii, *a later addition:* "To scholars with an interest in saga analysis it has long been apparent that [Achilles'] association with the Trojan War is not original. It may indeed have come about at a comparatively recent stage of the tradition" (*MI*, p. 42).

p. xxiii, *Even a man whose grandfather:* 6.218ff.

p. xxiii, *The best men choose one thing:* Hermann Diels and Walther Kranz, *Die Fragmente der Vorsokratiker* (Berlin 1906), p. 66, fragment 29.

p. xxiv, *a reprehensible crime:* In Book 3 Menelaus says, "Lord Zeus, grant me revenge on the man who wronged me, / Paris, and let me kill him with my own hands, / so that, for all generations, a man may shudder / at doing harm to the host who offered him friendship" (3.330–33). Two centuries later, even more pointedly, Herodotus has the Egyptian king Proteus say to Paris: "You are clearly the most wicked of men, since you accepted hospitality from a friend and then committed the gravest outrage: you slept with your host's wife. And as if that wasn't enough, after exciting her passion you stole her away and sailed off. And not just with her: you also stole a great deal of your host's property" (*Histories* 2.115).

Homer may well have known the story of the Judgment of Paris, but he doesn't mention it in the *Iliad* (24.29–30 in the Greek text are very probably a rhapsode's interpolation; see pp. 426–27). And in fact everything else in the poem argues against that story. Everyone in the poem agrees that the crime was Paris's fault. If Homer had included the Judgment of Paris in the *Iliad*, it would have been Aphrodite's fault. Paris may have made a foolish decision in choosing her over Hera and Athena (though any choice would have been disastrous, given the vanity and vindictiveness of all three goddesses), but from that point on in the story, he would have had no choice, since Helen was his reward for picking Aphrodite, and therefore he couldn't help committing the crime.

p. xxiv, *his son's action is the cause of the war:* 7.353.

p. xxiv, *a great curse:* 3.45.

p. xxiv, *hated / by every one of the Trojans:* 3.428–29.

p. xxiv, *Menelaus and Odysseus went on an embassy to Troy:* 3.192–209.

p. xxiv, *dissuaded the Trojan assembly:* 11.121.

p. xxv, *no possible good / can happen to us:* 7.335–36.

p. xxv, *all the Trojans:* 7.373–74.

p. xxv, *passionate arguments:* The strongest of these is Hector's:

> "What nearer debt in all humanity
> Than wife is to the husband? If this law
> Of nature be corrupted through affection,
> And that great minds, of partial indulgence

> To their benumbed wills, resist the same,
> There is a law in each well-order'd nation
> To curb those raging appetites that are
> Most disobedient and refractory.
> If Helen then be wife to Sparta's king,
> As it is known she is, these moral laws
> Of nature and of nations speak aloud
> To have her back return'd: thus to persist
> In doing wrong extenuates not wrong,
> But makes it much more heavy. Hector's opinion
> Is this in way of truth; . . ."

Yet even in Shakespeare's scene, there is a strange leap of unreason at this point, and Hector continues in this way:

> "yet ne'ertheless,
> My spritely brethren, I propend to you
> In resolution to keep Helen still,
> For 'tis a cause that hath no mean dependance
> Upon our joint and several dignities."
> *Troilus and Cressida*, Act II, Scene 2.

p. xxv, *considers giving Helen back*: 22.112–14.

p. xxv, *The Trojans' refusal to make things right*: Homer makes the Trojans doubly responsible for their own destruction by breaking their solemn oath to preserve the truce in Book 3. Both Achaeans and Trojans pray that

> "whichever army is first to betray this oath
> by breaking the truce, may their brains be spilled on the ground
> as this wine is spilled—their brains and the brains of their children;
> and may their wives become other men's slaves and whores." (3.282–85)

p. xxv, *The Egyptians' priests: Histories* 2.120.

p. xxvi, *her beauty / pierces the heart*: This phrase is not in the Greek. I took *ainōs*, "dreadfully," in another direction here to give the line a gravity appropriate to the statement.

p. xxvi, *"Don't believe them! They're rotten!"*: Chana Bloch, "Watching," in *The Secrets of the Tribe* (New York 1980), p. 3.

pp. xxvi–xxvii, *character is fate*: Diels-Kranz, p. 78, fragment 119.

p. xxix, *the battle shouts and the fighting*: 1.482.

p. xxix, *the sheer pleasure of killing*: "in the delight of war, as you slaughter Trojans," 16.82.

p. xxx, *Death, as Dr. Johnson said:* "Depend upon it, Sir, when a man knows he is to be hanged in a fortnight, it concentrates his mind wonderfully." James Boswell, *The Life of Samuel Johnson*, entry for September 19, 1777.

p. xxx, *foams at the mouth:* 15.562.

p. xxx, *My heart has been struck:* 13.72–74.

p. xxxii, *The battle scenes hardly ever:* D. S. Carne-Ross, *New York Review of Books* 21.20, December 12, 1974.

p. xxxiii, *not a trace of erotic feelings between them:* By contrast, the relationship between Gilgamesh and Enkidu is filled with homoeroticism, and in Tablet XII the sexuality is explicit. See my *Gilgamesh* (New York 2004), pp. 23–24 and 218–19. For the similarities between *Gilgamesh* and the *Iliad,* see M. L. West, *The East Face of Helicon* (Oxford 1997), pp. 336ff.

p. xxxiii, *may my bones:* 23.82–83.

p. xxxiii, *the soul of Jonathan was knit with the soul of David:* 1 Samuel 18:1.

p. xxxiii, *Your love for me was wonderful:* 2 Samuel 1:26.

p. xxxiii, *confidant:* 23.76–77.

p. xxxiii, *allowing him to be his son's attendant:* 23.89.

p. xxxiv, *a little girl tugging at her mother's skirts:* 16.5–8.

p. xxxv, *ashamed to show her face on Olympus:* 24.85–86.

p. xxxv, *lawful wife:* 19.304–5.

p. xxxvi, *my wife, my darling:* 9.333.

p. xxxvi, *I . . . loved this woman, with all my heart:* 9.340–41. It is true that Achilles later says, "I wish that Ártemis had taken an arrow / and shot her down on my ship the day that I won her / after destroying Lyrnéssus; then all those many / comrades would still be with us, the ones who were slaughtered / in battle while I was furious" (19.56–60), but this statement is an expression of his impotent grief at the death of Patroclus, not of his feelings for Briseïs.

p. xxxvi, *hate[s] like the gates of Hades:* 9.310–11.

p. xxxvi, *amusing themselves on the seashore:* 2.715–16.

p. xxxvii, *the god's marvelous craftsmanship:* 19.20.

p. xxxvii, *Achilles wishes that both armies:* "I wish that not one of the Trojans remained alive, / and not one of the Argives, but that you [Patroclus] and I were the only / ones to survive and smash Troy's towers to rubble" (16.89–91).

p. xxxvii, *a useless burden upon the earth:* 18.90.

p. xxxvii, *To be choked with hatred:* In "A Prayer for My Daughter," he says that his mind

> . . . knows that to be choked with hate
> May well be of all evil chances chief.
> If there's no hatred in a mind
> Assault and battery of the wind
> Can never tear the linnet from the leaf.

This thought leads to one of the most profound passages in all of English-language poetry:

> Considering that, all hatred driven hence,
> The soul recovers radical innocence
> And learns at last that it is self-delighting,
> Self-appeasing, self-affrighting,
> And that its own sweet will is Heaven's will.

p. xxxviii, *her terrible blazing eyes:* 1.204.

p. xxxviii, *I was out of my mind with rage:* 9.110.

p. xxxviii, *King Agamemnon is absolutely / at fault:* 13.107–8.

p. xxxix, *Nothing is worth my life:* 9.404.

p. xxxix, *which, far sweeter / than trickling honey:* 18.93–94.

p. xxxix, *of all the gods, only Hades:* 9.155–56.

p. xl, *Whoever is stiff and inflexible: Tao Te Ching: A New English Version* by Stephen Mitchell (New York 1988), chapter 76.

p. xl, *the loneliest character in the* Iliad: Homer calls her "Helen of Argos," never "Helen of Troy." She is an outsider in Priam's family and in Trojan society; hated, blamed, and despised by her brothers- and sisters- and mother-in-law; treated kindly only by Hector and Priam. In one scene, a goddess inserts into her heart a longing for the city and family she left; but on her own, that is not what she longs for. The fact that she is the "daughter of Zeus" doesn't make her any more honored in Troy or less of an outsider. In any case, she shows no awareness of being Zeus's daughter; and Zeus, for his part, far from being concerned for her welfare (as he is for his son Sarpedon, the Lycian commander), doesn't even mention her.

p. xl, *they shudder at it:* 24.768.

p. xl, *is a fool:* 6.358.

p. xl, *a proper sense of the people's outrage:* 6.357.

p. xl, *the enchanting gifts / of Aphrodite the golden:* 3.58–59.

p. xli, *whoever wins will take [her] away:* 3.128.

p. xli, *Brother-in-law of mine:* 6.349–50.

p. xli, *through my fault:* 6.363.

p. xli, *Zeus has brought us an evil fate:* 6.364–65.

p. xlii, *these evils are as the gods have ordained them:* 6.355.

p. xliii, *with a raucous shouting, like cranes:* 3.2.

p. xliv, *the one defender of Troy:* 6.407.

p. xliv, *honored by them like a god:* 22.384.

p. xliv, *not gentle in combat:* 24.731–32.

p. xliv, *an ancient scholiast:* Quoted in Richardson, *The Iliad: A Commentary,* p. 118. (I have made one minor change in the translation.)

p. xlv, *that this miserable war:* 6.334–35.

p. xlv, *No man of any sense could ever belittle:* 6.520–21.

p. xlv, *In Plato's* Ion: *Ion* 535e.

p. xlvi, *which moves Hector to stroke her face:* The Greek doesn't specify which part of her body Hector strokes; the literal meaning is "he stroked her with his hand." But the same line in Book 1, which describes Thetis stroking Achilles (cf. 18.54), implies that it is Andromache's face or hair, rather than her hand, that is being stroked here.

p. xlvi, *much more and much less than pity:* I have appropriated some phrases in this sentence and the next one from Hugo von Hofmannsthal's "Lord Chandos Letter" (in German called simply "Ein Brief").

p. xlvi, *Nothing can explain the power of such moments over us:* Introduction to *Anna Karenina* (Norwalk 1975), p. x.

p. xlvii, *I do not blame you:* 3.152–53.

p. xlvii, *Paris committed that act of madness:* 24.23. See note on pp. 426–27.

p. xlvii, *down to Death's house:* 22.417.

p. xlvii, *I will go down to my son in the grave, mourning:* Genesis 37:35, from *Genesis: A New Translation of the Classic Biblical Stories* by Stephen Mitchell (New York 1996), p. 83.

p. xlvii, *inexpressibly beautiful:* Aylmer Maude, *The Life of Tolstoy: First Fifty Years* (London 1908), p. 172.

p. xlvii, *the wolf to dwell with the lamb:* "The wolf shall dwell with the lamb, and the leopard shall lie down with the kid" (Isaiah 11:6), a verse that is eerily reminiscent of the opposite feeling in one of Achilles' last speeches to Hector:

> "Don't talk to me of agreements, you son of a bitch.
> No solemn oaths are sworn between lions and men;
> wolves and lambs don't bargain to make a truce
> but hate one another for all time."   (22.253–56)

p. xlviii, *of a handsome young prince:* 24.338–39.

p. xlviii, *pass through the gates of Hades:* 23.71.

p. l, *he gently pushed him away:* Simone Weil badly misreads this gesture as a mode of unconscious brutality on Achilles' part.

p. l, *the young men's tunics:* 18.578–79.

p. l, *Achilles has lost all pity:* 24.38.

p. l, *So do not provoke my grieving heart:* 24.560–62.

p. lii, *to make love with a woman:* 24.125.

p. liii, *Achilles will sleep with his beloved Briseïs forever:* It might be objected that Achilles appears again, or his ghost does, in Book 11 of the *Odyssey*. But West and most Homeric scholars believe that the *Odyssey* was written by a different poet from the author of the *Iliad*. So the *Odyssey*'s Achilles is in the same category as Dante's Ulisse or Goethe's Helena.

p. liii, *It must give pleasure:* This is the title of the third section of Wallace Stevens's long poem "Notes Toward a Supreme Fiction."

p. liii, *a joy to be savored:* For example, *Odyssey* 8.91 and 368.

p. liii, *shaken and exalted:* Carne-Ross, *op. cit.*

p. liv, *its extraordinary artistic precision, calm, and purity:* Friedrich Nietzsche, "Homers Wettkampf," in *Werke in drei Bänden* (München 1954), 3, p. 292.

p. liv, *I am always glad to return to the* Iliad: To Friedrich Schiller, May 12, 1798.

p. liv, *made Schiller say:* Caroline von Wolzogen and Christian Gottfried Körner, *Schillers Leben* (Stuttgart 1845), p. 335.

p. lv, *To men, some things are good:* Diels-Kranz, p. 76, fragment 102.

About the Greek Text

p. lvii, *far inferior:* It accepts the received text for the most part and rarely tries to determine which verses are interpolated. In addition, its data are notoriously unreliable, and it is badly out of date (for example, its third edition [1920] is able to cite just 103 ancient papyri, whereas West cites 1,543).

p. lvii, *fiercely complicated:* West gives a helpful overview in "The Textual Criticism and Editing of Homer."

p. lvii, *interpolations by rhapsodes:* Here are a few examples that West gives (line numbers in this section refer to the Greek text):

1. 13.748–50:

    Hector was pleased at the good advice of his comrade;
    [*and he leaped to the ground from his chariot, in full armor;*]
    he agreed with him, and he answered him with these words:

The problem with the interpolation is that Hector is not in his chariot in the first place. (In the parallel passage from which this line is taken, 12.80–81, he is.)

2. 2.484–93:

Homer's famous invocation to the Muses:

> Tell me now, Muses, who have your homes on Olympus—
> since you are divine, and present, and know all things,
> while *we* hear only a rumor, and we know nothing—
> who were the lords and commanders of the Achaeans?
> As for the common soldiers, they were so many
> that I could not name them even if I had ten tongues,
> even if I had ten mouths, an unwearying voice,
> and my heart were of bronze. And now I will tell the names
> of all the captains, and how many ships came with them.

And here is the expanded passage:

> Tell me now, Muses, who have your homes on Olympus—
> since you are divine, and present, and know all things,
> while *we* hear only a rumor, and we know nothing—
> who were the lords and commanders of the Achaeans?
> As for the common soldiers, they were so many
> that I could not name them even if I had ten tongues,
> even if I had ten mouths, an unwearying voice,
> and my heart were of bronze, [*unless the Olympian Muses,
> daughters of Zeus, were to call to my mind all those
> who came to Ilion*]. Now I will tell the names
> of all the captains, and how many ships came with them.

The fifth to sixth line above literally means "I could not name the multitudes." What has happened here is that a rhapsode misinterpreted the Greek word *plēthun*, "multitudes," thinking that it referred to the multitudes of leaders, not the multitudes of common soldiers; by adding the explanation, he was trying to make explicit what he thought was implicit in the line about the multitudes. But the poet's point is that he could never name all the soldiers (with or without the Muses' help—there were just too many of them); he will name only the leaders. Omitting the gloss restores the passage to its original clarity. (It is easier to see from a literal translation how this passage was spliced in, since in Greek the lines form two complete hexameters:

> not even if I had ten tongues, and ten mouths,
> and an unbreakable voice, and a heart of bronze,
> [*unless the Olympian Muses, daughters of Zeus, who carries the storm shield,
> were to call to my mind how many came beneath Ilion*].
> Now I will tell the leaders of the ships and all the ships.)

3. 24.22–30:

> And so Achilles kept trying to mutilate him
> day after day; but the gods felt pity for Hector,

and they even asked Hermes to steal the corpse. But while this
found favor with all the others, it did not please Hera
or Poseidon or the gray-eyed daughter of Zeus;
they hated the Trojans as passionately as they did
on the day when Paris committed that act of madness
[*—he offended those goddesses when they came to his shepherd's cottage*
and he picked the one who furthered his ruinous lust].

"That act of madness" refers to Paris's seduction of Helen, as does the same phrase in 6.356 (*Alexandrou henek' atēs*, which I translate there as "through Paris's folly"); but with the interpolation the reference is now to the Judgment of Paris, which is never mentioned elsewhere in the *Iliad*. This is an attempt to explain the two goddesses' hatred, though it doesn't explain Poseidon's. In any case, "it seems unlikely," according to West, that the poet "would introduce his only reference to the Judgment of Paris at this late stage," when he had an obvious chance to do so in 4.31–36. (See note to 4.30–31, p. 436.)

4. 6.429–39. In one of the most deeply moving scenes in the *Iliad,* Andromache ends her long speech to Hector with these words:

"Hector, you are my everything now: my father,
my mother, my brother—and my beloved husband.
Have pity on me. Stay with me here on the tower.
Don't make your child an orphan, your wife a widow."

And here is the passage with the interpolated lines (although West doesn't bracket these lines, he casts doubt on them in his supplementary volume):

"Hector, you are my everything now: my father,
my mother, my brother to me—and my beloved husband.
Have pity on me. Stay with me here on the tower;
Don't make your child an orphan, your wife a widow.
[*As for the army, station it by the fig tree*
where the city is most vulnerable and the wall
easiest to scale. Three times their best men have tried,
led by the two Ajaxes and Idómeneus
and the sons of Atreus and brave Diomedes;
either some skilled soothsayer told them about it
or maybe it was their own idea to attack.]"

Not only is it out of character for Andromache to be offering her husband military advice, as the ancient critic Aristarchus pointed out; it is rude and presumptuous. Aristarchus made two other points: Hector replies as if these lines had never been uttered, and the wall's vulnerability in this place is unattested anywhere else in the poem. Certainly the passage changes the whole tone of Andromache's impassioned plea. There are few greater anticlimaxes in all of literature.

p. lvii, *Wherever West has deleted or bracketed a passage:* The one exception is 3:18–20, since West's later opinion is that these verses are original.

p. lvii, *others of his books: Studies in the Text and Transmission of the Iliad* and *The Making of the Iliad.*

About This Translation

p. lix, *Nobody will give a damn:* Homer, *The Iliad,* trans. Michael Reck (New York 1994), p. 12.

p. lix, *Rilke's* Duino Elegies: For example, one my favorite passages, toward the end of "The First Elegy," begins in this way:

> *Freilich ist es seltsam, die Erde nich mehr zu bewohnen,*
> *kaum erlernte Gebräuche nicht mehr zu üben,*
> *Rosen, und andern eigens versprechenden Dingen*
> *nicht die Bedeutung menschlicher Zukunft zu geben;*
> *das, was man war in unendlich ängstlichen Händen,*
> *nicht mehr zu sein, und selbst den eigenen Namen*
> *wegzulassen wie ein zerbrochenes Spielzeug.*

> Of course, it is strange to inhabit the earth no longer,
> to give up customs you barely had time to learn,
> not to see roses and other promising Things
> in terms of a human future; no longer to be
> what you were in infinitely anxious hands; to leave
> even your own first name behind you, as lightly
> as a young child will abandon a broken toy.

> *The Selected Poetry of Rainer Maria Rilke,* ed. and trans. Stephen Mitchell (Random House 1982), pp. 154–55.

Wallace Stevens also uses this kind of five-beat line in such profound and beautiful late poems as "This Solitude of Cataracts," "The World as Meditation," "Long and Sluggish Lines," and "Large Red Man Reading":

> There were ghosts that returned to earth to hear his phrases,
> As he sat there reading, aloud, the great blue tabulae.

p. lix, *Matthew Arnold's famous advice:* From his essay "On Translating Homer."

p. lx, *An improper share of the reader's attention:* For example, in his own translation of the end of Book 8 (the lines actually sound like pentameters, unless you come down hard on the initial syllables), he confidently omits the epithet for dawn in the last line, which literally means "[the horses] stood beside the chariots and waited for fine-throned dawn":

> As numerous as are the stars on a clear night,
> So shone forth, in front of Troy, by the bed of Xanthus,
> Between that and the ships, the Trojans' numerous fires.
> In the plain there were kindled a thousand fires: by each one
> There sate fifty men, in the ruddy light of the fire:
> By their chariots stood the steeds, and champ'd the white barley
> While their masters sate by the fire, and waited for Morning.

Tennyson, too, in his "Specimen of a Translation of the Iliad in Blank Verse," omits the epithet in this line, as he does in the first:

> As when in heaven the stars about the moon
> Look beautiful, when all the winds are laid,
> And every height comes out, and jutting peak
> And valley, and the immeasurable heavens
> Break open to their highest, and all the stars
> Shine, and the Shepherd gladdens in his heart:
> So many a fire between the ships and stream
> Of Xanthus blazed before the towers of Troy,
> A thousand on the plain; and close by each
> Sat fifty in the blaze of burning fire;
> And champing golden grain, the horses stood
> Hard by their chariots, waiting for the dawn.

p. lx, *First he attacked the mules:* 1.50 (1.52 in my translation).

p. lx, *sometimes inappropriate to it:* Here are a few more examples (line numbers refer to the Greek text): *godlike* Paris is panic-stricken at seeing Menelaus (3.30), *laughter-loving* Aphrodite whimpers on her mother's lap (5.375), *glorious* Ajax spits out cow dung (23.779).

p. lx, *godlike Priam:* 24.483 (24.472–73 in my translation: "just so was Achilles astounded when he saw Priam, / that godlike man").

p. lx, *best left untranslated:* "In fact, we must recognize that it is hardly possible [to reproduce in translation the true meaning of the fixed epithet], because a modern writer cannot expect his audience to become familiar with the noun-epithet formula, and that is the essential condition for a real understanding of the epithet" (Milman Parry, *The Making of Homeric Verse*, p. 171).

p. lx, *soon ceases . . . to seek for any active force:* Ibid., p. 373.

p. lxi, *a bramble of possibilities:* I also consulted a number of translations. Of these, the old Samuel Butler version taught me the most, notably about what to omit. The prose translations by Martin Hammond and by E. V. Rieu (as revised and updated by Peter Jones with D. C. H. Rieu) were also particularly helpful. In addition, I read the Loeb Library translation by A. T. Murray (as revised by William F. Wyatt) and the verse translations by Robert Fagles, Robert Fitzgerald, Ian Johnston, Richmond Lattimore, and Stanley Lombardo.

p. lxi, *master woodworker Ch'ing:* See the marvelous story in *The Second Book of the Tao,* compiled and adapted from the Chuang-tzu and the Chung Yung, with commentaries by Stephen Mitchell (New York 2009), p. 92.

Notes on the Translation

Line numbers in this section refer to the translation, except in quoted passages, where they refer to the Greek text. I have changed the spelling of names in quoted passages to conform with the spelling in this translation.

1.1 goddess: The Muse, who is the poet's inspiration. "An initial invocation to the Muse or Muses is conventional for epic poems and for the literary kind of hymn, as is the request to 'sing of'—that means, through the poet—the main theme which is to be outlined" (Kirk 1, p. 51).

1.3 Hades: The god of the underworld.

1.7 that king of men: "Although Agamemnon is called *anax* ('lord') and *basileus* ('king'), the poet tells us that there are other *anaktes* (2.405, 777) and *basilēes* (2.445). . . . The Atreidae [sons of Atreus, viz. Agamemnon and Menelaus] are said to be marshals of the host, but in fact the precise hierarchy of power in the Greek camp is a matter for dispute among the Greeks. Achilles, Ajax, Diomedes, and the others are all kings in their respective communities. However, on the expedition to recover Menelaus's wife, the Atreidae have taken charge. Achilles resents this state of affairs (158–60) and clearly does not see himself as subordinate to either of them. It may seem strange that, throughout the *Iliad*, it is Agamemnon who is presented as commander-in-chief rather than his brother, who was the aggrieved party. However, it is likely that, in the tradition as Homer found it, Agamemnon had already acquired a special ascendency as king of Mycenae with all its gold and a plethora of subject cities (11.46; 9.149–56)" (Pulleyn, pp. 123, 126–27).

1.13–14 the god's / golden staff adorned with his sacred ribbons: "The staff is a sign of divinely approved authority and inviolability and as such is borne by kings (2.86), priests (1.15, 28), seers (*Od.* 11.91), heralds (7.277), orators (23.568), and judges (1.238; 18.505). . . . [The ribbons] are long woolen garlands which would normally hang on a statue (or other sacred object) to mark its sanctity. . . . Chryses has detached them from a statue [of Apollo] and fixed them to a staff as a further mark of his power" (Pulleyn, pp. 125–26).

1.39 *Mouse-god:* "The Greeks linked mice and epidemic illness. The story related by the scholiast on this line tells of Apollo destroying armies of mice that were devastating the land. If the god can ward off mice, and therefore plague, perhaps he can also be asked to do the reverse, so that this is why Chryses summons him as the 'mouse-god' " (Pulleyn, p. 135).

1.117 *Chryséïs:* "Chryseïs" is not a proper name in Greek; it means "the daughter of Chryses," as "Briseïs" means "the daughter of Briseus." "In an unspecified 'ancient' author . . . the two girls were named as Astynome and Hippodameia" (*MI*, p. 86).

1.263 *Períthoüs, Dryas . . . :* "These are Lapiths from Thessaly, famous in myth and art for the fight that broke out when the centaurs become drunk at King Perithous' wedding to Hippodamia and tried to rape her and the other women. Theseus of Athens, an old friend and ally, helped Perithous against them; the basic story . . . ends in the centaurs being driven out of their home on Mt. Pelion and across to the Pindos region" (Kirk 1, p. 80).

1.266 *centaurs:* Creatures who were half man, half horse, and notorious for their violence.

1.321 *heralds:* Their functions "included the taking of messages, arranging of sacrifices, and general assistance to the kings" (Willcock 1, p. 193).

1.363 *the Old Man of the Sea:* "The verse is repeated at 18.36, the context of which shows her father to be Nereus (who is not named directly in Homer), since her sisters there are Nereids (18.52). The ancient sea-god has other names and aspects, Proteus at *Od.* 4.365 and 385, Phorcus at *Od.* 1.72, 13.96, and 345" (Kirk 1, p. 90).

1.371 *Thebē:* One of the cities around Troy captured and plundered by Achilles (see 9.336–37). The king of Thebē, Eëtion, was the father of Hector's wife, Andromache. Chryseïs was taken captive here, and Briseïs in Lyrnessus at about the same time. "Among the loot from Thebē is the *phorminx* [lyre] played by Achilles at 9.188, his horse Pedasus at 16.152f., and an iron weight offered by him as a prize at 23.826f. and previously thrown by Eëtion" (Kirk 2, p. 211).

1.416 *Ocean:* The river Ocean was the circumference of the earth.

1.417 *Ethiopians:* A mythical race who lived at ease at the far eastern end of the earth and who sometimes entertained the gods at their feasts.

1.426 *forestays:* A pair of ropes running from the top of the mast to the front of the ship.

1.426 *mast-crutch:* A piece of wood standing up from the stern of the ship, into which the mast was lowered.

1.577 *He picked me up by one foot:* "The description is full of charm and subtle meaning, and it is a sign of Milton's genius that he could even improve on it" (Kirk 1, p. 113). The passage in *Paradise Lost* is:

> Nor was his name unheard or unador'd
> In ancient *Greece*; and in *Ausonian* land
> Men called him *Mulciber*; and how he fell
> From Heav'n, they fabl'd, thrown by angry *Jove*
> Sheer o're the Chrystal Battlements: from Morn
> To Noon he fell, from Noon to dewy Eve,
> A Summers day; and with the setting Sun
> Dropt from the Zenith like a falling Star,
> On *Lemnos* th' *Ægæan* Ile: (1.738–45)

1.580 *Sintians:* A Thracian tribe who were the earliest inhabitants of Lemnos.

1.583 *nectar:* The wine of the gods.

1.585 *inexhaustible laughter:* The gods are entertained by Hephaestus's limping ineptitude as a wine server, especially since the usual servers and cupbearers are Hēbē, a beautiful goddess, and Ganymede, the most beautiful of men (see note to 5.250).

2.48 The plot and the motivation become quite confused here and for the next several hundred lines. This, according to West, is because most of Book 2 "consists of secondary insertions. In parts there is more than one layer of expansion, and revision has been done by a more complicated process than simple addition.... This has left difficulties in the continuity of the narrative more severe than in any other rhapsody [i.e., book of the *Iliad*]; ... they have long exercised critics and must trouble any attentive reader" (*MI*, p. 100).

2.172 *Eurýbates:* This is Eurybates of Ithaca, not the Eurybates whom Agamemnon had sent to Achilles in Book 1.

2.283 *Aulis:* A port in Boeotia where the Achaean fleet had assembled before sailing for Troy.

2.429 *the shield of almighty Zeus:* In Greek, *aegis*, which can be translated "storm shield": a shield or breastplate used by Athena, Apollo, or Zeus to encourage or terrify an army. It is described quite differently in 5.669–73.

2.442 *Asian wetlands:* "Asia" here means the coast of Asia Minor.

2.465–815 The Catalogue of Ships is a separate and possibly much older text that has been incorporated into the *Iliad*, with many inconsistencies. "For the Achaean part (494–759) [the poet] has adapted the catalogue from another poem in his repertory, an account of the Gathering at Aulis at the beginning of the war" (*MI*, p. 112).

2.552 *his struggles and groans over Helen:* His groans are of anguish at losing his beloved wife, and also of shame at the humiliation of it. As for his struggles—this is the tenth year of a great war. (The Greek can also mean "Helen's struggles and groans.")

2.673 *would soon recall him:* "Philoctetes came to Troy soon after the end of the *Iliad* story, brought by the Greeks from Lemnos because of a prophecy that Troy could not be taken without the bow and arrows of Heracles, which were in his possession" (Willcock 1, pp. 211–2).

2.678 *Asclépius:* The archetypal healer, son of Apollo and student of the centaur Chiron.

2.697 *the dread river of oaths:* The Styx, the river that forms the boundary between earth and the underworld, is "the greatest / and most terrible oath that any immortal can take" (15.38–39).

2.725 *Typhǽus:* A monster fathered by Tartarus and Gaia. He tried to destroy Zeus, who imprisoned him under Mount Etna.

2.754 *Myrína, the peerless dancer:* "Supposedly one of the Amazons who had fought against the Phrygians (3.189)" (Willcock 1, p. 213).

2.815 *Xanthus:* A river in Lycia, not to be confused with the Trojan river Xanthus (which was also called the Scamander) or with Achilles' immortal horse Xanthus or with the Trojan Xanthus, son of Phǽnops, who is killed by Diomedes in Book 5.

3.5 *Pygmy troops:* Pygmies means "fist-like men," from the Greek *pugmē*, "fist." "Behind the myth there may be real knowledge of the diminutive tribes . . . that possibly reached the Greeks through Egyptian informants" (Krieter-Spiro, p. 14). "The strange idea of their war with the cranes was perhaps derived from a lost Egyptian folk-tale" (Kirk 1, p. 265).

3.19 *Menelaus caught sight of him:* According to West, the battle between Paris and Menelaus, like the Catalogue of Ships in Book 2, "would have been more appropriate at the beginning of the war and might represent an independent song in [Homer]'s repertory that he has transferred from the first year of the conflict to the tenth" (*MI*, p. 34).

3.65 *her possessions:* "The possessions, including some that were strictly perhaps Menelaus's rather than hers, which Helen and Paris took with them from Lacedaemon" (Kirk 1, p. 274).

3.154 *Tell me now, what is the name:* "Rationally, Priam should by this time know who was who, but his first opportunity in the *Iliad* is treated as the first overall. . . . It has been conjectured that an analogous scene had occurred in earlier poetry in the context of the Achaeans' first attack on the city . . . and/or of the attack on Thebes" (*MI*, p. 131).

3.169 *if the life I seem to have lived then was ever real:* An expression of someone remembering happier days, equivalent to "unless it was all a dream." I have translated the same Greek phrase differently at 11.712–13: "That is who I once used to be—if that life / was ever real," and 24.418: "My son (if he ever existed) . . ."

3.173 *Phrygia:* A kingdom in west central Asia Minor.

3.178 *Amazons:* "In epic the Amazons are described as a tribe of women who engage in war—an activity which otherwise defines men. In the cyclic *Aethiopis* the Amazons joined the Trojans against the Achaeans, and Achilles eventually killed their queen, Penthesileia" (Graziosi and Haubold, p. 130).

3.187 *Helen, daughter of Zeus:* Homer never refers to the myth about Zeus impregnating Leda in the form of a swan. "We cannot guarantee that Homer and other early sources in which Leda is the real mother [of Helen] did not know this story, but its unusual nature is surely better explained as a later conflation of two separate traditions, one in which Leda is the mother, the other in which two divinities mate as birds. Our earliest reference of any sort to Zeus becoming a swan to engage Leda's attention is Euripedes' *Helen*" (Timothy Gantz, *Early Greek Myth* [Baltimore 1993], p. 320).

3.217–18 *Menelaus / would entertain him whenever he came from Crete:* "Menelaus had connections with Crete through his mother Aërope. It was to attend her father Catreus' obsequies that he went off to Crete when Paris was staying in his house, opening the door for the seduction of Helen" (*MI* 133).

3.222 *my mother's sons:* In the *Odyssey* (11.298–99), Castor and Pollux (Polydeuces) are said to be the sons of Leda and Tyndareus.

3.261 *gods of the world below:* Hades and Persephone.

3.275 *slit the lambs' throats:* "Most of the sacrifices described by Homer are, in effect, meals shared between men and gods. An animal is ritually killed, its flesh cut up and roasted, a portion of the meat dedicated to the god for whose benefit the sacrifice is made, and the rest eaten by the human participants. But one type of sacrifice is performed according to a different rite. Here and in 19.252–68 Agamemnon makes a sacrifice in which the meat is not roasted and there is no shared meal. This sacrifice has the purpose of giving the most solemn weight to a request to the gods that perjurers will be punished" (Hooker, p. 62).

3.311 *greaves:* Armor to protect the legs. "Heroic greaves are surely envisaged as being of bronze; those in the arming scenes have silver . . . ankle-guards of some kind to which they were . . . attached, and therefore most probably to another metal object" (Kirk 1, p. 315).

4.30–31 *What harm has King Priam done you, / or the sons of Priam, to make you so wildly rage:* Hera's reason for hating the Trojans is never stated in the *Iliad.* "Zeus finds Hera's hostility to Troy excessive; he does not say she has no reason for it at all. But if the poet knows the story of the Judgment of Paris . . . he is resolved to exclude it, otherwise he would surely have made Zeus taunt Hera about it here. The allusion in 24.29f. is probably interpolated. . . . [24.29–30] represent an attempt to supply the explanation at least for Hera and Athena, but it seems unlikely that [the poet] would introduce his only reference to the Judgment of Paris at this late stage . . . , or that he would have contemptuously dismissed the δῶρ' ἐρατὰ χρυσῆς Ἀφροδίτης (3.64) as μαχλοσύνη. I regard these two lines as a rhapsode's interpolation. Perhaps the same rhapsode altered 28 from its formulaic form" (*MI*, pp. 139–40, 412).

4.44 *Ilion:* Another name for Troy. The Homeric form is actually "Ilios," but poets in English, from Chaucer and Shakespeare through Tennyson and Pound, have written "Ilion" or the more Latinate "Ilium."

4.172 *loin-guard:* "A waist-cloth or apron, probably of leather" (Cunliffe, p. 176).

4.173 *plaited kilt underneath:* "Apparently some kind of metal guard worn round the waist under the ζωστήρ [belt], ζῶμα [loin-guard], and θώρηξ [breastplate]" (Cunliffe, p. 272).

4.201 *Chiron:* "The most humane of the centaurs" (11.781). He was famous for his intelligence and his knowledge of the healing arts, and was the teacher of many heroes, including Achilles, Heracles, and Theseus.

4.252 *Ajax and Teucer:* Literally, "the two Ajaxes." This phrase usually refers to Ajax the Tall, son of Telamon, and Ajax the Smaller, son of Oïleus. But occasionally it "can refer to the greater Ajax *and his half-brother Teucer; so* definitely [here] ... and also 13.197 (despite 13.203). ... The Locrian Ajax's light-armed contingent ... would hardly be described as 'bristling with shields and spears' " (Kirk 1, pp. 158, 359). See *MI*, pp. 144, 270.

4.341 *Tydeus:* One of the Seven against Thebes, along with Sthenelus's father, Capaneus. After Oedipus, king of Thebes, discovered his guilt and blinded himself, he was mistreated by his two sons, Eteocles and Polynices, so he cursed them. To avoid bloodshed, they agreed to rule Thebes alternately, for one year at a time. After the first year Eteocles refused to give up power as he had promised, so Polynices raised an army, led by the Seven, to take Thebes by force. They failed, and all seven (in other versions, six) commanders were killed. Ten years later their sons, the Epigoni (Diomedes and Sthenelus among them), wanting to avenge the death of their fathers, attacked Thebes and captured it.

4.353 *Thebes:* A city in Boeotia, in northern Greece; in Mycenean times it had been a very rich city. It is to be distinguished from the very rich city of Thebes in Egypt (see note to 9.382). Thebē, referred to in 1.371 and elsewhere, is a smaller city near Troy.

5.5 *like the star of late summer:* Sirius, the brightest star in the night sky. It is also known as the "Dog Star" because of its prominence in the constellation Canis Major.

5.100 *who called me from Lycia:* This Lycia, at the foot of Mount Ida near Troy, is not to be confused with the larger country called Lycia in the southwest corner of Asia Minor. The southern Lycians, led by Sarpedon, are, along with the Dardanians, the principal Trojan allies.

5.212 *Tros:* The first king of Troy, Aeneas' great-great-grandfather and Priam's great-grandfather. See note to 5.582.

5.250 *Gánymede:* One of the three sons of Tros,

> the most handsome of mortal men, and because of his beauty
> the gods snatched him up to heaven, so he could be
> Zeus's wine-steward and live among the immortals. (20.233–35 in the
>   Greek text)

5.312 *Enýo:* A goddess of war.

5.359 *Otus and Ephiáltes:* Gigantic twins fathered by Poseidon (at age nine they were fifty-four feet tall). Their story is told in the *Odyssey*, 11.305–20.

5.365 *Héracles* (Latin, Hercules): The son of Zeus and Alcmena, and the greatest of the Greek heroes. See note to 8.338–39.

5.582 *who once came here to claim Laómedon's horses:* As punishment for rebelling against Zeus, Poseidon and Apollo had been sent to Earth stripped of their divinity and in servitude to King Laomedon, grandson of Tros and father of Priam. They built the walls of Troy for him, but he defrauded them of their pay (21.418ff.), so Poseidon sent a sea monster to terrorize the land. Laomedon was about to sacrifice his daughter Hesione to the monster in the hope of appeasing Poseidon, but he offered the immortal horses of Tros as a reward to whoever killed the monster. Heracles rescued her, but Laomedon tried to cheat him by giving him mortal horses instead. In return, Heracles attacked and devastated Troy, killing Laomedon and all his sons except for Priam. Telamon took Hesione as a war prize and married her; Teucer was their son.

5.596 *Death, the pale horseman:* The reference is probably to Hades' rape of Persephone.

5.672 *Gorgon:* A female monster who had hair of poisonous snakes and whose face turned the onlooker to stone. After Perseus killed the Gorgon Medusa, he cut off her head and gave it to Athena to put on her shield.

5.706 *ambrosia:* Literally, "immortality"; a plant that is the food of the gods. It is also used in the *Iliad* as a perfume, a cleansing cosmetic, and an embalming preservative.

5.729 *an envoy to Thebes:* See note to 4.341. Adrastus, king of Argos, gave shelter to Polynices and helped him raise an army to attack Thebes.

5.770 *tamer of horses:* A conventional epithet of heroes (Greek *hippodamos*), used most often for Diomedes and Hector, and also for the Trojans. Its most famous occurrence is as the last word of the *Iliad*.

5.800 *you yourself gave birth:* According to legend, Zeus impregnated the Titaness Metis, but since it had been prophesied that he would have a son more powerful than himself, he tricked Metis into becoming a fly and swallowed her. The child, a daughter, grew inside Zeus, and eventually Metis began to make a helmet and robe for her. The hammering caused Zeus a severe headache, and Prometheus (or, according to different sources, Hephaestus, Hermes, or Palaemon) split Zeus's head open with an axe. Athena leaped out, fully grown and armed.

6.48 *iron skillfully worked:* In the Bronze Age iron was a rare and precious metal.

6.58 *not even the baby boy:* "The scholiasts were much exercised by the 'beast-liness' of [Agamemnon's] words. . . . They try to justify him by rehearsing his own arguments and by drawing attention to the Trojans' violation of the truce in Book 4" (Graziosi and Haubold, p. 91). The relevant passage is:

> "whichever army is first to betray this oath
> by breaking the truce, may their brains be spilled on the ground
> as this wine is spilled—their brains and the brains of their children;
> and may their dear wives be other men's slaves and whores."   (3.282–85)

6.132 *Lycúrgus:* A king of the Edoni in Thrace. He banned the cult of Dionysus and imprisoned Dionysus' followers, the Maenads. Dionysus decreed that the land would remain barren as long as Lycurgus went unpunished, so his people had him torn apart by wild horses. (See also 7.141–48.)

6.157 *Sísyphus:* King of Ephyra (Corinth). He was greedy and cunning and lived by robbery and murder. Because of this, or because he betrayed Zeus's secrets, he was punished in the underworld by having to roll a huge rock up a hill, but before he could ever get to the top, the rock would roll back down again.

6.173–74 *a folded tablet inscribed / with many murderous symbols:* This is the only mention of writing in the *Iliad* or the *Odyssey*.

6.177 *the river Xanthus:* See note to 2.815.

6.189 *Bellérophon killed her:* According to other legends, he first had to tame the winged horse Pegasus, "beloved by the Muses of Mount Helicon, for whom he had created the well Hippocrene by stamping his moon-shaped hoof. . . . He overcame the Chimaera by flying above her on Pegasus's back, riddling her with arrows, and then thrusting between her jaws a lump of lead which he had fixed to the point of his spear. The Chimaera's fiery breath melted the lead, which trickled down her throat, searing her vitals" (Robert Graves, *The Greek Myths* [Harmondsworth 1960], p. 253).

6.190 *Sólymi:* The original inhabitants of Lycia.

6.197 *a god's offspring:* He was rumored to be the son of Poseidon.

6.205 *Bellérophon came to be hated by all the gods:* At the height of his fame Bellerophon in his hubris tried to fly to Olympus, but Zeus sent a gadfly that stung Pegasus under the tail, making him buck and throw Bellerophon down to Earth. Lamed by the fall, Bellerophon wandered until his death, homeless, blind, and despised by all men.

6.218 *guest-friend:* "In those distant days of separate communities, when a stranger could be in considerable danger, some security was provided by a system of family connections, sometimes called 'guest-friendship.' *xeinos (xenos)* means a stranger, but also a host or guest. The tie of having been entertained in somebody's house in a strange land was remembered even into following generations; and the relationship was watched over by Zeus *xeinios* (625)" (Willcock 2, p. 220).

6.219 *Œneus:* King of Calydon, a city in Aetolia, in northwestern Greece. He was the father of Meleager (see 9.538ff.) and also, by a different woman, the father of Tydeus and grandfather of Diomedes.

6.227 *that time the Achaean army was slaughtered at Thebes:* See note to 4.341.

6.296 *Sidon:* A principal city of Phoenicia, famous for its glass and its purple dyes.

6.298 *one of these robes:* "[Hecuba's] choice is disastrous: she picks a garment woven by Sidonian women who were abducted by Paris on his way home, after he had already taken Helen. . . . [The] history of this particular garment was not likely to please Athena: it evoked the rape of Helen. . . ." (Graziosi and Haubold, p. 28).

6.343 *Just now my wife was gently urging me back:* In fact, her words (3.404–11) were anything but gentle.

6.347 *or else you go first:* "Paris asks Hector to wait while he gets ready for battle and then suddenly changes his mind: Hector should go right ahead. We can easily imagine Hector's look at the mere suggestion that he should stay around, while his soldiers die (for the sake of Paris) on the battlefield. . . . Here as elsewhere Homer's poetry is so vivid that we can visualize not just the speaker but also the reaction of his interlocutor. . . ." (*Ibid.*, pp. 24, 174).

6.400 *Cilícians:* There was also a country called Cilicia in southeast Asia Minor. The Cilicians ruled by Andromache's father live just south of Troy, beneath a spur of Mount Ida.

6.496 *turning around to look back:* "The implication must be that Hector is looking at her and is still standing by the Scaean Gates" (Graziosi and Haubold, p. 24).

7.434 *the wall that I and Apollo:* See note to 5.582.

8.177–80 *Nestor's great shield . . . his finely wrought breastplate:* A strange passage. Why would the loss of Nestor's shield and Diomedes' breastplate make the Achaeans sail off immediately? "There has been no previous mention of these special pieces of armament, and they will not be heard of again. Diomedes was evidently not wearing this corslet three days before, when he exchanged his armour with Glaucus; it can hardly be part of the golden armour that he received from Glaucus" (*MI*, p. 205).

8.211 *Lemnos:* The Achaeans had stopped at the island of Lemnos on their way to Troy and abandoned Philoctetes there (2.670–73).

8.268 *tripod:* "A three-legged . . . metal implement, sometimes on wheels, on which a cauldron was placed, which was then heated over the fire for cooking or to boil water. The tripod was highly esteemed as a prize; seven of them are included in Agamemnon's promised recompense to Achilles at 9.122, and they appear again in Priam's offer to Achilles at 24.274–7; see also *Od.* 4.128–35" (Wilson, p. 195). At the funeral games for Patroclus the prizes for the wrestling contest are

> for the winner, a large tripod to stand on the fire—
> its value was set at twelve oxen; and for the loser
> he placed in their midst a woman skilled in the arts
> of spinning and weaving, valued as worth four oxen. (23.714–17)

8.338–39 *the tasks / of Eurýstheus:* Driven insane by Hera, Heracles killed his own children. To expiate the crime, he was required to carry out ten tasks set by his enemy, King Eurystheus. Heracles accomplished all ten, but Eurystheus discounted the second (killing the Lernaean Hydra) and fifth (cleansing the Augean Stables) and set two more tasks: bringing back the Golden Apples of the Hesperides and capturing Cerberus.

8.343 *the dog of Hades:* Cerberus, the three-headed dog that guards the gates of the underworld to prevent the dead who have crossed the river Styx from escaping.

8.432 *Ĭápetus and Cronus:* Titans, sons of Uranus, and fathers, respectively, of Prometheus and Zeus. Cronus had castrated and deposed Uranus, and was in turn deposed by Zeus and imprisoned in Tartarus.

9.138 *Orestes:* His killing of Aegisthus in revenge for the murder of his father is mentioned several times in the *Odyssey.*

9.141 *Íphianássa:* "Homer's names for Agamemnon's daughters are different from those of classical times, with no mention of Electra or Iphigenia, who are also not to be found in the Odyssey. . . . Iphianassa here has sometimes been thought to be the equivalent of the later Iphigenia; but if this is right, then Homer cannot have known the story which became famous later of Agamemnon sacrificing Iphigenia at Aulis before his fleet set sail from Greece to Troy" (Wilson, p. 220).

9.143 *bride-price:* "Normally Homer talks in terms of 'bride-price' rather than 'dowry': the bridegroom must pay the bride's father, e.g. the touching account of Iphidamas, 11.241–7. . . . At other times the poems seem to envisage the reverse, dowry, system. . . . Sometimes no doubt both things happened, or both families contributed to set up the new couple" (Griffin, p. 92).

9.186 *Éétion's city:* Thebē. See note to 1.371.

9.326 *Troad:* The region around Troy.

9.382 *Orchómenos or of Egyptian Thebes:* Orchomenos, in Boeotia, was, with the Boeotian Thebes, one of the leading cities in Mycenean times. The Egyptian Thebes, "the modern Luxor, 400 or so miles down from the mouth of the Nile, had once been the capital of Egypt, and its wealth is mentioned several times in the *Odyssey*, e.g. at 3.301 and 4.127, which is almost equivalent to 382 here" (Wilson, p. 234).

9.408 *Pytho:* "Apollo's great center at Delphi, on the lower slopes of Mount Parnassus in northern Greece. . . . The word Pytho . . . was supposed to have come from Apollo's exploit in slaying the Python, a mighty dragon, when he established his sanctuary there. The wealth of the place will have derived from the dedications that had been made to Apollo" (Wilson, p. 235).

9.529 *Œneus:* See note to 6.219.

9.557–58 *against Lord Apollo / for the sake of his wife:* "After Idas had carried Marpessa away from her father Evenus, Apollo wished to carry her away from Idas. Idas resisted him, and Zeus intervened, asking Marpessa to make her own choice between the two, at which Marpessa chose Idas" (Wilson, p. 243).

9.567 *when Meleáger had killed her brother:* In a dispute over the spoils of the Calydonian Boar.

9.571 *the Fury:* The Furies (in Greek, *Erinyes*, "Angry Ones") are the spirits of vengeance "that under the ground / punish the dead who have broken their solemn vows" (19.265–66). They also punish family offenses, including violence of younger brother against elder (15.188).

9.637 *blood-price:* "The kinsmen of a murdered man were bound to avenge his death, unless the killer left the community. . . . At some times or in some places it was possible to come to a financial arrangement" (Griffin, pp. 142–43).

9.650 *some outcast who has no rights:* "A landless man who arrived on the run and has no legal position" (Griffin, p. 144).

11.1 *Lord Tithónus:* The son of King Laomedon of Troy (and thus a brother of Priam) by a water nymph named Strymo. The Titaness Dawn (in Greek, *Eos*) kidnapped him and kept him as her lover.

11.20 *Cínyras:* Son of Apollo and king of Cyprus, famous for his wealth and, later, as the founder of the cult of Aphrodite at Paphos. On Cyprus he was revered as the inventor of the arts and of musical instruments. Before the Trojan War, he was visited by Menelaus, Odysseus, and the herald Talthybius, who tried to persuade him to join the allies.

11.166–67 *the tomb / of Ilus:* This Ilus, son of Dardanus, died childless. His brother, Erichthonius, was the father of Tros, who was the father of the Ilus who was the father of Laomedon, Priam's father. "His tomb, the fig-tree (167), the oak (170) and the 'rise' . . . are the permanent landmarks of the *Iliad's* geography of the Trojan plain. . . . The fig-tree was near the city, the tomb in the middle of the plain" (Hainsworth, p. 243).

11.311 *the two sons of Merops:* Adrestus and Amphius; they are named at 2.770.

11.660 *Ctéatus and Eúrytus:* Cteatus and Eurytus were famous warriors, twins, nominally sons of Actor, but their real father was Poseidon. Their sons Amphimachus and Thalpius were leaders of the Elean contingent at 2.576–84; Amphimachus is killed at 13.178–81. Also see note to 23.646.

13.4 *looking far north:* The poet "reveals a geographical horizon that extends beyond the Danube to the lands of steppe pastoralists. These are not fabulous people but real ones that Greek explorers encountered after penetrating into the Black Sea and beyond the mouth of the Danube" (*MI*, p. 18).

13.5 *Mysians:* These are not the Mysians of 2.796, the Trojan allies from Asia Minor, but a northern tribe from the European side of the Hellespont.

13.356 *Cassándra:* She makes one other brief appearance at 24.692–99, and her murder by Clytemnestra is mentioned at *Odyssey* 11.421–23. Homer says nothing about the prophetic ability that was so famous in later Greek literature.

13.520–21 *the vein that runs / along the spinal cord, all the way up to the neck:* In reality there is no such vein.

13.588–89 *his eyeballs, dripping with blood, / fell at his feet on the ground:* "Homer's descriptions of wounds are usually realistic . . . but occasionally impossible and grotesque. This . . . is an example of the latter. The eyes cannot in fact drop out of the head" (Willcock 2, p. 219). This happens again when Patroclus kills Cebriones at 16.678.

13.627 *like a dead worm:* A worm writhes when it is hurt, but stretches out when it is dead.

13.630 *his father:* A famous example of "Homer nodding": the poet forgets that Pylaemenes was killed by Menelaus at 5.522–24.

13.750 *had come from Ascánia on the previous day:* "This contradicts the Catalogue, as Ascanius was already leader of the men from Ascania there, and the action of the *Iliad* has lasted some four days. . . . The reason for the slip is no doubt that Homer is using a stock theme involving the pathos of war, that these men only arrived at the front yesterday" (Willcock 2, p. 224).

14.112 *Adrástus:* The king of Argos, leader of the assault on Thebes. Both Tydeus and Polynices married daughters of his. See note to 4.341.

14.189 *Tethys:* A Titaness and goddess of the sea, daughter of Uranus and Gaia, and both sister and wife of Oceanus. During the Wars of the Titans, when Zeus overthrew his father, Cronos, Hera lived in the palace of Oceanus and Tethys, who had received her from her mother, Rhea, and were keeping her safe.

14.244 *Night:* Sleep doesn't mention that Night is his mother.

14.253 *Graces:* Goddesses of beauty, grace, happiness, dance, and song; attendants of Hera and Aphrodite. Another Grace, Charis, is married to Hephaestus (18.359–60).

14.256 *Styx:* "When Zeus declared war on the Titans, offering rewards to any who would join him, Styx was first to come, at her father Oceanus's suggestion; she brought her children Victory and Power, who dwell for ever with Zeus. As a reward, he made her the *orkos* [oath] of the gods, and with reason: if Styx and her children change sides, the Titans will oust the Olympians. So Hera utters the dreadful curse that if she neglects her promise, the entire divine order is to be overturned" (Janko, p. 194).

14.300 *Ixíon's wife:* Her name was Dia. Ixion was the king of the Lapiths. Because he killed his father-in-law, he was shunned and despised. Zeus took pity on him and brought him to Olympus, but Ixion tried to rape Hera, so he was cast down and bound to a fiery wheel for eternity.

14.301 *Piríthoüs:* He is mentioned in 1.263 and 2.684.

14.302 *Dánaë:* Daughter of King Acrisius of Argos. When the king heard a prophecy that he would one day be killed by a son born to his daughter, he locked Danae in a bronze tower. But Zeus came to her as a shower of gold and impregnated her. Soon afterward she gave birth to the hero Perseus.

14.303 *Perseus:* Founder of Mycenae. He killed the Gorgon Medusa and rescued Andromeda from a sea monster.

14.303 *Phoenix:* The eponymous ancestor of the Phoenicians.

14.304 *Minos and Rhadamánthys:* Brothers, kings of Crete, and judges of the dead in the underworld. See 13.432.

14.305 *Sémelē:* Daughter of Cadmus and Harmonia, king and queen of Thebes. After Zeus took her as a lover, she demanded that he reveal himself to her in all his glory. When he did, she was burned to ashes.

14.305 *Alcména:* See note to 19.96.

14.307 *Dionýsus:* God of wine and ecstasy.

14.308 *Deméter:* Goddess of grain and fertility, and mother of Persephone.

14.308 *Leto:* Mother of Apollo and Artemis.

15.80 *Themis:* The noun means "what is established or sanctioned by tradition." "A gift of the gods and a mark of civilized existence, sometimes it means right custom, proper procedure, social order, and sometimes merely the will of the gods (as revealed by an omen, for example) with little of the idea of right . . . custom, tradition, folk-ways, *mores,* whatever we may call it, the enormous power of 'it is (or is not) done' " (M. I. Finley, *The World of Odysseus* [New York 1978], pp. 78, 82). The goddess Themis "presides at divine conclaves: hence Hesiod makes her Zeus's second wife . . . , Zeus bids her call the gods together (20.4) and they both preside over assemblies in general. . . . As a Titan who sided with [Zeus] . . . she shares his counsels . . . and protects his power" (Janko 238).

15.100 *Ascálaphus:* He was killed at 13.494–96.

15.377 *cord:* "A device employed by carpenters, etc., a line rubbed with chalk or the like and drawn tight along a surface so as to leave on its removal a straight line marked thereon for the workman's guidance" (Cunliffe, p. 363).

15.389 *his dear cousin:* Caletor's father, Clytius, is King Priam's brother and one of the elders of Troy (3.136).

15.513 *your cousin:* Melanippus's father, Hicetaon, and Dolops's father, Lampus, are brothers of Priam.

15.590 *Eurýstheus:* See note to 8.338–39.

16.139 *Xanthus and Bálius*: Poseidon gave Peleus the immortal horses as a wedding present (23.278–79). Chiron's wedding present was the ash-wood spear (16.132–33). A third present was the "indestructible armor" forged by Hephaestus (17.194–95).

16.212 *lord of Pelásgia*: Achilles comes from Pelasgian Argos (2.634).

16.290 *Amisódarus*: The king of Lycia who was the father-in-law of Prœtus (6.160ff.) Amisodarus's sons are Bellerophon's brothers-in-law and Sarpedon's uncles.

17.206 *something you shouldn't have done*: "There is no impropriety in taking the armor of a dead foe. What Zeus means is that Hector does not have the status to wear the immortal arms of Achilles" (Willcock 2, p. 258).

17.263 *As at the mouth of a river*: "A simile famous in antiquity for its sound-effects. [The ancient scholiast writes,] 'He has compared the noise not only to the flowing of a river or to the sea surf, but he has combined them both. And one can see the great surf of the sea hurled against the current of the river, and roaring as if beaten back, and the beaches on either side of the river resounding, which he has imitated. . . . ' This simile caused both Plato and Solon, [the scholia] report, to burn their own poetry in despair" (Edwards, p. 88).

17.566 *Eëtion*: "Presumably this Eëtion is not Andromache's father, king of Thebē, whose seven sons were killed by Achilles (6.421–24); there was also an Eëtion of Imbros who ransomed Priam's son Lycaon (21.42–43)" (Edwards, p. 118).

18.371 *for saving me*: "It is not clear whether this is the same fall as that described in 1.592–93, when Zeus threw him off Olympus; nor is it clear whether Hephaestus' lameness was caused by the fall, or whether he was lame from birth" (Willcock 2, p. 286).

18.375 *Eurýnomē*: "Eurynome is mentioned by Hesiod among the daughters of Oceanus and Tethus . . . and as mother (by Zeus) of the Charites. . . . The amiable Hephaestus is courteously giving prominence to his mother-in-law" (Edwards, p. 193).

18.407 *forced to marry a human*: Homer gives no reason, but "in the *Kypria* . . . Thetis rejected Zeus's advances in order to please Hera, and for that reason . . . Zeus in anger condemned her to marry a mortal" (Gantz, p. 228).

18.476 *two men were disputing*: "The killer is claiming the right to pay ransom . . . in full . . . on the grounds of mitigated homicide, the amount to be fixed by the court. The other party is claiming and choosing the right to take revenge, as in cases of aggravated homicide. The court must set the 'limit' . . . of the penalty, i.e. whether it should be revenge or ransom, and also the appropriate 'limit' of either revenge or ransom" (Edwards, p. 216).

18.556 *Linus*: The son of Apollo and one of the Muses. According to the geographer Pausanias, he was killed by his father because he had rivaled him in his singing. He was universally mourned, and laments (*linoi*) were sung in his honor. Rilke mentions him in the conclusion of "The First Duino Elegy":

> *Schließlich brauchen sie uns nicht mehr, die Früheentrückten,*
> *man entwöhnt sich des Irdischen sanft, wie man den Brüsten*
> *milde der Mutter entwächst. Aber wir, die so große*
> *Geheimnisse brauchen, denen aus Trauer so oft*
> *seliger Fortschritt entspringt—: könnten wir sein ohne sie?*
> *Ist die Sage umsonst, daß einst in der Klage um Linos*
> *wagende erste Musik dürre Erstarrung durchdrang;*
> *daß erst im erschrockenen Raum, dem ein beinah göttlicher Jüngling*
> *plötzlich für immer enttrat, das Leere in jene*
> *Schwingung geriet, die uns jetzt hinreißt und tröstet und hilft.*

> In the end, those who were carried off early no longer need us:
> they are weaned from earth's sorrows and joys, as gently as children
> outgrow the soft breasts of their mothers. But we, who do need
> such great mysteries, we for whom grief is so often
> the source of our spirit's growth—: could we exist without *them*?
> Is the legend meaningless that tells how, in the lament for Linus,
> the daring first notes of song pierced through the barren numbness;
> and then in the startled space which a youth as lovely as a god
> had suddenly left forever, the Void felt for the first time
> that harmony which now enraptures and comforts and helps us.

The Selected Poetry of Rainer Maria Rilke, pp. 154–55.

18.575 *Dædalus*: The archetypal artist and master builder. He built the device by which Minos's wife Pasiphae mated with the bull to produce the Minotaur, and also the labyrinth where the Minotaur was kept, and he gave Minos's daughter Ariadne the thread that allowed Theseus to find his way out of the labyrinth.

19.90 *Madness*: The Greek word is *atē*, which can also be translated as "delusion" or "(mental) blindness." "If a man act[ed] in an inexplicable and self-damaging way, it was deduced that something external to himself had taken over his decision-making faculty. This outside force is commonly said to be sent by Zeus, because Zeus is ultimately responsible for everything. However, ascribing the blame to *atē* does not absolve the doer from responsibility for his actions" (Willcock 2, pp. 273–74).

19.96 *Alcména:* She was the daughter of Electryon, king of Mycenae, who was the son of Perseus, and she was married to her cousin and uncle Amphitryon, king of Thebes. She was wiser and more beautiful than any other mortal woman, and famously faithful, so Zeus could seduce her only by taking the form of her husband. He extended one night of lovemaking into three to produce Heracles, and when Amphitryon learned from Tiresias that Heracles had been fathered by Zeus, he never slept with his wife again for fear of the god's reaction. Hera, jealous as usual, prolonged Alcmena's labor and sent snakes to kill the infant, but Heracles strangled them in his cradle.

19.102 *has come from my very own loins:* "Zeus's pronouncement comes true because both Heracles and Eurystheus are of his lineage, though only the former is his son; Perseus, son of Zeus, fathered both Alcmena's father Electryon and Sthenelus, father of Eurystheus" (Edwards, p. 250).

20.89 *Leléges:* The people of Pedasus.

20.135 *sea monster:* See note to 5.582.

20.233 *innocent:* This refers "to Laomedon's outrageous behavior toward Poseidon and Apollo (12.441–57); Aeneas is not descended from Laomedon" (who was Priam's father and a cousin of Aeneas's grandfather). "The abduction of Helen by the Trojan prince Paris may also not be held against the Dardanians" (Edwards, p. 325).

20.239 *Dárdanus:* Son of Zeus, great-great-great-great-grandfather of Aeneas and of Hector.

20.344 *Polydórus, his young brother:* He was the son of Priam and Laothoë, and thus Hector's half-brother.

21.43 *Eunéüs:* King of Lemnos, son of Jason and Hypsipyle. See 23.754–61 for an account of the silver mixing bowl that Euneus gave to Patroclus as ransom for Lycaon.

21.44 *Éétion of Imbros:* Not to be confused with Andromache's father, Éétion, who "had ruled the Cilícians in Thebē under the wooded / slopes of Mount Placus" (6.402–3).

21.183 *the mightiest river of all, Achelóüs:* The longest river in Greece; it rises in the Pindus Mountains of central Epirus, divides Aetolia from Acarnania, and empties into the Ionian Sea.

21.420 *to work for Laómedon:* See note to 5.582.

21.455 *allowed you to kill any mother you wish in childbirth:* As the goddess of childbirth, Artemis is responsible for deaths as well as for safe deliveries.

22.30 *Oríon's Dog:* Sirius, the brightest star in the night sky. Its heliacal rising marked the flooding of the Nile in Egypt and the "dog days" of late summer for the Greeks.

22.147 *One spring flows:* "The present tenses imply features to be seen in [the poet's] own day. The hot and cold sources of the Scamander of course belong up in the mountains. . . . [He] must have known of them by hearsay . . . and wrongly attached them to the city" (*MI*, p. 386).

22.151 *the wide troughs:* "Washing-troughs, on the other hand, are genuine; they are located on the western side of the lower town, where a large fig-tree now grows. . . . They are fed by an underground spring, which [the poet] evidently confused (whether by error or creative fiction) with the hot and cold springs he had heard of" (*MI*, pp. 386–87).

22.465 *her husband's sisters:* Laodice, Cassandra, etc.

22.465 *brother's wives:* Helen, for one.

23.261 *funeral games:* "Funeral games with horse races were an ancient institution" to honor the dead (*MI*, p. 387).

23.290 *Eumélus:* See 2.661–65; for his horses, see 2.704–10.

23.355 *Aríon:* A fabulously swift immortal horse sired by Poseidon, by whose help Adrastus, king of Argos, escaped from before Thebes. According to later legend, Arion's mane was green.

23.356 *Laómedon's horses:* See 5.249–55 and note to 5.582.

23.564 *took from Asteropǽus:* See 21.172.

23.646 *sons of Actor:* See note to 11.660. In other sources Cteatus and Eurytus are described as Siamese twins, their bodies joined below the waist.

23.674 *Epéüs:* According to the *Odyssey* (8.493, 11.523) he later made the Trojan horse, with the help of Athena.

23.691 *when Œdipus fell:* Apparently in battle: a very different conclusion, of course, from the one we have in Sophocles' *Oedipus at Colonus*.

23.692 *his cousin:* Euryalus's father, Mecisteus, was the brother of Adrastus, whose daughter Deipyle married Diomedes' father, Tydeus, and became the mother of Diomedes. In addition Diomedes married Deipyle's sister Ægialia.

23.715 *its value was set at twelve oxen:* At 6.240 Diomedes' bronze armor is said to be worth nine oxen and Glaucus's golden armor a hundred oxen.

23.717 *valued as worth four oxen:* "Contrast *Od.* 1.431, where Euryclea was bought for twenty, evidently an unusually high price" (Richardson, p. 247).

23.749 *equal prizes:* "[The poet] does not explain how the prizes were made equal; neither a tripod nor a woman is much use if cut in half" (*MI*, p. 407).

23.759 *Eunéüs:* See note to 21.43.

23.858 *throwing-stick:* It had a string attached to it and a weight at the other end; the herdsman threw it when he wanted to drive a cow back into the herd.

24.53 *gave her in marriage:* See 18.406–9 for a different aspect of the story.

24.146 *Hermes:* "Hermes is appropriate not as a universal escort but more particularly as a god of wayfarers . . . and accomplice of sneak-thieves . . . , able to smuggle them past defences and guards" (*MI*, p. 417).

24.454 *it would be most offensive:* "In the *Iliad,* only the remote Ethiopians have the privilege of giving hospitality to the gods in their true form, but in the *Odyssey* the Phaeacians can also do so (7.201–6). In the past, however, the gods came in person to the wedding-feast of Peleus and Thetis (*Il.* 24.62–63)" (Richardson, p. 320).

24.487 *other wives in my palace:* "It is fairly clear that Homer is depicting Priam as a polygamous ruler, in contract to Greek custom. . . . Altes' daughter Laothoe . . . was mentioned at 21.84–85, 22.46–48, as mother of Lycaon and Polydorus. At 8.302–5 we hear of Castianira, mother of Gorgythion. Of Priam's fifty sons, twenty-two are mentioned in the *Iliad.* Two (Mestor and Troilus) died earlier in the war (257), eleven are killed in the course of the poem, and the remaining nine are named at 249–51. If we exclude the three children said to be from other wives (Lycaon, Polydorus and Gorgythion) we are left with nineteen, and so it is possible that all the nineteen sons of Hecuba are mentioned by the poet in the course of his narrative, although only five are explicitly said to be hers (Hector, Paris, Antiphus, Deiphobus, Polites)" (Richardson, pp. 325–26).

24.535 *Macar:* The founding king of Lesbos.

24.612 *she still continues:* "The origin of the story was clearly a rock-image on Mt. Sipylus, identified as the sorrowing Niobe, the water flowing down its face being her tears" (Richardson, p. 341).

24.641 *with a hint:* "Achilles knows that his guest must leave by night, and his speech hints at the danger of his remaining. He knows too that a god has escorted Priam . . . and he guesses that the same god will help him return, as in fact happens. He thus avoids a farewell in which he and Priam would have to be together in the presence of Hector's body. . . . So by making Priam sleep in the *aithousa* [porch or colonnade] he eases the old man's departure. But it would be undignified and inhospitable for him to do so more openly; hence the polite deception of these lines" (Macleod, p. 143).

24.753 *killed with his gentle arrows:* A sudden, painless death was ascribed to the "gentle arrows" of Apollo or Artemis (the former bringing death to men, the latter to women).

Notes on the Greek Text

The text that I have translated is *Homeri Ilias,* edited by Martin L. West. I have omitted all verses that are deleted in his edition or bracketed as probable interpolations. Any divergences are indicated below. (Line numbers in this section refer to the Greek text.)

Alternative Readings

2.291 †ἀνιηθέντα νέεσθαι†: marked as corrupt by West; read ἀνίη τ' ἐνθάδε ἧσθαι (cj. Pfudel), which West considers the least unlikely conjecture.

3.126 μαρμαρέην: Read πορφυρέην with Zenodotus, Aristophanes, Aristarchus, and two of the codices.

4.235 ψεύδεσσι: Read ψευδέσσι with Aristarchus, Ptolomaeus Ascalonita, and the vulgate.

7.21 ἐκκατιδών: Read ἐκκατιών (Payne Knight's emendation); West, *Studies in the Text and Transmission of the Iliad* (hereafter *Studies*), p. 199.

9.73 πᾶσά: Read πᾶσί. West's apparatus; *Studies,* p. 206.

13.134 †ἐπτύσσοντο†: Read ἐπλίσσοντο. *Studies,* p. 222.

14.173 †κινυμένοιο Διὸς: Read κινυμένης Ζηνὸς. *Studies,* p. 227.

14.396 †ποτὶ: Read πέλει. *Studies,* p. 228.

16.382 †κέκλετο: Read κέκλιτο. *Studies,* p. 238.

16.710 πολλὸν: Read τυτθὸν with Zenodotus. *Studies,* p. 240.

17.264 δέ τ' ἄκραι: Read δὲ μακραί. West's apparatus; *Studies,* p. 241.

23.871 †ὡς ἴθυνεν†: Read ᾧ ῥ' ἴθυνεν. West's apparatus; *Studies,* pp. 275–76.

23.49 ὄτρυνε: Read ὄτρυνον. *MI,* p. 395.

Omissions

1.209: *MI*, p. 89.

1.396–406 (athetized by Zenodotus): *MI*, p. 94.

2.141: *MI*, p. 104.

2.260: *MI*, p. 107.

2.319: *MI*, p. 108.

2.572: *Studies*, p. 181; *MI*, p. 117.

3.18–20: I have retained these lines. Though West brackets them in his text, his later opinion is that they are presupposed by 17 (*MI*, p. 128).

3.108–10: (athetized by Aristarchus): These lines are superfluous and contradict 106, which implies that *some* young men—though not Priam's sons—are responsible people.

3.201: *MI*, pp. 132–33.

3.343: *MI*, p. 135.

4.177: West's apparatus; *Studies*, p. 189.

5.313: *Studies*, p. 191.

5.338: *Studies*, pp. 191–92.

5.462–70: *MI*, p. 161.

5.604: *MI*, p. 164.

5.774: *MI*, p. 169.

5.820–21: West's apparatus; *Studies*, p. 195.

6.433–39: *Studies*, pp. 198–99.

7.156: *MI*, p. 191.

7.410: *MI*, p. 196.

7.466–81: West brackets these verses in *MI*, p. 198.

8.189–90: West's apparatus; *Studies,* p. 202.

8.359: *Studies,* p. 202.

8.385–87, 390–91, 393–96: *Studies,* p. 203.

8.410: *MI,* p. 210.

8.532–34, 538–41: West's apparatus; *Studies,* p. 204.

9.32–39: *MI,* p. 215.

9.350: *MI,* p. 222.

9.425–26: *MI,* p. 224.

9.616: "616 is unexpectedly lavish. Heyne and others have deleted 616 as a later insertion, plausibly" (Griffin, p. 141).

11.272: *Studies,* p. 212.

11.299–306: West's apparatus; *Studies,* p. 212.

11.354: *MI,* p. 254.

11.603–7: *Studies,* p. 214.

11.810: West's apparatus; *Studies,* p. 214.

12.153: West's apparatus; *Studies,* p. 217.

12.175–81: *Studies,* pp. 216–19.

13.418–23: *MI,* p. 279.

13.694–700: West's apparatus.

14.279: *Studies,* pp. 227–28.

16.74–79: *MI,* p. 314.

16.268–77: *MI,* pp. 317–18.

16.675: *MI,* p. 325.

17.657–67: *MI,* p. 341.

18.106: "The correction of the preceding line is needless, and not like the character of Achilles" (Leaf 2, p. 276). He is a great speaker (as he was trained to be, 9.442–43), and he undoubtedly knows it, as everyone else does; Nestor's statement in 1.258 isn't merely polite.

20.213–43, 246–55: *Studies*, pp. 255–56.

21.202–4: *MI*, p. 377.

21.250: *MI*, p. 379.

22.323: *MI*, p. 389.

22.371: *Studies*, p. 263.

22.485–99, 506–7: West's apparatus; *Studies*, pp. 265–66.

23.74: West's apparatus; *Studies*, p. 266.

23.104: *Studies*, pp. 267–68.

23.296–300: *MI*, p. 401.

24.6–9: *MI*, p. 411; Macleod, p. 85.

24.640: *MI*, p. 424.

Pronouncing Glossary of Major and Secondary Characters*, Peoples, and Places

Acamas (**a**-ka-mas): Trojan, son of Antenor, comrade of Aeneas, killed by Meriones. (In this glossary, "Trojan" may refer to an actual Trojan, or to a Dardanian, a Lycian, or another of the Trojan allies.)

Achaea (a-**kee**-uh): The land we call Greece.

Achaeans (a-**kee**-uhnz): The people of Achaea. Synonymous with Argives and Danaans.

Achilles (a-**kil**-eez): Achaean, son of Peleus, king of Phthia, and of the sea goddess Thetis; comrade of Patroclus; commander of the Myrmidons.

Aeneas (a-**nee**-uhs): Trojan, son of Anchises and Aphrodite, commander of the Dardanians.

Agamemnon (a-ga-**mem**-non): Achaean, son of Atreus, brother of Menelaus; king of Mycenae and leading commander of the Achaeans.

Agenor (a-**jee**-nor): Trojan, son of Antenor, one of the principal Trojan commanders.

Ajax (**ay**-jaks) the Smaller: Achaean, son of Oïleus, commander of the Locrians.

Ajax (**ay**-jaks) the Tall: Achaean, son of Telamon, one of the principal Achaean commanders and their greatest fighter after Achilles.

---

*A "secondary character" is defined here as one who has a speaking part in the *Iliad*.

Alcimus (**al**-sim-us): Achaean, son of Laerces, one of the Myrmidon commanders; also know as Alcimedon.

Andromache (an-**drom**-a-kee): Trojan, daughter of Eëtion, wife of Hector.

Antenor (an-**tee**-nor): Trojan, counselor to Priam, husband of Theano, father of many sons who take part in the fighting.

Antilochus (an-**til**-o-kus): Achaean, son of Nestor, friend of Achilles.

Aphrodite (af-roh-**dye**-tee): Daughter of Zeus and Dione, goddess of love, mother of Aeneas.

Apollo (a-**pol**-oh): Son of Zeus and Leto, twin brother of Artemis, patron of music and the arts, chief protector of the Trojans. Also known as Phoebus Apollo.

Ares (**air**-eez): Son of Zeus and Hera, god of war, protector of the Trojans.

Argives (**ar**-gyvz): Another name for Achaeans.

Argos (**ar**-gos): Can refer to a city, ruled by Diomedes; a larger region, ruled by Agamemnon; or all of mainland Greece.

Artemis (**ar**-tem-is): Daughter of Zeus and Leto, twin sister of Apollo, goddess of the hunt.

Asius (**ay**-si-us): Trojan, son of Hyrtacus, father of Adamas and Phaenops, commander of the Trojan allies from Percote, killed by Idomeneus.

Asteropaeus (as-ter-oh-**pee**-us): Trojan, son of Pelegon, commander of the Paeonians, killed by Achilles.

Athena (a-**thee**-na): Daughter of Zeus; goddess of wisdom, handicrafts, and war; chief protector of the Achaeans, with Hera. Also known as Pallas Athena.

Automedon (aw-**tom**-e-don): Achaean, son of Diores, friend and charioteer of Achilles and Patroclus.

Briseïs (brye-**see**-is): Trojan, daughter of Briseus, a captive awarded to Achilles after he captured Lyrnessus.

Calchas (**kal**-kas): Achaean, son of Thestor, prophet, "the wisest of those who scan the flight patterns of birds."

Cebriones (se-**brye**-o-neez): Trojan, bastard son of Priam, killed by Patroclus.

Charis (**ka**-ris): One of the Graces, wife of Hephaestus.

Chryses (**krye**-seez): Trojan, priest of Apollo, father of Chryseis, who is Agamemnon's captive.

Danäans (**dan**-ay-uhnz): Another name for Achaeans.

Dardanians (dar-**day**-nee-uhnz): Trojan allies, led by Aeneas.

Deïphobus (dee-**ih**-fo-bus): Trojan, son of Priam and Hecuba, one of the chief Trojan commanders.

Diomedes (dye-oh-**mee**-deez): Achaean, son of Tydeus, ruler of Argos, one of the chief Achaean commanders, wounded by Paris.

Dionē (dye-**oh**-nee): Mother of Aphrodite.

Epeans (e-**pee**-uhnz): A people of the northwestern Peloponnese.

Euphorbus (yoo-**for**-bus): Trojan, son of Panthous and Phrontis, who wounds Patroclus and is killed by Menelaus.

Eurypylus (yoo-**rip**-i-lus): Achaean, son of Euaemon, commander of one of the contingents from Thessaly.

Glaucus (**glaw**-kus): Trojan, son of Hippolochus, friend of Sarpedon, co-commander of the Lycians, wounded by Teucer.

Hēbē (**hee**-bee): Goddess of youth, cupbearer for the gods.

Hector (**hek**-tor): Trojan, son of Priam and Hecuba, husband of Andromache, chief commander of the Trojans, killed by Achilles.

Hecuba (**hek**-yoo-buh): Trojan, daughter of Dymas, wife of Priam and queen of Troy, mother of nineteen sons, including Hector, Paris, Helenus, and Deïphobus.

Helen (**hel**-en): Achaean, daughter of Zeus, wife of Menelaus, and later of Paris; her abduction from Lacedaemon was the cause of the Trojan War.

Helenus (**hel**-en-us): Trojan, son of Priam and Hecuba, prophet and warrior.

Hellespont (**hel**-e-spont): The long, narrow strait that divides Thrace from the Troad. Also known as the Dardanelles.

Hephaestus (he-**fees**-tus or he-**fes**-tus): Son of Zeus and Hera, god of fire, "the master craftsman, the crippled god."

Hera (**heer**-a): Queen of the gods, daughter of Cronus and Rhea, and both sister and wife of Zeus, mother of Ares and Hephaestus, chief protector of the Achaeans, with Athena.

Hermes (**her**-meez): Son of Zeus, god of wayfarers, patron of sneak-thieves.

Hippolochus (hi-**pol**-o-kus): Trojan, son of Antimachus, killed by Agamemnon.

Ida (**eye**-da): Mountain near Troy, from which Zeus looks down on the war.

Idaeus (eye-**dee**-us): Trojan, herald of Priam.

Idomeneus (eye-**dom**-en-yoos): Achaean, son of Deucalion, commander of the contingent from Crete.

Ilion (**il**-i-on): Troy.

Iris (**eye**-ris): Goddess of rainbows, messenger of Zeus.

Lacedaemon (la-suh-**dee**-muhn): City and land ruled by Menelaus, in the southern Peloponnese.

Lapiths (**la**-piths): A tribe from Thessaly, in northeastern Greece.

Locrians (**lok**-ree-uhnz): People of Locris, in north central and northeastern Greece, ruled by Ajax the Smaller.

Lycaon (lye-**kay**-uhn): Trojan, son of Priam and Laothoë, killed by Achilles.

Lycians (**li**-shuhnz): Trojan allies, people of Lycia (**li**-sha), a region on the southern coast of Asia Minor, ruled by Sarpedon and Glaucus.

Menelaus (men-e-**lay**-us): Achaean, son of Atreus, king of Lacedaemon, brother of Agamemnon, husband of Helen.

Menestheus (men-**es**-thyoos): Achaean, son of Peteos, commander of the Athenians.

Meriones (me-**rye**-o-neez): Achaean, son of Molus, friend of Idomeneus, second in command of the Cretan forces.

Mycenae (mye-**see**-nee): Agamemnon's capital, just north of the city of Argos.

Myrmidons (**mer**-mi-donz): A tribe from Thessaly, in northeastern Greece.

Nestor (**nes**-tuhr): Achaean, son of Neleus, commander of the contingent from Pylos, father of Antilochus and Thrasymedes, the oldest of the Achaean commanders.

Odysseus (oh-**dis**-yoos): Achaean, son of Laertes, commander of the contingent from Ithaca.

Olympus (oh-**lim**-pus): Mountain in northeastern Thessaly, home of the gods.

Pandarus (**pan**-da-rus): Trojan, son of Lycaon, commander of the troops from Zelea, killed by Diomedes.

Paris (**par**-is): Trojan, son of Priam and Hecuba, younger brother of Hector; his abduction of Helen caused the Trojan War.

Patroclus (pa-**trok**-lus): Achaean, son of Menoetius, beloved friend of Achilles, killed by Hector.

Peneleos (pee-**nel**-ee-os): Achaean, commander of the Boeotians, along with Leïtus.

Pergamus (**per**-ga-mus): The citadel of Troy.

Phoenix (**fee**-niks): Achaean, son of Amyntor, tutor and friend of Achilles.

Phthia (**fthye**-a): Region in southern Thessaly ruled by Peleus, home of Achilles.

Pisander (pye-**san**-der): Trojan, son of Antimachus, killed by Agamemnon.

Polydamas (pol-**id**-a-mas): Trojan, son of Panthous and Phrontis.

Poseidon (poh-**sye**-don): Son of Cronus and Rhea, younger brother of Zeus, god of the sea.

Priam (**prye**-am): King of Troy, son of Laomedon, husband of Hecuba, father of Hector, Paris, Helenus, Deïphobus, and many other sons who appear in the *Iliad*.

Pylians (**pye**-li-unz): People of Pylos (**pye**-los), Nestor's capital, in the southwestern Peloponnese.

Sarpedon (sar-**pee**-don): Trojan, son of Zeus and Laodamia, friend of Glaucus and co-commander of the Lycians, killed by Patroclus.

Scaean (**see**-an) Gates: The main gates of Troy.

Scamander (ska-**man**-der): Chief river of the Trojan plain, called Xanthus by the gods.

Simoïs (**sim**-oh-is): River of Troy, tributary of the Scamander.

Sthenelus (**sthen**-e-lus): Achaean, son of Capaneus, co-commander, with Diomedes and Euryalus, of the contingent from Argos.

Talthybius (tal-**thi**-bee-us): Achaean, herald of Agamemnon.

Teucer (**tyoo**-ser): Achaean, bastard son of Telamon, half-brother of Ajax the Tall.

Theano (thee-**ay**-noh): Trojan, daughter of Cisseus, wife of Antenor, priestess of Athena.

Themis (**them**-is): Goddess of order and custom.

Thersites (ther-**sye**-teez): Achaean who rails at Agamemnon and is beaten by Odysseus.

Thetis (**thee**-tis): Daughter of Nereus, the Old Man of the Sea, wife of Peleus, mother of Achilles.

Thoas (**thoh**-as): Achaean, son of Andraemon, commander of the Aetolians.

Tlepolemus (tle-**pol**-e-mus): Achaean, son of Heracles, commander of the contingent from Rhodes, killed by Sarpedon.

Troad (**troh**-ad): The province of Troy in western Asia Minor.

Xanthus (**zan**-thus): 1. Another name for the river Scamander. 2. One of Achilles' immortal horses, along with Balios, sired by the west wind, Zephyrus, out of the storm-mare Podargē.

Zeus (**zoos**): King of the gods, son of Cronus and Rhea, husband of Hera, father of many gods and humans.

Bibliography

Apthorp, M. J. *The Manuscript Evidence for Interpolation in Homer.* Heidelberg 1980.

Arnold, Matthew. *On Translating Homer.* London 1861.

Bolling, G. M. *The External Evidence for Interpolation in Homer.* Oxford 1925.

Cunliffe, Richard John. *A Lexicon of the Homeric Dialect.* Norman 1963.

Graziosi, Barbara, and Johannes Haubold. *Homer Iliad Book VI.* Cambridge 2010.

Griffin, Jasper. *Homer Iliad Book Nine.* Oxford 1995.

Hooker, J. T. *Homer: Iliad III.* London 1991.

Kirk, G. S. *The Iliad: A Commentary,* I: Books 1–4. Cambridge 1985.

——, II: Books 5–8. Cambridge 1990.

——, III: Books 9–12 (Bryan Hainsworth). Cambridge 1993.

——, IV: Books 13–16 (Richard Janko). Cambridge 1992.

——, V: Books 17–20 (Mark W. Edwards). Cambridge 1991.

——, VI: Books 21–24 (Nicholas Richardson). Cambridge 1993.

Latacz, Joachim, ed. *Homers Ilias Gesamtkommentar,* Band I, Erster Gesang, Faszikel 2 (Joachim Latacz, René Nünlist, und Magdalene Stoevesandt). München 2000.

——, Band II, Zweiter Gesang, Faszikel 2 (Joachim Latacz, Claude Brügger, Magdalene Stoevesandt, and Edzard Visser). München 2003.

——, Band III, Dritter Gesang, Faszikel 2 (Martha Krieter-Spiro). Berlin 2009.

——, Band IV, Sechster Gesang, Faszikel 2 (Magdalene Stoevesandt). Berlin 2008.

——, Band VI, Neunzehnter Gesang, Faszikel 2 (Marina Coray). Berlin 2009.

——, Band VIII, Vierundzwanzigster Gesang, Faszikel 2 (Claude Brügger). Berlin 2009.

Leaf, Walter. *The Iliad,* 2nd ed., 2 vols. London 1900–1902.

Macleod, C. W. *Homer Iliad Book XXIV.* Cambridge 1982.

Parry, Anne Amory. *Blameless Aegisthus: A Study of AMYMΩN and Other Homeric Epithets.* Leiden 1973.

Parry, Milman. *The Making of Homeric Verse: The Collected Papers of Milman Parry.* Ed. Adam Parry. Oxford 1971.

Pulleyn, Simon. *Homer Iliad Book One.* Oxford 2000.

Weil, Simone. "L'Iliade ou le poème de la force." *Les Cahiers du Sud* (Marseille), décembre 1940-janvier 1941.

West, M. L. *Homeri Ilias.* 2 vols. Stuttgart 1998–2000.

————, "The Invention of Homer." *Classical Quarterly* 49.2 (1999), 364–82.

————, *The Making of the Iliad.* Oxford 2011.

————, "The Singing of Homer and the Modes of Early Greek Music." *Journal of Hellenic Studies,* 101 (1981), 113–29.

————, "Some Homeric Words." *Glotta 76* (2001), 118–35.

————, *Studies in the Text and Transmission of the Iliad.* München 2001.

————, "The Textual Criticism and Editing of Homer." In G. W. Most, ed., *Editing Texts/Texte edieren.* Göttingen 1998, 95–110.

————, *Textual Criticism and Editorial Technique.* Stuttgart 1973.

Willcock, M. M. *Homer: Iliad I-XII.* London 1978.

————, *Homer: Iliad XIII-XXIV.* London 1984.

Wilson, C. H., *Homer: Iliad Books VIII and IX.* Warminster 1996.

Acknowledgments

M y heartfelt thanks to the following:

Professor Martin L. West responded to an email from a total stranger, and over the course of more than two years answered my many queries about the Greek text with the patience and generosity of a bodhisattva. In addition, he sent me a prepublication copy of his *The Making of the Iliad,* so that I would have time to digest its insights. For his unhoped-for guidance, as well as for the illumination that his books have offered, I am deeply grateful.

Michael Katz, my old friend and literary agent, to whom this book is dedicated, served as its advocate and was his usual self—my highest praise.

Richard Lawrence Cohen read the whole book and gave me the benefit of his astuteness and his fine novelist's ear.

Robert Lamberton read Books 1 and 4 along with the Greek text; his meticulous response taught me a great deal about Homeric scholarship.

Elaine Pagels and John Tarrant read the introduction and gave me some wonderfully insightful criticisms.

Leslie Meredith, my editor, read the manuscript with her usual attentiveness and asked all the right questions. Kirsty Dunseath took good care of the British edition.

Judith Hoover for the American edition and David Atkinson for the British did a meticulous job of copyediting; Eric Fuentecilla (jacket) and Ellen Sasahara (interior) made the American edition as beautiful as I could have wished, and Steve Marking did the same for the British; and Jeffrey L. Ward designed and drew the handsome map.

The late Professor Sir Hugh Lloyd-Jones's article about translations of the *Iliad* in the *New York Review of Books* (38, 4, February 14, 1991; I read it in April, 2008) convinced me that there was a need for something better than what we had and started me on this adventure.

The late Adam Parry had lunch with me one day when I was a graduate student at Yale in 1966. I remember nothing of our conversation but his passion for Greek, a little of which rubbed off on me, I think.

Katie, my wife, without doing anything, permeates everything I do. It is a privilege to live with her. (If you think I'm exaggerating, read *A Thousand Names for Joy.*)

About the Translator

Stephen Mitchell was born in Brooklyn in 1943, educated at Amherst, the Sorbonne, and Yale, and de-educated through intensive Zen practice. His many books include the bestselling *Tao Te Ching, Gilgamesh,* and *The Second Book of the Tao,* as well as *The Gospel According to Jesus, Bhagavad Gita, The Book of Job,* and *Meetings with the Archangel.* He is married to Byron Katie and cowrote two of her bestselling books: *Loving What Is* and *A Thousand Names for Joy.* You can read extensive excerpts from all his books on his website, www.stephenmitchellbooks.com.